SOUTHERN BIOGRAPHY SERIES
Bertram Wyatt-Brown, Editor

# SENATOR ALBER

## TENNESSEE MAVE

## KYLE LONGLEY

### WITH A FOREWORD BY AL GORE, JR.

LOUISIANA STATE UNIVERSITY PRESS

BATON ROUGE

GORE, SR.

RICK

Copyright ©2004 by Louisiana State University Press
All rights reserved
Manufactured in the United States of America
FIRST PRINTING

DESIGNER: Andrew Shurtz
TYPEFACES: Janson Text, ITC Franklin Gothic
TYPESETTER: Coghill Composition Co., Inc.
PRINTER AND BINDER: Thomson-Shore, Inc.

Library of Congress Cataloging-in-Publication Data

Longley, Kyle.
  Senator Albert Gore, Sr.: Tennessee maverick / Kyle Longley.
      p.   cm. — (Southern biography series)
   Includes bibliographical references and index.
      ISBN 0-8071-2980-1 (hardcover : alk. paper)
    1. Gore, Albert, 1907–  2. Legislators—United States—Biography.   3. United
States.  Congress. Senate—Biography.   4. Tennessee—Politics and government—1951–
I. Title.  II. Series.
E748.G689L66   2004
328.73'092—dc22

                                                                          2004011048

*To my parents, Joe and Chan*

# CONTENTS

FOREWORD, by Al Gore, Jr.   xi

PREFACE   xiii

Introduction   1

1  The Boy from Possum Hollow   8

2  Mr. Gore Goes to Washington   41

3  In the New World of Atoms, the Cold War, and the Fair Deal   69

4  Joining the Millionaires' Club   102

5  A Time of Peril on Many Fronts   134

6  Living in Camelot   158

7  In the Midst of the Great Society and Beyond   182

8  Target Number One   217

9  Life out of the Limelight   241

Epilogue   271

NOTES   275

BIBLIOGRAPHY   317

INDEX   335

# ILLUSTRATIONS

*following page* 68

Pauline and Albert around the time of their marriage, 1937

Mr. and Mrs. Gore with Nancy at the beach, early 1940s

Young Al with his father, mid-1950s

Portrait of Albert Gore, early 1950s

Senators John F. Kennedy, Hubert Humphrey, and Albert Gore

Senator Lyndon B. Johnson and Lady Bird Johnson on the campaign trail with Senator Gore

Senator Gore with President Johnson in the Oval Office

Gore campaigning for the Senate, 1970

Senator Gore with his family, 1970

Father and son celebrating Al Gore Jr.'s 1976 congressional victory

The senator with President Jimmy Carter and Jim Sasser

Karenna and her grandfather on the occasion of her wedding

# FOREWORD

I AM PLEASED that Kyle Longley has come forward with a scholarly presentation highlighting the career of my late father, Albert Gore, Sr. As a son, I continue to miss him in a personal way. And as a citizen, I wish that our nation could hear his voice again right now as we struggle with pressing issues in these perilous times.

My father personified the American dream. He never forgot what it was like to grow up on a hard-scrabble farm in the Appalachian foothills, or what it was like to try to instill in feisty students in a one-room school a desire to learn, or what it was like finally to earn a college degree after holding a variety of jobs during hard economic times. Those experiences made him what he was, and they were experiences he recalled vividly many times as he shared them with my sister and me when we were young.

Many of those who have scrutinized my father's thirty-two years in Washington have referred to his independence, his courage, his talent, his perseverance, his righteousness, and his idealized sense of public service as a sacred trust. He was a man of honor and incredible dedication. It seems clear to me that we need more men and women in government today who demonstrate similar traits.

One of my fascinations in growing up was listening to my father speak at public functions. On the campaign trail, he was a spirited, colorful orator of the old school. Whether it was on the courthouse lawn in a county seat town or in the United States Senate, his remarks—usually with a challenging conclusion but sprinkled with animated humor—were not soon forgotten by those who heard him.

As this biography reveals, many of the important legislative issues that captured my father's attention coincided with significant events in American history, covering the crucial period leading up to World War II and extending through the cold war and the Vietnam War. Professor Longley admirably digs deeply to explore my father's stances on important matters both domestically and internationally. A visionary, my father was often ahead of his time with his informed but sometimes immovable positions on legislation. Indeed, he was sometimes stubborn in holding to fixed conclusions about issues—especially when he felt an important principle was involved—often to his political detriment. But, in retrospect, history has been kind to him.

My father loved his country and dedicated his adult life to making it better. To borrow an old Tennessee saying, he was "something else!" Through exhaustive research and clarity of language, Professor Longley has been able to offer readers a keen insight into the fascinating career of Albert Gore, Sr.

AL GORE, JR.

*May 2004*

# PREFACE

IN NOVEMBER 2000, a week after the presidential election, I traveled to Murfreesboro and Middle Tennessee State University on a research trip. The entire country remained transfixed on the Florida recount. In the ensuing debates, one of the perplexing questions asked was why Vice President Al Gore had failed to carry his home state, which would have made the events in Florida irrelevant. As I drove back to Murfreesboro from an interview in Nashville, a car suddenly sped by with a prominent Bush/Cheney bumper sticker. On the back window, written in large characters with shoe polish, was "God, Guts, and Guns = Republican Platform."

Though the person driving the car may not have realized it, he had taken the saying from a Ku Klux Klan slogan: "God, Guts, and Guns Made America Free. Let's Keep All Three." As I thought about the matter, I recognized a historical continuity. In 1970, Bill Brock defeated Senator Albert Gore Sr. by running a campaign that bore a striking resemblance to George W. Bush's. The Republicans in 2000 had taken Tennessee by attacking Gore on school prayer and abortion, racially sensitive issues of vouchers and gun control, and national defense. In 1970, the Republicans had assailed the elder Gore's votes on gun control and school prayer, his opposition to the Vietnam War, and his support of civil rights. The margin of defeat in Tennessee was remarkably similar for the two men. These facts reinforced to me the value of my writing a biography of the elder Gore.

I had not been attracted to the topic until I made a trip to Middle Tennessee State University in 1994 for a job interview. While there, I met Jim Neal, the archivist of Senator Gore's papers. Knowing my interest in U.S. foreign relations, he encouraged me to investigate the possibility of writing a biography of Senator Gore. He pointed out that there were several articles, theses, and dissertations about him, but no monographs. I filed the recommendation away because at the time I was finishing a study of the U.S. relationship with José Figueres, the Costa Rican nationalist and progressive leader. I took a different job and did not have the opportunity to explore the suggestion immediately.

It would be a couple of more years before I finished my other work, but I kept Dr. Neal's suggestion in the back of my mind. I did a little reading and became more interested. Once I dove fully into the subject in late 1997, I came away with a new appreciation of Senator Gore. Beyond his relationship with his son, he was a fascinating character in his own right, and I could not believe the good fortune that no one had written a full-length biography of him.

I am indebted to many people in the long and arduous task of completing this work. First, there is the long list of archivists and personnel at many different sites. In particular, I must thank Jim Neal and his successor Lisa Pruitt, as well as their assistant Betty Rowland, at the Gore Center for their innumerable hours of helping me sift through the thousands of folders and boxes in Senator Gore's collection. Many others, including Michael Parrish at the LBJ Library (now at Baylor University), Donald Ritchie in the Senate Historical Office, and David Haight at the Dwight Eisenhower Library, helped me as I gathered information at depositories throughout the country. I must also thank Dr. Parrish and Dr. Ritchie for taking the time to read the manuscript and make insightful comments and recommendations.

There are other scholars who helped shape this manuscript into its final form. They include colleagues Robert Johnson, Randall Woods, Jeff Woods, LeRoy Ashby, Robert Brigham, Walter LaFeber, Jim Siekmeier, Michael Martin, Tony Badger, James Gardner, Elizabeth Cobbs-Hoffman, Dewey Grantham, Hugh Davis Graham, Marshall Eakin, Thomas Schwartz, Patrick Cox, and Nick Sarantakes. My past and current colleagues at Arizona State University including Vicki Ruiz, Brooks Simpson, Ed Escobar, Gayle Gullett, Philip Vandermeer, and Peter Iverson have been particularly supportive and provided numerous insights. I also benefited from the assistance of several graduate students, including Eve Carr, Jaime Ruiz, Richard Kitchen, and Bruce Zachary, each of whom helped with the project at various times. I am especially grateful to my department chair, Noel Stowe, who assisted in finding additional research funds to complete this project.

Very special thanks go to George Herring, my doctoral mentor at the University of Kentucky, who took the time to read the manuscript and make recommendations that significantly improved it. He remains my most important intellectual influence, as well as a close friend. Also, I want to extend my gratitude to one of my undergraduate professors at Angelo State University, Dr. Shirley Eoff, who took many hours out of her busy schedule to provide some wonderful copyediting recommendations.

One of the most exciting aspects of this project was meeting the people who lived during the period I have described and who interacted with Senator Gore. In particular, Jim and Mary Sasser, Jack Robinson Sr., Theodore Brown Jr., Tamara Trexler Moxley, and Karenna Gore Schiff were extremely supportive of the project. Others including Bill Allen, John Seigenthaler, Larry Daugherty, Martin Peretz, Wayne Whitt, Steve Owens, Emmett Edwards, Jane Holmes Dixon, Pam Eakes, and Gilbert Merritt shared their knowledge and insights about the senator. Finally, I want to thank Vice President Al Gore for taking time out of his busy schedule to help me better understand his father. The personal insight these people provided helped me draw a more complete picture of the senator and his family.

I also owe special thanks to Louisiana State University Press. Bertram Wyatt-Brown, editor of the Southern Biography Series, provided invaluable guidance in refining and improving the manuscript. Sylvia Frank Rodrigue, Greg Peters, and Lee Sioles have been very helpful in facilitating production of the book. Also, anonymous readers provided comments that greatly improved the text. Finally, Glenn Perkins gave substantial assistance as the copyeditor who tightened and refined the final product. I cannot speak more highly of a press and staff who were professional, courteous, and really assisted in turning this into a better book.

As is so often the case, sacrifices were asked of those close to me to allow me to complete the work. This is especially true of my wife, Maria, and my young son, Sean. Countless times, Maria waited for me to return from research trips or to exit my office after many hours of typing away at the computer. Without her I never would have been able to complete my work. In addition, this project has been around as long as Sean has been alive. I have seen him move from the playpen to more energetic pursuits as an active little boy, all the while having to accept numerous times that I had to work rather than wrestle or play outside. His knocks at my office door always tore at me. I hope he will grow to understand more about his father's absences when he is older.

Finally, I want to dedicate this book to my parents, Joe and Chan. I share a gratitude with Vice President Gore that I never worried about the foundations of my home and that I would always have supportive parents, no matter what my endeavor. They have been wonderful examples of people and parents, both sacrificing themselves in public service to innumerable communities throughout the state of Texas. Without them, I would never have been able to reach my current position. They truly are great people and role models for me and many others. I only hope that I can be half as effective as a spouse and parent.

# SENATOR ALBERT GORE, SR.

# INTRODUCTION

THERE WAS weeping and gnashing of teeth throughout the South in 1954. The Supreme Court had issued the *Brown v. Board of Education* decision that overturned the concept of "separate but equal" and opened challenges to segregation throughout the region. Angry white southerners banded together in groups such as the Southern Citizens' Councils and Ku Klux Klan, determined to protect segregation by any necessary means. As the anger mounted, novelist William Faulkner warned that the "south is armed for revolt" and observed that all ammunition and weapons had disappeared from store shelves. He told a journalist that "these white people will accept another civil war knowing they're going to lose."[1]

By early 1956, southern politicians led by Strom Thurmond of South Carolina, Richard Russell of Georgia, and Harry Byrd of Virginia had decided to exploit the conflict for political gain. Throughout the congressional session, they had gathered in Southern Caucus meetings to work on a document, "A Declaration of Constitutional Principles." Ultimately, the group produced what became known as the "Southern Manifesto," a formal declaration against the *Brown* decision. In many ways, the manifesto was a crucial test of the potential of Byrd's principle of "massive resistance," which would require a unified southern front to have any chance at success.

An important challenge to the unified southern front came in March 1956 when Thurmond decided to put Tennessee senator Albert Gore on the spot. He and his allies had already lined up the support of every southern senator except Gore, Estes Kefauver of Tennessee, and Lyndon Johnson of Texas. Still, they hoped that Gore would cave in and support the measure, following the example of other southern moderates, including Lister Hill of Alabama and J. William Fulbright of Arkansas.

The cagey, confrontational Thurmond planned to ambush Gore on the Senate floor to achieve the most dramatic effect and force Gore to sign. His staff alerted southern journalists that he would present the Tennessean with a copy of the Southern Manifesto on March 10. That day, the reporters gathered in the gallery to watch the confrontation as if they were spectators in the old Roman Coliseum. They understood the significance of the decision for Gore and knew that there was potential for fireworks between the two strong-willed men.

The reporters leaned over the edge of the observers' gallery as Gore entered the Senate chamber and walked toward his desk. They watched Thurmond stalk him like a lion after prey. At the right moment, the South Carolinian sprung at Gore, holding up a document and bellowing for everyone to hear, "Albert, we'd like you to sign the Southern Manifesto with the rest of us." For a moment, Gore looked at him, stunned perhaps by his audacity and totally unprepared for the public spectacle. After a moment, he regained his composure. Then he looked straight at Thurmond and loudly responded with an emphatic "Hell no!"[2]

This episode was one of Albert Gore's defining moments as a legislator. He had faced intense pressure from his constituents to oppose the *Brown* decision and defend segregation. Nevertheless, he had refused to bend under what he later characterized as "a dangerous, deceptive propaganda move which encouraged southerners to defy the government and to disobey its laws."[3] He made up his mind and firmly stood his ground. It was neither the first nor the last time that he made an unpopular decision. In many ways, his stand against the Southern Manifesto exemplified the type of legislator that he had become, and which he remained when he took a progressive approach to civil rights, international relations, and economic development that angered many fellow Tennesseans. One observer later commented that he was a man "who has deeply offended, at one time or another, nearly every lobby and special interest on Capitol Hill."[4]

Gore's maverick nature ensured that he never achieved the national stature and recognition of some of his contemporaries, including John Kennedy, Johnson, or Fulbright. In fact, most people recognize him as the father of former vice president Al Gore, rather than for his own accomplishments. He himself recognized the fact that his son had eclipsed him in the public eye. After retiring to his home in Carthage in the 1990s, he would meet people at the family-owned antique store where he sometimes worked. Some would remember the old times, he recalled, but many would also then "ask about my son. Al's name is a household word now. So that makes me popular I guess."[5]

There are many reasons for undertaking a full-scale biography of Albert Gore, in addition to understanding the father Al referred to as "the greatest man I ever knew in my life."[6] Examining Gore's career provides insight into the national political movements of his time. He shared ideas with an entire generation of politicians including Kennedy, Johnson, Kefauver, Hubert Humphrey (D-MN), Eugene McCarthy (D-MN), Wayne Morse (I-OR), George Mc-

Govern (D-SD), Mike Monroney (D-OK), Paul Douglas (D-IL), and Mike Mansfield (D-MT). These progressive and liberal politicians helped shape many of the socioeconomic and political policies of the United States from the end of World War II through the 1970s. They contributed to the government's expanding responsibility for the well-being of Americans in areas of health care, education, and economic security. In addition, they assisted in the transformation of the United States into the greatest world power in the postwar era.

Leaders of public opinion would characterize these politicians as leaders of the modern American liberal movement because they sought an expanded government role in the economy and society and emphasized Keynesian principles to increase jobs and production and to pay for social programs that benefited the historically disadvantaged. The liberal coalition was primarily urban; had a well-educated leadership; relied heavily for support on ethnic minorities and interest groups, including labor; and typically believed that the United States should pursue an active role in international affairs. By the late 1940s, most liberals shared most Americans' conviction that the United States should oppose vigorously the expansion of communism as a matter of principle and self-protection.[7]

Gore shared many of the liberals' ideas. Strongly influenced by the internationalists including his political mentor, Cordell Hull, and Woodrow Wilson, he supported foreign trade and U.S. involvement in international organizations such as the United Nations. For many years, he backed U.S. efforts to contain communism, although by the end of his career he became a very vocal critic of specific applications of U.S. foreign policy for betraying core American values. He also believed that the government could and should help individuals fully recognize their potential and create a better America.

There were also significant differences between Gore and the liberal leaders. He was no Keynesian; he opposed government debt and argued that government competition for money ensured higher interest rates. He preferred taxing those with exorbitant wealth to reduce the burden on the majority while still providing necessary social programs. Also, he was not a member of the liberal establishment, belonging to neither the primarily northeastern educated elite nor the ethnic minority blocs that constituted the foundations of the modern American liberal community.

Gore's political ideas reflect the complexity of the generation that shaped America in the face of conservative opposition in the postwar era. He was a progressive whose rural roots imbued him with populist ideas. He believed in the government helping its citizens through increased business regulation, equitable distribution of the tax burden, and support of the laborer over managers and owners. Social justice needed to be rooted in economic opportunity, with government ensuring better working conditions, improved health care, and access to education. His political commitments continued the populist and progressive impulses of the late nineteenth and early twentieth centuries, which encouraged him to support some, though not all, postwar liberal programs.[8]

The Tennessean's contributions during his tenure in national office highlight the trend toward congressional activism in the postwar area. He helped sponsor legislation that created the National Interstate Highway System and Medicare, backed programs that expanded the Tennessee Valley Authority (TVA) and Social Security, and fought for tax equity and campaign finance reform. In the area of civil rights, he proved an ally of those promoting change; only once did he fail to back significant legislation.

In foreign relations, he ardently supported U.S. participation in the United Nations and the North Atlantic Treaty Organization. He was at the forefront in pushing to end atmospheric nuclear testing and calling for early efforts at arms control. In the early 1960s he criticized U.S. involvement in Vietnam and encouraged diplomatic recognition of Red China. Working with Fulbright, Morse, Ernest Gruening (D-AK), and Frank Church (D-ID), Gore played a prominent role in shaping U.S. foreign policy in the postwar era.

In addition to being a significant actor on the national level, Gore also played a substantial role in southern politics. Unlike most progressive and liberal politicians of his day, he came from the South and understood its legacy of defeat, racism, and elitism. He was proud of his roots, although he recognized the shortcomings of the leadership and the divisive role race played in preventing the South from realizing its fullest potential. An overarching goal, one that he sought even after leaving office, was to help southerners emerge from their provincialism and become an important progressive, rather than reactionary, force on the national scene. He urged them to bring positive southern virtues to the forefront of American society, thus "letting their glory out" and making the region a more fundamental part of the nation.

This placed Gore squarely in the movement that became known as "southern liberalism." Southern liberals included political leaders such as Estes Kefauver and Frank Clement of Tennessee, Claude Pepper of Florida, Frank Porter Graham of North Carolina, Ralph Yarborough of Texas, and Brooks Hays of Arkansas.[9] Unlike many of their conservative counterparts, typically residing within the Democratic Party, southern liberals believed that the federal government had a substantial responsibility in improving the plight of its citizens, especially those in the many underdeveloped areas of the South. As a result, they backed many of the programs of the New Deal, Fair Deal, and Great Society programs, in particular the TVA, Social Security, Medicare, and improved education and health care plans.

The main issue that separated southern liberals from other southerners was civil rights.[10] While northern liberals such as Humphrey, Douglas, Kennedy, and McCarthy faced some criticism from constituents and other legislators over the issue, they never experienced the direct challenges confronted by southerners who opposed segregation. In the North, the issue had political benefits, especially among the ever-expanding African American voting bloc. In the South, however, supporting equal rights carried potential consequences. Nonetheless, a small group of people, typically in the border states, assumed leadership in the efforts to overcome white opposition. By far, this stance, more than anything else, stamped the tag of "southern liberal" on men such as Gore.

Fighting for economic justice and moving away from the old politics of racial divisiveness, Gore and his contemporaries made it acceptable for white southern politicians to support civil rights and progressive ideas.[11] Their legacy paved the way for Jimmy Carter of Georgia, Dale Bumpers of Arkansas, Howell Heflin of Alabama, Reubin Askew of Florida, and John C. West of South Carolina. These heirs would join with an emerging group of prominent African American politicians, such as Barbara Jordan of Texas and Andrew Young of Georgia, to change the dynamics of southern politics.

This generation in turn would pass the torch to a new generation including Jim Sasser of Tennessee, Bob Graham of Florida, Chuck Robb of Virginia, Bill Clinton of Arkansas, John Edwards of North Carolina, and Al Gore. The impact was obvious. President Clinton told reporters in 1998 that the elder Gore was "the embodiment of everything public service ought to be. He was a teacher, he was a progressive, he helped to connect the South with the rest of America." Gore was "a great patriot, a great public servant, a man who was truly a real role model for the young people like me in the South in the 1960s."[12]

Additionally, Gore and his southern liberal contemporaries prompted change by incorporating the South more fully into the fabric of the United States. At the onset of Gore's career, the South was the most impoverished and underdeveloped region of the United States. By the time of his death, it had evolved into a more urban, progressive area that housed cultural and economic centers such as Atlanta, Charlotte, Nashville, Dallas, Houston, and Miami. The work of the southern liberals made this advancement possible.

At the same time, Gore's life and work exemplify the political consequences of challenging those he characterized as the new southern Bourbons. The white backlash against him in the 1970 election, mostly by former Democrats from working-class and middle-class roots, demonstrated that there remained an ongoing battle within southern politics. During his Senate tenure, Gore battled southern conservatives including Thurmond, Herman Talmadge (D-GA), James Eastland (D-MS), and George Wallace (D-AL). In turn, these men helped lay the groundwork for white, states' rights Democrats to move into the Republican Party.

Much as Gore and his allies passed on the mantle to a new generation of southern liberals, the southern conservatives bred their own powerful offspring. Jesse Helms of North Carolina, Trent Lott of Mississippi, Tom Delay and Dick Armey of Texas, and Newt Gingrich and Bob Barr of Georgia rose within the ranks of the Republican Party to become important national figures. While the new breed has played the race card more subtly, their fight against the progressives and liberals extends a continuum in southern politics throughout the twentieth century. The remarkable power of the southerners in Washington today makes understanding this political progression even more important.[13]

Finally, Gore's life and career provide significant insights into the history of Tennessee during the twentieth century. Long-time editorial writer for the *Nashville Tennessean* Larry Daugherty noted that Gore's death in 1998 "marked the formal end of a remarkable era of Tennessee politics." "Gore was one of the last of Tennessee's Roosevelt Democrats to hold office," he observed, "men unafraid of the word liberal, if it meant they stood up against powerful corporate and political interests in favor of ordinary people."[14]

During Gore's life, Tennessee underwent significant changes. The stranglehold of the Boss Edward Crump machine in Memphis that largely dominated Tennessee politics during the first half of the twentieth century was broken. Men like Gordon Browning, Kefauver, and Gore chipped away at it steadily, and Gore's defeat of Kenneth McKellar in 1952 hammered the final nail in the coffin. This change helped ensure that Tennessee truly became a two-party state, as the Republicans gained significant ground in western Tennessee during the 1950s. By the 1960s the Republican Party could elect senators and governors in Tennessee for the first time in many years.[15]

Other changes followed. Court-ordered desegregation met resistance, but Tennessee escaped many of the violent confrontations afflicting neighboring states. The enlightened views on race and courageous leadership of Gore, Kefauver, and Governor Frank Clement helped the state avoid the conflicts that engulfed Arkansas, Alabama, and Mississippi during the 1950s and 1960s. Leadership from the top flowed down, and Tennessee's spokesmen differed significantly from senators such as Russell and John McClellan of Arkansas and governors like Orval Faubus of Arkansas and Ross Barnett of Mississippi. While there was resistance to integration in Tennessee, it never approximated the disorder and brutality that took place elsewhere.

Gore, Kefauver, and Clement ensured that a new generation of progressive Tennessee politicians could move to the forefront without relying on race baiting and states' rights rhetoric. That new generation included Sasser, Bob Clement, Bart Gordon, Harold Ford Jr., and Al Gore. Continuing the traditions of Gore and his allies on public works, education, and civil rights, they remain an important part of the modern political scene in Tennessee.

The biographical component of this book is framed within a social, economic, cultural, and political study of the period Gore's life encompassed and provides a good snapshot of the "American Century." Born in 1909, he lived for nearly ninety years. Like many of his generation, he moved away from farms with no indoor toilets, electricity, and running water into a world that included automobiles, television, and microwave ovens. In the space of a generation, America became an urban-based industrial giant and the preponderant world leader.

Albert Gore's career also provides other insights into U.S. history in the twentieth century. Very few people would have predicted at his birth in 1909 that the son of a small farmer from the Upper Cumberland would rise to become a U.S. senator. The road was often hard and full of disappointments, but through perseverance, hard work, and good timing, he made a relatively rapid ascent into the circles of power. His life and his career provide an interesting, and oftentimes inspiring, study of commitment, conscience, and public service. To borrow Adlai Stevenson Jr.'s characterization of Harry Truman, Gore was "an object lesson in the vitality of popular government; an example of the ability of this society to yield up, from the most unremarkable origins, the most remarkable men."[16]

# 1 THE BOY FROM POSSUM HOLLOW

WHILE LIVING in Detroit as a teenager after leaving high school, Albert Gore recalled that "I pondered upon my own happy childhood and wondered why it had been so. I concluded it was because we lived apart from the world, relatively isolated and therefore dependent entirely upon one another. Although the chores were heavy and discipline absolute, there was love in our family and reverence for each other."[1]

The values instilled in Albert Gore by his family, when combined with good fortune, helped the young man chase his dreams. In between, there would be many struggles for the young man from Possum Hollow. He worked as a teacher in various locations to support himself while he attended Middle Tennessee State Teacher's College (MTSTC). Always ambitious, he failed in his first run for public office, becoming unemployed at the height of the Great Depression. However, good luck together with determination landed him a job as Smith County superintendent of schools, a law degree through night courses at the YMCA in Nashville, and ultimately a position as Tennessee commissioner of labor. In the meantime, he married and started a family before winning a congressional seat in 1938.

Gore's family lived in the Upper Cumberland region of Tennessee. In his youth, it was a beautiful, wild region dominated by the Cumberland River, which cut a swath through the rolling valleys with lush green grass and tall trees. The farther one moved up the river toward Kentucky, the more difficult the land became, as people struggled to carve out farmlands and livelihoods. Down the river, people were nearer population centers like Nashville and had more readily available and fertile lands. Still, the region was a place described by one commentator as "not the old cotton kingdom ruled by the slavocracy's modern Faulknerian heirs, but the hard-scrabble hill country where tough, independent men had to tear a living out of the soil."[2] The majority of inhabitants farmed and tenaciously held the rural and religious values of their forefathers.

The Gores emigrated from England to America in the early eighteenth century, eventually moving to land around New Market, Virginia, where Gore's great-great-grandfather, John, was born in 1761. At the age of eighteen, he joined the Continental Army. After service in South Carolina, he fell ill and received a furlough. He married and moved the family to Jefferson County, Tennessee, in 1792. Four years later, when Tennessee joined the Union, Gore became a justice for Jefferson County. The family, including eight children, moved to the Roaring River area in Jackson County. John Gore later served in the Tennessee General Assembly as a representative, beginning a standard for public life in the family.[3]

The next two generations of Gore's descendants remained in the vicinity. Most were farmers with large families. Albert Gore's great-grandfather, Mounce Gore, had four children including Gore's grandfather, Charles Claiborne Gore Sr., who moved to nearby Smith County. He would sire twelve children, among them Albert Gore's father, Allen, who was born in 1869. He married Margie Denny of Smith County in 1894 and produced five children. Albert, the third, was born near Granville in Jackson County on December 26, 1907, the day of his parents' wedding anniversary. His older brother, Reginald, was twelve years his senior, and a sister, Amanda, was halfway between them in age. His two younger sisters, Laura Bettie and Grace, were born in 1909 and 1912.[4]

The future senator later recalled that he lived in "a self-giving, self-respecting household." He characterized his father as a "rather strict" man who demanded obedience and maintained a powerful position as head of the house. Conversely, he portrayed his mother as "extremely kind and gentle," although she also demanded respect from her children. When asked about how his parents had molded him, Gore recalled that "they influenced all decisions, their way of life, manners at the table, courtesy to visitors, the work and the play."[5]

Soon after Albert's birth, the Gore family moved to the little hamlet of Possum Hollow, south of Carthage in Smith County, approximately fifty miles east of Nashville. On a very cold New Year's Eve day, the family loaded all its possessions onto two wagons and a buggy. His parents put Gore and his sister Bettie in the foot room of the buggy and buried them under a lap rug on which was painted a dog with a glass eye. The children peeked out occasionally to see the countryside. They finally arrived at their new house near midnight and found that the seller had not vacated the premises. Fortunately, there was enough room, and the family stayed the night. Thus started Albert Gore's life in Smith County, an area to which he remained tied until his death in 1998.[6]

Albert worked hard on the farm. His family was relatively self-sufficient, only going to the store for materials like spices, sugar, and cloth. They had beef cattle and participated in a beef club where ten to twenty families banded together and butchered the animals and then distributed some to each family. The

Gores also had pigs and chickens, and Albert and Reggie became skilled hunters and supplemented the diet with turkey, squirrels, rabbits, and white-crest chicken hawks. Their mother kept a garden and canned foods for the winter and also churned butter, selling the excess to earn spending money. The family used everything including the ashes from fires, which they mixed with water to produce soap. Overall, the family was fairly prosperous compared to many of their neighbors.[7]

Among his many chores, Gore rose at 4 A.M. and started the fire in the wood-burning stove. As he grew older, his routine expanded to include helping his father with plowing, mending fences, and taking care of the livestock. Since his brother was twelve years older and left home when Albert was young, his days in the fields and barn were full. The work did not, however, keep him out of trouble. Once, his father and a neighbor assigned him and two neighbor boys to hoe some corn near the creek. It was a very hot day, so they decided to go swimming instead. When the two men came to inspect the job, they found the boys in the water. "All of us got a thrashing," Gore remembered.[8]

The central features of life in Possum Hollow were school, religion, and the outdoors. "I was stimulated by the isolated life I lived in an isolated community where every boy was pretty well on his own out in the woods and on the lonesome hills," Gore recalled. He believed that the solitude created an independence and self-reliance for people in the area, as they were "left upon their own talents and skills to succeed and to achieve."[9]

A family friend, Charles Bartlett, recognized the physical manifestation of this independence in Gore, as well as in many of the people of his generation from the area. "He does have the distant look in his eye. It's a mountain thing. It's the look of people who don't quite trust anybody."[10] Living in a small community where everyone knew each other contributed to this guarded nature. The personality trait would remain throughout Gore's life. Although he was gregarious, there was always a distance that prevented him from revealing too much of himself, except to his family and close friends. Many would characterize this as aloofness or arrogance, but it went much deeper than that to the environment in which he grew up.

As in so many other such hamlets, the church sewed the community together. The Gores were Baptists, the dominant denomination in the Upper Cumberland. Southern Baptists believed that the Bible was the divinely inspired word of God, and it played a fundamental role in most households as a source of learning, as well as a record of marriages, births, and deaths. Their literal interpretation of the Bible also ensured a belief in severe punishment for sin, on earth and in the afterlife. Additionally, the Baptists promoted abstinence from alcohol, tobacco, gambling, premarital sex, and dishonesty.[11] The church leaders glorified hard work, claiming that it strengthened character, and most leaders promoted Christ's belief in justice and caring for others, although racism and anti-Semitism remained. Most families tried to live the blueprint provided in the Bible, and those in the Gore family were devout Christians.[12]

The other institution that established standards of conduct and reinforced beliefs was school.[13] Early on, Gore developed a love for his schoolwork. In an event he described as one of his "brightest moments," he entered a one-room schoolhouse for the first grade. He proudly stressed that at the end of the first week, he went in front of the school body and recited the alphabet and numbers up to one hundred. The teacher, Mary Litchford, bragged on him. Gore ran home at a brisk pace to tell his father about the recognition. He admitted that "a small fire was lit" by his success, one that made him study harder.[14] At even this early age, Gore demonstrated a strong commitment to set himself apart from others.

The one-room schoolhouse allowed him to progress quickly. Since he often finished his studies early, he had a chance to listen to the teacher give the lessons to the students in grades ahead of him. He liked history and literature, which stirred his imagination, especially books on Tennessee and its heroes, as well as on traditional American icons like George Washington, Thomas Jefferson, and Abraham Lincoln. Every morning during the time between lighting the fire and sunrise, he read whatever he could find. "I loved to read everything of a historical character," he admitted, "though in the early days the books were quite limited. Nevertheless, whatever I could lay my hand on I read."[15]

His early reading also helped shape his view of the world. When asked in the mid-1970s who his political heroes were, Gore responded that "Andrew Jackson was foremost . . . And in an earlier period, Jefferson." He added that he knew Sam Houston was "one of my predecessors in Congress," from the hills around Carthage. These leaders, along with James Polk and Davy Crockett, both Tennesseans, profoundly influenced the future senator.[16]

Jefferson, whom Gore often quoted during his political career, particularly impressed the young Tennessean. Jefferson saw the strength of American democracy in the independent-minded, democratic, and egalitarian American yeoman farmer. In 1787, he had written that "those who labour in the earth are the chosen people of God, if ever he had a chosen people." He distrusted city dwellers and their perceived greed and speculation, and he feared people such as Alexander Hamilton, whom he associated with a large centralized government that primarily represented the elites. Finally, he wanted people to be "free to regulate their own pursuits of industry and improvement."[17]

Equally as important to Gore was the influence of Andrew Jackson. One observer correctly characterized Jackson as ambitious, courageous, dedicated to his duty, and driven as president by his "unshakable belief that he represented the people against the aristocracy and privilege." Jackson once commented that he believed "that just laws can make no distinction of privilege between the rich and the poor. And that, when men of high standing attempt to trample upon the rights of the weak they are the fittest objects for example and punishment."[18]

Jackson and his successors, including James K. Polk, helped establish a political culture in Tennessee, one that particularly influenced Middle Tennessee and the Upper Cumberland. They abhorred the elites, especially in the banking and industrial centers of the Northeast. These leaders were self-made men who wanted continued opportunity for ambitious people like themselves. Furthermore, they often took controversial stands for the day and prided themselves in challenging the establishment. Gore would in many ways emulate Jackson, his successors, and their dedication to the ideals of duty and honor.

As Gore matured, his love of learning set him apart, but at the same time he was mischievous and pugnacious. He reminisced about hating his middle name of Arnold because "every Saturday afternoon when I went to town, I wound up fighting some dude who kept calling me Benedict Arnold." He earned money by hunting and trapping polecats and other animals and selling their skins. He learned to swim in the local rivers. He remembered ordering some water wings from Sears-Roebuck and trying them in the creek. "In the deepest part of the current, I lost my wings, and I learned then and there how to swim," he recalled. He began to excel in sports, especially baseball and basketball. With practice, he became a good enough pitcher that people encouraged him to try to make a career out of the sport, and he later earned $5 per game pitching for different towns during the Great Depression.[19]

Throughout his life, Gore showed great dedication to anything that interested him, almost to the point of obsession. Once, after the annual commencement ceremonies at his school, a fiddler, Uncle Berry Agee, who "sure drew a wicked bow," entranced him with country classics including "Turkey in the Straw" and "Old Joe Clark." The people dancing and stamping their feet and clapping their hands impressed the young boy. Afterward, Albert pestered his mother to buy him a fiddle. Ultimately, she took some money from the family's small savings and gave it to Reggie to buy a fiddle at a pawnshop in Nashville. He paid $4 for it and brought it home to Albert. "I recall how sad and disappointed I was when I drew the bow, and what came forth did not sound at all like Uncle Berry," he remembered. To compensate, he traveled "some distance away" after a day's work to the only man in the area who could teach the instrument. Heartened that the man told him he had a natural ear, Gore began practicing and playing to anyone that would listen. The noise became so bad that his father asked him to practice away from the house so he could go to sleep. After many hours of practice, Gore became a fairly good fiddler.[20]

Soon, Gore was playing with local bands at various functions. The activity became more than a hobby, but his father brought him back to earth. At one point, the family hosted a hoedown for their neighbors and invited several musicians. Among them was "Old Peg," the best mandolin player in the area, who arrived in a broken-down buggy pulled by a mangy horse. After a wonderful party, it came time for Old Peg to leave. As his cart wobbled away, Gore's father put his hand on his son's shoulder and told him, "Son, there goes your future." Gore noted that "this quiet and understated admonition shocked me as few things in my life have." While he continued to play the fiddle for much of his life, he turned his attentions elsewhere for a career. That focus soon turned toward politics. One day, he saw on some utility poles and trees signs announcing his cousin's run for a position in the state legislature. "In my childish imagination I was fascinated by the prospect of seeing my own picture there some day," Gore recalled. One friend, Donald Lee Hackett, remembered that as they worked in the fields, sometimes he and Gore's father would turn around and not see Albert. Eventually, they would find him "on a stump somewhere speaking to an imaginary crowd."[21]

Thus began the quest of a young Tennessean for the ultimate goal. Like many people in his generation, he wanted more than a farmer's life. The media, especially newspapers, magazines, and radio, promoted a more industrial way of life that glamorized more lucrative and exciting careers. Gore did not want to leave his home but wanted a profession that would allow him some of the world's comforts while maintaining the lifestyle of a gentleman farmer and cattleman. He mapped out his path early and, once decided, relentlessly pursued it.

Unlike many of his neighbors, Albert Gore had a high school education and other advantages. In 1925, he graduated from Gordonsville High School after only three years. His family instilled in him the values of hard work, loyalty, honesty, and integrity, and he had the self-confidence and drive to succeed. Many around him recognized Albert as a man on the move.

After graduating, Gore began searching for work outside the family farm. He admitted that "there was but one way to go from Possum Hollow—that was up and out!" and that "you couldn't get out except by going up, and once you got out, you still were pretty far down that pole."[22] To achieve his goals, he focused on teaching, although ultimately he wanted to practice law. "I came to love the profession," he noted, "and I enjoyed it and developed a pride in education."[23] For the next eleven years, he would teach and then become an administrator, all the while learning about life and politics.

Once he made the decision to teach, he pestered his father about enrolling at MTSTC to take an intensive instructor preparation course that the state required for a teaching certificate. Reluctantly, his father agreed, although he really wanted the young man to stay on the farm and help him with the summer chores. Nevertheless, they loaded up one morning and trucked off to Murfreesboro, some fifty miles away. Gore quickly finished the program, although he admitted upon earning his certificate that he was not a particularly qualified or skilled teacher.[24]

He returned home to Possum Hollow without a job. A chance visit by an uncle, Charlie Gore, who was chairman of the school board in Overton County, led to Gore's first position. One of the teachers in the system had resigned, and a job was available in the little hamlet of High Land. Gore jumped at the chance and rode with his uncle to Livingston, the county seat. To get to High Land, his uncle drove him as far as the roads allowed him, but Gore walked the last five miles up the mountain to a fork in the road. Unsure of which branch to take, he sat down and waited, playing his fiddle to pass the time. After a short wait, a man came by and told him that he was on his way to church and offered to take the new teacher along. The man carried Gore's belongings with the exception of his prized fiddle, which he kept close at hand.[25]

High Land at the time was also known as "Booze" because the most popular form of manufacturing was the production of moonshine. It was located not far from Byrdstown, the birthplace of Rep. Cordell Hull, and near Pall Mall, the home of the celebrated Tennessee war hero Alvin York. Gore called it a "beautiful little place," with only a few houses "scattered underneath huge beech trees along each side of a ravine. There were a general store and an old grist mill with a big wooden water wheel—and the one-room schoolhouse, which was also used for religious services."[26]

He immediately went to church with his guide and joined the choir, where he remembered sitting between a man with a large Adam's apple and long neck and a lovely, brown-eyed woman named Orpha Ledbetter. Despite being dismayed with his own performance, he enjoyed singing in a choir. The pastor called on "Professor Gore" to make some opening remarks, which he later characterized as his "dismal debut" as a public figure.[27]

The next day he opened school at 8 o'clock. Instead of the expected twenty-five students, more than forty arrived, including the lovely Orpha. He acknowledged that her presence created his first challenge in private versus public interest but that he managed to remain professional despite his infatuation with her. He started teaching "everything from ABCs to the eighth grade," even classes with which he had no experience, but he recalled the new materials as rather simple and manageable. It was a classic setting in which many rural Americans learned during the time.[28]

Gore described the period as his "Appalachian Spring." He boarded with a relative, Arkley Gore, who lived with his wife and daughter in a small two-room home with an attached lean-to. He paid them a dollar a day, which he took from his $75-a-month salary. Arkley Gore worked in a coal mine five miles away and also maintained a small farm. He left early in the morning on muleback and returned late at night, covered in coal dust. The poverty was extreme. During Gore's four-month stay, the family had processed meat only once, although he supplemented their diet by hunting in the mountains. He concluded that "the hardship of life was driven home to me in many ways." Later, as commissioner of labor, he would remember this experience and try to address the problems of men such as his cousin.[29]

After a semester of teaching, Gore had enough money to enter the University of Tennessee. He admitted that he knew he would attend school, "but finding the means to do so was somewhat difficult." In Knoxville, the money was tight as he mailed his shirts back home for his mother to launder and iron, returning them by mail because it was cheaper. To earn his meals, he waited tables at a restaurant on Gay Street downtown. When he started, the owner lectured him to eat only a reasonable amount. One day, however, he decided to have a piece of pie à la mode. The owner caught him and fired him for having an inordinate appetite.[30]

He spent the semester studying and particularly enjoyed the classes on English and history, but he found the college experience rather disappointing. "I had been an omnivorous reader," Gore stressed, "and things were not as new as I had anticipated except in the limited science and mathematical studies." He did not venture too far in the latter, although he noted that "later on in life when I found it necessary to try to understand complicated economic matters, accounting reports and business reports, discount and cash flow, . . . I found that the limited training I had in mathematics stood me in very good stead."[31]

The experience in Knoxville ended when the money ran out, and he returned home to earn tuition.

After a failed trip to earn money in Detroit during the summer and without funds to return to school that fall, Gore landed a teaching position in yet another one-room schoolhouse, at Little Creek in Smith County. He rented a room in a small four-room frame whitewashed house for $35 a month, which contrasted greatly with the extreme poverty of Arkley Gore's home. The family had a fertile, small creek-bottom plot, and the head of the household had a small veteran's pension and worked as a substitute mail carrier. Gore earned $85 a month, and by January he had enough money to go back to school.[32]

He returned to the university because "throughout my life, I have sought promotion." Ambitious and goal-oriented, he had his eyes on some day becoming principal of a four-teacher school in Pleasant Shade, and ultimately superintendent of schools of Smith County. Yet he realized he needed more education and, equally important, the validation of having a college degree, which would allow him to go to law school.[33]

In the winter of 1928 Gore enrolled again at MTSTC, which was closer to home and allowed him to focus on teaching. For the next four years, he would attend, although rarely in two consecutive terms, as he normally studied in the spring and summer terms if he had the money and taught during the fall. Nonetheless, he enjoyed college, especially athletic contests, dating, and friendships. He also learned some valuable information and skills and clearly benefited from the experience.[34]

Although he continued to enjoy history and English, he struggled at times. In one English class, he earned failing marks from a teacher who informed him that he lacked solid grammar and writing skills. With his typical tenacity, Gore asked for and received additional instruction. After much work, he passed the course and became "a stickler for correct punctuation, sentence structure, and paragraphing."[35]

He did not like all the subjects, especially education classes, which he complained were only marginally helpful. Such an attitude affected his grades. One fifth-grade student, Katherine Holden, who attended the campus training school, remembered stories circulated about Gore's teaching practices and his unorthodox approaches that particularly infuriated one supervisor. "I do not know if this is true," she recalled, "but the tale was that he was the only person that ever flunked practice teaching."[36]

At college, Gore admitted not being the "most docile and sedate" student. He made friends easily and was popular. A roommate, Lawrence Freeman, emphasized that "he was a real politician from day one. He was very likeable. I think he spent most of his time politicking instead of school." Still, another roommate, Rollie Holden, stressed that Gore was a good student when motivated and "was always pushing, he wanted to do better things."[37]

Gore was also a practical joker. One caper involved a trip to a local store where he bought some paper bags. When someone snored too loudly, he would fill a bag with water, walk slowly down the hall and throw the water on the person, then race back to his room and pretend to be asleep. His classmates sometimes turned the tables on him. On one occasion, someone crept into his room and stole his pajamas. The next day, Gore found them run up the flag pole in front of the Old Main. No one knew for sure how and when, but he eventually retrieved them.[38]

Gore also participated in organized activities. He was a member of the basketball and baseball squads and found time to participate in the drama club. A schoolmate, Baxter Hobgood, remembered that they cooperated in a production of *All's Quiet on the Western Front*. Gore worked with the lighting, did some of the directing, and had a part in the play. The production received a resounding standing ovation. At another performance, *Journey's End*, Gore played a young lieutenant. As he passed away in the final scene, a friend remembered, "Albert died beautifully. But as the curtain started closing, he reached out from his deathbed, held back the curtain, and died a little more. Albert always did like the limelight."[39]

While working and going to school, Gore actively participated in politics. In the 1928 presidential race between the Republican Herbert Hoover and Democrat Al Smith, the former governor of New York, Gore campaigned against Herbert Hoover, even before he was old enough to vote. He made his first political speech for Smith when a local congressman visited the school where Gore was the principal.[40]

Despite Gore's efforts, Hoover won Tennessee and the country. Many Tennesseans refused to support Smith because he was a Catholic, and Gore remembered his pastor giving a sermon on "Romanism and Rum, War, and Ruin." Lawrenceburg native Mabel Pittard also recalled that the word started spreading in her town that the Catholics planned to take over the country. People began hoarding guns and preparing to defend the country against the papal conspiracy. Many Americans shared such sentiments, especially in the South and the rural areas of the Midwest. Republicans played on these fears and made promises of continued economic prosperity to win the presidency easily in 1928, with 84 percent of the electoral vote and 58 percent of the popular vote.[41]

Why did Gore support such an unpopular candidate? The answer lies partly in the traditional Democratic orientation of Middle Tennessee but also in a hybrid ideology that had taken root in him. While the ideals of Jefferson and Jackson were significant and sometimes held sway, Gore's principles largely had been shaped by the two major reform movements of the late nineteenth and early twentieth centuries, populism and progressivism.

The Populist movement of the 1880s and 1890s had swept the agricultural areas of the South and Midwest. Efforts to organize farmers, and later labor, into a third party evolved from economic depressions and the unresponsiveness of the two major parties to their plight. By 1892, reformers banded together in the Populist Party to promote lower tariffs, public ownership of railroads and the communication system, and labor's rights. One Populist, Ignatius Donnelly, caught the essence of the movement with his declaration that "we believe that the powers of government—in other words, of the people—should be expanded . . . as rapidly and as far as the good sense of intelligent people and the teachings of experience shall justify to the end that oppression, injustice, and poverty shall eventually cease in the land."[42]

The Populist Party disappeared in 1896 when it fused with the Democratic Party and supported presidential candidate William Jennings Bryan. Nevertheless, the Populists had a long-term influence on U.S. history as their principles helped shape men such as Gore, Ralph Yarborough, and Lyndon Johnson. The Tennessean characterized populism as "an outstanding liberal movement" that based its appeal on "an equitable tax rate, opposition to favoritism for business . . . equitable money policies and forward looking farm and labor programs." "As one who believes there is much merit in this Populist heritage," he recalled, "it always seemed to me perfectly logical that government should play an active role in the nation's business affairs, and I have never lost faith in the government's ability to guarantee economic justice to all people."[43]

That the Populists supported Bryan highlights why he became one of Gore's heroes. The three-time presidential aspirant and congressman from Nebraska won much acclaim for his oratory skills. One of his most famous speeches was the "Cross of Gold" given at the Democratic National Convention in 1896. Opposing the gold standard, Bryan emphasized that "the humblest citizen in all the land, when clad in the armor of a righteous cause, is stronger than all the hosts of error." He argued that "there are two ideas of government. There are those who believe that, if you will only legislate to make the well-to-do prosperous, their prosperity will leak through on those below." By contrast, Democrats believed "that if you legislate to make the masses prosperous . . . their prosperity will find its way up through every class which rests upon them."[44]

Bryan also served as something of a role model in foreign policy. An internationalist, he supported the U.S. intervention in Cuba and later the Wilson administration's efforts to join the League of Nations. Yet he also recognized the constraints of American power. In 1900, in Indianapolis's Military Park, he stood with his running mate, Adlai E. Stevenson, and condemned the U.S. intervention in the Philippines. He emphasized that "imperialism would be profitable to the army contractors; it would be profitable to the ship owners, who carry live soldiers to the Philippines and bring dead soldiers back; it would be profitable to those who seize upon the franchises," but not to most Americans. He called for Filipino independence, which would allow the United States to become "a republic standing erect while empires all around are bowed beneath the weight of their own armaments—a republic whose flag is loved while other flags are only feared."[45]

Bryan had a long career as he became a prominent speaker on the "Chautauqua" speaking circuit, whose motto was "Religious-Democratic Faith in the Popularization of Knowledge." Lecturers spoke on various subjects in tents, opera houses, and other meeting sites to people who typically paid a quarter a person or one dollar for the family. Many people attended, including a young Estes Kefauver who heard Bryan in his hometown of Madisonville, Tennessee. Kefauver later wrote: "The experience I best remember at Madisonville when I was in Grammar and High School were [sic] once when William Jennings Bryan came with the Chautauqua. After that I studied all of his books and speeches."[46]

Others, including a young Albert Gore, read reprints of Bryan's speeches. Gore recalled that part of his political education was when his father would sit on the front porch after supper and read the newspaper. Many times he would "stop to discuss some new development. Often he would refer to William Jennings Bryan, whose achievements as 'the Great Commoner' are still cherished in the memory of the people of my state." "The Bryan to whom my father referred . . . was not the ineffectual Secretary of State under Wilson," according to Gore, "nor the pitiful old man of the 'monkey trial,' but the dynamic Cross of Gold Populist."[47]

Bryan acted as a bridge between the Populists and the progressives of the early twentieth century and helped shape Gore's views. The progressives were often urban-centered professionals from both parties, driven by humanitarian impulses to create a better society. Typically, the progressives started at the local level, then extended their interests to the state and, finally, the national level. They would achieve many successes at rationalizing a society that had been turned upside down by the rapid industrialization at the end of the nineteenth century.[48]

In the South, progressives focused on creating a "New South." Their goals were to industrialize and modernize the region through reform. They made significant gains in several areas, including improvement of mental health and prison facilities, better infrastructure and educational opportunities, and limits on the power of the corporations, especially the railroads and banking industries. Finally, some southern progressives fought for social justice, which included supporting antilynching laws, although most southern reformers at the time neglected African American concerns.[49]

While the southern progressives were revolutionary in some ways, they still believed in many southern traditions. One, historian Clement Eaton, recalled that while a student at the University of North Carolina he belonged to "a group of young liberals who felt that they had emancipated themselves from the shackles of old authority." Still, he noted that despite this new freedom, "we accepted unconcernedly some of the ruling assumptions of the society in which we had been reared." These included a slow and gradual approach toward change that attempted to reconcile progress and tradition.[50]

Progressive ideals took firm root in Gore's political philosophy. Like the progressives, he wanted to improve the plight of his fellow citizens and believed that gradual change protected "good" southern institutions. He also shared progressive ideas about the benefits of education, better infrastructure, and improved health care.[51] To Gore, only economic progress with compassion, rather than unbridled capitalism, would help the South evolve from its backwardness. This progressive impulse would make it much easier for him later to support the New Deal, Fair Deal, and Great Society programs.

Several progressives influenced Gore, especially Woodrow Wilson, whom he characterized as "a role model." Wilson was the classic progressive. The son of a Presbyterian minister, born in Virginia but raised in South Carolina, he earned a doctorate in political science from Johns Hopkins. Eventually, he became president of Princeton University and then Democratic governor of New Jersey in 1910.[52]

Over time, Wilson formulated ideas about the role of government, as he called on the Democratic Party to be "at once conservative in respect of the law and radical in respect of the service we mean to render to people." He added that the party's actions should focus on "the individual, not the corporation, the single living person, not the artificial group of persons existing merely by permission of law." Private monopoly was intolerable to him, and he promoted "wise regulation" that would remove obstacles "that now beset us in our search for justice and equality and fair chances of fortune for the individuals who make up our modern society."[53]

When Wilson won the presidency in 1912, he worked with other progressives to implement his ideas. Accomplishments during Wilson's administration included reduced tariffs, the Federal Reserve Act, the Clayton Anti-Trust Bill, and the Sixteenth Amendment (a federal income tax). Congress and state legislatures also approved the Seventeenth Amendment (direct election of senators) and Nineteenth Amendment (women's suffrage). Other victories occurred, although Wilson often moved slowly, fearful that the programs were paternalistic or unconstitutional.

The area where Wilson most shaped an entire generation of politicians was foreign relations. He was an internationalist who outlined many of his views in his famous "Fourteen Points." To a joint session of Congress in January 1918, he pushed for a just and lasting peace after World War I. He called for open covenants of peace, the "absolute" freedom of navigation of the seas, the removal of trade barriers, self-determination in former colonies, and the creation of an international body of nations "formed under specific covenants for the purpose of affording mutual guarantees of political independence and territorial integrity to great and small states alike."[54]

Although he failed to win support for a League of Nations and often ignored his own rhetoric with interventions in the Caribbean, Wilson's policies were highly influential. He helped mold an entire generation of leaders, including Franklin Roosevelt, Cordell Hull, J. William Fulbright, and Gore, who believed that the United States should reject its historical isolationism, especially in the aftermath of the Great Depression and rise of the fascists.[55] Wilson's ideals became a cornerstone for U.S. foreign relations after 1941, when a new generation of leaders assumed power in Washington.

Bryan, Wilson, and other reformers left an indelible mark on Gore and provided the foundations of his political philosophy, which changed little during his career. They typically challenged the vested interests in the name of the common man. They were idealistic, hoping that the government, in tandem with individuals, could raise the standards of living for all Americans. In foreign policy, they supported increased economic exchanges and a more rational world system that brought nations together to promote peace and stability. Thus, Gore became part of a long-term transition in U.S. politics, one that was underway prior to the Great Depression and a dominant force after 1945.

Gore's political ambitions momentarily took a back seat in late 1929 as the Great Depression wreaked havoc on the country and world. There were many causes of the calamity including poor lending practices in the bank industry, an overinflation of the stock market, weak markets in Europe, and the ongoing depression in the agricultural sector. The administrations of Warren G. Harding and Calvin Coolidge, led by Secretary of the Treasury Andrew Mellon, had constructed tax laws that provided little relief to the majority of Americans and exacerbated structural problems. The burden fell on President Hoover to deal with the massive catastrophe, a role in which he failed miserably.[56]

The depression struck the Gore family like everyone else. Allen Gore had been fairly prosperous and had paid off his mortgage. Afterward, he deposited his surpluses in three banks in Watertown, Alexandria, and Rome, building up a nest egg of nearly $8,000. Within a few days of the Wall Street crash, however, banks began failing throughout the region, including those where Allen Gore put his money. He never recovered a single dollar.[57]

While the family was comparatively self-sufficient, they still needed to buy supplies such as cloth, sugar, and spices. Without cash, Allen Gore decided to send some of his cattle and hogs to market in Nashville. He hired a driver to transport the animals, but the man returned and told Gore that the livestock did not bring enough at auction to pay for his hauling bill.[58]

Albert Gore watched the depression result in "bankruptcy, mortgage foreclosures, desperation, fear and want." He remembered a man telling him that he had lost his job and could not find another. The bank had foreclosed on his house and the store repossessed his furniture. His wife had lost her washing machine, which had helped support the family. Because of the conditions, the man sent his wife to live with her parents and placed his children in an orphanage.[59] Such stories had a profound impact on Gore. As the crisis worsened, many people sought refuge in the cities but few found relief, and desperation, hunger, and hopelessness ruled for nearly a decade, shaping the perspectives of a whole generation.

Fortunately, the Gore family had enough to eat and a place to live. Albert continued to teach and go to school when he earned enough money for a semester. He became the principal of a four-room school and continued to live with his family, which eased his financial burden. Over time, his vision of holding a higher office reemerged as he had continued participating in local Democratic Party activities and planning for his own run for superintendent of schools.

At the height of the depression in 1932, he made a fateful decision. Twenty-five years old and full of vigor, he decided to challenge the long-time superintendent of schools in Smith County, Lee Huffines, who had held the office since 1915, with only one four-year interruption. During this time, Huffines had created a great deal of opposition, and the young Gore hoped to take advantage of this, believing that he had many ideas that could improve the school district's performance.

He started to campaign early. One of his college roommates, Rollie Holden, observed that Gore always received a lot of mail and always seemed to be reading and writing letters. He remembered one night asking Albert to go out, but he responded that he could not because he had some more correspondence. When asked why, Gore answered that the letters were from his students back home and that "I am going to run for county superintendent next year, and I expect all of those kids to get their mothers and fathers to vote for me."[60]

As in later elections, Gore campaigned tirelessly, speaking at picnics, barbeques, graduations, and other public ceremonies. None was too remote or small for him as he followed the advice of Judge Joseph M. Gardenhire, who had told him to "never turn down the opportunity to speak. There will always be two or three fools in the audience who will think it was a good one."[61] When he had no speaking engagements, Gore went door to door.

He also established a precedent for himself during the election. He noted that Huffines had been challenged before in "bitter personality conflicts, charges back and forth." Instead, Gore focused on the issues and avoided personal attacks. While maybe not the most expedient course of action, Gore refused to take the campaign to a personal level, a pattern he followed for many years.

He made quite a race against the incumbent. On election night, he stood with a large crowd in front of the old stone courthouse in Carthage, not far from the bluffs overlooking the Cumberland River. The editor of the county newspaper had erected a large blackboard with results on which people trained their car lights. As the returns arrived, it showed Gore winning by more than one hundred votes. Then the officials counted the absentee ballots, and he lost by 184 votes. Huffines had sent a team of his supporters to Detroit, Akron, and other northern cities where Smith County residents lived temporarily to gather votes. Gore admitted that he had not thought of it, and there was nothing illegal about the strategy; "I just didn't do it." He concluded that "I learned that you look for votes and you get votes from whatever sources you legally can do so. I later profited by the experiences."[62]

Defeated, the young man depended on Huffines for a job. He soon visited the superintendent and later recalled him as a very friendly man, especially since

Gore had waged a clean campaign. Gore asked for a position as a teacher, having the audacity to request a job in a large community that had voted against him during the election. The superintendent declined, responding, "I'm not going to put you there, you'd beat me next time."[63]

At the height of the depression, Gore was unemployed and living in a devastated nation. After his defeat, Gore worked on the farm. He went to the market where he received less than $100 for a summer's work. The sale of his goods left a lasting impression on him. There, he saw men unable to feed or clothe their families. "I recognized the face of poverty: grown men who were so desperate," he observed, "the tears streamed down their cheeks as they stood with me at the window to receive their meager checks for a full year's work." Standing there, he "vowed to remember the ignominy of their plight."[64]

The lack of a teaching job following his loss in the election led Gore to observe that "my own condition was embarrassing" although "never desperate." He went to the Dupont rayon plant in Old Hickory and stood in line for a week without receiving an interview. Then, he tried unsuccessfully to borrow $40 from a Carthage bank to travel to Detroit and try his luck in the factories. Finally, a furniture man, Bill Tuley, hired him as a door-to-door salesman. Each day, he had routes where he loaded a high-sided truck with goods such as carpets, kitchen goods, and anything that he thought he might trade for produce or animals. For his work, he earned $12.50 a week.[65]

While he was working as a door-to-door salesman, good fortune shone on Gore. He took advantage of an opportunity one day by accepting some tobacco in exchange for goods. Tuley was from west Tennessee and knew little about the product, so Gore offered to buy it for $20. He agreed and promised to deduct it from his next two paychecks. The following day, Gore graded and prepared the tobacco and sold it for $38. Afterward, he paid his debt and quit his job.[66]

With only a few dollars to his name, Gore began buying and selling tobacco. Because he had so little money, typically he waited until the end of the day before giving the farmer a check so that he could not deposit it immediately. He then negotiated with the local banker not to cash the check until he had sold the product. Almost every morning, Gore rushed to the bank and deposited his earnings. The ingenuity and hard work paid off. By the end of the season, he had earned nearly $1,000, which he described as "burning a hole in my pocket." With the proceeds, Gore made a wise investment in a small farm outside of Carthage, putting him closer to the center of power in his district.[67]

The industrious young man also decided to reward himself by taking a trip to Washington to visit his congressman, J. Ridley Mitchell. After disembarking his railroad car in Union Station, he proceeded to the Dodge Hotel, carrying most of his belongings in a new suitcase he had bought for 98 cents. While only pasteboard, it was painted to look like leather. Unfortunately, during his walk to the hotel, a downpour descended on him. The paint wore off and dripped down as the suitcase fell apart. He arrived at the hotel with his arms full of clothes, almost everything he owned, and took a room.[68]

The next day, he dressed up in his finest suit and set off to Mitchell's office. Gore characterized him as quite a character, noting "there was a saying in the old Fourth District that he was the only Congressman who could promise every constituent a post office and then make him happy not to get it." Mitchell greeted him enthusiastically and told him how much he respected his father and grandfather and then gave Gore a pass for the congressional gallery. For three days, he observed the speeches and legislative processes. Finally, he traveled home, firmly convinced that he "could do anything they were doing."[69]

On his return from Washington, Gore continued to scratch out a living. He soon received a break, albeit an unfortunate one. In April 1933, doctors diagnosed Huffines with terminal cancer. Lying on his deathbed, the superintendent asked his supporters to pressure the county court to appoint Gore as his replacement because he had run a clean campaign. Soon after Huffines's death, Gore became the new leader of schools for Smith County.

The way that Gore obtained his position was significant for several reasons. He noted that his running a clean and "gentlemanly contest" created few enemies and helped him solidify support among various factions in his county. These people became valuable allies in future political races. Equally as important, he stressed that he learned a "fruitful lesson": "to minimize the personal angle in campaigns, and to engage in principles not in personalities."[70]

In early 1933, Franklin D. Roosevelt became president of the United States. During the fall campaign, Gore had supported Roosevelt, stressing "the need for change"; "the opportunity and necessity for reform seemed so imperative that I was ready to join any movement in that direction." He attended rallies and made several speeches condemning Hoover and praising Roosevelt, recalling that he was "exulted in the battle because I felt that the country needed a change from our terrible economic hardships."[71]

The new president had promised a New Deal. While sitting with some friends in a barbershop in Carthage, Gore heard Roosevelt declare in a radio address that "All we have to fear is fear itself." He noted that "the strength of that matchless voice and the confidence and determination in his words seemed to reach every part of our community and to awaken hope where none had been." To him, the "election of Franklin D. Roosevelt rolled like an irresistible tide" over the country, giving hope to all Americans.[72]

Roosevelt fulfilled his promise to provide action. In his first two years in office, he created projects such as the Civilian Conservation Corps (CCC), which put young men to work throughout the country, and he reformed the banking industry and stock market through the Federal Deposit Insurance Corporation (FDIC) and the Securities and Exchange Commission (SEC). To help the country's farmers, the Agricultural Adjustment Act (AAA) tried to prevent overproduction and raise commodity prices, and labor received benefits under the Wagner Act. Of particular interest to the people of the Upper Cumberland was the creation of the Tennessee Valley Authority (TVA), which would construct dams, manage flood control and navigation, and stabilize agricultural development while simultaneously providing cheap electricity. For many Americans, the New Deal instilled hope and helped prevent the terrible political upheavals sweeping the world in the 1930s.[73]

The New Deal impressed Gore, who stressed that with the exception of the elite and "hard-shell" Republicans, even the southern conservatives greeted Roosevelt's proposals favorably. "Among my acquaintances, enthusiasm was deep and genuine," Gore remembered. Building on the Populist and progressive beliefs that the federal government, under proper leadership, could help the majority of Americans, Gore thought that Roosevelt capitalized on the "roots of social justice. He nourished them on pure water and cheap electricity—and they quickly sprouted."[74]

Another reason the people in Upper Cumberland supported the New Deal so heartily was because one of their own, Cordell Hull, had become Secretary of State. Born in Overton County in 1871, Hull had lived primarily in Carthage, the son of a comparatively affluent merchant; at age twenty he had graduated from Cumberland Law School. A devoted Democrat, he made his first partisan speech at seventeen. From a position as circuit judge, he won a seat in the state legislature at twenty-two and moved on to the House of Representatives in 1906, a seat he held with only one interruption until 1930 when he was elected to the Senate.[75] A cautious but progressive politician, Hull focused on issues dear to his constituents, including tariffs, trade, and the income tax, which he co-sponsored as a constitutional amendment. He also backed organized labor, the eight-hour workday, and child labor laws. Deliberate in his actions and hard working, Hull remained a prominent player in the Democratic Party throughout the 1920s and 1930s. For his efforts, Roosevelt put him in charge of the State Department.[76]

Hull set a standard for aspiring young politicians in the Upper Cumberland. Although he lacked charisma, he worked extremely hard and resisted the temptations of Washington's darker sides. One observer noted that "he made a fine personal impression with his old-fashioned Southern chivalry and his slow drawl . . . He possessed a rigid sense of morality, was a devoted husband, preferred old friends to suave dilettantes, and had an abiding distaste for social engagement. When given the choice, after a day's work on Capitol Hill, he preferred to spend a quiet evening at home, occasionally enjoying a very mild rye highball."[77]

The Gore family had personal ties to Hull. Allen Gore and Hull had "run the river," going down the Cumberland on rafts of logs and then traveling home on the steamboat together. Gore recalled that "around the fireside, Hull was a hero" and "my father was his supporter." The family took Hull's loss for Congress in 1920 very hard and supported him after he retook the office in 1922. When Hull ran for the Senate in 1930, the Gores enthusiastically supported him.[78]

Hull provided young Albert Gore a good role model. In the early 1940s, *Collier's* reported that a young Gore remembered going to Carthage on a mule to the miller. While standing on top of a sack of corn, he watched Hull working among stacks of books in his garden, which overlooked the Cumberland River. "Only a country lad who had fought a contrary mule and plowed the rocky, unproductive Cumberland mountainsides," the reporter observed, "with only the privilege of going to mill on Saturday for recreation, could appreciate the contrast between a mountain farmer and a congressman . . . Young Gore decided to be a congressman."[79]

Recognizing the significance of political connections, Gore nurtured ties with Hull. While serving as a principal at Pleasant Shade, Gore would drive the twelve miles to Carthage after work to learn from the senator. "By that time, Judge Hull, as everybody called him, would have finished his mail and his lunch," Gore remembered, "and now and then would be up under the trees in the courthouse, talking with the checker players and other people. I would sit nearby and listen to him, and I became greatly impressed."[80]

Hull helped shape Gore's political principles. In many ways, he bridged the gap between the progressive movement and the New Deal. His two major areas of interest were the income tax and the tariff, both of which became primary areas of interest to Gore as a representative of the Fourth District. Later, when

Gore arrived in Washington, Hull became a political mentor he described as an "anchor" during his early years in the capital.[81] Throughout Gore's career, Hull's portrait hung prominently in his office.

While concerned with the national scene, Gore focused on his job as superintendent of schools. First, he worked to pay the teachers in cash rather than in county warrants. Before he took office, the banks refused to honor the warrants, forcing teachers to wait for the county tax collector to gather enough revenue to compensate them. Desperate for cash, teachers sometimes sold their warrants, such as one young man who traded a $100 promissory note for $60 cash. Gore went to the banks and arranged loans to pay the checks immediately.[82]

He also focused on improving school transportation systems and consolidating and streamlining operations to balance the budget. These efforts included purchasing buses to take children from the more remote areas to better locations. Although he believed that one- and two-room schools had many benefits, the smaller schools were economically inefficient. He approached the county court for money to purchase buses. After an all-day fight, Gore won, and the school district bought its first school buses.[83]

Finally, he used federal programs to help the community and schools. Gore sponsored a works project that leveled the football field by pick and shovel. He stressed that before that the field had been eight feet lower on a "down-hill-drag" corner, one he called "our favorite touchdown corner." While machinery could have done the job quicker and more efficiently, Gore wanted to provide more people with work.[84] Such tasks, along with the daily duties of monitoring teachers and maintaining good community relations, took a lot of time and energy.

Still, Gore had bigger plans, and he continued working in the local Democratic Party. As at other important junctures in his life, he received a big break as a result of his hard work and good timing. In 1934, the Young Democrats met to discuss the midterm elections. At the meetings, one of the campaign managers of a candidate sponsored by Memphis Boss Edward Crump's machine sought the group's endorsement. Gore organized the opposition, arguing the Young Democrats should not back any particular candidate. He won, sparking interest among some of the people watching the convention. Soon after, Rep. Gordon Browning, who wanted a Senate seat, approached Gore and asked him to manage his campaign. While the twenty-seven-year-old Gore complained that he lacked qualifications, Browning persisted, and Gore ultimately accepted.[85]

One person described Browning's choice as a good one because "Gore proved to be intelligent, aggressive, and willing to learn." With Gore as the campaign chair, Browning challenged Senator Nathan Bachman, who had the support of Boss Crump. Crump had dominated Tennessee politics for years by maintaining a coalition between western Tennessee Democrats and Republicans in east Tennessee. Browning focused on the issues, rather than attacking Bachman as Crump's puppet. He supported aid to disabled veterans, various New Deal programs, and the TVA. With Gore at his side, he criss-crossed the state, making speeches and shaking hands. Despite a spirited effort, Browning lost the August primary.[86]

During the campaign, Gore gained some valuable experience. It gave the future senator his first exposure to a statewide race and allowed him to create many long-term connections with prominent Tennessee Democrats. Gore also received an appointment as chair of the speakers' bureau of the Democratic party nominees, largely resulting from a custom of placating the losing side. He used this position well by making sure that Congressman Mitchell received special preference in talking in the larger towns with media outlets. Nevertheless, as one observer noted, when the "congressman was not scheduled to speak in his own district, Gore accepted those engagements, and began to be 'mentioned' for Congress."[87]

Despite Gore's successes, times were hard for most Americans. In 1934 the depression appeared unending. Farm prices remained low, and many people in the cities survived by relying on charity. Throughout the world, economies continued to fail and democracies collapsed from the weight of the calamity. It took a young man with energy and determination to succeed in such a setting. Gore was such a man, and with the help of his family and good luck, he continued to gain ground.

Through all his travails, Gore still maintained a good sense of humor, although one with an edge. One Saturday night he organized a barn party near the Cumberland River in Carthage. In advance, he planted a suggestion that he had seen a bunch of rattlesnakes in the area. As the partygoers stood by a fire, he attached a fish hook to the pant leg of a friend, Walter Merriman. At the end of the line, he tied a large black snake that he had killed earlier. Waiting for the right moment, he shouted "Snake!" and pointed at the dead one several feet from Merriman. The startled man jumped up and ran away. Desperately fleeing, he found that the more he ran, the more the attached snake chased him. He ran so hard that the fish hook ultimately went through the pants and sank into his flesh. Believing that the snake had bitten him, he passed out. The story became a local legend, and it took Gore several months to repair the friendship.[88]

Although he was buried in politics and his job, Gore believed that he needed to add to his résumé if he wanted to become a congressman. Despite his intense schedule, he began traveling to Nashville to attend law classes at the local YMCA. Three evenings a week, he made the fifty-two-mile trip on Highway 70. There, he studied for three hours and then returned to Carthage. "I literally drove a distance around the world to get my law degree," he boasted later.[89]

Obtaining a law degree was important, but a more significant event occurred during his studies in Nashville. Each night, he would go to the café in the Andrew Jackson Hotel to get some coffee to help him stay awake on his return trip. Soon, he reported that the coffee tasted bad "unless a certain beautiful blue-eyed girl served it."[90] After many talks, Gore began escorting the woman back to her residence at the local YWCA. It was the beginning of a lifelong romance.

The young woman was Pauline LaFon, who later reminded Gore that they had actually met when a friend of hers had introduced them as he campaigned with Browning in 1934. She had been raised in a small farm community in Weakley County in western Tennessee, near Palmersville. Her family bore a striking resemblance to Gore's, as her father was a small store owner and farmer who had moved to the area from Arkansas in 1911. Pauline had been born soon after, in 1912. Like most children, she had many chores, and for recreation she played basketball and waded in the creeks to escape the heat and humidity of the summertime. The family members were devout Christians, attending the local Church of Christ, a conservative hybrid of Southern Baptists.[91]

When Pauline was thirteen, the family moved to Jackson after her father developed a debilitating disease that hampered the use of one of his arms. He took an administrative job with the local highway department, handing out gasoline tickets to road crews and patrolmen. To help the family meet its financial obligations, her mother, Maude, kept a small garden and rented rooms to boarders in their modest home. Pauline worked hard, helping her mother by cooking and cleaning and looking after the other children, especially Thelma, who was blind. Years later, her brother Whit (who became a Madison County circuit judge) called her "the heart of the family. She just always had a burning desire to better herself. She probably had more guts than anyone I'd ever seen."[92]

In Jackson, Pauline attended high school, where her friends remembered her as serious and determined. One classmate, Nell Lowe Nuckolls, recalled that "she was very studious . . . She worked hard . . . She was a very genuine friend, a very sincere person with a good sense of humor." Another person observed that she was "not the class clown or over-involved, join-every-club type that usually dominates friends' memories." Her name did not appear often in the Jackson High yearbook, nor was she listed in the class prophecy or will. The "Who's Who" stressed that while other girls primped and giggled, Pauline "spent her time 'keeping house' and listed her ambition as 'to make her husband happy.' "[93]

Initially, she had tried to conform to the standards of society for women of the time by marrying a local man, but the union ended quickly. After the failed attempt to meet expectations, she focused on a nontraditional route. A defining event was that both her grandmother and mother had suffered discrimination because of their gender. "I was greatly influenced by the stories my father told me about his struggles helping both my mother and his mother with their problems inheriting land rightly belonging to them instead of all of it going to their brothers. As a young child, I thought about such inequalities and thought that was something I would like to help change," she recalled. Had she been a lawyer, she argued, "I could have helped with that."[94]

To accomplish her goals, she attended Union College, a small Baptist institution, in Jackson. To earn money for school, she worked as a waitress in a tearoom on the courthouse square. Many of the customers were lawyers, so she listened to them talk and before it was over, she believed that "I could do anything that they did." Law also held a special place for her because she knew that she "didn't have to take any more math."[95] In two years, she finished her studies, helping Thelma at Union at the same time.

After college, she gained entrance into Vanderbilt Law School. To pay her way, she borrowed $200 from the local Rotary Club. Her brother Whit emphasized that "she had a real ambition" and added that she was a feminist before it was in vogue and "a leading person in the fight for women's rights."[96]

While attending Vanderbilt, she lived at the YWCA. In the morning, she attended classes and studied until she took the trolley to the Jackson Hotel café at 5:30 where she worked until 10:00. Fellow students remembered her as having beautiful blue eyes and a no-nonsense demeanor. One person who competed against her in moot court noted that "she wanted results . . . She wasn't satisfied leaving anything halfway." Within three years, she would be the only female graduate in the class of 1936.[97]

While waiting on tables, she met the young superintendent of schools for Smith County. Her first opinion was that he was charming but that "he was serious even then. I couldn't tempt him to leave any serious work, no matter how fancy a party we were invited to."[98] Despite her initial opinion, the two became a couple after the long talks and walks back to the YWCA. It was the start of a lifelong commitment in which they would share the tremendous ups and downs of personal, political, and professional lives.

Pauline's influence on her husband was significant. Albert later described her as "keenly astute, enormously loyal, I guess most of all, a very sensitive person; her political judgment is excellent. She could sense trouble many times more quickly than I. And, as adroitly she remembers people, names, faces, personalities excellently, better than I." He characterized their life as one of mutuality, and his need for her and stories reinforce it. Once, Pauline grew exasperated and told him, "I think I'll leave." Without hesitating, he responded: "Why that's a good idea. I believe that I will go with you."[99]

Others stressed Pauline's enormous influence on her husband and her contribution to their political life. Journalist David Halberstam, a family friend, characterized Pauline as the one "looking out from behind for the guys with knives." He added that Pauline was "smarter, tougher, more calculating."[100] She would remain throughout their political lives an important adviser and confidant and later performed a similar role for her son Al when he entered politics.

Pauline recognized Albert's strengths. She emphasized that "there are two kinds of men. One, the wife is in the background. But Albert wanted me right up front with him." The couple in many ways had a unique relationship, far ahead of its time. Their son Al noted later that "of all the lessons he taught me as a father, perhaps the most powerful was the way he loved my mother." Al added that he always treated her as an equal and was proud of her. "But it went way beyond that," he added. "When I was growing up, it never once occurred to me that the foundation upon which my security depended would ever shake. As I grew older, I learned from them the value of a true, loving partnership that lasts for life."[101]

Despite their attraction, Albert and Pauline hesitated to marry. Pauline wanted to try her hand at law after graduation, where she had been only the tenth female graduate in the history of Vanderbilt Law School. Gore had a full plate with his jobs and flowering political career. Like many people of the time, they waited, partly because of the economic catastrophe that caused many people to seek some financial stability before starting a family.

While deciding their paths, the two studied hard for the bar exam. The big day came and passed. Both were nervous as they waited for their scores. During a trip through Memphis, Pauline found out they had passed and earned entrance to the Tennessee bar. Gore liked to joke that it was "by the slimmest, thinnest margin, she made a grade of 84 on her test and I made 84 1/4. By that narrow margin, I maintained a position as head of the household."[102]

With her degree in hand and a strong recommendation from the dean of the law school, Pauline took a job in Texarkana, Arkansas, with a fellow Vanderbilt graduate. Despite not wanting to leave Albert, she emphasized that "I had worked so hard and built up my hopes so . . . I knew I'd be sorry if I didn't give this job a try." She packed her bags and moved to Arkansas to work to pay off her school loans by taking on many types of cases, including divorce cases, which at the time were very difficult and a bold move for a young female lawyer.[103]

Gore also tried his hand at law, although he never relinquished his position as superintendent of schools. On the Monday after the Nashville paper published that he had passed the bar exam, a fellow named Joe called him over near the courthouse. They went behind a tree, which was the habit when people wanted to talk confidentially. Joe told him that he heard that Gore was now a lawyer and inquired about him possibly taking his case. A well-known bootlegger who went to court about every three months, Joe was in trouble again. Since Joe was his first potential client, Gore pondered what he should charge, fearful of asking too little and aggravating the other lawyers, but not wanting to ask too much. He settled on $10. Exasperated, Joe walked away muttering, "Hell, I can get a good lawyer for that."[104]

Gore had a few more clients, but he really did not practice long because fate again intervened and took him in another direction. In 1936, Gordon Browning decided to run for governor. While not serving as his campaign chairman as in 1934, Gore vigorously supported Browning, who promised administrative reforms, the establishment of a conservation agency, and other progressive changes. He also appeared willing to challenge the patronage stranglehold of the Crump machine.[105] After winning, Browning asked Gore to join his cabinet as commissioner of labor. Gore accepted, and the twenty-nine-year-old took the position in the fall of 1936.

He jumped into the job with his usual enthusiasm and vigor. It was new and challenging because he had experience only with farm labor. When some of the organized labor leaders complained about his appointment, Gore went to Rogersville and took an apprenticeship as a pressman. Within a short time, he became a licensed pressman's assistant and gained union membership, carrying his union card wherever he went. The job took him to the major cities and industries across the state where he worked with businessmen, laborers, union leaders, and politicians to implement several programs.[106]

A major drain on his time and energy was the administration of the office. Requests for positions poured in from lawyers, accountants, and clerical personnel. He resisted the pressure to dispense patronage, even from family members such as his uncle, Charlie Gore, who was in the Tennessee House. Nevertheless, he was a good politician who often encouraged people to stop by and meet with him to discuss future opportunities.[107]

Others encouraged him to change the attitude of the office toward labor. A friend, C. W. Heard, complained that "labor in Tennessee has been sold down the river by a flock of so-called leaders without vision, ability or conscience, who have been led captive by machine politicians from time immemorial." He called on Gore to establish stronger ties with labor, in particular with Steve Nance, president of the Georgia Federation of Labor and CIO and regional director.[108] Gore complied in many cases and started a relationship with industrial labor, albeit one that had some bumps in the road, as he remained primarily a farm man for many years.

Learning and administering the Mine Inspection Law became one of Gore's first chores. Strongly influenced by having lived with Arkley Gore, he took the job very seriously. The Mine Inspection Office had a horrible record with high numbers of accidents and deaths. "I didn't know anything about coal mining but I made it my business to find out about it," Gore recalled. "I went down in the mines," he added, "and I had people who knew mining to explain where the hazards were, what the dangers were, where inspection was needed to make the mines safe." He found out that many of the inspectors were political hacks who asked to see the company's records but never did actual inspections. With Browning's approval, he fired them all and replaced them with professionals who were engineers or former miners. He also helped purchase testing equipment and required rigorous examination of conditions. Hostility arose, but Gore observed that "the only shield one could erect against such animus was the conviction that social reforms must be carried out even if they offend the vested interests."[109]

His most important piece of work was the development and implementation of the unemployment compensation program required by the Social Security Act and National Unemployment Act. Working tirelessly and traveling to Washington often to consult with national planners, Gore established a viable system. Throughout, he battled state politicians, including Senator Kenneth McKellar, who tried interfering in its administration. Gore wrote a friend that he preferred avoiding conflict but that "when someone insults me by an assault upon the honesty of my efforts and attempts to prevent the proper performance of my duties, I, like the mountain ancestors of whom I am proud, first feel an impulse to fight and fight hard." Over time, he would succeed; his plan became a model, and leaders ordered states that failed to meet national standards to study the Tennessee plan.[110]

Gore also enforced federal codes and also monitored the Fair Labor Standards Bill, which ultimately created a national minimum wage law. The young commissioner watched as some congressional representatives, many with ties to conservative southern business organizations such as the Southern States Industrial Council, denounced the act for strangling industry. Rep. Eugene Cox (D-GA) called it a terrible measure that "would throw a million out of work," while Martin Dies (D-TX) announced that "there is a racial question here. Under this measure what is prescribed for one race must be prescribed for the other. And you cannot prescribe the same wage for the black man as for the white man." Gore noted that Roosevelt "was not content to lose this fight," and the bill passed. Much to his delight, Gore highlighted that "there is no record to show that it 'throttled' industry."[111]

One of Gore's most significant acts during his tenure as commissioner of labor had nothing to do with work. On May 15, 1937, Albert and Pauline traveled to Tompkinsville, Kentucky, right across the Tennessee-Kentucky line, and married. The two had maintained their relationship after Pauline moved to Texarkana. Gore visited and found an unhappy Pauline. While she lived in a nice home with a widow and her two daughters, her workplace was extremely hostile and her boss consistently harassed her. She wrote a mentor at Vanderbilt that her boss "was impossible for me to work with. I am doing everything I can to make him fire me." He responded that she should quit and prevent any blot on her record. Pauline did not make the incident publicly known until many years later, but the event soured her on the practice of law, and she returned to Nashville after seven months.[112]

The marriage officially united the two as Pauline proved an able supporter of Albert. With her background in the law, she provided significant input on the unemployment compensation system and other issues. She was happy to help her husband: "Of course, I was interested in anything he was doing because we were newly married. Both ambitious. I was not only ambitious for myself but for him also. I was pleased that things were coming along for him."[113] She also soon discovered that she was expecting a child. By early 1938, she was a mother to Nancy LaFon Gore. Her priorities had shifted dramatically, and she readily accepted the new responsibilities. For both Albert and Pauline, the family and dedication to each other through the good and bad times would remain a cornerstone of their marriage until his death in 1998.

Gore continued as commissioner of labor until 1938. Working hard at being a family man and politician, he also prepared for the future by remaining active in the Democratic Party. He cemented his position among many party loyalists by backing the TVA, Social Security, the AAA, and particularly Roosevelt's dedication to the minimum wage and increasing the inheritance tax, graduated corporation income tax, and a gift tax on fortunes.[114]

Despite his support of the New Deal, Gore remained independent-minded. By 1938, Gore had soured on some of Roosevelt's efforts, especially those to purge conservative Senator Walter George (D-GA) and Senator Millard Tydings (D-MD) from the Democratic Party, as well as the president's court packing scheme. In particular, he criticized the fact that Crump and McKellar controlled the patronage associated with works projects. Roosevelt needed southern congressional support, and he understood the value of pork-barrel politics. "At times, this practice served to entrench the conservatives and hamper liberals," Gore lamented. Gore also opposed the fashion in which many of the New Deal programs became law. Most went to the House in gag-rule fashion, limiting debates and amendments, which he asserted created a "kind of undemocratic practice, [which] even when used in an emergency, is questionable because it prevents the collective judgment and will of Congress from being applied during the legislative process and stifles any opportunity to improve laws."[115]

Still, Gore's criticisms of the New Deal were minor compared to those of the conservative opponents who attacked Roosevelt's programs for being socialist, communist, fascist, and any other political anathema to the American way of life. In the South, the conservatives appealed to the tradition of states' rights and condemned federal interference in the economic and political well-being of the region. Senator Carter Glass (D-VA) called the New Deal "an utterly dangerous effort of the federal government to transport Hitlerism into every corner of the nation."[116] The majority of the strongest opponents were wealthy industrialists or political leaders whom the New Deal coalition threatened to displace. Birmingham chemical manufacturer Theodore Swann argued that "Sherman's march to the sea was no more destructive than the NRA is going to be to the South. Before it is over, we may have secession."[117]

Gore disagreed, believing that despite its shortcomings, the New Deal worked and that "the doctrine of states' rights . . . was only a smokescreen for inaction."[118] As labor commissioner, Gore battled men like Swann in the coal mines and manufacturing industries throughout his state. He viewed them as greedy and unconcerned with the welfare of the majority. In addition, he believed in a Jeffersonian ideal of the superiority of the producer. Such views would remain a consistent feature in Gore's philosophy.

His first trip to Washington and subsequent visits during his tenure as commissioner of labor made Gore covet higher office. "For my own part, I exulted in the search for solutions and longed for an opportunity to go to Washington and have a part in the great drama," he recalled.[119] Still, he recognized the futility of challenging J. Ridley Mitchell for the Fourth District congressional seat because the congressman had a good record and incumbency would make it very difficult to unseat him.

In 1938, good fortune again shone on Gore. A friend from a local newspaper told him that Mitchell had decided to run for the Senate. Without hesitating, Gore told him to take down his statement that he would seek Mitchell's seat. The paper was about to go to press, so Gore was the first to announce, and his story appeared alongside that of Mitchell's declaration. Gore admitted that the announcement "aggravated some of my colleagues and friends because they were older and thought they should have been first."[120]

Gore's announcement caught some people off guard, including Pauline. "He didn't tell me. It was early one morning and he had gone to the office," she remembered. "He announced before he even called me." She admitted knowing that he harbored such ambitions, but "I was surprised that it came at the time. But, I didn't know how to take it. I knew it affected me or whatever career I might have. I knew that before I married."[121]

Gore recognized it would be a hard campaign and that it was a gamble. He resigned his position as commissioner of labor, giving up the best job he ever had. Soon, he started off on a three-month-long campaign with a new wife and baby girl. He faced five other candidates in a large district that covered eighteen counties with a population of 300,000, and he encountered strong opposition from those tied to the "federal crowd," people allied with various factions in the state, including Crump and McKellar. He had some advantages, however, including his record as school superintendent and commissioner of labor, as well as Governor Browning's support. The Gore family had a good name in the area, and his kinship ties reached deep. It was a tough challenge, but one he and Pauline believed they could meet.

To finance his effort, Gore traveled to the bank in Carthage and mortgaged his small farm. Starting with $3,000 in a campaign war chest and great energy and determination, he set out on a tireless campaign schedule that took him to all the parts of the district. Pauline arranged speaking engagements by calling towns ahead of time and asking party leaders and backers to get people to attend the speech, whether on the courthouse lawn, at a picnic, or at any social gathering. Afterward, she telephoned people in the area phone book and encouraged them to come and listen. Then, the family drove by car from place to place as Albert often spoke at several events each day.[122] He had only a small political organization, mainly family members and close friends, but they were loyal foot soldiers for this election and many years to come.

In his campaign for the Democratic nomination, Gore concentrated on issues that meant a lot to the farmers and small merchants of the region. In particular, he hammered home that he supported Hull's programs of reciprocal trade and low tariffs. On the New Deal, he highlighted his backing of the TVA and efforts to help farmers with price supports. During the campaign, Gore relied on two slogans. The first was, "Economics is only arithmetic writ large," and the other was advice that he received from an old man: "Son, always start from where you're at."[123] These homespun words of wisdom resonated with crowds.

Gore soon found a signature way to differentiate himself from the other candidates. Initially, Pauline prohibited him from taking his fiddle along when he campaigned. Since he was twenty-nine and looked younger, his advisers wanted him to always wear a dark coat and "to never play that damn fiddle because if you do you will appear undignified."[124] They argued persuasively that his opponents would draw a comparison to Emperor Nero, saying that he played while the country burned. Some advisers also feared that people would accuse him of copying Texas governor "Pappy" O'Daniel, who had won fame for his hillbilly music and "Pass the Biscuit" campaign. For a time, Gore resisted the temptation.

That he was well known throughout the region for his fiddle playing prevented him from completely escaping his roots. In a visit to Jamestown in June 1938, Gore spoke to a standing-room-only crowd in the courthouse. Talking on reciprocal trade, a subject he admitted bored many, he saw a man coming down the aisle carrying a fiddle, followed by a man with a guitar and banjo. He knew both from his days as a player. Pauline saw them also and shook her head no. Still, one said, "Here, Albert, play us a tune." For a moment, he thought about it before launching into a speech on how important the election was to his family and how he had mortgaged his home for a chance to go to Congress. After securing promises to vote for him from the majority of the crowd, he took the fiddle and played "Turkey in the Straw." Thirty minutes later, he put down the fiddle and talked about politics for a while. As his wife predicted, the next day the *Nashville Tennessean* published a story in which his opponents compared him to Nero.[125]

Despite the attacks, Gore continued playing, and he hired a band to accompany him throughout the district and play while he worked the crowd. Then, he made a speech followed by more music in which he often joined the band in songs such as "Cotton-Eyed Joe" and "Shake the Foot." Donald Lee Hackett, a member of the band, complained that Gore "really liked to put on a show, and he'd get all out of time, rolling up the bow and jumping around."[126] Despite maybe less-than-spectacular performances, such enthusiasm attracted large crowds for the fiddle-playing congressional candidate. It provided Gore a perfect forum for his speeches in which he stressed serious topics such as the TVA and reciprocal trade but also maintained a tie to the farmer and small businessman who represented the majority of people in the Fourth District.

By September, the primary race concluded. As all the candidates gathered in Murfreesboro where most had their headquarters, it became apparent that Gore had won. His supporters began clamoring for a speech. As he rose, "a benign old gentleman laid his hand on my arm," Gore remembered, and told him, "I have just come from the headquarters of one. He is the picture of dejection. His wife is crying. He probably will never be a candidate again. It is the end of his ambition." Gore recalled that "I lost my sense of elation. I could think only of the defeated candidates and their wives, and how my wife and I would have felt had I been among them." At that moment, he chose to praise his opponents and regret that all could not have been selected. "I often wonder what sort of fool I should have made of myself except for the admonition of that gracious old gentleman," he commented years later.[127]

Once Gore won the primary, he faced no serious challenge in the general election because the Republicans rarely fielded a strong candidate in the Fourth District. He and Pauline decided to travel to Washington to search for living quarters and meet people. They visited with various politicians who gave a variety of advice, including Vice President John Nance Garner. The blunt-talking Texan welcomed Gore with a large glass of bourbon, which he declined. "Young man, I never saw a Congressman defeated for something he didn't say and didn't do," the vice president bellowed. Gore noted that "the more I thought about this suggestion to do and say as little as possible in order to keep on being elected, the less I liked it."[128]

During the same trip, he established himself as a good entertainer. The people running Constitution Hall invited the young congressman-elect to play.

One evening, he played "Soldier's Joy" on the fiddle to the delight of a large crowd that included Eleanor Roosevelt.[129]

The victory in the November 1938 election was a watershed. Once in Congress, most legislators found it difficult to lose reelection. Only those who lost touch with their constituency or became involved in scandal failed. Incumbency provided access to power, which most legislators used to their advantage. They also gained immediate media and personal exposure, providing them with opportunities to continue to reach most people. Other advantages included ties to the leadership of the state and national political parties, which provided financial assistance and programs for the districts of the successful legislator. From this point forward, Gore would face few challenges in the Fourth District because he proved a very capable legislator.

# 2   MR. GORE GOES TO WASHINGTON

A SHORT TIME after arriving in Washington, Gore received a special invitation to visit the White House. The young congressman's opposition to President Roosevelt's housing bill was the reason for the honor. The thirty-two-year-old Gore arrived with a new briefcase full of documents, prepared to point out to the president the shortcomings of his public housing bill. Instead of the anticipated discussion on housing, the charming Roosevelt shared with Gore his vision for relieving the desperate economic plight of America's farmers and workers. The discussion of an annual wage and full employment "was such music to the ears of a young Populist from Tennessee" that Gore never got around to explaining his position on the housing bill. He was so distracted that a presidential aide had to retrieve the unopened briefcase he had left behind in the Oval Room on his departure.[1]

This visit to the White House would not be his last. Gore arrived in Washington in January 1939, an important juncture in U.S. history. The ravages of the Great Depression, while still felt, had subsided somewhat. The nation's focus remained on economic recovery, but the New Deal had stalled. Increasingly, international relations took center stage, especially fascist aggression in Europe and Asia. Within a short time, the country would find itself embroiled in a world war, and Gore would become involved in a whole series of issues including price controls, the development of the atomic bomb, and preparations for the postwar world. As with most members of his generation, World War II dramatically changed his life and attitudes.

Congressman Gore's journey to the nation's capital had commenced soon after Christmas Day 1938, when he, Pauline, Nancy, and Nancy's nurse, Ocie Bell, bundled up and piled into the car for the drive to Washington. As the car pulled away, it was unlikely that his father gave him the sendoff that Sam Johnson gave his son, Lyndon: "Now you get up there, support FDR all the way, never shimmy and give 'em hell."[2] The two-day trip from Carthage through the Appalachian Mountains and up the Shenandoah Valley to Arlington, Virginia, took on symbolic significance as little Nancy took her first steps along the way. Once there, the Gore family rented a room for $62.50 a month and began their life in Washington society.[3]

The young couple was frugal, much like the entire generation that matured during the Great Depression. Gore's congressional salary was $7,500 per year, by far his largest earnings to date, and would have been sufficient to purchase a home. It was the bustling Washington of the New Deal, housing was readily available, and a home would have been a good investment. Yet Gore's political principles dictated that the family would rent because he believed that as long as he represented the people of Tennessee, he should maintain his permanent residence in Carthage.[4]

Gore began preparing for the upcoming session by hiring a staff and moving into his office. Pauline played a substantial role by helping him organize the office. She would run the day-to-day operations and allow him to concentrate on studying the issues. With staff members, she helped with the mail, greeted constituents, and handled everyday duties.

In the early stages of his career, Gore's most significant influence was Cordell Hull. A frequent adviser to Tennessee legislators, Hull told Gore to keep his mouth shut early and "learn the rules of the congress procedure, make friends of all congressmen whether Democrat or Republican and don't be afraid to speak on all subjects before the House plus study the issues and be knowledgeable on them." Hull also advised Gore to "try to be a master of one subject" and told another Tennessee congressman, Estes Kefauver, that once he had found his niche with the federal income tax and reciprocal trade, "I read everything I could on it, and made about a speech a year." "Take a lot of time in deciding how you will stand on issues," Hull suggested, and "never let your constituents down."[5]

Following Hull's advice, in the first seven months of his term, Gore cast his votes but was not very active on the floor. "As in my father's household, the youngsters were to be seen and not heard," he later recalled.[6] He was appointed to the House Banking and Currency Committee, which over time proved a more exciting and challenging position than it initially appeared. For the most part, however, the pace remained slow.

Gore's only notable stance in the first few months occurred in April when he vocally opposed an additional $1,046,000 appropriation sought by New York representatives for expenditures at the 1938 New York World's Fair. Gore entered the fray after one of the legislators supporting the bill, Sol Bloom, insulted him. The Tennessean had asked Bloom to help him secure a Capitol policeman job for a constituent. Before he could finish the request, Bloom cut him off, blurting out: "How impertinent for a freshman to ask for a policeman! Impossible!"[7]

Gore turned the tables on Bloom not long after. In the floor debates, the New York congressmen argued that the fair's director, Grover Whalen, had promised European participants additional funds. Gore complained that Whalen had pledged the money without congressional approval and noted the same appropriation could employ forty thousand WPA workers in Tennessee. With a coalition of other freshman congressmen in tow, Gore prepared amendments, such as $30,000 to the Carthage Fair, Lebanon Mule Day, and Petersburg Colt Show. Ultimately, he sidetracked the appropriation in committee, and only the intervention of House Speaker Sam Rayburn (D-TX) mended fences. "Democrats have a way of getting together; my constituent graduated in his policeman's uniform, and I attended the New York World's Fair at the personal invitation of Congressman Bloom," Gore recalled.[8]

The first confrontation paled in comparison to his next one, as Gore decided that "when I hit I would hit hard." His maiden speech came in August 1939, regarding a bill sponsored by the Roosevelt administration expanding the borrowing power of the U.S. Housing Authority. He opposed it for several reasons, including its costs and eligibility restrictions that favored people of means. Furthermore, during hearings on the bill, Gore felt that the public housing administrator, Nathan Straus, "gave me condescending short shrift, if not downright rude treatment, when I asked some critical questions about the public housing bill."[9] Gore responded to this perceived affront by challenging the administration in committee, but the bill nevertheless passed to the floor.

Despite Roosevelt's special invitation to the White House and efforts at persuasion, Gore remained steadfast. In August 1939, the bill went to the floor for debate. When Democratic leaders refused to give Gore any time to speak against it, he turned to Minority Leader Joe Martin (R-MA) for floor time. When his turn came, he delivered a broadside described by one journalist as "a rip-snorting ten-minute speech." In it, he denounced the Housing Authority for failing to return any revenue to the government, adding that the appropriation would cost five times as much as the $800 million requested when finally completed. "My 18-month-old baby," he concluded, "will be lucky to see one of these contracts consummated."[10]

The *New York Times* reported that the address "stopped the show" and that House members gave Gore "an ovation of proportions such as is usually reserved for elder statesmen."[11] Some analysts credited Gore's speech with changing the minds of several congressmen, and opponents defeated the appropriation, 191 to 170.

While Gore regretted working with conservative Democrats and Republicans, he had felt strongly enough about the provisions of the bill to buck the party leadership and the president. It was the first in a long string of stands on his principles that provoked conflict with friend and foe alike, and the opening confrontation set a pattern that recurred throughout his career in Congress. People began to recognize him as a man who voted his conscience, even in the face of extreme pressures from his party and the president. Unlike Lyndon Johnson, a compromiser who benefited from his ability to maintain disparate coalitions and ingratiate himself into the good graces of those in power, Gore had a strong independent streak.

During the first few months of his term, Gore concentrated primarily on domestic issues, but events in Europe dramatically altered America's focus. On September 1, 1939, Germany invaded Poland, leading to a declaration of war on Hitler by France and Great Britain. Two days later, Roosevelt made a radio address, declaring, "The nation will remain a neutral nation, but I cannot ask that every American remain neutral in thought as well." Less than three weeks later, Roosevelt requested that Congress repeal the arms embargo as mandated by the Neutrality Act of 1935, an action that favored the Allies, who possessed superior naval power and an ability to buy and transport American goods.[12]

The debates on the repeal of sections of the Neutrality Act raged in October and November 1939, with opponents such as Senator Arthur Vandenberg (R-MI) warning that the United States could not be "an arsenal for one belligerent without becoming a target for another." Another senator asserted that "we want to sell guns to make a profit, even if it bathes the earth in mothers' tears."[13]

From the start, Gore sided with Roosevelt, believing that the fascists posed a serious threat. The administration asked him to make a lead-off speech on a bill to repeal the arms embargo. In it, Gore underscored the effectiveness of the German mechanized and technologically superior forces, which required the prevention of the "unpreparedness which existed in 1917." The embargo, he argued, endangered American interests by helping the aggressors and hurting the democracies. He closed by arguing that international peace and domestic tranquility required "the repeal of this abominable thing."[14]

After much wrangling, the Fourth Neutrality Act passed the Senate by a vote of 63–39 and the House by 243–181. It annulled the arms embargo and permitted the British and French to obtain American war materials on a "cash and carry" and "come and get it" basis. Furthermore, the repeal primed the pump of the American economy by infusing cash into war industries and bought time for the United States to prepare for war.[15]

When Gore returned from the Christmas recess in early 1940, he became embroiled in the contentious debates on reciprocal trade treaties. Leading the supporters of the renewal of the agreements was Hull, who had supported the idea of reducing tariffs and facilitating trade since making his first political speech in 1888. To the farmers of the Upper Cumberland and other areas of the Mississippi and Ohio River valleys, the battle for lower tariffs and increased trade had existed since the beginning of the Republic. They believed that increased trade benefited the majority of Americans, especially farmers and consumers, while undermining international conflict that decreased when discriminatory barriers declined.[16]

Throughout his political career, Hull had promoted lower tariffs and more open international trade, passing these ideas along to Gore. When Hull took over the State Department in 1933, he prodded Roosevelt into supporting the Reciprocal Trade Agreement Act, which gave the president authority to negotiate bilateral treaties that lowered or raised tariffs by as much as 50 percent without congressional approval. Despite some opposition, Congress approved the new international trade agreements that worked to expand "foreign markets . . . as a means of assisting in the present emergency in restoring the American standard of living."[17]

The reciprocal trade agreements were widely used throughout the 1930s, and by 1940 the United States had negotiated sixteen reciprocal treaties with those countries importing more U.S. goods than countries without such agreements. Despite the economic benefits, the protectionists opposed renewals and claimed the agreements undermined U.S. industry by allowing foreigners to dump inexpensive foreign goods on the U.S. market while not ensuring proper health safeguards.

The battle was hard fought, and Gore played a role in helping defeat twenty-four amendments to the extension. In one exchange, he challenged charges by Rep. Francis Culkin (R-NY), who argued that Hull's program had caused an outbreak of typhus in southern states by allowing entry of Argentine corn. Gore countered with a report by the Pan American Bureau of Sanitation that noted typhus outbreaks in Alabama, Florida, and Georgia in 1922, long before the reciprocal trade program started. With the support of Gore and others, the extension passed 216–168 in the House and 42–37 in the Senate.[18]

This was not Gore's last battle on reciprocal trade or open markets. A whole generation of southern leaders supported Hull's position, including Gore. In their view, agricultural interests needed protection from overproduction and lack of markets in the 1920s that had led to depression in the farm sector. To Gore, the government should not favor industry over farmers or consumers who benefited from open markets and low tariffs but must find a balance between industry and agriculture and ensure prosperity for all Americans, not just special interest groups.[19]

In the midst of the debates, Gore had to campaign for reelection in 1940. Increasingly, he returned home to make speeches and attend events. In April 1940, he made a particularly enlightening address in Murfreesboro, entitled "The Mission of Our Generation." He praised Roosevelt's efforts to deal with the nation's economic and political problems, stressing that "socialization of education, roads, and certain other endeavors has been necessary and good. In the progress of democracy and human beings, it is possible that certain further socialization, properly proscribed and bounded, may be desirable, but basically and fundamentally and theoretically representative democracy depends upon private enterprise and an enlightened citizenship." In particular, he emphasized the importance of education, calling the free public-school system essential and urging that a college education be available for anyone seeking it. "To refuse to accept social obligations for the welfare of the people as a whole," he added, "along with the assumption of industrial and commercial leadership, would be dishonoring of the trust and opportunity offered us."[20]

In the area of international relations, Gore incorporated a great deal of Christian symbolism and patriotism. "World events make it imperative that the United States stand unshaken in the storm as a citadel of democracy and freedom toward which the people of the world may look, like the star of Bethlehem, to guide and light their way," he told the audience. Then, he called on his listeners to expand the ideas of loving their neighbors and following the golden rule so that the march of American democracy and society could continue until the point where Americans "proudly say to the world, 'Behold our democracy.'"[21]

The speech demonstrated that Gore remained under the influence of the ideas infused into him by his family, church, and community, as well as populism, progressivism, and Jeffersonian and Jacksonian ideals. It highlighted his strong belief in the interdependence of America and the rest of the world, as he encouraged the United States to assume its proper role as a leader. Also, it was imbued with a strong sense of American exceptionalism, which permeated American thought and institutions, and of God's divine mission for the United States in the world. While he would grow in many areas, especially regarding his world view, these fundamental ideas remained with him long after 1940.

As Gore campaigned for himself and Roosevelt, against the Republican challenger, Wendell Willkie, events in Europe and Asia grabbed America's attention. In June 1940, the French surrendered to the Germans, and the Nazis overran all of Western Europe except Great Britain. In response, Roosevelt moved closer toward a pro-Allied position by transferring fifty World War I–vintage destroyers to the British in return for leases on British naval bases in the Caribbean and North Atlantic. Several weeks later, he signed into law the first peacetime draft in U.S. history.[22]

Gore strongly supported the president's plans, and he borrowed a tactic from Roosevelt that provided him a medium to back the president's actions. In September, he inaugurated a weekly Sunday program on WSM, the Nashville radio station and home of the Grand Ole Opry, which broadcast all over Tennessee and its neighboring states. Gore wanted to reach his constituency every week and provide information and his opinion on important issues. As a former teacher, he sought to educate the public and allow his constituents to participate more fully in the national discourse.

He also wanted to provide leadership, taking the advice of Hull, who had told him that "any Congressman worth his salt should be able to furnish leadership in his district and at the same time perform a much broader duty to the nation as a whole." He later mused that "we are often inclined to underestimate the crucial importance of leadership in a democracy . . . In such a pluralistic system, leadership is essential. Without it, the individual flounders in a sea of meaningless choices."[23]

Many people tuned in to Gore's talks on Sunday mornings for information about what was happening in Washington and the world. Sally Howell, a future history professor at Middle Tennessee State University, recalled sitting with her father at the radio and listening to Gore talk about the important issues of the day. Before Gore's show, country-and-western superstars the Carter Family had a musical program. June Carter Cash liked to tell how her family members would "wince" when Gore arrived early and joined in the singing.[24] For more than a decade, he continued the program, using the format to educate listeners as well as to further his political ambitions.

In the summer congressional session, Gore began his annual defense of one of the most significant projects in his state, the Tennessee Valley Authority. Since its inception in 1933, the TVA had become an integral part of the lives of people in seven states, including Tennessee. Numerous dams, locks, and power plants had sprung up throughout the region, creating thousands of jobs and providing cheap electricity to hundreds of thousands of people. It was enormously popular, especially among those who benefited most from the massive government expenditures.[25]

Despite its popularity, each year, TVA opponents would battle over the agency's appropriations. Critics included the senior Tennessee senator, Kenneth McKellar, whom the Roosevelt administration had not asked to help as an original sponsor of the legislation creating the TVA. Furthermore, he did not like that he had little say in the patronage and complained that the TVA ignored his recommendations for appointments.[26] Most of the opponents, however, denounced the TVA as a socialist organization that competed with private utilities and undermined individual initiatives.

The battle in summer 1940 involved those opposed to an additional $25 million appropriation, designed primarily to build new dams and increase operations in defense industries reliant on the TVA power, in particular the aluminum industry. Rep. Andrew Schiffler (R-WV) adopted the most common attack. "The Tennessee Valley Authority," he argued, "and the projects under its control do not represent the sound philosophy that supports our American way of life. To take by taxation from some of their capital for the enrichment of another group is unfair and un-American."[27]

Gore counterattacked by stressing the viability of the proposed project and potential for significant increases in electrical production. He also worked with other supporters to defend the program. At one stage, Gore teamed with Joe Starnes (D-AL) to highlight that the funding would allow an increase in power from 683,000 kilowatts to 903,000 kilowatts, all of which would power private and defense industries. The TVA supporters successfully fought the opposition to the additional expenditure, and the budget increased to a total of $65 million.[28] This would mark Gore's first defense of the TVA, but hardly his last.

By late 1940, almost all attention had turned to preparedness for war as the British struggled to survive at the height of the Battle of Britain. In early December, Prime Minister Winston Churchill urgently requested food and war materials but explained that London could no longer pay cash. In response, Roosevelt and his secretary of the Treasury, Henry Morgenthau Jr., devised a solution of loaning materials through a lend-lease plan. At a press conference on December 17, FDR declared Great Britain's survival was vital to American national security and criticized the traditional forms of war financing as "nonsense" and based on the "foolish old dollar sign." Later, he would call on the United States to become "the great arsenal of democracy."[29]

The White House and its supporters designated the lend-lease bill as H.R. 1776, "An Act to Promote the Defense of the United States," and it gave the president the right to provide materials to any country that he deemed vital to U.S. defense. An outcry arose in Congress from isolationists and those allied with America First. Senator Burton K. Wheeler (D-MT) called lend-lease "the

New Deal's triple 'A' foreign policy—it will plow under every fourth American boy." Senator Robert Taft (R-OH) commented that "lending war equipment is a good deal like lending chewing gum. You don't want it back."[30]

In the House, Gore found himself in conflict with the isolationists such as Hamilton Fish (R-NY), whom he recalled "I came to detest, not as a personality but as the embodiment of isolationist philosophy with which I thoroughly disagreed." For Gore, the fight would help repudiate the isolationism that had allowed the rise of the fascists. He told his radio audience that "this bill gives this Nation, through its chosen leader, a stronger, a more flexible, and more ready hand in playing this tragic game in which the liberty and freedom of mankind are at stake."[31]

Debate lasted over a month, as Gore allied with proponents of the bill to win victory in a final count of 317–71 in the House and 60–31 in the Senate. Celebrations followed among internationalists such as Gore who believed that "the final enactment of the Aid-to-Britain Bill marked an end to an era of isolationism which began with the rejection of the Versailles Treaty by the United States Senate in 1919."[32]

Though the times were grave, the mood in Washington was not always somber, and Albert and Pauline participated in the occasional social event. At times, some of Gore's colleagues joined to share common interests. In March 1941, Rep. Luther Patrick (D-AL) and Gore informed the White House that they would like to host a program of humorous sketches and fiddling in May. Although Gore eventually withdrew because of more pressing engagements, he developed a reputation in Washington for his musical skills and often played for his colleagues and others.[33]

As war preparations continued, Gore had the opportunity to help shape economic policy. Believing that a strong economy helped the military, he devoted himself to trying to organize it. Walking a fine line between socialism and the free market, Gore and other members of the Banking and Currency Committee worked with the Roosevelt administration to develop plans to manage the economy effectively and prevent inflation and shortages. With his usual zest and energy, Gore followed Hull's advice and concentrated on this important, often complex, legislation.

In the fall, action on the economic bills began in earnest. The administration asked for legislation that would allow Leon Henderson, head of the Office of Price Control (OPC), to set prices on several important commodities to control inflation. Relying on the support of the chairman of the Banking and Currency

Committee, Henry Steagall (D-AL), the administration pushed H.R. 5479, also named the Henderson Bill, in the House in September and October.[34]

Gore immediately clashed with the administration over it, announcing that "except for the maiming and slaughter of human beings, inflation with its inevitable counterpart—depression—is the most destructive consequence of war."[35] One of the most important sources of his ideas was Bernard Baruch, the well-known businessman and financier who had been director of the War Industries Board during World War I. After reading his influential book, *American Industry in the War*, Gore had contacted him and the two began a long-term friendship. On the advice of Baruch, he began calling for further price ceilings and wage controls than the Roosevelt administration proposed.

Gore spent many hours formulating his own bill, introduced on October 6, 1941, and known as H.R. 5760. Believing the Henderson Bill was too narrow, he proposed a much more detailed plan that included ceilings on the wholesale prices of all commodities and limitations on salaries for any employer with more than eight employees, especially defense contractors. The bill gave broad discretionary powers to Henderson and his office to adjust for regional differences and excluded nonessential items such as toothpaste or hairpins. Finally, it carried punishments for black market transactions and guaranteed the right to strike. The provisions would remain in effect until June 30, 1943, when Congress could decide to adjust or do away with the bill, depending on the state of affairs.[36]

The battle between Gore and the administration ensured publicity for the Tennessean. In an interview with a *Newsweek* reporter in late October 1941, Gore promoted his price control plan. The reporter walked away from the interview with several interesting observations. First, he noted that "for all his posing as a dirt farmer at election time, he looks more like the man in the arrow Collar ads." To the reporter, Gore was "charming, ingratiating, shrewd but not slick; he rambles along from cliche to cliche, managing from time to time to inject into them an apparently homespun sincerity." Finally, he believed that "he is definitely on the make and perhaps a trifle too hasty in his desire to arrive."[37]

Until the end, Gore hoped to change Roosevelt's opinion. With that in mind he entered the fray when the House began debates on November 24, 1941. With only a few allies, including his friend Mike Monroney (D-OK), Gore pushed his proposal by repeating many of his earlier criticisms of the Steagall plan, warning that the selective method "would hit the fire at the high places and splash it all over the ranch and burn the whole ranch up." He cautioned that other problems threatened the national defense plans, especially the civilian producer who would avoid conversion until coerced, and he claimed that the selective method encouraged speculation and hoarding.[38]

Underlying his critique was the belief that another Great Depression would follow if the country reacted slowly. He reminded his colleagues of the last period of wartime inflation and the ultimate failure of all the banks within a ten-mile radius of his home, which plunged innocent people "into the abyss of desperation and despair": "I hope that we can provide better leadership than to allow a repetition of that."[39]

Gore's plan never stood a chance in the face of opposition from FDR, the Republicans, and organized labor. Still, even opponents applauded Gore's courage of conviction, including Earl Michener (R-MI), who acknowledged that "this body cannot have too many members of the intelligence, industry, integrity, and courage of the gentleman from Tennessee." The famous economist John Kenneth Galbraith would praise Gore's efforts, calling him "a young and exceptionally able congressman."[40]

Despite his defeat, Gore believed that eventually the country would adopt a more comprehensive program, especially if it entered the war. This major legislative battle further highlighted several of the young congressman's traits. First, he took on a very complex and complicated issue in which he believed and developed a coherent plan to address it. As was often the case, he was ahead of the curve on the matter. Second, he focused primarily on the workers and the poor who suffered most from inflation; attention to these underrepresented groups remained a guiding principle throughout his career. Finally, Gore's ambition was apparent; he had made it clear that he would buck the leadership to establish himself as an up-and-comer in the House.

The U.S. government focused primarily on Europe, but many people, including Cordell Hull, saw an equally looming threat in the Far East, especially after Roosevelt responded to Japanese expansionism in Southeast Asia by signing an executive order freezing all Japanese assets in the United States and instituting shortly thereafter a trade embargo, which placed the United States and Japan on a collision course. Gore acknowledged in October that the Japanese had little oil and that their military machine desperately needed it but that any attempt to move into the Dutch East Indies and exploit its oil reserves "would lead to shooting." He observed that "Washington is calm over the threat of war with Japan" but that "the calm may be ominous."[41]

On Sunday, December 7, 1941, after Japanese planes destroyed a significant part of the U.S. Pacific fleet at Pearl Harbor, Gore made his regular broadcast on WSM. "Never in the history of civilized man has any Nation resorted to such brazen treachery as Japan has practiced upon the United States. Not only did she follow Hitler's example of lulling his victim into a sense of false security by talking peace while preparing for war, Japan's representatives were actually talking peace to our government in Washington when the vicious attack was launched upon us." He roared that "there is no choice for us now but war . . . The die is cast. The battle is on. Let the storm rage. Let the tempest roar. America will prove worthy of her destiny."[42]

The next day, Gore took his place in a joint session of Congress and listened to Roosevelt's famous "Day of Infamy" speech. Sitting in the packed room, Gore heard the angry president denounce the Japanese attack. Soon after, he voted for the declaration of war.[43] A few days later, Germany declared war on the United States, thrusting the United States firmly into the world war.

By the time Congress returned to a full session in early January 1942, an aura of gloom hung over the country. The Japanese offensive continued in the Far East while in Europe the Germans had advanced to a few miles from Moscow. German submarines devastated Allied shipping in the North Atlantic. Fear of sabotage and direct attacks gripped the United States. Still, Americans believed in their cause, and millions began to flood into the military and defense factories.[44]

As the war progressed, Gore focused on war profiteers. In March, he voiced his opinion that "the government is being flinched and robbed. I warn both the labor lords and industrial barons that the patience of the American people is worn threadbare." Testifying before the Naval Affairs Committee, Gore attacked the "scandalous increases" in the salaries and bonuses of some businessmen. These included Bror Dahlbert, president of Celotex Corporation, who had received a bonus of $46,000 in addition to his $36,000 salary in 1940 and a $157,000 bonus in 1941. At the Cessna Aircraft Company, salary increases for company executives exceeded 700 percent. In response, Gore supported a new bill limiting the profits of defense contractors and called on the IRS to collect any excess profits.[45]

After the hearings, Gore took the issue to the public. He told a national audience that "exorbitant profits create labor unrest, hinder the sale of war bonds to the general public, add to inflation pressures, and undermine the morale of our soldiers who feel that the cause for which they are called upon to make so great a sacrifice should not be used by so many fellow citizens for selfish gain." To battle the problem, he advocated rigid price controls, statutory limits on profits from war contracts, and across-the-board ceilings on salaries and wages.[46]

Gore and others succeeded in curtailing some wartime profiteering. Soon after the hearings, a Cleveland company, Jack and Heintz, which had been under the microscope, announced the voluntary limitation of its profits to 6 percent and a drastic salary cut for the company's top three executives. The officers also agreed to investigate the huge bonuses paid to the president of the company and his secretary.[47]

As her husband focused on war profiteering, Pauline joined the war effort. She heard that Eleanor Roosevelt was receiving thousands of letters from concerned women and family members regarding their husbands, sons, and their livelihood. "People poured out their hearts to Mrs. Roosevelt, wanting hope from her that hope was somewhere to be found," Pauline recalled. She volunteered to work in Mrs. Roosevelt's office and help respond to the letters and enjoyed the opportunity to assist Eleanor, whom she greatly admired.[48]

Throughout the spring, U.S. forces fought defensive battles in the Atlantic and Pacific theaters. In April, the country suffered a devastating loss when the last U.S. holdouts surrendered on the Bataan peninsula in the Philippines. Such defeats sparked great outpourings of hatred for the Japanese. Admiral William "Bull" Halsey vowed that by the end of the war, the only place he wanted Japanese spoken was in hell. He would push his men with slogans such as "Kill Japs, kill Japs, kill more Japs." The U.S. Marines developed their own mantra: "Remember Pearl Harbor—keep 'em dying."[49]

This animosity encouraged swift actions against Japanese Americans and legal immigrants. General John L. DeWitt of the Western Defense Command echoed a sentiment felt by many that "a Jap's a Jap . . . It makes no difference whether he is an American citizen or not . . . There is no way to determine their loyalty." In response, the Roosevelt administration issued Executive Order 9066 in February 1942, which allowed the War Department to create zones where the military could determine the undesirability of resident peoples. Soon after, the army began the relocation of Japanese Americans to concentration camps throughout the Southwest.[50]

Gore told his radio audience that 9066 was "a historic order" that demonstrated that "the President has his sleeves rolled up and is determined to do his utmost, is determined to use the power of his office to safeguard us against Fifth column work from inside our own country. All power to him." While noting that most Japanese Americans were loyal, he asked: "But who can tell them apart? A Jap is a Jap. And to most of us, they all look alike." While avoiding the extremism of some who called for their deaths, he emphasized that "as long as they behave, they should be treated well; but for goodness sakes, let them be put where they cannot stab us in the back by internal sabotage [sic]."[51]

While supporting internment, Gore avoided the hard-line racism that called for the complete extermination of the Japanese. In the aftermath of the May 1942 victory at Coral Sea, Gore told his audience that "while we are exulting over the sinking of the Japanese vessels let us pause for a moment and think how strange it is that we derive so much joy at hearing that so many Japanese, or so many Italians, or so many Germans were killed." He admitted that the deaths were necessary, "but why should they be? The mothers of these brown enemies love them just as all mothers love their sons. Isn't it a terrible thing that a few men like Hitler, and Mussolini, and the Japanese Mikkido [sic] should so seize control of the people in those countries as to hurl them at us, declaring our destruction as their mission?"[52]

While Gore had supported FDR in many areas, his opposition to the housing and the price control bills had created some hostility to him in the White House. In May, Frank Kent published an article in the *Washington Star* hinting that members of the administration planned to support a challenger in the Fourth District of Tennessee. Alvin York, fresh from the rebirth of his legend in the movie *Sergeant York*, had told several people that "I figure Albert Gore is young and could fill a place in the fighting forces. So it looks like it might be a good thing if I could take his place in Congress."[53]

Even before Roosevelt could respond to the rumors, Gore astutely telegraphed the president and informed him that he had read the Kent column but that he gave the rumors no credence. Roosevelt wrote to an aide after receiving the telegram: "How can this be got—not by us—to Kent's attention?" The assistant responded that "I have already talked to Albert. He says he has no opponent and just wanted you to know that he is not swallowing any of Frank Kent's line."[54]

Roosevelt and his close aides appeared oblivious to plots against Gore by some in the administration. A Treasury Department official, Harold N. Graves, had contacted a Tennessee political consultant, George Fort Milton, and requested some information on Gore and potential opponents. Milton replied that McKellar and Gore were at odds but that he had talked with Kefauver, who reported that the people in the Fourth District liked Gore's anti-millionaire, anti–labor union leaders positions and that "they are proud of 'Our Albert' for having gotten into the front-page headlines." While acknowledging that York had been mentioned as a potential challenger, he added, "I doubt if York could beat him—his conduct at home has been so greedy and grasping that he has lost most of Fentress County and Fourth District friends." He concluded that there was not "much question of Gore's reelection."[55]

Soon after, Roosevelt demonstrated his faith in the young congressman. Early on, the brilliant German scientist Albert Einstein had warned Roosevelt that the Germans planned to create an atomic weapon. Spurred by the report of the doomsday device, the administration began plans for a U.S. version. By the summer 1942, work on the Manhattan Project began at several sites throughout the United States, one of which bordered on the Fourth District in Oak Ridge, Tennessee. One day, Sam Rayburn called Gore into his office with a small group of men. In the meeting, the Speaker of the House asked the Tennessean to serve on a secret committee to spearhead congressional appropriations for development of the bomb. Gore agreed, and the committee of five men began efforts to funnel money into the project.[56]

Throughout the war, Gore worked in secrecy. The members shepherded various appropriation bills through the House and Senate. Outside the committee, only small groups laboring on the project in Tennessee, Illinois, and New Mexico, and a select number of Roosevelt's advisers, knew anything about the multibillion-dollar enterprise. Gore learned a lot about the process of constructing the bomb, mainly through his relationship with David Lilienthal of the Atomic Energy Commission (AEC), whom Gore had known since he worked for the TVA. As the project gained momentum, Lilienthal approached him and asked if he wanted to return to school. When Gore responded yes, he arranged for experts from the AEC to instruct the congressman on the science and engineering aspects of the project. As part of the process couriers periodically would visit the Gore family residence in Arlington. The presence of the men, often heavily armed, carrying top-secret documents both alarmed and amused Nancy. Gore noted later that "I became, if not an apt, surely an avid student of the subject matter."[57]

Despite this dabbling in atomic energy, Gore's primary concern remained price controls. In the *Washington Daily News* and the *Saturday Evening Post*, he continued to push his plan by holding up Canada as a model, observing "of particular embarrassment to Mr. Henderson, Canada for two years had tried the selective plan . . . and had discarded it as inadequate." To his delight, Canada had adopted virtually the same system he proposed, implementing across-the-board freezes on wages and prices. Gore highlighted the plan's flexibility, its reliance on women to serve as "guardians of the law," and its provision for reporting price gouging and other forms of non-compliance. He advocated adapting the Canadian example as soon as feasible.[58]

In September 1942, Gore demonstrated his persistence by reintroducing his proposal for an all-inclusive price control bill, but it met strong resistance. That month, however, Roosevelt requested changes to the Price Control Act that greatly expanded price and wage controls. Gore supported the changes and urged Congress to act quickly to prevent inflation that could undermine morale. He worried that people not working in the defense industry had suffered most and would continue to do so without significant changes. "Are we going to let the rich man or the fellow who happens to be making a profit or drawing high wages of a war job fill his coal bin and live comfortably and snug," he asked, "while those who are not fortunate enough to get a war job or otherwise have more money to spend suffer from cold and deprivation?" He emphasized that "we mustn't allow that to happen . . . We must protect the weak . . . That is what government is for."[59] Ultimately, Congress accepted many of the changes.

In other areas, Gore cooperated with the president. In one particular incident, William P. Lambertson (R-KS) charged that the president's son, Marine Lt. Colonel James Roosevelt, had received preferential treatment. Rayburn called Gore to his office and told him to prepare a response. When the Kansan spoke again, the Speaker recognized Gore, who admitted later that "I took Lambertson's hide off." He castigated Lambertson for putting "himself and the Chamber to shame" and pointed out that the president had four sons in the armed services. Also, he highlighted that James Roosevelt had led a Marine raider battalion in a dangerous attack on the Japanese stronghold of Makin Island in August 1942. "We hear further the very integrity of the armed services challenged. Any man who states that a commander at the orders of the Commander-in-Chief, or the commander himself, withdrew one as a special favor from points of danger undermines the integrity and the morale of the armed forces of the United States. I brand it as a disservice and call upon the gentleman to apologize to these boys," Gore bellowed.[60]

The Kansan backed down and never repeated the accusation. In fact, a challenger defeated him in the next election. Afterward, during one of the congressional recesses, Gore was at home in Carthage. Standing out in the front yard, he saw a car pull up in the driveway and park. Lambertson emerged and walked toward him. "I didn't know whether he came to shoot me or to exchange old times," Gore recalled. Fortunately, the political adversaries did not come to blows, and Gore described the visit as pleasant.[61]

Gore also supported the administration's efforts to finance the war, even as antitax conservatives offended his populist sensibilities with their proposals. In March, legislators led by Rep. Wesley E. Disney (D-OK) tried to push through a plan that increased the debt ceiling limitation and removed the $25,000 salary limits. While the administration accepted raising the debt limitation, it opposed removing salary limits, and debates on the House floor soon followed as Disney complained that the administration's position was "government by directive as against government by law."[62]

Gore immediately joined the fray, contending that the removal of the salary limits would cause discontent among the laborers and farmers. He emphasized that Eugene Grace, director of Bethlehem Steel, had received large government contracts and drawn a salary of $537,724 the preceding year. Rep. Walter Knutson (R-MN) responded that Grace had paid $400,000 in taxes, living expenses, and charitable giving. To this, Gore retorted that "to say that any comparison of the boy who is dying today for $50 a month with a man who is making steel which he shoots cannot be made. The latter is in a favored position when all he has after taxes is $100,000." Gore won such resounding applause from other House members that Knutson accused him of demagoguery. The Tennessean proudly responded that it had taken five years in the House to earn such a characterization.[63]

On another front, Gore clashed with conservative Republicans over the Ruml plan. In 1942, Congress had passed a Revenue Act that created payroll deductions for taxes. The problem that resulted was that in early 1943, people would have to pay taxes at the same time that they would start having money withheld. Beardsley Ruml, chairman of the New York Federal Reserve Board, proposed absolving most people of their 1942 obligations. Immediately, the administration criticized the plan for ignoring the inevitable cost of the war and raising the debt significantly while allowing the wealthy to receive the largest proportion of the tax forgiveness.[64]

Although it made good political sense to support the Ruml plan, Gore challenged it. Along with several colleagues, he emphasized that the Ruml plan would wipe out 77 percent of the tax burden for a person making $2,000 net income while for millionaires it would amount to 320 percent. He and his allies also complained that it would delay the payment of the huge debt and shift the burden more squarely onto the shoulders of the lower and middle classes. Gore told his colleagues that "this Ruml Plan looks like a redistribution of wealth in the wrong direction."[65] Despite his efforts, the Ruml plan passed.

Gore clashed with conservatives and Republicans over reciprocal trade treaties that came up for renewal in spring 1943. On his radio show, on the floor of

Congress, and elsewhere, he supported the efforts of Hull and others to renew the reciprocal trade agreements. He wrote in *Collier's* in April that "Congress will soon have to make a decision that may determine when—and if—we shall have another war." Gore lumped the opponents into two categories, those who believed in the need to create a self-sufficient nation and those representing special interests affected by trade. He especially criticized the latter for its "self greed," which resulted in higher prices for American consumers. While recognizing the difficulties some industries faced, he maintained that "what it all boils down to is this: If we have to see a couple of hundred men lose their jobs in order to give a couple of thousand work, I think it's the patriotic and decent thing to do for the country's sake."[66]

Outside of the immediate benefits for the domestic economy, Gore situated the reciprocal trade agreements within the larger scope of international relations, calling them "a ray of light in a dark, war-omened decade." Looking to the postwar era, he believed that the United States would become the preponderant economic power, increasing the need for access to markets and resources. The United States needed to accept leadership, and any "rejection of this duty and privilege would mean that economic warfare would continue, thus rendering any military peace futile and only temporary." He admitted that the trade agreement was not a panacea but clearly a positive step forward.[67] A few months later, Congress easily approved the bill that extended the reciprocal trade agreements for another two years.

While international issues dominated Congress's agenda in the spring of 1943, domestic issues remained important. Organized labor had begun to make more demands as prices rose, and Congress failed to place limitations on the profits of the owners, leading many to question the equal distribution of sacrifice. In 1943, work stoppages plagued the country as more than 3,800 "wildcat strikes" resulted in the loss of 13.5 million man-days. The most contentious were those led by John L. Lewis and United Mine Workers (UMW). The coal miners, demanding better pay and working conditions, staged a series of walkouts, leading the Roosevelt administration to seize the mines to keep them operating.[68]

The UMW actions angered Gore. While sympathizing with the workers, he believed that the war efforts took precedence. To him, Lewis undermined national security by threatening economic stabilization programs. In his radio broadcast in early May, he emphasized that the "Japs have not stopped us. Hitler hasn't stopped us. John L. Lewis threatens to stop us." Chastising Lewis for defying the commander-in-chief, he claimed that Lewis "has placed himself and his imperious will above the law, above the government and above the safety and welfare of his country. The darkest dungeon in the dirtiest prison in America would be too good for him."[69]

A month later, Gore blasted Lewis on the floor of the House during debates over the Smith-Connally Act, which called for government seizure of strike-bound plants, required strikers to give formal notice of an action, and called for thirty-day cooling-off periods. Criticizing the stranglehold the UMW had over the individual workers, Gore called on the government to break not only the strike but the "toils of Lewis' tyranny over 500,000 of our fellow Americans." He highlighted the sacrifices of farmers and other laborers and observed that "by our action on this bill, Lewis and every other home-grown dictator must be made amenable to the law."[70]

Soon after, Congress passed the Smith-Connally Act and then overrode Roosevelt's veto. Gore told his listeners that "except for the votes declaring war, I have not seen Congress as tense and excited in my five years in Washington." He regretted the tension between the president and Congress but emphasized that "these strikes must stop . . . Dilly-dallying, pussy-footing and pacifying must end." While momentarily putting labor on the defensive, the Roosevelt administration worked by the end of the year to ensure that the miners received almost all of their demands.[71]

His stand against the UMW combined with his positions on reciprocal trade, war profiteering, and price controls won Gore support throughout Tennessee. In June, the *Chattanooga Times* praised his recent speech before the local Rotary Club. The editorial writer stated that "love of country beats strong in the hearts of men born in the lovely rolling hills around Carthage in upper Tennessee." He pointed out that Gore had avoided the tendency "to tear down" and focused instead on building up, adding that "it should be a source of great gratification to Tennessee that this state's delegation in the House of Representatives is perhaps the strongest from any state in the Union." Noting that several of the Tennessee congressmen had attracted national attention, the writer emphasized that "this is particularly true of Albert Gore, and Rotarians who heard him yesterday could well understand why this is true."[72]

While solidifying his position at home, Gore continued speaking out on many national issues, including supporting the efforts of a fellow southerner. In the spring of 1943, a freshman Democratic representative from Arkansas, J. William Fulbright, had introduced a House resolution that called for Congress to issue a statement favoring the "creation of appropriate international machinery with power adequate to prevent future aggression and to maintain lasting peace, and as favoring participation of the United States herein."[73]

The issue remained in limbo until September, when contentious debates began on the Fulbright resolution. Vocal opposition emerged, especially from isolationists and virulently anticommunist organizations and individuals. Rep. Clare E. Hoffman (R-MI) argued that the adoption of the Fulbright resolution would mean "that we repeal the Declaration of Independence." Hamilton Fish (R-NY) called it a "pious declaration" and sneered "let's win the war and then fight it out with our allies."[74]

The internationalist Gore fought hard for its passage. When Daniel Reed (R-NY) complained that the resolution would force the United States to surrender its sovereignty, Gore noted the failure of the United States in the last war to assume leadership and called the Senate's action a "run-out" that ensured future conflict. Gore believed the whole world, especially the neutral nations, looked to the U.S. Congress for guidance and leadership. "If the whole Congress would now go on record as favoring United States participation in an international organization to keep peace and let the world know it," he contended, "I believe it might be one of the great victories of the war."[75]

The sentiment in the country and Congress clearly supported U.S. participation in an international organization in the postwar era. In the House, the Fulbright resolution passed 360–29, while a similarly worded resolution in the Senate sponsored by Senator Tom Connally (D-TX) carried 85–5. While nonbinding, the resolution put Congress on record in support of the international peace organization. Most members of Congress, including Gore, believed that it bound the administration morally to the cause of peace and would prevent infighting at the end of the war if the issue festered and isolationists gained more credibility as victory appeared imminent.[76]

As debates on postwar questions continued, Gore faced some tough personal issues. While millions of American men and women had joined the fighting, until 1943 Gore had watched as a spectator from the House floor. However, in the fall, he contemplated a change as he watched friends and family members serve. Though thirty-six, he was healthy and believed that he had an obligation. He also had his brother's example of service in World War I, and older men than he, including Alvin York, had volunteered. In October, he opposed the Wheeler Bill, which would allow fathers to defer military service, arguing that military planners should make the decision. Instead, he had backed a plan to compensate married soldiers with additional funds—$50 per month for a wife, $30 for the first child, and $20 for each additional child.[77] This stand further caused him to rethink his own commitment, as he feared that such votes made him look hypocritical, especially if he was unwilling to volunteer himself.

Wanting to avoid charges that he had avoided service and eager to serve as an example, on December 29, 1943, Gore waived his congressional draft immunity and requested a leave of absence; he was the first congressman to do so. He had announced earlier in the month during a speech to the American Legion in Nashville that "as for me, I am ready to go along with the thousands of other fathers and take my chances and do my part in the armed services." Refusing to resign from Congress, he argued that like other soldiers, "I would like to come back to as much as possible of what it has taken a lifetime to attain." When he showed up for induction at Fort Oglethorpe, he chose to enter as a private, although his education and experience clearly qualified him for officer status. In a gesture of support, fellow Carthaginian Wash Reed, a father of seven, joined Gore at the induction center.[78]

For a month, Gore and Pauline prepared for his entry into the army. He received orders to report to Camp Shelby, Mississippi, for basic training, but plans stalled when Attorney General Francis Biddle interpreted the law as requiring a legislator to resign his seat on entry into the military. However, President Roosevelt intervened before Gore had to choose between competing obligations. The administration, anticipating difficult legislative battles, wanted a stalwart in the House. Equally important, Gore had top-secret knowledge of the atomic program and posed a security risk at a significant juncture in the war. Roosevelt summoned Gore to the White House, and after some discussion, Gore emerged and announced that FDR had told him that "you are needed here and can best serve here, and I hope you will stay." In response, Gore remarked, "Who am I to say or gainsay where I can best serve? I stay." Instead of joining full time, Gore entered the enlisted reserve and returned to his duties on Capitol Hill.[79]

After deciding to stay in Congress, Gore concentrated on important domestic legislation including the G.I. Bill of Rights, which provided money for education, loans, unemployment compensation, employment training, and hospitals for veterans.[80] The Senate passed the bill unanimously after forty minutes of debate. In the House, however, the representatives debated for six days. Ultimately, Gore supported a compromise bill, which he described as sensible, although he warned that the reconversion was "not an overnight job." Cognizant of the lessons of World War I, Gore reminded his colleagues "that unless there is a well-designed national program for integrating these 10,000,000 or more servicemen into our national life, it might create a glut and stagnation of our economy that would have disastrous effects." No one disagreed, and the bill passed 388–0.[81]

Soon after, Gore found himself defending the administration against Republican charges that the president had purposefully allowed the Japanese to destroy the American fleet in Pearl Harbor to secure a declaration of war on the Axis powers. With the election approaching, the Republicans wanted, at the least, to level charges of ineptitude. Rep. Forest Harness (R-IN) argued that if the president was innocent, he "should be cleared promptly," but that if Roosevelt was "culpable in directing our military activities in Hawaii, the American people should have the true facts before they are called upon to pass judgment on his fitness for re-election to a fourth term as President."[82]

In the ensuing debates, Gore attacked the anti-Roosevelt Republicans. When Fish denounced Roosevelt for replacing Admiral J. O. Richardson, who had warned against stationing the fleet at Pearl Harbor, Gore turned the tables on the New Yorker. He chastised the isolationists for their role in keeping the country from adequately preparing for war. "No one has accused the gentleman personally of being responsible for Pearl Harbor," he retorted, "but certainly, as I see it, Pearl Harbor and the war can partially be laid to the record and the philosophy of the gentleman's party." He added that the inadequate preparation, "which, if it had been different, might have made Pearl Harbor impossible is a matter of paper and ink." The charges and countercharges flew throughout the summer, but the furor ultimately died down as the House and Senate passed extensions, called witnesses, and established a formal investigation, but failed to produce any smoking guns.[83]

The investigation had partisan overtones as the 1944 presidential election approached. During the summer and early fall, Gore campaigned for Roosevelt's unprecedented fourth term against Republican nominee New York governor Thomas E. Dewey. The moderate Republican was an internationalist who accepted many New Deal programs, although he believed that the New Deal had gone too far. As they campaigned, the Republicans contrasted Roosevelt's age with Dewey's youth and vitality. To balance the ticket, the Republicans nominated the conservative Ohio governor John Bricker as vice president, a man who specialized in charging the administration with being soft on communism.[84]

Gore and many other Democrats mobilized against the Republicans. In May, Gore made a speech in Pennsylvania in which he focused on the upcoming election. He discussed the "yardstick for fitness for the job" and, in his typical style, used a homespun story to highlight differences between FDR and Dewey.

He told of talking with a farmer friend who generally wasted little breath in making his point. He informed Gore that it was "never a good idea to change horses in the middle of the stream. But if I ever come to that pass where I've got to consider it, I will sure draw the line to changing to a Shetland pony." Gore told the audience it really was not an attack on Dewey's physical stature but more on "what he has done to qualify him for the Presidency at this critical time."[85]

Gore and other Democrats also emphasized the recent history of the Republican Party and questioned whether Dewey and his party could accomplish the job. The Republicans, according to Gore, had put the country "on to the skids," and their record included the "Teapot Dome, post-war inflation, synthetic boom and the awful bust-up, depression days when men were selling apples on the streets of America." He also observed that President Hoover was one of Dewey's closest advisers. "I do not think the country wants any more of Herbert Hoover," he proclaimed, "not even a Tom Thumb facsimile."[86]

Gore could not afford to focus exclusively on FDR's reelection, as his own political future appeared to be in doubt. Rumors relating to his war record posed a potential threat. A party regular from Trousdale County, James Donoho, wrote FDR in June 1944 and remarked that "it is being said that before [Gore] waived exemption and was inducted in the Army he knew that you, as Commander-in-Chief, would not let him go into the military service." He asked for the facts about Gore's efforts to enlist, emphasizing that he did not believe the charges of evasion but wanted proof to dispute them. While no record of Roosevelt's response exists, Gore and his allies understood that he needed to campaign to maintain his prominence in his district and address such criticisms.[87]

Running on his record, Gore made public appearances throughout his district in the summer of 1944. He told crowds that "six years ago you trusted and selected me to be your representative in Congress. I have tried, my friends, I have tried to be worthy of that trust, I come back to you now for an accounting. I come back to you not without having made mistakes . . . But I do come with a record of earnest, sincere effort." He highlighted his support for Roosevelt and Hull in foreign affairs and mobilizing the country for war. In addition, he stressed his record on securing parity for farm goods and pointed to his backing of the G.I. Bill and other measures intended to help the country prepare for peace. He concluded that the next Congress most likely would write the peace and that it was important for people to elect representatives "of capacity, vision, and courage."[88]

As the election approached in October, Gore continued attacking Dewey and noting the Democrats' accomplishments since 1933. In a speech in Columbus, Ohio, he warned the crowd that while Dewey was a sincere internationalist, the Republicans held within their ranks such prominent isolationists as Fish, who would become chairman of the Rules Committee in the House, and Hiram Johnson (R-CA), who would chair the Senate Foreign Relations Committee if the Republicans took control of Congress. He recalled that the Republicans after World War I "succeeded in steering us into a rut going the wrong way" and commented that "the hope of America and the world for a lasting peace would be dimmed by another Harding in the White House."[89]

The Democrats' arguments resonated with the American people in November 1944. In the presidential election, Roosevelt received 53.5 percent of the vote, taking thirty-six states, including all of the South. His coalition of urban ethnic groups, labor, and lower- and middle-income voters overwhelmed the Republicans' base of the upper-income and midwestern Protestants. The Democrats gained twenty-five seats in the House and maintained the status quo in the Senate. Gore also won handily in the general election and returned to his seat in the House.[90]

Soon after winning reelection, Gore finally fulfilled his goal of entering the armed services. On December 3, he submitted his letter of resignation from the 78th Congress to Governor Prentice Cooper and informed Rayburn of his decision, noting that the rulings from the courts allowed him to retain his recently elected position in the 79th Congress. He began preparations to shift from enlisted reserve to active duty as a private, telling his weekly radio audience that Kefauver would take his place while he served.[91]

In early 1945, Private Gore moved into the military. Bryce Harlow, one of Roosevelt's administrators and later a member of the Johnson administration, reported that he had the task of shepherding special people through the army including Gore, Johnson, and John Fogarty (D-RI). He remembered that his job was "to get them in for a special basic training, and in for a special little advanced training, and then for a special shipment to a combat area, and a special escort through a combat area, special return to the United States and special discharge." The urgency, he believed, was that "these were all dynamic political soldiers, true to the faith of Roosevelt and could be counted upon to wage his fights in the House." Roosevelt feared that the lack of a war record would hurt their political aspirations, so he made sure that the congressmen had one, albeit a very limited one.[92]

Gore completed his training at Fort Meade near Washington and was sent to Europe with a special War Department assignment to help in the prosecution of suspected war criminals and other military court cases. In addition, he was to study the occupied areas and develop a report for Congress on the challenges facing America in the war-ravaged region. At the age of thirty-eight, he left the United States for the first time.[93]

Once in Europe, he began following the front-line troops. Under enemy fire on several occasions, Gore found that the death and destruction rather than the fighting impressed him. "German dead, civilians and soldiers, horses, cows, dogs, stinking to high heaven, litter the streets and buildings," he remembered, adding "all semblances of law and order have vanished with the retreating Nazis."[94]

The congressman devoted much of his time in Europe to prosecuting German citizens accused of various crimes. When U.S. troops occupied an area, the American military officials required all citizens to turn over firearms, ammunition, and radio transmitters, and they implemented curfews. When someone violated the laws, military courts convened. While the German civilians had the right to counsel and the ability to cross-examine the prosecution's witnesses, Gore characterized the whole process as oftentimes a "seemingly summary procedure" with "loose rules of evidence." Still, Gore complained that "the sentences for serious offenses may tend to be too light, while too much attention may be given to technicalities."[95]

As he traveled around the countryside, he made several observations. First, the Autobahn caught his attention. He noted the complexities of its construction and how well the Germans organized it to facilitate efficient movement, especially for the German war machine. Exposure to the German roads system influenced him and General Dwight D. Eisenhower, and both later took an active role in the creation of America's interstate highway system.[96]

Gore also found that the German people were generally submissive, as their lives had been "reduced to the bare essentials of living." Still, he discovered some dangerous currents. One of his interpreters, a young Russian who had lived in Germany all his life, talked openly about the "nice life under Hitler before the war" including the dances, food, money to spend, beer, vacations, and work.[97]

The young man's attitude startled Gore, who feared that many Germans would "forget the vicious excesses, the racial hatred, the mass murder of innocents committed by Nazi Germans. They will blame us . . . for the havoc wrought by the war." To him, the Allies had to destroy the militaristic spirit, or the war had accomplished nothing. This required reorientation of the Germans, especially the children, through education and creation of viable democratic institutions in the country in the postwar period.[98]

After two months, Gore returned home in March. The *New York Times* reported that "he was frequently under fire and in the course of the offensive crossed the Roer River on a footbridge with infantry troops." It added that "only a few high-ranking officers knew he was a member of the Congress" and that "the disclosure of the nature of his service came today after he had been called to confer with Lieutenant General W. B. Smith, Chief of Staff to General Dwight D. Eisenhower, and other staff officers." Finally, the story noted that the military leaders were happy the congressman had been in Germany so that he could report back to the civilian leaders the magnitude of the problems facing them.[99]

Once home, Gore immediately presented his findings on the American occupation of Germany to Congress. In a statement titled the "Military Government of Occupied Germany," Gore told his colleagues about what he had seen and learned during his service. He noted that "collectively, the German Nation has committed unspeakable crimes against the very principles upon which civilization is based." "There must be punishment," he added, "justice cannot be done without punishment . . . We must act in the light of the terrible fact that twice in the last 25 years Germany has brought immeasurable destruction and suffering to the world."[100]

In much of his presentation, Gore focused on the gravity of the problems facing the United States in Western Europe. Millions of mines made crop production hazardous, and the infrastructure was devastated. He predicted that the developing American zone would occupy one-third of the area but would have one-half the population, as Germans fled the advancing Russians. To him, one of the most pressing problems was the nearly 3 million refugees who had been forcibly taken from their homelands. The repatriation and temporary care of these peoples would place an immense strain on U.S. resources.[101]

Gore also stressed the magnitude of the task facing the United States regarding economic reconstruction. Citing the aftermath of World War I when the German economy had collapsed from the weight of the war debts and reparations, Gore encouraged the United States to adopt proactive measures. He called for tight controls and argued that orthodox financial means would not suffice and that the Allies should maintain the Reichsmark by "rigid controls." He recommended that the United States force wealthy German citizens and institutions to provide credit to maintain the currency.[102]

The goals of the occupation of Germany concerned Gore. People such as

Secretary of the Treasury Henry Morgenthau had called for the complete pastoralization of Germany to prevent future aggression. Gore proposed a moderate path that encouraged creation of a new Germany that worked peacefully within the community of nations. "Every day I was in Germany I was impressed over and over with the enormity of this undertaking," he told his colleagues, "the greatest political experiment in the history—a metamorphosis of the political ideals, standards, practices, and aspirations of an entire nation of proud, industrious, smart, and remarkably homogenous people." He warned, however, it would take U.S. and UN patience and effort to achieve the necessary change.[103]

Soon after returning from Europe, Gore suffered a profound loss together with the rest of the country. On April 12, President Roosevelt died while vacationing in Warm Springs, Georgia. The news shocked the country. The man who had taken them through the depression and World War II, and who most believed would lead them into the postwar era, was no longer alive. Lyndon Johnson fought back tears in the corridor of the Capitol when he learned of FDR's death, stating that "he was always like a Daddy to me. I don't know that I'd ever have come to Congress if it hadn't been for him. But I do know I got my first great desire for public office because of him."[104]

Most Americans shared Johnson's sense of grief and loss. On his weekly radio show on WSM, Gore reflected on Roosevelt's death. "On street cars, in the cafes, in government buildings, there was a hushed silence which bespoke more eloquently than words not only the deep and tender regard in which the President was held by the common people, . . . but it told also of the void in their hearts as well as in their country left by the silence of this eloquent voice of the people, this brilliant intellect with a passion for human welfare, this leader with vision and courage." Later, he recalled that not everyone shared his view, especially southern conservative business interests, but he still believed "the mass of the people never wavered in their affection. Roosevelt—glamorous, charming, inspiring and dedicated—remained the people's hero."[105]

Gore correctly appraised the situation. Roosevelt remained for many Americans a hero who had risen to power and saved the country from economic depression and fascism. He had accomplished many feats and altered the way a whole generation of Americans looked at government. For many years, men such as Gore, Johnson, and others who had come to power during the New Deal sustained FDR's vision. Only after the memories of Roosevelt and his accomplishments began to fade from the public consciousness would these politicians come under attack for their beliefs on the role of government.

Roosevelt's death marked an end to an era. While the war continued for another five months, victory appeared assured. During the four years preceding, Gore had risen to national prominence through his stands on price controls, wage limits, and international affairs. People around him recognized his potential, and increasingly he was in demand as a speaker on a wide range of issues throughout the country. Clearly, the young congressman from Tennessee was a political star on the rise, full of ambition and talent. The war had provided him opportunities to test his mettle and hone his political skills. In 1945, his popularity appeared as strong as ever in his home district. However, new challenges awaited the country and Gore as the war ended, and the specter of hostilities with the Soviet Union, the reconstruction of the world economy, and looming domestic economic problems thrust themselves to the forefront.

Pauline and Albert around the time of their marriage, 1937
*Courtesy Karenna Gore Schiff*

Mr. and Mrs. Gore with Nancy at the beach, early 1940s
*Courtesy Tennessee State Library and Archives*

Young Al with his father, mid-1950s
*Courtesy Karenna Gore Schiff*

Portrait of Albert Gore, early 1950s
*Courtesy Tennessee State Library and Archives*

Senators John F. Kennedy, Hubert Humphrey, and Albert Gore at the Chicago
Democratic National Convention, August 1956
*LBJ Library Photo by unknown*

Senator Lyndon B. Johnson and Lady Bird Johnson on the campaign trail with Senator Gore, Knoxville, Tennessee, 1960

*LBJ Library Photo by Frank Muto*

Senator Gore with President Johnson in the Oval Office, 1968

*LBJ Library Photo by Yoichi Okamoto*

Gore campaigning for the Senate, 1970

Senator Gore with his wife, Pauline; daughter Nancy and her husband, Frank
Hunger; and son Al Jr. with his wife, Tipper, 1970

Father and son celebrating Al Gore Jr.'s 1976 victory for the congressional
seat previously held by his father

*Copyright Nashville Public Library, Special Collections Division, Nashville, TN.
Used by permission.*

The senator with President Jimmy Carter and Jim Sasser aboard Air Force
One, 1980

*Courtesy Jimmy Carter Library*

Karenna and her grandfather on the occasion of her wedding, July 12, 1997, at the vice-presidential residence.

*Courtesy Karenna Gore Schiff*

# 3   IN THE NEW WORLD OF ATOMS, THE COLD WAR, AND THE FAIR DEAL

GORE REMINISCED that although he generally supported Truman's administration, there were some "little irritants—his conduct, the cronyism . . . his excesses such as his language—these humiliated me to some extent." Overall,
however, he thought Truman "made a great President. He surely had identification with the people, the mass of the people, and I admired that in him."[1]

The period of the Truman presidency proved especially challenging for the
United States on many fronts, and Gore found himself often working with the
new president on significant issues including reconversion to a peacetime economy, protection of New Deal programs, and expansion of basic access to jobs
and education. The wartime alliance between the United States and the Soviet
Union crumbled and anticommunism returned as a cornerstone of U.S. foreign
policy, sparking an intense domestic debate. Throughout this time, Gore concentrated on doing a good job in the House, especially on matters of importance
to his district and Tennessee. All the while he built alliances across the state. He
made his decisions with the ultimate goal of moving into the Senate, and by
1951 he was ready to challenge McKellar in a spirited contest.

When Truman inherited the presidency in April 1945, he had only served as
vice president for a few months and had little experience to prepare him for
leading the country. The former Missouri senator had limited foreign policy
experience because Roosevelt had avoided taking him into his confidence, not
even briefing him about the atomic bomb. While Germany's surrender appeared imminent, the Japanese continued to resist. Since sustaining the wartime
alliance had been difficult for the accomplished diplomat Roosevelt, many questioned whether Truman was up to the task.

A lot of people, including Gore, held this uncertain view of the new president. Soon after Truman took office, Gore told his WSM audience that "those
of us who know him well know him to be a good, honest, sound American . . .
He comes from humble parentage. He comes from a life and a strata that is as
typical of America as Andrew Johnson when he became President after Abraham Lincoln's assassination. Raised as a farm boy, he worked at various odd
jobs, operated a little business of his own, advanced from one job to another,

. . . but none very important until he reached the United States Senate, where he did a truly great job."[2]

Gore recalled his first meeting with Truman in 1940. At the party's request, he went to Missouri to speak to a Democratic meeting in Kansas City to help bolster Truman's reelection bid. During his stay, Truman traveled over from Independence and took the young representative out to lunch to discuss politics. After a nice meal, Gore made his speech and returned to Washington. "It certainly never occurred to me that I was eating the sandwich and drinking the coca-cola with the next President of the United States," he recalled. In a move that impressed the Tennessean, Truman always went out of his way to speak and shake hands when they saw each other.[3]

Foreign affairs dominated Truman's attention as he took office. Within two weeks after Roosevelt's death, forty-six Allied countries gathered in San Francisco to form the United Nations. Secretary of State Edward Stettinius Jr. led a bipartisan American delegation, although Hull (who was ill) acted as senior adviser. The delegates immediately began to debate issues such as regional security pacts and the veto power of the individual nations of the Security Council.[4]

Internationalists like Gore vocally supported U.S. participation in the UN. In late April, he told the graduating class of Crossville High School that "next Wednesday a historical convention or conference begins in San Francisco." He acknowledged that stories of war dominated the history books but that "there are chapters about men who have devoted much of their lives in trying to find a formula to keep peace." The conference represented a chance to take a monumental step forward. Gore also stressed that future wars likely would involve the United States because of new technological advances. "If we who serve on the home front should shirk or falter in the effort to vouch safe [sic] peace," he concluded, "we would break faith with every American who has died or suffered in this war."[5]

The U.S. policy failures after World War I made approval of the UN vital to Gore. "It is a source of gratification that the outlook for ratification is bright," Gore told his constituents. He warned that most Americans had supported the League of Nations but that "after long Committee hearings, after long drawn-out debates, enough doubts were raised, enough partisan fires were fanned into flaming heat, enough bickering jealousies and narrow attitudes had their sway, that the League of Nations Treaty was finally killed in the Senate."[6]

Despite heated debates in San Francisco, the delegates compromised on a number of contentious items. President Truman sent the treaty to the Senate where a few senators objected to the United States surrendering some of its sovereignty. Tom Connally (D-TX) and Arthur Vandenberg (R-MI), however, led the Senate to approve the treaty 89–2.[7] People throughout the country greeted the ratification as a turning point in the history of U.S. international relations.

As the United States moved toward preparing for the postwar era, the Japanese continued to resist. Gore visited the Pacific in July as part of a congressional commission to determine what bases the United States should retain. He made stops at Iwo Jima, Guadalcanal, and Okinawa, where General Joseph Stilwell, commander of the invasion force of Japan, provided a briefing. He showed the congressmen a large map of Japan with the invasion sites and predicted at least 200,000 American and 500,000 Japanese deaths in the battle for the mainland. Gore later remarked that as he flew over the large Allied fleet preparing for attack, he knew that many men including friends and constituents would die in the assault.[8]

The committee's last stop was Manila where General Douglas MacArthur hosted a dinner. Afterward, MacArthur briefed the delegation, but unlike Stilwell, he forecast that the war would end before the men reached home. The date was August 6, 1945. When Gore and the others arrived in Honolulu the following day, the papers ran the headline, "Atom Bomb Dropped." Later, Gore reminisced that the announcement stopped him in his tracks as he realized that the work on the Manhattan Project had come to fruition. The weapon of mass destruction had killed more than 130,000 Japanese, as well as 23 American prisoners-of-war at Hiroshima.[9]

Three days later, Gore and his colleagues landed in Los Angeles and discovered that the United States had dropped a second atomic bomb on Nagasaki on August 9, killing another sixty thousand Japanese. The atomic bombs combined with Russia's declaration of war against the Japanese ensured Tokyo's surrender on August 13.[10]

Years after, critics argued that Truman needlessly dropped the bombs on Japan, pointing to Tokyo's peace overtures through the Russians prior to August 6. They also speculated that a demonstration of the bomb on an unpopulated area would have ensured Japan's surrender.[11] Others believed that Truman used the bombs to intimidate the Russians. Regardless, Gore defended Truman. "I remembered those 200,000 American boys we did not lose and those 500,000 Japanese who were not killed," he later told an interviewer.[12]

With Japan's surrender, the United States faced the arduous task of reconverting the economy, and many feared the problems of overproduction and unemployment that plagued the country after 1918. While business leaders and farm groups pressed Truman and Congress to remove price controls, Gore advised caution and told an audience in Jackson, Tennessee, in early October that the country should fear inflation. To illustrate the point, he recalled that when he was a child "somebody was always pulling the prank of throwing a dipper of water into the air over my head with the shout, 'all that goes up comes down' . . . [O]f course it did. It always does, and the coming down hurts perhaps more than the going up . . . [I]rksome as controls and regimentation are to all of us, we have no sensible choice but to restrain ourselves until the danger is past and relax the controls gradually until such time that we can safely depend on the workings of the law of supply and demand."[13]

As during the war, Gore teamed with Bernard Baruch to promote price controls. Baruch openly praised Gore for the "brave fight" for the overall price control bill, calling it "a good fight that was lost." Throughout 1945, the two men corresponded, discussing plans to prevent an economic collapse. In October, Gore published in the *Congressional Record* a letter from Baruch that outlined his ideas for economic stability. First, the financier called on the government to create a balance sheet of present debts, productive capacity, and other important economic indicators. This would allow the country to avoid exporting too many goods, prevent inflation, and ensure that aid "did not assist in foreign nationalization and increased competition." Second, he denounced the "scuttle and run" policy of those calling for an immediate end to controls: "The miracle of American production can save the situation now, as it did in war, but it must hurry, hurry, hurry."[14]

Gore and others fought tenaciously in Congress to prevent the dismantling of the price and wage control laws, and they succeeded temporarily, buying the country time to adjust. While opponents used terms such as "socialist" or "fascist" to criticize the policy, the wisdom of the strategy became apparent over time. When the price controls disappeared in the summer of 1946, inflation rose precipitously.

While debates on conversion continued, Gore also found himself involved deeply in national politics. Republicans focused on unseating the Democrats in 1946. They believed that the American people had tired of the restrictive wartime practices and wanted to return to Republican values of limited government and lower taxes. Many wanted to roll back the New Deal, arguing it violated American principles of free enterprise, while others wanted a harder line against the Soviets. They anxiously anticipated the midterm congressional elections.[15]

In response, the Democrats and Gore fought back. One of his first attacks on the Republicans occurred in December 1945 when he rose to the floor and called the recently released Republican platform a "sorry apology for a program" and a "pussyfooting conglomeration of words." He noted that the Republicans agreed with 80 percent of the plans President Truman promoted, including the United Nations and opposition to Soviet expansion. "I want to congratulate my Republican colleagues for standing so bravely on the burning deck and saying, 'We oppose those who would destroy us.' Well, who would not?"[16]

Such speeches and Gore's closeness to Sam Rayburn paid significant dividends in early 1946. The powerful House Speaker selected a group of fifteen young Democrats to respond to Republican charges and chose Gore as leader of the group, which included Mike Monroney (D-OK), Brooks Hays (D-AR), and Mike Mansfield (D-MT). They received orders to instill "aggressiveness into the Democratic Party's progressivism." Gore emphasized that membership was open but that "we are not necessarily 100 per cent New Dealers or 100 per cent Liberals. We are 100 per cent good Democrats and we don't intend to sit around idly while the Republicans jump all over our party."[17]

Gore spearheaded group operations, relying on information provided by a research analyst through a special pipeline into the Democratic National Committee's office. At times, the group chose speakers for the floor. On an issue of providing economic assistance to Italy, for example, it selected a spokesman who represented a large Italian American constituency. After floor debates ended, the group mailed synopses to constituents to highlight Democratic positions.[18]

Gore also went on the campaign trail, becoming an increasingly popular party speaker. At a meeting of Ohio Women Democrats in Akron, he emphasized the need for Democrats to remember their progressive roots. He quoted Thomas Jefferson: "Laws and institutions must go hand in hand with the progress of the human mind. As that becomes more developed, more enlightened, as new discoveries are made, new truths disclosed, and manner and opinions change with the change of circumstances, institutions must advance also, and keep pace with the times." The Republican Party, he lamented, was meanwhile "settling ever deeper into the mold of conservatism" and had focused on "putting on the brakes" of progress. Gore reminded his audience that the Republicans led the country into depression and that when disaster struck, it was the Democratic Party that developed a bold and dynamic response. "The outcome of the election will—I firmly believe—determine the kind of a country we shall have to live in during the crucial years that lie ahead."[19]

With the election cycle in full swing, Gore soon found himself speaking out on a very controversial subject. In the fall of 1946, liberal Democratic and Republican senators tried to remove Mississippi senator Theodore G. Bilbo, who had created many enemies with statements such as, "If I can succeed eventually in resettling the great majority of the Negroes in West Africa . . . I propose to do it." When Eleanor Roosevelt protested, he retorted that "I might entertain the proposition of crowning Eleanor queen of Great Liberia." On another occasion in 1946, he bragged on the radio about belonging to the Ku Klux Klan, telling them that "once a Kluxer, always a Kluxer." His attitudes and actions led one author to describe him as the "Archangel of White Supremacy."[20]

Gore disliked Bilbo and had criticized his filibuster against Fair Employment Practices Commission (FEPC) appropriations, telling his constituents that "there is nothing democratic or fair about a filibuster."[21] However, during the attempts to oust Bilbo for campaign funds misappropriation and electoral irregularities in December 1946, Gore emphasized that "Senator Bilbo is a kind of a man for whom I would never vote, but the majority of people voting in Miss. chose to vote for him." He worried aloud that "the Senate will be going pretty far to say that the people in Miss. shall not have the right to elect the man of their choice to represent them in that body" and warned that liberal opposition to Bilbo only strengthened his position among racists who dominated Mississippi.[22] Ultimately, the Senate refused to seat Bilbo after his reelection, and he died soon after from cancer.

The Bilbo question was one of the first times that Gore spoke openly on the explosive issue of civil rights. His opposition to the filibuster, one of the prime weapons of southern segregationists, was very unpopular, as was his support of antilynching laws and efforts to abolish the poll tax. Many southerners saw such actions as the first steps to destroy their segregated culture. They often ostracized those southerners who took such positions as subversives and turncoats and sometimes helped orchestrate an early career change for these politicians.

Gore recognized the volatility of the civil rights issue in state and regional politics and typically preferred to avoid the subject. The Fourth District had only a small minority population, so issues of civil rights had limited political value. While lacking the blatant racism that existed in western Tennessee, most whites in the Upper Cumberland believed in segregation and maintenance of the status quo. Also, that there was a smaller African-American population in Tennessee than other areas of the South made reaching out to that portion of the population even more difficult.

Gore sought a middle ground on the racial issue, as he already was eyeing a run for the Senate in 1948. The ultimate winner of the seat, Estes Kefauver, succinctly pointed out the problem. While many viewed the Chattanooga congressman as one of the South's strongest progressives, Kefauver was also a political realist who once told a reporter regarding race issues that "I don't want to be a dead statesman." To another, he emphasized that "you have to get elected before you can do any good up there." Gore agreed, arguing that "I based my appeal for black support upon a liberal economic record—full employment at decent wages, social security, TVA, health, housing, etc.—and let the sleeping dogs be as best I could."[23] In this way, he believed that he served all Tennesseans regardless of race and stymied men like Bilbo.

Despite all the emphasis on important issues of the day, the work of a representative was often very ordinary, and Gore found himself doing a variety of small favors for his constituents. He helped an elementary-school teacher from Cookeville obtain copies of President Truman's portrait to hang in her classroom. On another occasion, he forwarded a letter from a Robley D. Webb of Winfield, Tennessee, to President Truman to encourage the president to consider a pension bill to provide disability checks to Webb and his family of eight. Gore even hand-delivered a bottle of Jack Daniels no. 7 pre-Prohibition whiskey from a Nashville doctor to the president.[24]

When Gore returned to Washington for the new session in early 1947, he was a member of the minority party for the first time. During the 1946 election, Republican candidates viciously attacked the New Deal for its "regimentation," and "radicalism" and criticized Truman with slogans such as "To Err is Truman" and "Under Truman: Two Families in Every Garage." Senator Robert Taft of Ohio emphasized that "the main issue of the election was the restoration of freedom and the elimination or reduction of constantly increasing interference with family life and with business by autocratic government bureaus and autocratic labor unions."[25] These ideas appealed to many conservative Democrats as well, and the stage was set for bitter conflicts throughout the 80th Congress.

The first major battle related to a Republican effort to cut taxes. The chairman of the House Ways and Means Committee, Harold Knutson of Minnesota, introduced legislation for a 20 percent across-the-board tax cut as a way to "stop the New Deal practice of using tax laws to punish its enemies and promote social innovations."[26] To pay for it, Knutson and his allies promised to slash billions of dollars in federal spending to balance the budget.

Everything about the Knutson plan offended Gore's populist sensibilities. Baruch agreed that the plan was irresponsible, calling it "an awful boner." Gore and many others believed it failed to pay down the huge war debt and would

ensure major cuts in social spending. Furthermore, the tax plan unfairly benefited the wealthy with the top 4 percent receiving 36 percent of the tax cut and
was "grossly unfair, unsound, and unequitable." Gore stressed that Americans
could not sacrifice the basic principle of taxation according to ability to pay and
noted that with the money that the wealthy man has left he "will have enough
. . . to buy a yacht, I mean another yacht . . . pay his membership in his golf
club, take a cruise, a vacation, and still have $5,000 left with which to gamble in
the stock market." By contrast, the man earning $1,200 received an increase of
$11.40, allowing him "to buy a cheap spring hat for his wife." Gore warned that
"the philosophies of the Knutson bill" bore a striking comparison to the 1920s
tax bills that had carried the country into a depression.[27]

As he battled the Republicans on taxes, Gore also found himself defending
one of the showcases of the New Deal, the TVA. It remained a popular target,
and opponents received the support of Tennessee Democratic senators Kenneth
McKellar and Tom Stewart. In early February, Gore defended the TVA, noting
that Stewart had made "charges ranging from illegality to communism to illicit
love." "The question of private versus public power has been settled in the Valley of Tennessee. The TVA is all we got and the people who must depend upon
it for electricity," he argued, and we "do not want this highly technical business
run by hacks of a vicious political machine nor do they want it to become a
partisan football."[28]

The first battle developed over the appointment of Gordon Clapp as head
of the TVA. Gore testified in front of the Senate Public Works Committee in
February 1947, defending Clapp against several charges, including that Clapp
had Communist sympathies. In response, Gore told the committee that he had
known him for many years and that "without exception, I have found him honest, forthright, efficient, patriotic and able." "I, for one, am going to be careful
about blackmailing the name of innocent people with false charges," he told his
constituents.[29]

The focus on communism signaled a new direction for the country's foreign
relations. Since 1946, relations with the Soviet Union had deteriorated. George
Kennan, a foreign service officer at the U.S. embassy in Moscow, had argued
that Stalin was a brutal, xenophobic, and aggressive dictator. He urged the
United States to "draw the line" and contain Soviet expansion. The catchword
of the time became, according to Secretary of State James Byrnes, a policy of
"patience and firmness."[30]

Events unfolding in early 1947 pushed the Truman administration to heed
Kennan's warnings. In March, Truman requested $400 million in military and

economic assistance for Greece and Turkey. "I believe that it must be the policy of the United States to support free peoples who are resisting attempted subjugation by armed minorities or by outside pressures," he told the nation as part of the speech that became known as the Truman Doctrine.[31]

Critics immediately assailed Truman for aiding antidemocratic forces; others feared that the emphasis on military assistance was unnecessarily provocative. Nevertheless, Gore praised Truman's initiative, observing that "the doctrine of the foreign policy which he outlined was literally breath-taking in its scope. The course which the President chose and which now the American people and the American Congress must back up or repudiate is a course of affirmative action and not a course of appeasement."[32] When the final vote on the appropriation occurred, he cast his ballot with the majority that passed it in May.

The Truman Doctrine marked a turning point in U.S. foreign policy, as Washington adopted a unilateral course to defend governments from Soviet domination. Few people raised alarms about the costs and commitments the United States would need to make to contain the Soviets. Over time, it became an open-ended policy. Gore, like most Americans, never questioned the decision, remembering the lessons of appeasing the fascists. A number of years would pass before he and other legislators began to criticize the basic tenets of the policy.

The growing anticommunist paranoia also affected domestic affairs. Pro-business, pro-management Republicans had launched a major assault on organized labor, culminating in the Taft-Hartley Bill. It outlawed closed shops and secondary boycotts in related industries, prohibited labor union political contributions, and established "cooling-off" periods for eighty days if a strike threatened national security. The House and Senate passed the bill by large majorities, with Gore standing with the majority, but Truman vetoed it. Afterward, the president told a radio audience that "we do not need—and we do not want—legislation which will take fundamental rights away from our working people."[33]

Joining with most southern and western Democrats and the Republicans, Gore voted for the successful override. Gore's support of amendments and the extension of Taft-Hartley would weaken over the years, especially when he set his sights on higher office and needed the support of the fledgling union movement in Tennessee. It appeared contradictory that he would support working-class issues on taxes, Social Security, the TVA, and working conditions, but not unions. At this point, he clearly differentiated between organized labor and workers and maintained a strong ambivalence toward the former.

The summer was quiet as Congress recessed, but new battles began immediately in the fall, most revolving around foreign policy. Conditions in Western Europe during 1947 continued to deteriorate as the Communist parties in Italy and France appeared likely to seize power at the ballot box.[34]

The administration responded quickly. In June, Secretary of State George Marshall made a speech at Harvard University in which he proposed having the European nations, including the Soviet Union and its satellites, submit plans for economic revitalization with U.S. grants. Almost immediately, Knutson chastised Truman and his allies for being "the one-worlders, the do-gooders, and the internationalists." Potential presidential nominee Robert Taft supported annual appropriations but called the Marshall Plan "a kind of five-year plan, like Stalin's or a European TVA."[35]

During the three-month-long battle, Gore stood arm and arm with the president. In early December 1947, he told his radio audience that "the speed of transportation and communication, the awful destructiveness and power that had been released by modern science . . . and the determined revolutionary threat of international communism" had forced the United States to accept a leadership role. While there were no guarantees of success, Gore argued that to fail to help Western Europe would likely ensure war. To make his point, he compared opposition to the Marshall Plan to the America First Committee in 1941, hypothesizing that if the United States had followed that group's isolationist path, "America might now be under the heel of a conquering dictator."[36]

Despite dogged efforts by some Republicans to derail the Marshall Plan, Congress approved it in late March by a vote of 329–74 in the House and 69–17 in the Senate. Within a year, more than $4 billion began flowing to Western Europe, the majority to Britain, France, and Allied zones of Germany. The investment immediately paid dividends for the Europeans and the U.S. economy, as many agreements required purchasing American products. In the final analysis, the Marshall Plan was successful, creating much goodwill in Europe and stabilizing several democracies. At the same time, it also marched Washington into deeper foreign commitments and created more animosity between the East and West as Stalin responded with a Russian form of the plan for Eastern Europe.[37]

While some bipartisanship characterized foreign policy issues in early 1948, domestic issues remained contentious. The Republicans continued pushing a tax cut and attacking New Deal programs, while Truman and the progressive

Democrats became more combative. Although Truman was "a bit more conservative and a bit less audacious than his great predecessor," Gore liked many of the president's ideas. He criticized Taft as the archetypal Republican, "the embodiment of that type of conservatism which clings to, if not longs for, the conditions of the past, which intrinsically opposes change, which is inherently timid and distrustful of the future, which is so basically over cautious that in leadership finds it all too difficult to be constructive or visionary."[38]

Despite Gore's support for Truman, he feared a disastrous electoral outcome for the Democrats. In late February 1948, he reported that Truman's defeat appeared likely. The president's initial indecision on Palestine had alienated Jewish voters, while his call for ending poll taxes and desegregating the military had angered white southerners. Noting Hull's observation that "six months is a lifetime in politics," Gore worried that only the Republicans could help the Democrats win. In a rather somber mood, he took out his fiddle and told his radio audience that "since I am so blue and regretful about all these unfortunate developments, as I am sure many of you are, I have invited my friends [several congressmen] in and we are just going to play a few tunes for you." They opened with the melancholy song, "Flow Gently, Sweet Afton."[39]

The confrontations with the Republicans and the disheartening position of the Democrats in 1947 increased Gore's anti-Republican sentiments. He admitted by 1948 that he had "become more partisan than when I arrived." Explaining the change, he acknowledged the sharp policy differences between the two parties. "I saw that the leadership of the Republican party talked a popular game, but their real loyalty, down deep their real dedication, was to the policies and programs in favor of the vested interests."[40] While many conservative southerners often crossed lines and voted with the Republicans, Gore remained part of the bloc of progressive southerners such as Hays, Monroney, Kefauver, Lyndon Johnson, and others who supported most Fair Deal programs.

While political battles raged in Washington and world affairs gripped Americans, Albert and Pauline focused on family matters. For many years they had tried adding to the family but failed. Finally, in 1947, Pauline learned that she was pregnant. The family, including Nancy, was overjoyed at the prospect of a new sibling. Finally, on March 31, 1948, the thirty-six-year-old Pauline traveled to Columbia Hospital for Women where she gave birth to a nine-pound, two-ounce baby boy. Later, Pauline told interviewers that the conditions surrounding his birth made him "kind of a miracle to us."

The news of the birth spread quickly. Ten-year-old Nancy stayed at home with the nurse and called family and friends. The *Nashville Tennessean* ran a headline: "Well, Mr. Gore, Here He Is—On Page 1." Several months earlier, Gore had extracted a promise from its editors after Kefauver had a baby girl and they put the story on the inside pages. "If I have a boy baby, I don't want the news buried inside the paper, I want it on page 1 where it belongs," he crowed. The editors complied after he called them with the information, and the headline dominated the left-hand corner of the front page. As one author observed, "Before he was home from the hospital, Al Gore had won a news cycle for his father."[41]

The major challenge of the young man's birth was the choice of names. Pauline fought in what she characterized as a "battle royal" for the traditional Albert Gore Jr. The congressman resisted, fearing it would be a burden to him in the future. "He was adamant about it," Pauline recalled. As was often the case within the inner circle of the Gore family, debate led to compromise. They ultimately decided on Albert but would leave the decision up to the boy on what he would accept. For the time, he would simply be "Little Al."[42]

The son's birth brought great joy to his parents. Though they loved the vivacious and talented Nancy, a son was a special source of pride. He would acquire many of Albert and Pauline's qualities, each of which drove him to succeed to please his overachieving and intelligent parents. Being the son of an up-and-coming politician brought intense pressure and scrutiny. His father and mother's high expectations pushed him to confront all challenges head-on. Al was a product of Washington, but the family worked hard to keep him grounded in his Tennessee roots. From the start, they groomed him for great things.

The competition in the *Tennessean* over baby announcements mirrored that within the Tennessee congressional delegation. Gore had been eyeing a challenge to Senator Tom Stewart after everyone avoided a clash with the senior senator, Kenneth McKellar, in 1946. The rising stars in Tennessee politics, Gore and Kefauver included, lined up to challenge the junior senator.

Kefauver ultimately beat Gore to the punch. After announcing his candidacy, Kefauver traveled to Memphis to challenge Edward Crump's political machine. The Memphis boss commented that Kefauver reminded him "of the pet coon that puts its foot in an open drawer in your room, but invariably turns its head while its foot is feeling around in the drawer. The coon hopes, through its cunning by turning its head, he will deceive any onlookers as to where his foot is and what it is into." The Ivy League–educated Kefauver turned the slight to his advantage. At the meeting of his supporters, he donned a coonskin cap. His action became an immediate hit among the press and constituents and thrust him into the limelight.[43]

During the primary, Gore publicly remained out of the three-way race between Kefauver, Stewart, and Judge John A. Mitchell of Cookeville, whom Crump decided to back. While despising the Crump machine, Gore wanted to avoid alienating powerful men, although he openly backed his old mentor, Gordon Browning, for the gubernatorial race. The primary was nasty. Crump's cronies lambasted Kefauver as "a darling of the Communists and Communist sympathizers" and called him a "warm supporter" of the FEPC.[44] Despite such charges, the Chattanooga congressman won the nomination by forty thousand votes. With Browning's concurrent victory, the power of the Crump machine appeared broken, which boded well for future challenges to its allies, including McKellar.

During the general campaign between the Republican B. Carroll Reece and Kefauver, Gore actively campaigned for Kefauver. In one of his more memorable speeches in Gallatin, he provided the Kefauver entourage with a chuckle. During his talk, he reached a frenzied pitch and quoted Shakespeare. "He who steals my good name steals trash," Gore loudly exclaimed. Pauline quickly recognized the error and exclaimed, "Oh no, Albert! That's not it, Albert!" Undeterred, Gore continued: "but he who steals my purse steals that which enriches him not, but makes me poor indeed!" While the Kefauvers bit their lips to prevent from laughing, Gore finished. Much to Pauline's delight, it appeared few in the crowd caught the error.[45] In fact, Kefauver later made a similar error with his Shakespeare. It mattered not; Kefauver easily defeated Reece and became Tennessee's junior senator.

Much has been made of the relationship between Kefauver and Gore. It was competitive but remained comparatively cordial as they shared ideas on civil rights, the TVA, education, and foreign policy. Certainly, there were differences and disagreements. Gore called Kefauver more "urbane," highlighting his Ivy League education, while promoting himself as more "provincial." Furthermore, Kefauver was a more natural politician, one who frequently told people what they wanted to hear and proved much more skilled at personal touches like having his staff send cards on occasions of birthdays, marriages, or deaths.[46] Gore resisted such actions, believing they were insincere and costly.

If there was a difference that caused some rifts, it was Kefauver's marital infidelities and alcohol abuse. While both vices were rampant in Washington among his future friends, including John F. Kennedy, Gore avoided them and stressed that Kefauver "had certain interests and entrees and affinities that I did not enjoy."[47] Gore was a teetotaler most of his life and always a dedicated family man. It added fuel to his belief that he was a better candidate, but Kefauver beat him to the punch time and time again. Still, there was no overt animosity, and the two men cooperated closely on many issues until Kefauver's death in 1963.

While the Tennessee races developed, most eyes remained fixed on the presidential election. In the summer, Gore characterized the Republican nominee, Thomas Dewey, as "an efficient administrator of public affairs" as governor of New York, which he thought was important for the job of president. Yet he also observed that someone could characterize Dewey as "a cold, calculating producer of efficiency without too much regard to the humanities and statesmanship involved."[48]

While Dewey appeared an imposing challenger, internal divisions threatened to tear apart the Democratic Party. Henry Wallace bolted the party to lead the Progressive Party, which called for more conciliation toward the Soviet Union and "progressive capitalism." On the other side, southern Democrats angry over Truman's support of civil rights formed the Dixiecrat Party and nominated South Carolina governor Strom Thurmond for president. Its platform pushed states' rights and opposition to civil rights. In both cases, the Democratic Party lost important elements of their winning coalition from the New Deal.[49]

Despite the divisions, Truman and party stalwarts concentrated on running a campaign that focused as much on the Republican Congress as on Dewey. Traveling throughout the country, Truman called the 80th Congress a "do nothing" group and "gluttons of privilege" who believed in "low prices for farmers, cheap wages for labor, and high profits for big corporations." In another speech, he labeled Republican leaders as "cunning men" who aimed to "put the Government of the United States under the control of men like themselves. They want a return of the Wall Street economic dictatorship."[50]

As Gore stumped Tennessee with Kefauver, he also campaigned for the Truman ticket, which included Kentucky senator Alben Barkley as the vice-presidential nominee. The president's attacks on the privileged interests of the Republican Party fit well with Gore's own views. He recognized, however, that Truman had an uphill fight, telling his constituents in October 1948 that Dewey "appeared very confident" of winning and seemed more intent on promoting Republican Senate candidates. While noting that Dewey disagreed with these people on many issues, Gore stressed that despite the sharp differences, the partisan Dewey had "chosen to try to elect men who stand for nearly everything he is against."[51]

Much to everyone's surprise, Truman staged a massive comeback and won, taking 24,105,812 votes and 303 electoral votes to Dewey's 21,970,065 and 189, while Thurmond took 1,169,021 (39 electoral votes) and Wallace 1,157,172 (no electoral votes). In addition, the Democrats regained control of Congress, going from a six-seat deficit in the Senate to a twelve-person majority and from a 246–188 disadvantage in the House to a 263–171 advantage.[52] Running against the 80th Congress had succeeded and sent a resounding message to conservatives that many people remained committed to the New Deal and Fair Deal.

Gore and his friends savored the victory, and he praised Truman as a "scrappy, persistent, tireless candidate who dodged no issue, who hit and hit hard at the record of the Republican party not only during the 80th Congress but also during the administration of former President Herbert Hoover." According to Gore, Dewey had ducked the issues to talk in generalities and that the "sweeping victory of the Democratic Party in last Tuesday's election has far reaching meaning for you and me." To him, it meant an improved TVA, the expansion of Social Security, housing projects, and a strengthened national defense.[53]

Gore also saw the 1948 election as an important turning point in the history of the South. He later called the Dixiecrats "nothing more or less than the old Bourbon leaders of the South who believed that by 'hollering nigger' and waving the flag they could once more control the Southern states"; they were "clearly doomed to failure." The Dixiecrat Party signaled to Gore the final break between the southern Bourbons and the Democrats and opened the door to a "regularized two-party system" in the South. Over time Thurmond, whom Gore particularly disliked, would bolt the party and carry many like-minded southerners with him.[54] The process of desertion to the Republican Party had begun in earnest in 1948 and would have significant ramifications in postwar politics.

The election of 1948 marked another watershed in American history. The electorate reinforced their support for the government playing a strong role in domestic welfare and national defense. This New Deal/Fair Deal generation would remain a major force in politics and the electorate for two more decades. It was within this setting that Gore had risen and would continue his climb up the ladder. He had served well in the first Truman administration, solidifying his position in the Democratic Party and within the state of Tennessee. This process would continue through the challenging period that was to follow as Gore planned for his step up from the House to the Senate.

The new term in 1949 began with a flurry of activity over the budget and taxes. Truman recommended a $41.9 billion appropriation, which Gore considered "astronomical" but necessary for national security. He told his constituents that little room existed for cuts in government, but he promised to remove waste. In a bold move, he also called for increased taxes. "Yes, Siree, taxes are high and plenty high and hard to pay, but one resolution I have, and that is that during this period of prosperity and maximum employment I will vote for taxes sufficient to pay for the cost of government and at the same time make a substantial payment upon our public debt." He continued to hammer home his theme of taxation according to the ability to pay. "I do not know how this nation as a whole could have prospered so well without it. We have too much concentration of wealth in a few families and corporations as it is, far too much, but had it not been made possible, back in 1914, then the concentration would have been even more pronounced than it now is."[55] He would fight to put the burden on those most able to handle it, thus challenging conservative orthodoxy.

U.S.–Soviet relations also remained an important issue. The Soviet intervention in Czechoslovakia and the war scare over Berlin in 1948 had accelerated calls for an alliance between Western Europe and the United States. After much negotiation, twelve nations including the United States, France, and Great Britain signed a pact in 1949 that committed each to consider "an armed attack against one or more of them" as "an attack against all" and required that each "will assist the Party or Parties so attacked by taking forthwith, individually and in concert with other Parties, such action as it deems necessary, including the use of force." To assuage concerns about a loss of sovereignty, the treaty also pledged each country to follow its own constitutional measures when making decisions.[56]

As was often the case, Gore spoke in favor of the Truman administration's internationalist foreign policies, despite having no vote on the matter. He emphasized that the treaty expressed a Western determination to prevent aggression and unify nations in promoting peace and preventing more destructive conflicts. "The North Atlantic Pact is not the final answer nor will the problem likely be solved in our time. But lest we be discouraged let us reflect upon the progress that has been made just recently."[57]

With backing from most important Senate Republicans, NATO passed easily in the Senate, 82–13. By July 1949, President Truman signed the treaty, an important milestone in American history. For the first time since the Franco-American Alliance of 1778, the United States had entered a formal entangling alliance, and military containment of the Soviet Union became a direct military commitment, one with important consequences for the United States during the next four decades.[58]

Gore also weighed in on the controversial issue of public education. He reported that a federal education bill had been stalled due to a controversy on the division of funds to private schools. "I believe strongly in religious freedom . . . But I hold that the only sure way to safeguard the inalienable right of religious freedom is to steadfastly maintain the absolute separation of church and state," he asserted in a radio broadcast. Thus, he opposed any federal funds for private schools. He admitted he had put Nancy in a private school after she returned from Tennessee because of problems of coordinating schedules, but "the taxpayers of the country are not called upon nor do I think they should be called upon to provide this special privilege. It is a privilege for which I must pay."[59]

The issue of the separation of church and state remained an important one for Gore for many years. Because he was the representative of a state dominated by conservative Protestants, the question was not controversial—most of the debate centered on aid to parochial schools. Yet the issue became more complex, especially when school prayer, teaching of the Bible in the public schools, and desegregation became political hot potatoes in the early 1960s and private Protestant schools became more prevalent. Gore stayed consistent in his opposition to blending church and state activities, even when his position became more difficult to defend to conservatives in Tennessee.

One of the most controversial issues Gore faced in the summer of 1949 involved agricultural supports. Since the establishment of the AAA in 1933, government aid to farmers had been a hotly debated issue. Programs of price supports and subsidies to reduce acreage in production were especially important to legislators from farming areas like the Fourth District of Tennessee. In the postwar period, conservatives sought to reduce the ever-increasing expenditures while rural leaders countered that the Great Depression had been facilitated in large part by the agricultural community's problems during the 1920s. Each year, politicians clashed over the size of the appropriations and proposed reforms in the benefit programs.

In 1949, a major battle broke out when Republicans pushed two plans, including Title I of the Agricultural Act of 1948, proposed by Rep. Clifford Hope (R-KS), which retained an inflexible 90 percent of parity price supports for another year. Senator George Aiken (R-VT) offered an alternative proposal with a flexible system of price supports, creating a lower limit of 60 percent and upper level of 90 percent apportioned according to supply and demand. Most southerners supported the Hope bill because tobacco and cotton farmers feared flexible parity, and both parties agreed to support a merger of the two bills during the national campaign in 1948.[60]

While the two sides debated, the secretary of agriculture, Charles F.

Brannan, dropped a bombshell in April 1949 by proposing a new system based on an "income support" formula. Instead of price supports and production limits, he wanted full production and market-based prices. In return, the federal government would make direct cash payments to farmers for perishable commodities, with the goal of a maximum of $26,100 worth of subsidies per farm. To him, the plan would allow production to grow and lower consumer prices while preventing upheaval in the agricultural community.[61]

The battle over the Brannan plan began in earnest in July, and Gore found himself at odds with the administration. A long-time supporter of farm subsidies, Gore argued that "we cannot afford to run the risk with the farmer's welfare . . . by taking this leap in the dark and throwing overboard a program that has been built out of sixteen years of experience and farmer cooperation." He characterized Brannan's plan as "a crazy impractical scheme" and told his constituents that he would fight until it disappeared.[62]

During the debates, Gore vigorously attacked the Brannan plan by focusing on the possible cost, especially if the prices of goods fluctuated. He highlighted that $3 per hundred increase in hog price supports would drain the treasury of $500 million. He admitted that the present system, one dating back to the Steagall Bill that he had supported in 1941, had flaws but that it had been refined over the years. To scrap it would be to invite many problems. When several Democratic supporters of the bill accused him of sounding like a Republican, Gore ignored them and continued his attacks.[63]

The administration continued pushing the Brannan plan. When the White House offered to make a trial run on several commodities, Gore countered with legislation extending the current program for one year and called the administration's compromise "an admission of the basic fault of the bill." Soon, the Brannan plan died, and Gore's plan passed by a vote of 239–170. *Life* ran a photo of Gore in "people of the week" with the caption: "Biggest fight in Congress last week came when Representative Gore (D., Tenn.), usually an administration stalwart, introduced a bill to scrap the Truman Brannan farm plan . . . and keep up present support system. Gore won."[64]

Gore concluded after the victory that "if we can accomplish this trick of high farm income but low food prices in the grocery store without the outpouring of billions of dollars from the United States Treasury then I think we will have discovered something as great as would be the discovery of perpetual motion." Holding out an olive branch, he praised his opponents for fighting for what they believed was best. "I just disagree and expressed my disagreement in the hardest fight I have made in my 11 years in Congress."[65]

In challenging the Brannan plan Gore continued demonstrating his maverick streak, even in the face of extreme party pressure. He also won a great deal of publicity for himself, especially among the important agricultural interests in Tennessee who had opposed the plan. This was good news for a man looking ahead toward a run for the Senate in 1952, for which it was essential to develop more ties outside of the Fourth District. Gore was an ambitious man with a sense of what he believed was right, but it helped that in this instance the fight corresponded with his personal goals.

While his opposition to the Brannan plan won Gore support in Tennessee, another controversy developed that had more down sides for an aspiring southern politician. In the spring of 1950, the administration introduced new legislation to strengthen the Fair Employment Practices Commission. It immediately met strong opposition as Rep. Charles E. Bennett (D-FL) blamed the legislation on the Communists and "a lot of pretty wild people, with pretty long hair" determined to destroy the South's "traditional democracy." Rep. Clare E. Hoffman (R-MI) called the effort "another step toward dictatorship" designed to promote "social intermingling." In response, supporters such as Herman Edelsberg of the Anti-Defamation League argued "the bill is not aimed at prejudice, the bill is aimed at discrimination, at overt acts which you might call the bitter fruits of prejudice."[66]

Gore took the middle ground on the issue. "There is no denying that serious discrimination is practiced against some of our minority racial groups," he admitted, but in recent years there had been "very, very rapid strides in the direction of understanding, tolerance and Christian brotherhood." To him, only time and education would ensure equality, and the FEPC replaced these ideas with "the force of the Federal government . . . I do not believe this problem can be solved by such force bill methods."[67]

Does his opposition to the FEPC mean that Gore shared the racist views of many Tennesseans? The answer is clearly no. Like many progressive-minded southerners, he viewed the mistreatment and lack of opportunities for African Americans as appalling. On a personal level, Pauline and Albert treated African Americans with respect and equality, and personal experiences reinforced this view. Later, Gore told the story of how he and his family would travel from Washington to Tennessee during his service in the House. His daughter's nanny, Ocie Bell Hunt, who was black, often accompanied them. This created many complications for the family because owners of the motels and service stations prohibited Hunt from using their facilities. Gore would always ask gasoline station attendants if she could use the facilities. If they replied no, he moved to another. Lodging was even more difficult. Eventually Gore found an owner near a midway point who allowed them to stay if they arrived after dark. To avoid problems, the family often chose to make the 650-mile trip in one day. Gore lamented that he would never forget "such unbelievable cruelty."[68]

The stand on the FEPC provides insights into Gore's consistent view on civil rights for the next two decades. He personally believed in equality for all Americans regardless of race and supported efforts to strengthen the protections guaranteed all citizens under the Constitution. Nevertheless, he was a southern politician with aspirations for higher office who knew that taking a strong stand on the subject would cost him dearly. At the same time, he believed that the South could change when people like himself and Pauline taught their children and those around them the benefits of equality for everyone and avoided the race-baiting and demagoguery so typical of southern leaders like Bilbo and Thurmond. He thought it would take generations to secure the needed change and that coercion would ensure violent resistance and not address the root problems of discrimination.

Even during these major political battles, Gore continued to position himself for the Senate race in 1952. In early 1950, a rumor floated around the state that Kefauver was dominating Gore and making most of his decisions. It was most likely perpetuated by those who saw Gore as a potential rival and wanted to link him to the perceived "liberal" Kefauver. Harry Woodbury of the *Memphis Commercial Appeal* ran a story repeating the rumor, leading Gore to immediately complain that "were I a novice here, I could understand how such a rumor might get started . . . but after having served in Congress 14 years, each year of which I have a record of independence in thought and action, I am wholly unable to understand it."[69] Nevertheless, the issue would remain one that Gore felt he had to address for another two years.

One of the biggest controversies for Gore developed in spring 1950. For years, the charge that Communists had infiltrated the government during the New Deal had been a political minefield. The House Un-American Activities Committee (HUAC) became a national theater, as witnesses from universities, the media, and government paraded before it to defend their political beliefs against a hostile audience.[70]

The most famous of the Red hunters stepped into the limelight in February. The junior Republican senator from Wisconsin, Joseph McCarthy, traveled to Wheeling, West Virginia, and declared that "one thing to remember in discussing the Communists in our Government is that we are not dealing with spies who get 30 pieces of silver to steal the blueprint of a new weapon. We are dealing with a far more sinister type of activity because it permits the enemy to guide and shape our policy." Then, according to reporters, he waved a piece of paper and boasted that he had a list of 205 known Communists working in the State Department. In response, the Senate impaneled a subcommittee of the Senate Foreign Relations Committee headed by Senator Millard Tydings (D-MD) to investigate the charges.[71]

Never one to run away from controversy, Gore tried to educate his constituents on the issue. He hated McCarthy's partisanship and bullying tactics and believed they undermined government operations. When the hearings started, he quickly complimented the bravery of one of the first witnesses, Dorothy Kenyon. The former New York municipal judge and member of the UN Commission on Women had been accused of Communist sympathies by McCarthy. Testifying before the committee, Kenyon held her ground and denied the charges, admitting to nothing more than her liberalism. In public, she called McCarthy "an unmitigated liar" and the "worm from Wisconsin." Gore praised her, quoting Rudyard Kipling's "The Female of the Species." "When the Hymalayan peasant meets the he-bears in his pride, he shouts to scare the monster, who will often turn aside. But the she-bear thus accosted, rends the peasant tooth and nail, for the female is more deadly than the male." He added he enjoyed the cartoon in the Washington papers showing McCarthy hiding under the bed when Kenyon entered the room.[72]

In his own manner, Gore continued attacking McCarthy, especially in his WSM broadcasts. "Senator McCarthy continues on his reckless and irresponsible way . . . The time for proving his many charges is overdue. He hasn't proven one yet and he seems to be laboring." Gore warned that the Wisconsin senator, however, had created doubts about U.S. diplomats, weakening their influence at home and abroad. Time and time again, he chastised McCarthy, Kenneth Wherry (R-NE), and Styles Bridges (R-NH) for undermining American confidence for partisan gain.[73]

McCarthy lost some momentum for a brief while in the spring of 1950. A few, like Gore, saw through the charade, but many did not. A devastating attack on the State Department, especially against experts in the fields of Latin American, Asian, and Southeast Asian relations (people with an understanding of the culture and indigenous origins of discontent), had disastrous effects. Many lost positions to Eurocentric diplomats blinded by Communist paranoia who misjudged subsequent events. As for Gore, he continued criticizing the Wisconsin senator, although until he entered the Senate in 1953, he possessed little power outside of his region to shape the debate. Still, the demagoguery, partisanship, and recklessness of McCarthy and his associates disgusted him.

A new crisis that fueled a new round of McCarthyism developed in late June 1950 when North Korean forces swept across the 38th parallel and attacked the south, which had received American support. The Truman administration responded quickly; the State Department drafted a Security Council Resolution accusing the North Koreans of aggression. "If we let Korea down, the Soviet [sic] will keep right on going and swallow up one piece of Asia after another," Truman warned. "If we were to let Asia go, the Near East would collapse and no telling what would happen in Europe."[74] Almost immediately, the UN Security Council condemned North Korea, and Truman ordered U.S. forces into action.[75]

Like most Americans, Gore praised Truman's decision to commit U.S. troops in South Korea. He spoke of his hope to avoid a major war but warned that "we must stay awake at night . . . there is no telling what the Russians will do." He reminded people of the failure of the League of Nations in responding to Japanese aggression in Manchuria in 1931, which in turn prompted Hitler and Mussolini to pursue "their mad adventurs [sic]." He concluded that "in this situation, given this set of facts, we can only hope and proceed on the assumption that there will be less chance of a major war if we and our associates in the United Nations make unmistakably clear to the Communist combine that the time of easy conquest has passed and that hereafter force will be met with force."[76]

While carefully monitoring the events in Korea, Gore focused much of his energy in the early fall on campaigning for Democrats in other Tennessee congressional districts. In particular, he assisted Frank Wilson in East Tennessee, traveling the region to help out against Howard Baker Sr. He made several appearances supporting Wilson, telling the candidate that "eight or ten speeches a day is but a usual gait for me. I do not know what you have in mind, but I will be glad to comply with your wishes." At the same time, he demonstrated a fairly keen understanding of the area when he suggested that he should avoid Scott County where Baker held a significant majority. He feared that an outsider would only incite the local Republicans to turn out on election day.[77]

As the election approached in October, he intensified his efforts. In a remark that could have cost Gore a lot of votes if people had known, he told Wilson that he would prefer campaigning in a rural district rather than attending a University of Tennessee football game. "I know I cannot help you by going to the ball game, and, to be perfectly frank with you, I am not too much of a football fan, anyway," he wrote Wilson.[78] For many Tennesseans, this would have been heresy, then and now.

Wilson ran a good race but lost. Nevertheless, Gore earned the gratitude of many East Tennessee Democrats for his efforts. Robert Cassell of Harriman thanked him for being a "wheel-horse," stressing that Wilson had "made a wonderful race and I don't know anybody who contributed as much to it as you did."[79] These contacts proved important over the next two years as Gore entered a major political battle in 1952.

Pauline served as an important ally in her husband's struggle for higher office. She began accepting more speaking engagements, primarily at women's groups, to shore up support for her husband even though he had not officially announced his intention to run. She was insightful and witty in her speeches. In Crossville, she opened with a story of a woman whom supposedly she had represented while a lawyer in Arkansas. The woman had lost a thumb in a car accident and wanted $20,000. When Pauline reported that such a sum was too large, the woman told her: "You just don't understand. I think the court will allow me $20,000. You see, that was the thumb I kept my husband under." Immediately, she followed with the warning: "Perhaps, for Albert's protection, I might warn you that he may not necessarily agree with what I have to say—as you know, maybe someone should warn him—for his protection—that even if he doesn't, he'd better not say much about it."[80]

The benefit of such a good partner was never lost on Albert Gore or close political and family friends. Pauline was a fine speaker with an excellent political sense. Had she lived fifty years later, she might have had the opportunity to be a political giant in Tennessee and the nation. In these times, however, she was content to help her husband fulfill his dreams.

The planning for the Senate campaign intensified in 1951 as Gore tried solidifying his position in western Tennessee. His brother-in-law Whit LaFon and others, many associated with the anti-Crump faction, began actively promoting him. Jack Woodall, secretary to Rep. Tom Murray, wrote in late 1951 that "I am keeping close contact with the people here in West Tennessee in your behalf and want to assure you that your popularity is increasing every day." On the opposite side of the state, Frank Wilson and others helped organize support by encouraging Gore to increase contacts with the Democratic executive committee and members of farm and labor organizations, as well as newspaper editors. Wilson especially promoted writing personal letters announcing his candidacy to the leaders of the groups and editors once he made the formal announcement.[81]

While planning his run, Gore watched the Korean War demoralize the country. After the successful Inchon assault in September 1950, the UN forces under General Douglas MacArthur had driven the North Koreans back across the 38th parallel and looked to reunify the country. Despite warnings from the Chinese about approaching their boundary, UN forces continued northward. In late October 1950, massive numbers of Chinese troops crossed the Yalu River and forced the UN troops to retreat. By early 1951, the lines had stabilized around the 38th parallel, and a war of attrition began.[82]

The failure to win victory and the protracted conflict raised serious doubts about the wisdom of U.S. policy in Korea and further fueled the Red Scare. Gore's constituents grew frustrated with the lack of victory, and one asked, "Can you please tell me why our boys do not get out of Korea? . . . I had a son in the last war and I sure do not want to send him over there knowing these boys do not have a chance."[83] Others feared the war's effect on the economy and government programs, while the more hawkish ones criticized Truman for not using all the force necessary to win, including atomic weapons.

Gore shared his constituents' frustrations, but he called on Americans to focus on building up their country to face the extreme challenge. To achieve peace and stability, he believed the United States needed atomic superiority, air and naval supremacy, and greater productive capacity without inflation and disunity. "The house is dark," he cautioned, "but by strength, courage and faith may be brought to light."[84]

The issue of Korea became even more controversial in April 1951. For months, problems had festered between MacArthur and Truman. The general requested permission to bomb Chinese sanctuaries in Manchuria, but the president denied it. Against the commander-in-chief's orders, MacArthur called for an attack on mainland China. Using members of Congress to promote his views of unifying Korea and allowing Nationalist forces to attack from Formosa, MacArthur clearly challenged civilian control. On April 10, Truman relieved him of command and replaced him with General Matthew Ridgway.[85]

Many Americans reacted angrily to MacArthur's reassignment, and thousands of letters flooded the White House protesting the hero's dismissal. Gore received his fair share of mail, including one letter from Memphis whose author argued that "I feel that this foolishness in high places has gone too far, and I ask you, in the best interests of our country, to do all in your power to impeach Harry Truman and Dean Acheson."[86]

Despite the unpopularity of Truman's decision, Gore supported him. While calling MacArthur "one of the brightest" generals in history, Gore acknowledged that the general had disobeyed a directive agreed on at an earlier meeting at Wake Island and whose plans could lead to an intractable war on the Asian mainland. He responded to one constituent that MacArthur's challenge to his commander-in-chief resulted in "but one choice under our constitution: The military must subordinate to civil government authority."[87]

Frustrations with Korea provoked Gore to offer the president some very dubious advice. Arguing that the United States should adopt extreme measures in Korea to end the "meat grinder of American manhood," Gore stressed, "I think the tragic situation today demands some dramatic and climatic use of some of these [atomic] weapons." In particular, he suggested that after removing Korean civilians and informing the enemy, the United States "dehumanize a belt across the Korean Peninsula by surface radiological contamination," with periodic recontamination of the area as needed until a settlement could be reached.[88] Of course, Truman rejected the advice.

Gore was an ardent Cold War warrior, but while he rejected the extreme measures of going to nuclear war with the Soviet Union over Korea, he wanted to end the bloodbath. Despite his attacks on McCarthy and others for their methods in the war against communism, he never wanted to allow himself to be attacked for being too soft on communism. Furthermore, he believed that technology, particularly atomic weapons and energy, remained a panacea to many of society's ills, including geopolitical conflict. Like most people of the time, he did not have a good understanding of the effects of radiation and fallout on the environment and people. Clearly, he believed too much in the ability of science and technology to solve problems without recognizing the inherent dangers. He demonstrated an ability to evolve intellectually and alter his positions, but often in his career he lacked the insight to anticipate problems with the new forms of technology.

While Korea occupied the attention of the country, Gore focused on improving his credentials in foreign affairs as he prepared to run for the Senate. He accompanied Vice President Barkley on a congressional fact-finding mission to the Middle East in 1951. Since the end of World War II, turmoil had engulfed the region, as traditional European colonial powers lost ground in the face of a rising tide of Arab nationalism. Contention over the creation of the nation of Israel added to the tension. In 1948, the Truman administration had supported its foundation, much to the great consternation of most of the region's people. That same year, Egypt, Syria, and Jordan waged an unsuccessful war of extermination against the Israelis. In the process, the Israelis seized more lands and created the first generation of Palestinian refugees, more than 800,000, whom neither Israel nor the Arab nations wanted.[89]

The trip strongly affected Gore, especially the conditions in the region. While admiring the beauty of the ruins of opulent civilizations, he decried the "tragic blight of humanity . . . the whole area seethes with unrest, filth, poverty, hunger, hate and strife." To one editor, he wrote, "Never before have I seen the problem of living, living bare living, so acute."[90]

He would remain interested and involved in issues of the Middle East, especially when he entered the Senate several years later. In particular, he became an advocate for changes in U.S. aid, especially relating to the refugee problem. This would not be his last trip to the region, and each time he would return befuddled by its complexities. The thorny question of the Middle East would perplex American policymakers, including Gore and many others, for generations.

As the election cycle approached, Gore increased efforts to strengthen his position. He contacted Frank Ahlgren, editor of the *Memphis Commercial Appeal* and committed foe of the Crump machine, and asked for help. He sought a "good" person from western Tennessee, preferably from the Memphis area, to head up his political organization and a capable person to do publicity. "In other words, Frank, I am starting into the organizational phase of my campaign and I need your help very much." He highlighted that he had worked "very, very hard" over the past two years, giving approximately 400 speeches throughout the state. "I know people far and wide and I believe many of them know me. I am slowing down my speaking campaign to devote the month of December largely to the organization."[91]

Gore recognized that the key to victory was western Tennessee. Kefauver's 1948 win demonstrated that Gore must take on the Crump machine to win. There was a progressive element of the society in western Tennessee that would find Gore's positions appealing. His ties to Kefauver, Browning, and others provided a good starting point. Seeking people from western Tennessee as campaign and publicity managers made perfect political sense. They would help him in Crump's backyard, allowing him to exploit McKellar's vulnerabilities.

In anticipation of the forthcoming battle, Gore solidified his position with the Kefauver supporters. In early December, he traveled to the Peabody Hotel in Memphis to attend a rally supporting Kefauver's run for the presidency. Gore praised Kefauver for stepping up and challenging "corruption, tyranny and autocracy" within his own party and the opponents'. In particular, he praised the work of the Senate Crime Investigating Committee headed by Kefauver which had pursued organized crime and the political machines that often allied with criminal organizations. "Human parasites, chiselers and influence peddlers have taken advantage of the Democratic Party. However, it is sound at heart; there is nothing wrong with the Democratic Party that cannot be cured with the Presidential nomination of Estes Kefauver." In conclusion, Gore told the audience that "I think we ought to send to the National Convention from Tennessee delegates with one instruction—stand for Estes Kefauver first, last, and until he's nominated for President."[92]

It was essential for Gore to identify himself with Kefauver. Their political principles mirrored one another's. By supporting Kefauver, Gore secured a powerful and popular ally with a strong state organization. Furthermore, Kefauver provided a model for a successful challenge to the Crump machine by defeating Stewart in 1948. Finally, Gore truly hoped someone would break down the national barriers against southern politicians winning the presidency. While currently focused on the Senate race, he was ambitious and wanted to continue climbing. The fact that no southerner had been nominated for president since before the Civil War weighed heavily. Gore and other southerners with aspirations to the presidency needed someone to crash the glass ceiling.

Throughout the Christmas break and early 1952, Gore made final preparations for an official entry into the race against the eighty-three-year-old senior senator. On February 2, 1952, he flew to Jackson, Tennessee, to make his announcement. "Tennesseans have the right this year to elect a United States Senator for a six-year term—I am the candidate for that post," he told the assembled press and supporters. He focused on his accomplishments, emphasizing his fights for the TVA and opposition to the Brannan plan, and in all areas he stressed that his efforts as a congressman had been for all of Tennessee, not only his district. "I will represent all the people fairly and to the fullest of my energy and ability," he stated. "My middle-of-the-road record, which does not particularly please either the extreme right or the extreme left, will be continued."[93]

Gore tried to run a positive campaign. In his first speech, he purposely avoided making any reference to McKellar, and in speeches and press releases, he referred to McKellar only in the past tense and simply in complimentary terms. Even on that first day, when reporters pointed out that Gore had landed at McKellar Field in Jackson, Gore responded, "yes, it is typical of the many things Senator McKellar has accomplished in his long tenure." He wanted to avoid aggravating those who respected the elder statesman but felt the state needed a change. The only time he indirectly attacked McKellar was when he said, "I have no political machine supporting me. I am running on my own."[94] It was an obvious slap at the Crump machine, a tactic that had served Kefauver and Browning well.

While campaigning whenever possible in the spring and early summer, Gore continued to participate actively in congressional affairs. He focused on the Bureau of Internal Revenue Reorganization headed by Rep. Percy Priest (D-TN), which sought to remove any political appointments in the organization. He worked to push the atomic energy program appropriation including $150 million for new steam power plants for the TVA to help the atomic program at Oak Ridge. He also backed resolutions that expanded federal spending on education, stressing that "I am willing to take chances because of the desperate inequities we face and faced, particularly, by the children of our region."[95]

While Gore had been running for the Senate since February, he did not make his opening address until early June, as the political season at the time ran primarily through the summer months, reducing the campaign cycle and expenditures. He spoke forcefully from the steps of the Smith County courthouse, telling the crowd that "speaking here today in the presence of so many who have known me as a boy, as a young school teacher, as a County Superintendent, and as a Congressman, I am quite naturally filled with great pride and even greater humility to be appearing in the role of a candidate for United States Senator." He highlighted the role of his father and mother in helping him reach this point and identified Hull as a "hero" whose "footprints" he would try to follow.[96]

In his speech, he focused on his positions more than on McKellar. "Though many sharp disagreements could be cited, I raise but one principal issue: Who is best fitted to serve the state and the nation in the United States for the next six years?" He announced, "I am against wasteful expenditures of the people's money on unsound and unworthy projects . . . I am against the patronage plunder of taxpayer's money . . . I am against the FEPC. I am against Socialized Medicine. I am against cost-plus profiteers, five-percenters, influence peddlers and subversive enemies who seek to prey upon and undermine our government."[97] Gore found issues that appealed to the base of the party and reached across to moderates who saw him as an honest, hard-working congressman.

The race issue proved a potentially very damaging one that Gore faced in this first Senate contest. Gore acknowledged that "most Southern politicians—progressive and conservative alike—felt compelled to holler 'Nigger' from time to time, and align themselves with the conservative establishment." He admitted during the campaign that he publicly recognized "the existence of discrimination (to do so was then a mark of a Southern progressive) and avoided race-baiting." Throughout, he conceded, he "let the sleeping dogs of racism lie as best I could."[98] Fortunately, McKellar never made it a major issue, and his people concentrated on the loss of seniority on the powerful Appropriations Committee if Gore won.

Despite his efforts to avoid controversy, events proved the volatility of the race issue. While campaigning in Tipton County in western Tennessee, Gore moved through the crowd, shaking everyone's hand. Afterward, one of his friends, Henry Vaughn, told him that he had just lost that area. When Gore asked why, Vaughn answered: "By shaking hands with the niggers." Gore merely responded that he "rejected this indignity and continued to shake hands with blacks and to solicit their support throughout the campaign." He remained, according to his own words, a moderate on race relations, but "I never broached the subject of racial integration."[99] In his mind, the social and economic issues that he supported crossed racial lines and would help working people of all colors.

The McKellar organization recognized the potent challenge early on and tried to find ways to discredit Gore. The appearance of placards with the phrase, "Thinking Feller, Vote for McKellar" alarmed the Gore organization. Signs appeared across the state, and the Gore family saw them daily. Albert recalled that he and Pauline decided that they needed a counterstrategy, so they returned to Carthage and sat down at the kitchen table. For hours, they brainstormed until finally Pauline added to the bottom of one of the signs, "Think Some More and Vote for Gore." Soon Gore's followers began scribbling this on the placards, which soon began disappearing as McKellar's people removed them.[100] The Gore camp had won the first battle.

There were other skirmishes over similar issues that may have appeared hokey to outsiders. Gore's advisers wanted to focus on the difference in age and energy, and they developed the "principle issue" with a short song tied to the tune "Hoop-dee-doo." It proclaimed: "Go with Gore—Albert Gore. He's wise and able and he's just forty-four."[101] Such strategies were "catchy" and more effective in the age before television coverage of campaigns.

Gore's style appeared quaint when compared to modern campaigns. Often, advance people would enter a town in a truck with bullhorns on top. According to Everett LaFon, Gore's brother-in-law, "One of us would drive to one town and ride around the square a couple of times, telling everybody Al Gore would be there in 20 minutes to make a speech." Another one would go to the next town. "We'd leap-frog from one town to the next. I've seen Albert Sr. give 10,

12 speeches—real speeches—in one day."[102] The indefatigable congressman traveled throughout the state, using the tried and true methods of the day to rally support.

McKellar also began campaigning more actively. During the 1948 contest, he had not even bothered to return to Tennessee and rarely even visited during the interim six years. To address charges that he was not fit to hold office, he returned to the state and made three speeches. In Crossville on July 14, ten thousand people heard a fifty-one-minute speech in which he guaranteed more federal funds for dams and roads. His followers continued hammering home that Tennessee would lose seniority if McKellar lost the nomination.[103]

While McKellar battled hard, Gore held the lead, and even some of the senator's allies recognized the handwriting on the wall. Crump had encouraged McKellar not to run, reporting that "I told him he had not been over the state for 10 years . . . I thought he had done enough for the people of Tennessee, and could so easily, so gracefully retire."[104] Without the strong support of the Crump machine, which had concentrated its energies against Browning, the McKellar camp found itself in dire straits.

The race went into August with Gore maintaining a lead according to most pundits. When primary day finally arrived, he won handily, taking nearly 60 percent of the vote. He even won a small majority in Shelby County, although the Crump machine helped Frank Clement defeat Browning. *Time* announced Gore's victory with the caption "44 v. 83" and included a picture of Gore with a fiddle under his chin and the caption, "An accomplished hillbilly fiddler, Gore used his talent in congressional campaigns, but shelved it in favor of dignity this year." *U.S. News and World Report* listed Gore's victory under "Upsets in the Senate: Old-Timers Lose Out" and stressed that Gore "brings a moderately conservative vote to the Senate."[105]

Gore's victory signaled a significant change in Tennessee politics. The old guard had been replaced by younger, more progressive politicians. Frank Clement's victory for the governor's mansion further indicated the change. Only thirty-two, Clement was a veteran and a former FBI agent who had served as counsel to the Railroad and Public Utilities Commission. More progressive than many Tennesseans, he backed better health and welfare benefits, advocated improved education, and avoided race-baiting. He would remain a prominent Tennessee politician for more than two decades.[106]

With the victory in the primary, Gore virtually had the position locked.[107] Republican Hobart Atkins offered little resistance, which allowed Gore to focus on the national election. During the summer, the Democrats had met and, despite the strong showing by Kefauver in the primaries, nominated Governor Adlai Stevenson of Illinois as their standard bearer. To balance the ticket, he selected Senator John Sparkman of Alabama as his running mate. The party united to demand the repeal of Taft-Hartley, continued agricultural supports, and an honorable exit from Korea. The articulate, intelligent Stevenson appeared an attractive candidate for the Democrats, who hoped to escape the shadow of an increasingly unpopular Truman.[108]

Gore had skipped the Democratic National Convention in Chicago, recognizing the problems that would develop if he did not take a strong stand in favor of Kefauver. Facing a Catch-22 situation, he avoided the controversy. Once the selection was made, he became a determined proponent of the Illinois governor in his battle against the Republican ticket of Dwight D. Eisenhower and Richard Nixon.

In late September, a friend in Memphis advised Gore that campaigning for the national ticket in Tennessee had few benefits. Eisenhower was popular and most Tennesseans looked suspiciously at the perceived liberalism of Stevenson. Gore concurred but maintained that "I am thoroughly convinced that the election of Gov. Stevenson as President of the United States is eminently preferable not only to Tennessee but for the United States." He called Eisenhower a "great military leader . . . but he has shown unexpectedly small aptitude for the many and the complex domestic problems of the country."[109] Gore feared a Republican onslaught on the New Deal if the Republicans controlled Congress and the White House.

At the same time, Gore found himself embroiled in a controversy regarding vice-presidential nominee Nixon. Journalists uncovered the existence of a secret fund of $18,000 that Nixon had collected under the guise of funding his anti-communist activities. Instead, he spent the money on everything from travel to hotel bills, even Christmas cards. Nixon rationalized that the monies had saved the government money, which he would have charged otherwise.[110]

An uproar followed as many people, including Eisenhower, condemned the action. At one point, the general even considered dropping Nixon from the ticket. Gore found himself right in the middle of the controversy when in late September, he publicly condemned Nixon's behavior. Soon, a whole series of letters defending the California senator flooded his office. In response, Gore wrote that he could not condone such actions by a member of Congress, especially when conflict of interest appeared likely. He stressed that he lived well on his $15,000 salary, which allowed him to expand his farm and build a small business. "I would not consider it right for me to be subsidized by a continuing fund contributed and subscribed to by a few of the people when my fundamental obligation is to all the people," he replied to one writer.[111]

Nixon survived the storm and went on national television to give his famous "Checkers" speech. In it, he highlighted his lack of a financial fortune and inability to provide his wife a "mink coat." He used his cocker spaniel, Checkers, a gift from a woman in Texas, to demonstrate that he needed assistance even in giving his daughters a dog. He told the audience that "regardless of what they say about it, we're going to keep it."[112] The tactic worked, and the White House received thousands of calls, telegrams, and letters urging Eisenhower to keep Nixon on the ticket.

Despite Nixon's slippery escape, Gore continued condemning him. When one of his constituents, a self-described independent, accused him of slandering the senator, Gore responded that "it seems to me that he slandered himself. A careful analysis of his own speeches in defense of his subsidization of a United States Senator by a few, which he admitted, will reveal the act as a very unfortunate example and precedent of conduct in high office." To another constituent, he complained, "What I resent most about this whole affair is the attempt to justify his wrong doing by lumping together legitimate campaign contributions, and legitimate outside category . . . in the same category as subsidization of a United States Senator such as the Nixon fund."[113]

Nixon had survived and remained a constant source of irritation to Gore and many others. From this point forward, they clashed repeatedly. To Gore, Nixon represented the worst features of the Republican Party. He was an economic conservative, a rabid anticommunist, an inherently corrupt politician, and a servant of special interests. While Gore respected Eisenhower, he would never maintain anything but disdain for Nixon. There would be many battles ahead between the new senator from Tennessee and the vice president.

The best efforts of Gore and many others could not change the outcome of the presidential race. Eisenhower crushed Stevenson by 6 million votes, winning the electoral college 442–89. Tennessee followed the trend and voted by a small margin for the Republicans. Eisenhower's coattails were long, giving the GOP control of the House and Senate. For the first time since 1932 the Republicans controlled the White House and Congress and, in the election of the president, had done so in a convincing manner.[114]

Gore still defeated Atkins easily, winning nearly 70 percent of the vote. While happy about his victory, he was upset with the results of the contest for the presidency. He wrote Baruch and blamed Eisenhower's victory largely on the extremists of the East and North who had used issues such as the FEPC to take a demagogic position that made the South out as a "whipping post." To him, party leaders needed to realize they could not ignore the South. He complained bitterly that "as it has been, only those who cater to extremist elements in the East and North could get the nomination. Our party must be restored as a national party, which it basically and truly is. It is only that the recent leadership . . . has oriented it to Harlems and Hamtramyks."[115]

Gore's frustration was off base. The Democratic Party was in transition, and the southern base often coexisted very precariously with the labor and urban base in the North and upper Midwest. Roosevelt had struggled to maintain the coalition, and Truman had moved toward the more liberal elements, pushed in part by men such as Hubert Humphrey of Minnesota and Herbert Lehman of New York. The economic and social conservatism of the southern Democrats created an uneasy tension. More moderate elements, including Gore, Kefauver, Johnson, and others, resided in border states, but the majority of southern Democrats bore few differences from their conservative Republican counterparts other than party affiliation. Gore correctly believed that the party needed the support of the South to win, but it also needed to escape the southern racism and conservatism to create an ideological alternative to the Republicans. Deep down, he knew this and practiced it, but his sense of southernness often affected his judgment.

The end of 1952 marked a significant turning point for Gore. He had risen from a one-room schoolteacher to one of the highest positions in the government of the United States. He had left behind the House, where he had helped in furthering the New Deal and Fair Deal and played a role in foreign affairs, including the development of the atomic weapon systems. In the Senate, he would face fewer obstacles to pushing his priorities, which would include tax reform and economic policy that benefited the common people. He looked even further to a higher office and, like most senators, had aspirations to the presidency. Never lacking for ambition, Gore dove headfirst into the deep end of the political pool.

# 4 JOINING THE MILLIONAIRES' CLUB

GORE LOVED to tell the story of a November 1952 trip through East Tennessee on his way to Washington. He arrived in a small town, fresh off his victory and walking with a little extra bounce in his step. He went in to a local store to buy a Coke. "Every eye was on him—the man who had beat Kenneth McKellar," he thought. One of the old farmers came up to him and looked him over. "I know you, don't I?" Gore smiled and responded that he guessed he did. "Why sure," the farmer replied, "you're the new preacher, ain't you?"[1] Only Tennesseans can humble their representatives so well.

Despite the momentary setback, Gore entered the Senate with great enthusiasm, believing that he would have more influence to push his ideas on taxes, agricultural policy, and foreign relations. Although he started slowly, he gained skill during his first few years in office. This learning experience fed his aspirations for higher office, which culminated at the 1956 Democratic National Convention in Chicago when he narrowly missed the vice-presidential nomination.

Gore moved into a Senate controlled by a very slim margin by the Republicans, entering with several future stars of the Democratic Party including John Kennedy, Montana's Mike Mansfield, and Washington's Henry Jackson.[2] Gore audaciously requested several prestigious committee assignments, including Finance, telling Senate minority leader Lyndon Johnson that "you may recall the role I played in keeping score on Republican bookkeeping ledger domain, hanging the label of 'phony economy' on their spurious claim of budget balancing." He also requested the Senate Foreign Relations Committee (SFRC), admitting that he had no qualifications "except a deep interest and a deep conviction that international collaboration and acts of collective security offer our best hopes of peace." He made only one negative condition, that he "not be assigned to a committee headed by Senator McCarthy."[3]

Despite his appeals, the steering committee placed Gore on traditional freshman assignments including the District of Columbia, Public Works, and the Joint Committee on Atomic Energy. Johnson acknowledged that "I know you would have been a valuable addition to any one of the three and I hope that the time is not too far off that better Committee assignments can be worked out."[4]

In these early stages, Gore had anticipated more from his Senate service, lamenting that it was rather like a cross between a country club and a fraternity that had certain rules and regulations and historic traditions that restricted junior members. He wrote Frank Ahlgren that "I must admit that the crust is a little thicker over on the Senate side and the breeze is a little colder than I had ever known before."[5]

Despite institutional limitations, Gore found a voice in foreign affairs. The Tennessean disliked many of Eisenhower's appointments, including Secretary of State John Foster Dulles. Ivy League–educated conservatives tied to large corporations dominated the new diplomatic appointments. Gore considered their rhetoric regarding "massive retaliation and liberation" as provocative at a time when the Soviet Union's intransigence appeared to be weakening, especially after Stalin died in 1953.[6]

Gore soon weighed in on the matter by sharply criticizing the U.S. ambassador to the United Nations, Henry Cabot Lodge Jr., for refusing to shake hands with Soviet foreign minister Andrei Y. Vishinsky. Afterward, a constituent complained: "How could you, an American criticise [sic] our Representative to the Abortion (called the UN) for not shaking the bloody hand of one of the murderers of Korea?" Gore responded that Lodge represented the American people, and he should not let his personal feelings affect his actions. He argued that it was important "to keep ajar the door for negotiation and understanding . . . Can you imagine Cordell Hull acting in any such manner?"[7]

Eisenhower's choices for economic leadership also offended Gore's populist sensibilities, especially Treasury Secretary George Humphrey, whom Gore called "a noted rightist."[8] In addition, the president nominated William M. Martin Jr.—a "big bankers' tool"—as chairman of the Federal Reserve. He feared that these appointments signaled a return to trickle-down economics and higher interest rate policies of previous Republican administrations. The junior senator from Tennessee remained committed to "taxation according to ability to pay" and low-interest policies to aid the majority of people, believing Republicans wanted to prevent "too many others climbing the ladder."[9]

Without trying, Gore soon found himself in the first major conflict of his Senate career. In late April 1953, the oil interests led by Senator Price Daniel (D-TX) pushed a bill to authorize a major giveaway of tidelands petroleum reserves to the states. The measure extended state control of submerged lands to nine miles, six beyond that requested by the Eisenhower administration. Many Democrats perceived this extension as a means for coastal states to drain precious resources from the national treasury and for the oil companies to escape paying significant federal taxes.[10]

Gore did not want to start his Senate career in the middle of such a fight. Major political players from both sides of the aisle supported the legislation, including Johnson. Besides, the issue really did not affect Tennessee. Nonetheless, he reported to Hull that "a quorum developed sooner than I expected" and he found himself the only opponent on the floor "without a moment's notice, or without a single note."[11]

Gore made a passionate appeal against what he characterized as a "giveaway." The *Chattanooga Times* recounted how he presented "a forceful argument and likewise displayed a cool wit." "His sallies so infuriated Herman Walker (R-ID)," the journalist observed, "that the Westerner clinched his fists and told the Tennessean: 'I am willing to take you on.'" Finally, the reporter noted that Gore "displayed a knowledge of the parliamentary rules and outflanked Senate Republican Whip [Leverett] Saltonstall of Massachusetts."[12]

The battle over the tidelands continued for five weeks as states' rights Republicans allied with coastal Democrats. At one point, Robert Taft staged a filibuster that ultimately ensured victory for the Daniel plan. It would not be the last time Gore found himself on the losing side, or his last confrontation with the petroleum industry. Yet he had cut his teeth on an important issue relating to taxes and federal control and performed admirably.

While he continued to try to learn the workings of the Senate, Gore also tended to personal affairs. He completed fairly mundane tasks such as sending $4 back home to Tennessee to renew his and Pauline's driver's licenses and arranging for care of his elderly parents. He wrote his uncle, Charlie Gore, to thank him for checking in on his mother and father, noting that "Papa has certainly made a remarkable comeback twice. I hope I can have just half as much strength at his age."[13]

The family also focused on its finances. Gore earned a comfortable salary, but both he and Pauline were children of the depression and continued to live frugally, investing their savings in the family farm and enterprises back in Carthage. The family moved into another modest two-bedroom apartment in Fairfax, still refusing to buy a residence outside of Tennessee. When a car salesman from home wrote Pauline offering a good deal on a new Lincoln, she responded that "I wish you could sell us one, especially since our Buick has 79,000 miles on it. But I am afraid if we push it along another year we are going to have to do so."[14]

Many of the senators at the time came from affluent families, such as John

Kennedy and J. William Fulbright. Their money allowed them the luxury of better homes, clothes, vacations, and country club memberships. They already had the benefit of prestigious educations and connections with the movers and shakers in American society, especially the eastern establishment journalists and businessmen.

Gore had none of these, and in some ways he tried to compensate. He began changing his speech patterns and sounding more like a dictionary or someone preparing for the college entrance exam than a normal, everyday Tennessean. Pauline convinced him to put away his fiddle, as no U.S. senator would play a hillbilly instrument. It was relegated to the closet, to be pulled out only occasionally for special events. Designed to ease his movement into Washington circles, casting off his favorite instrument represented a distancing from his roots, which eventually helped end his political career.

The family's modest means made their entry into Washington society difficult. Pauline pushed Albert to join the Washington social circle, where each night people could find a cocktail party or some other event to attend. For the most part, Albert did not like these gatherings. The main activities were gossip and back slapping, neither of which really appealed to him. Pauline recognized, and Albert grudgingly acknowledged, that advancement of his career demanded that they attend and connect with party leaders and donors. However, they lacked the clothes, jewelry, and home to blend in with the Washington crowd. The ever frugal Pauline found dresses she liked in expensive boutiques and then had similar ones made at a greatly reduced price. Likewise, the senator never bought expensive suits. The wardrobe limitations caused discomfort for the two self-made people from humble roots. Moreover, neither of the Gores really drank alcohol, nor had they acquired the expected social graces. In addition, their modest apartment would not allow them to host such parties of their own. While the couple eventually learned some of society's ins-and-outs over time, it was an often difficult transition.

Gore's failure to be fully accepted into the Washington social circle mirrored his relationships with fellow senators. Like many people in the Cumberland Valley, he maintained a small circle of friends, usually family members or loyal staffers. While he established a good relationship with Oklahoma senator Mike Monroney and he liked Kennedy and, later, Ralph Yarborough (D-TX), he was not particularly close to them socially. Others had hobbies, such as Fulbright's penchant for golf, but Gore had no such pastimes. Hard work— whether at the office, on the Senate floor, or on the farm during the summer—was the norm. He typically spent twelve hours each day at the office and then went home to the family at night.

Gore's inability or refusal to walk easily within the good ol' boys' world of the Senate was shaped by his own personality and background. He saw himself as a maverick, which he had demonstrated on many occasions in the House. This self-image reflected his perception of what people from Tennessee and the Upper Cumberland represented. "Several tags . . . have been attached to me during my political career," Gore recalled. "One of these is 'maverick,' and if one likes labels, this in some ways is an apt description." He admitted that the label applied to most Tennesseans because "they are opposed to running thoughtlessly with the herd, feel no need to follow the leader, and value their personal and social independence." As a result, only someone willing to buck the establishment, "not out of desire to build a political image, but out of the principle, can truly represent such a state."[15]

Others recognized Gore's maverick nature and his pride in maintaining it. His Senate chief of staff, Bill Allen, recalled that the senator liked to brag that if he found himself voting with the majority, he needed to reconsider his position. "Show Albert the grain," another friend observed, "so that he can go against it." Jack Robinson Sr., an aide in the 1950s, noted, "I'd look up on the board and see a vote that was 93 to 3, and I'd think, one of those [three] was going to be him." Even Pauline agreed: "I tried to persuade Albert [senior] not to butt at a stone wall just for the sheer joy of butting."[16]

There were problems with being a maverick, however. Fellow senators often valued conformity and consistency, making it difficult for a maverick to create effective political alliances. Gore believed that hard work and the justness of the cause would create winning coalitions. If he failed, then it was due to powerful political forces positioned against him. He generally remained a maverick throughout his career, though his ambition for higher office sometimes caused deviations from this path.

While he learned the ropes and the culture of the Senate, Gore turned his attention to the economy early in his first term. He criticized George Humphrey's efforts to tighten the money supply by increasing interest rates, complaining loudly that the policy hurt average Americans who depended on credit for routine purchases, including cars and homes, and really only benefited the bankers. In contrast to the Humphrey plan, he called for lower interest rates, reminding people that the last time the government adopted tight money policies, the country sank into the Great Depression. His Republican counterparts, led by Senator Prescott Bush of Connecticut, vigorously disagreed, but Gore remained consistent in his criticisms of the tight money policy.[17]

The Tennessee senator took the issue on the road as Democrats prepared for congressional elections in 1954. At a speech to a Democratic rally in Knoxville in the late summer, he again attacked the administration's tight money policy, arguing that there was no legitimate justification for it. "The only thing I can figure out is that like a Martin to a box—the Republicans took wing and flew straight to the nest of the vested interest. That is their record," he told the audience with a special populist zeal.[18]

Gore's actions on the tidelands and interest rates increased his visibility and attracted people seeking access to power. One of these was Armand Hammer, son of a Russian immigrant who had been a member of the American Socialist Party and ardent supporter of Vladimir Lenin. These connections helped Hammer become one of the first U.S. businessmen to win economic concessions in the Soviet Union in the early 1920s. Throughout the prewar period, he worked in a variety of enterprises including art consignments and asbestos mining, which he used to fund Soviet intelligence operations in the United States. While barely surviving financially, he played the role of a wealthy and capable American capitalist.[19]

During the 1940s Hammer became more successful as he secured a lucrative contract from the U.S. government for liquor concessions and married a wealthy New Jersey socialite. The money and visibility brought him into contact with prominent politicians, including Roosevelt. Over time, many Americans came to recognize him as a captain of industry, despite the fact that the FBI and British Intelligence knew of his early ties to the Soviet government. Nevertheless, unconfirmed rumors did not keep Hammer from mixing in prominent social and political circles.

A common interest in cattle brought Gore and Hammer together. In the Congress, a fraternity of cattlemen, including Lyndon Johnson, Robert Kerr (D-OK), Monroney, Wayne Morse (I-OR), and Gore, engaged in a friendly competition. For the majority of these senators it really was only a hobby, something that identified them as gentlemen landowners, rather than a profitable business venture. For Gore, it was his one true love. As one person observed, Gore would much rather "find a new black calf in the weeds than a golf ball in the grass."[20] He had started a small herd in the 1940s and continued acquiring better animals as his reputation as a breeder increased.

The particular breed he raised, Angus, was also Hammer's choice, and they crossed paths at cattle sales during the early 1950s. Drawn by a common interest, the two men became friends. Hammer tried to impress Gore with his wealth, but Albert and Pauline refused some of his magnanimous gestures, as Pauline's polite 1953 letter turning down Hammer's offer to let the family use his yacht for a vacation attests.[21]

Early on, Hammer and Gore collaborated in the cattle business. In October 1953, Hammer praised Gore for his two excellent cattle buys at the Ridglea sale. "At that rate," Hammer wrote, "I think you can do my buying as well." Over time, Hammer began leaving some of his cattle on the Gore farm in Tennessee. The senator charged a flat rate for the boarding, never much more than the costs of feed and maintenance based on the value of the animal and the attention it needed.[22] Hammer also participated in annual sales that became major events at the Gore farm in the 1950s and 1960s.

The relationship between Hammer and Gore has been the subject of much speculation, and even material for conservative efforts to damage Al Gore's reputation during the 2000 presidential campaign.[23] Hammer's ties to Albert provided access to power, although it was very limited during his early tenure because Gore lacked prestigious committee assignments for many years. Most around Gore and even his opponents believed that he was not a man who could be bought for any price. Did Hammer's relationship with Gore help the businessman? Clearly, it paid dividends when Gore defended Hammer against charges of Communist sympathies in the early 1960s and when Hammer's Occidental Petroleum needed the Federal Bureau of Investigation (FBI) to make a witness available during a court case. Yet the relationship was hardly quid pro quo. Their cooperation on the ranching endeavor produced only limited profits, and special investigations by the *Nashville Tennessean* and the FBI never turned up any impropriety.[24] Hammer hired Gore in 1972, but that was several years after he had left office. During his political career, Gore's relationship with Hammer differed little from those he had with many others, including Bernard Baruch. Not surprisingly, most businessmen shied away from a senator with populist impulses and gravitated toward men such as Johnson or pro-business members of the Republican Party instead.

While occasionally interacting with business elites, the senator tried to remain grounded during this first year in office. When Governor Clement sent him a specialized license plate that indicated he was a Tennessee senator, Gore refused it, claiming he preferred his Smith County plates. "I do not mean by this to suggest that I make surreptitious trips, though upon occasion my whereabouts might be subject to question," he jokingly wrote the governor.[25] Gore wanted to resist the temptations of special stature, especially at a time when he criticized those who relied on such devices. He also knew that no one in Smith County would be impressed. They had known him when he was an unemployed teacher and would not be influenced by superficial trappings of power. If anything, they might view him as getting a little uppity.

As 1954 began, Gore became increasingly critical of the Eisenhower administration. In late February, he spoke in Topeka, Kansas, and complained about Republican attacks on Democrats, telling the audience that "we've been called just about everything from traitors to sadists and accused of just about everything." He recalled a story of "an old country lawyer friend back in Tennessee who gave me some advice right after I got my law degree. Albert, if you've got a good case, go into court and try it quietly and confidently. But if you haven't got a case, yell and storm and raise all the Cain you can. If you make enough noise, you may sometime fool the jury." In Gore's mind, the Republicans were doing the same, although he cautioned against fighting back with the same tactics and encouraged his colleagues to focus on the party's "record of responsibility and constructive achievement."[26]

In the same speech, Gore questioned the true nature of the administration. Gore observed that in press conferences Eisenhower was warm and personable, but it was the "turn back faction," not the president, that set the policies. Humphrey and others pushed regressive taxes and discriminatory budget policies, making the administration like "Dr. Jeckell [sic] and Mr. Hyde," where the Mr. Hyde cut conservation efforts, school construction, and public assistance and health programs. According to Gore, "the gap between the preachment and the practice is wide."[27]

Privately, Gore expressed similar views of the president and his administration. As he wrote Edward Meeman of the Memphis Press-Scimitar, "almost invariably the President attempts to mount a pinnacle high above controversies and from the eminence shed a glowing light of good fellowship, tolerance, and patriotism . . . This has been carried to such an extreme that the level of his stance is generally above not only the real issues but also practicalities." As one example, Gore pointed out that while Eisenhower had pushed for more hospital construction and cancer research, there was little funding when the budget appeared.[28]

The actual character of Eisenhower would perplex Gore and many others for years. On the surface, he was a likeable and comparatively nonpartisan leader. Many believed his conservative advisers ran the show while he played golf and gave the administration a kinder, gentler face. People such as Gore liked Ike but not his policies, and as a result, they directed their venom toward

Dulles and Humphrey. For many years, dealing with the popular leader frustrated the best members of the Democratic Party.[29]

As Gore clashed with the Republicans, he found himself embroiled in a controversy with FBI director J. Edgar Hoover. Before 1954, Gore maintained a comparatively good relationship with Hoover and the FBI. In January 1947, an agent reported after a visit with Gore that "he seems to be very friendly to the Bureau and I am sure can be depended upon to render assistance when necessary." Four years later, Hoover wrote Gore that "it is reassuring to know that we have in you a stalwart supporter, and I trust that our efforts will continue to merit your approbation."[30]

Problems, however, developed in March 1954 when Gore engaged Paul Douglas (D-IL) in a conversation on the Senate floor regarding innuendos and rumors the FBI had circulated about a Gore family friend. Soon, Hoover's number-three man, Carl DeLoach, visited Gore's office. "Without showing any decency or courtesy, the Senator promptly began casting aspersions at the FBI and our activities," he reported. When the Tennessean complained that the FBI had "smeared innocent people" and that the agency "was not one-tenth of what it was cracked up to be," DeLoach responded that he had made the call as a common courtesy, not to hear such accusations. Undeterred, Gore continued attacking the FBI, leading DeLoach to complain that "he refused to listen to reason." As he left, DeLoach noticed that an administrative assistant from Gore's staff had been standing behind a door and taking notes the whole time.[31]

Hoover was furious and responded immediately, writing in the margins of the report that "our offices in Tennessee should be briefed re. Gore's attitude." He ordered "no contact without prior approval" and that "Gore's name should be placed on list not to be approached at any time."[32] From this point forward, Hoover directed his agents and the offices in Tennessee to monitor Gore's moves and speeches and to try to uncover information that might be used to embarrass or entrap the senator, although he had no apparent success.

Gore's troubles with the FBI soon paled before a brewing international crisis in Indochina. Since 1945, the United States had supported the French efforts to reestablish control over the region. The Viet Minh and Ho Chi Minh's ties to the Soviet Union combined with efforts to restore France as a bulwark against Communist expansion in Western Europe led the Truman and Eisenhower administrations to back the French, while Ho received assistance from the Chinese after Mao's victory in 1949. The bloody war pitted a committed enemy against a technologically superior European army. By 1954, Washington had sent military advisers and was annually paying three-fourths of the cost of the French war.[33]

A major crisis developed in the spring 1954. The French decided to try to draw the Viet Minh into a major confrontation at Dienbienphu. They landed fifteen thousand elite paratroopers and South Vietnamese supporters in the logistically isolated area and dared the Viet Minh to engage. Soon, General Vo Nguyen Giap obliged and moved fifty thousand troops into the area. A fifty-five-day siege ensued in which the French found themselves overwhelmed. By early April, a Viet Minh victory appeared inevitable if there were no massive foreign intervention.[34]

As the French struggled, debates broke out in the United States over Indochina. U.S. Air Force officials formulated plans to bomb Viet Minh supply lines and positions, and some even suggested using tactical nuclear strikes to relieve the French garrison. The Eisenhower administration explored other covert operations, although some advisers urged avoiding another Asian conflict, especially so soon after the end of the Korean War.[35]

As the internal debates continued, Gore expressed grave concern over the matter. In mid-April, he wrote a constituent that he had just returned from a two-hour conference on the issue. He reported "uncertainty as to the extent to which the French want us to become involved," adding that he feared direct involvement. He worried, however, that "the threat of communist domination of Southeast Asia is starkly real . . . Satisfactory answers to all the perplexing questions are hard to come by."[36]

The matter remained divisive. When Vice President Nixon commented that while unlikely, he could envision U.S. troops in Indochina, Gore lashed out, telling reporters that "the president is golfing in Georgia and the secretary of state is fishing at Duck Island while the vice president speaks. The vice president has no constitutional responsibility in the matter." He demanded that Eisenhower "make his policies clear with respect to our possible further involvement in Indochina."[37]

American leaders watched as the Viet Minh tightened the noose around the French. A day before the fortress fell on May 7, Gore wrote a constituent that he had not ruled out supporting U.S. military intervention, but "I do not feel that the problem can be solved by this alone; nor do I think this should be the first step." He said that he would await Eisenhower's recommendation before reaching a final decision.[38] It mattered not, as the Eisenhower administration let the French meet their doom.

The issue would not be resolved in 1954. That summer, Viet Minh and

French negotiators hammered out an agreement at Geneva that called for with-drawal of the French and temporary division of the country at the 17th parallel, with elections to reunify the country in 1956. The United States sent observers but refused to recognize the treaty. Ultimately, the Eisenhower administration helped create an anticommunist state in the south under Ngo Dinh Diem, a decision that effectively began an American commitment lasting more than thirty years and costing millions of lives and billions of dollars.

At this juncture, Gore demonstrated a willingness to support the use of U.S. troops, although very hesitantly. Like most Americans, he feared another inter-vention following so closely on the heels of the meat grinder in Korea, espe-cially with the specter of China looming on Vietnam's northern border. Deep down, Gore recognized that there were many levels to the conflict, especially local conditions that had shaped the war. He also would have had a very hard time supporting the deployment of U.S. forces to reestablish French colonial rule. While he would not publicly voice substantial concerns about U.S. support for the Diem regime in the mid-1950s, he worried about another intractable Asian conflict and its repercussions.

Concurrent with the Indochina crisis, one of the most contentious and dan-gerous issues for any southern politician emerged on the home front. The Na-tional Association for the Advancement of Colored People (NAACP) had initiated a series of lawsuits attacking segregation, obtaining its most significant victory on May 17, 1954, with *Brown v. Board of Education of Topeka*. In it, the Supreme Court overturned *Plessy v. Ferguson*, an 1896 ruling that had legalized the concept of "separate but equal" segregation. Chief Justice Earl Warren stressed: "We conclude that in the field of public education the doctrine of 'sep-arate but equal' has no place. Separate educational facilities are inherently un-equal." This decision effectively paved the way for legal challenges to all forms of public segregation.[39]

Loud voices of protest arose from southern racists. Even before the an-nouncement of the decision, South Carolina governor James F. Byrnes warned that if "the Supreme Court decides this case against our position, we will face a serious problem. Of only one thing can we be certain. South Carolina will not now, nor for some years to come, mix white and colored children in our schools." Senator James Eastland (D-MS) added that the South would neither "abide by nor obey this legislative decision by a political court."[40]

Like other moderates, Gore opposed segregation but feared the upheaval that would accompany integration efforts. In May 1954, he wrote Hugh John-son that he was happy that the Court had not immediately tried to force the issue. While admitting that he had no idea about the Court's timetable, he believed that it should take a number of years. "The customs and mores of the people are not easily set aside," he worried, "and those who think that public school segregation in the South can be abolished quickly, without violence and intensification of racial tensions, simply do not understand the situation."[41]

Despite his concerns, he believed strongly in the Constitution and observed that Congress now had little to do in the matter and that the battles would now be fought at the state and local levels. "So, our problem now is to find ways to cope successfully with this new order of things," he wrote Johnson. "We must find ways to progress in peace and harmony under the law." He remained fairly optimistic, believing that southerners would respect the rule of law. Also, he believed that there had been a significant "improvement in racial relations in the past half century" that would make the transition smoother than some thought.[42]

This theme of respect for the law of the land became a cornerstone of his support for the *Brown* decision. Publicly he maintained a middle-of-the-road position while privately he supported the decision. "I do not mean to imply that I am in agreement with the reasoning upon which the Court based its decision or on the results on which it contemplates," he told one constituent. "I think all of us must recognize, however, that the decision of the Court is, after all a decision by the highest Court of our land and that it cannot be completely ignored."[43] Gore took this position because he believed in respecting the law and political expediency demanded circumspection in a state with a virulent segregationist voting bloc and the smallest percentage of African American voters in the South.

Although they did not crusade actively for civil rights, Gore and others like him received their share of attacks from segregationists. Mississippi governor Ross Barnett equated the southern moderate with a burglar who "comes into your house and tells you that if you give him just a few valuables, he'll go away. Just sort of a 'token' burglar." Others agreed, including respected senator Richard Russell (D-GA), who exclaimed, "There can be no such thing as token integration. This is merely a device of the race mixers to obtain total and complete integration." Gore complained that such extremism "made moderation a hazardous political course."[44]

The *Brown* decision was monumental. It no longer allowed southern politicians to let sleeping dogs lie. It stirred the civil rights moment and forced people to take sides, creating an extremely volatile position for Gore and Kefauver, who represented a state with a relatively small minority community but very vocal and active racist groups. Civil rights issues would become even more important to Gore as his career progressed.

Gore increasingly found himself in the national spotlight over his confrontations with the Eisenhower administration and Senate colleagues. One of the most publicized occurred in late June 1954, during a battle over foreign trade issues. Eisenhower had asked for a three-year extension of the Reciprocal Trade Act and more authority to lower tariffs to facilitate trade. However, he had encountered substantial resistance from special interest groups in his own party and instead accepted a one-year extension approved by the House. When the legislation reached the Senate, Gore and others committed to foreign trade seized the initiative. With the support of eleven Democrats and an independent, Wayne Morse, Gore threatened to introduce an amendment to the one-year House extension that would reinstate Eisenhower's minimum request for three years and convey new powers to lower tariffs. As the president vacillated, Gore declared that "our foreign trade policy is too important to be sacrificed without a struggle."[45]

As was often the case, observers recognized that Gore had a fairly limited chance of success without the full support of the White House and prominent Republicans. Nevertheless, he received their praise. The *New Republic* noted that "in a rare display of political imagination, Senate Democrats have threatened to put the Republican leadership squarely on the spot with regard to a world trade program." At *Life*, the editors proclaimed "three cheers for all the Democrats willing to join Gore's plot to make the fight the President wouldn't. Sure Gore and Co. are interested in embarrassing the Republicans. But in this case the embarrassment of the Republican besides being richly earned, coincides with the interest of the nation."[46]

As predicted, it was a losing battle. Democrats and Republicans from pro-labor states controlled important positions on the Senate Finance Committee and House Ways and Means and united to block the measure.[47] The president avoided the matter, fearful of antagonizing important constituencies. Again, Gore had demonstrated his integrity on a matter very important to his constituents. Positive political capital was obtained even in defeat, and by waging such losing battles, Gore positioned himself for future confrontations on issues more likely to succeed. This particular struggle was a win-win for Gore, with the exception of potentially damaging his national aspirations by antagonizing labor.

Gore again found himself on the losing side in a major controversy that broke out in the summer of 1954. During the 1952 presidential campaign, the Republicans had promised to support the TVA, although this galled many

Republicans who characterized the New Deal and Fair Deal as "creeping socialism" or the more extreme "galloping socialism." Soon after the election, Johnson reported overhearing Eisenhower saying, "We will sell the *** **** thing."[48]

The foundations of the controversy were laid in May 1953. Two corporate executives of the Middle South Utilities Company, Edgar Dixon and Eugene Yates, sought concessions to provide power to the Memphis area and enlisted the assistance of George Woods of First Boston Corporation. On May 11, he visited Joseph Dodge, director of the budget, and stressed his belief that the government needed to withdraw from the power business. Soon after, A. H. Wenzell, First Boston's lobbyist in Washington, began pushing the Dixon-Yates contract, with Dodge ordering that the whole affair be kept secret and that no one in the TVA be alerted.[49]

In mid-June, President Eisenhower instructed the Atomic Energy Commission to negotiate a contract with Middle South Utilities Company. When several AEC board members opposed the plan, the administration informed them that the president could force their compliance. With the support of AEC chairman Lewis Strauss and prominent Republican senators, the contract moved forward.

Battle lines immediately developed in the Senate. The opposition saw this as an attack on public power. It had some advantages because Kefauver held an important position on the Judiciary Committee Subcommittee on Antitrust and Monopoly Legislation (JSAM) and had the support of other members, including William Langer (R-ND), who supported rural electrification. Congressmen from throughout the region rallied. "For 20 years the Old Guard in the Republican Party has been trying to destroy the TVA. Only now have they found a formula and a tool," Rep. Thomas Abernathy (D-MS) warned.[50]

On the other side, the Republican leadership and some Democrats pushed the Dixon-Yates proposal. Right-wing supporters equated the TVA with communism. Senator William Jenner (R-IN) denounced it as a "great showpiece of the Socialist economy." The *Oklahoma City Times* claimed that "the Socialist party in the United States was the chief promoter of the TVA program and related nationalized power programs." Democrats led by Fulbright and McClellan of Arkansas, where the alternative plant was to be built, also supported the contract.[51]

Gore straight away became a leading opponent of Dixon-Yates. As soon as the news broke, he called Eisenhower's decision "deplorable." On the Senate floor, he argued that the AEC should resist a questionable presidential order. "The three people most directly involved in the decision were a general, who is the manager of the AEC, an admiral, who is chairman, and a general who is in the White House. Perhaps to those gentlemen an order seemed appropriate." If President Truman had done the same, "the top would have been blown off the Capitol and impeachment proceedings probably would have been filed." Gore's characterization of the plan as a "Crooked Deal" appeared in front-page headlines of the *New York Times*.[52]

Despite some parliamentary defeats in the early stages, Gore and his allies refused to back down. On July 22, they stayed up until 4:30 A.M. to plan their strategy. Previously opposed to the filibuster, Gore became the leader of one. "We've got a whole new team; now the old hands can get some sleep," he told reporters. Thus began a four-day full debate on the atomic energy bill. Senate majority leader William Knowland (R-CA) tried breaking the filibuster, and the White House worried about potential public relations setbacks. Gore and his allies talked around the clock, with Gore holding the floor for seven hours at one point. Even when the Republican-controlled House voted 172–115 to uphold the contract, the filibuster continued.[53]

The efforts of Gore and his allies finally collapsed on July 26 when Johnson, who wanted to discuss farm policy, worked out a deal with Knowland that terminated debate in return for ending twenty-four-hour sessions. "Had our lines held firm," Gore lamented, "victory might have been won."[54] Yet without support from Johnson and other key Democrats, the anti–Dixon-Yates senators had to concede the issue.

Gore and his allies did win some victories ultimately. The Tennessean secured an amendment that prohibited the AEC from directly paying private contractors' income tax. In the conference committee, Clinton Anderson (D-NM) insisted the tax bill include guarantees that there be a compulsory licensing of atomic patents. He and others feared this provision would favor the large power companies and hurt rural cooperatives and public power producers. Johnson and others rallied to the cause and secured a victory on that specific point. AEC commissioner Eugene Zuckert later wrote that the debates on Dixon-Yates paved the way for "a victory that the public power advocates would not have tasted except for the rallying point offered by the Dixon-Yates controversy." Gore called the changes "one of the great victories I ever expect to see."[55]

Even though the first battle had ended in defeat, for Gore and his allies the war was far from over. Gore found himself on the losing side in a struggle against the powerful vested interests; still, he proved unwilling to compromise and felt he had the support of the majority of his constituents. The Dixon-Yates struggle led one observer to comment that "by convincing themselves of the justness of their cause in battle against a common enemy, the opponents of Dixon-Yates aroused themselves to a fever pitch in the months to come."[56]

Gore faced other issues in Tennessee. In August 1954, he received a letter from a Knoxville lawyer friend, Harry Asquith. He told about attending a Clement meeting in which his people had stressed that in the upcoming election they wanted to win as many votes as possible to demonstrate the governor's popularity and prepare him for future races. "I believe and I also believe that you realize that Frank Clement will definitely run against you four years from now," Asquith warned.[57]

Gore did not ignore such admonitions. Clement was an imposing figure who had a pulpit to demonstrate daily his leadership to Tennesseans, while information only trickled back about Gore's activities in Washington. Despite the challenges, Gore had some advantages, including incumbency, and a good working relationship with Kefauver who had won reelection easily. He had also won major publicity fighting against Dixon-Yates, leading the *Knoxville News-Sentinel* to declare that he had emerged "from this fracas with colors flying." Also, he had the support of several important newspapers, including the *Memphis Commercial Appeal.* In early August, an editorial underscored that "studied from almost any angle, Sen. Gore's first two years as a United States Senator have proved Tennessee voters, two years ago, a winner . . . Gore has shown himself to be one of the finest young additions to the Senate in many, many years."[58]

Gore made news through other means that helped him. In June 1954, the *Knoxville News-Sentinel* and other Tennessee papers reported some news about his son. Al had learned that a cousin had received a bow and arrow set. Relentlessly, the six-year-old pestered his father to take him to the store and purchase a similar kit. Finally, he wore his father down, and they headed to the store after work one day. To his disappointment, the store had closed, leading him to complain that if they had only run as he wanted then they would have made it. Early the next day, the senator took Al back and bought a bigger and better set. When his mother asked him about the purchase, he replied, "Why, Mama, I outtalked a Senator." The newspaper story concluded, "That's why Al Gore is a young man to be watched from here on in."[59]

That summer, Gore focused on national politics. With midterm elections approaching, he and other Democrats wanted to win back Congress. During this crucial time, Gore served as chairman for the speaker's bureau of the Democratic National Committee, made speeches throughout the country, and assisted in fundraising. Throughout the process, he pummeled the Republicans for their lack of a domestic agenda, their favoritism toward the wealthy, and their attacks on the TVA.

He made a representative speech on September 1 to a national radio audience. "The Republicans came to power promising a bold, dynamic program. Yet where boldness and action have been required, we have had weakness, timidity, and vacillation; where unity and clarity were indicated, the pattern has been one of discord and confusion. When all is said and done, the plain fact is we are drifting—just drifting at home and abroad." He highlighted the Republican tax bill, which gave 73 cents of every dollar to corporations, while people making under $5,000—80 percent of the population—received only 9 cents per dollar. "The Republicans seem to be proud to boast that they have maintained the status quo. Well, status quo is fancy Latin language for standing still."[60]

Gore's efforts won him national acclaim. The *Daily Oklahoman* called Gore a good selection. "From first to last the senator was courageous and altogether fair . . . such urbanity is rather unusual. Ordinarily the partisan audience that turns out to hear a partisan address is hungering and thirsting for blood. And as a usual thing the partisan orator gives the hearers exactly what they want to hear . . . But this was not so in the case of Senator Gore." Instead, the editors characterized him as speaking as a patriotic citizen, "and we suspect that his speech was all the more effective for that reason."[61]

The hard work by Gore and the DNC paid off in November. The Democrats regained control of the House by twenty-nine votes and the Senate by one vote (two if people counted Morse, who had declared himself an independent in 1953 but promised to vote with the Democrats). Bitterly, Nixon complained that "there were just too many turkeys running on the Republican ticket."[62] With the victory, Lyndon Johnson and Sam Rayburn returned to Senate and House leadership. Though the Democrats promised cooperation, the stage was set for conflict with Eisenhower.

The 1954 victory brought mixed results for Gore. His work on trade and public power in the preceding term and his role as prominent speaker for Democratic causes throughout the country had earned him acclaim. Yet, Johnson's rise to Senate majority leader created a strong undercurrent that definitely did not favor Gore. Both men were extremely ambitious and had their eyes on bigger prizes, and each watched the other very carefully.

Gore recognized the complexity of his relationship with Johnson. "We had several things in common, a Populist heritage, descent from landed gentry in scrabbly hill country—he in east Texas, I in the Appalachian foothills. Both had scrambled for education and both had taught as youngsters. Both came under the spell of FDR and entered politics early . . . And, of course, both of us loved our service in Congress, in politics, and in power." Still, he noted there were significant differences. "One was that I had grown stronger in Populist leanings and had become an inveterate enemy of special privilege, while Johnson had become a bedfellow of big money, oil, and military brass." The two could work together on public power and other issues, but Gore acknowledged that they often disagreed on taxes. "I wanted to eliminate special tax privileges, close the big tax loopholes that permit people to escape their fair share of the tax burden, but the creation and preservation of tax favoritisms had long been a strong arch of Johnson's Texas support and one of the keys to his rise to Senate leadership."[63]

The two senators often could work together, but the relationship was always uncomfortable. Many outsiders recognized the tensions. Russell Baker of the *New York Times* wrote that despite the outwardly friendly relations, the "two have a mysterious capacity for getting under each other's skin." He added that one Washington insider had commented that "when Gore and Johnson come together, it is like the meeting of a dog and cat." Senator George Smathers (D-FL) also noted the strain. He remembered that "Johnson picked his people just exactly why I don't know, but I know I was considered one of his favorites," but that "Johnson did not particularly care for Albert Gore." David Halberstam contended that policy disagreements existed, "but the difference between the two was personal as much as anything else, a lingering animosity. Johnson, above all else, liked to control and dominate other men, and Albert Gore is a loner, a man not to be controlled."[64]

The result was that Johnson always kept a watchful eye on Gore. In the 1950s especially, they maintained an outwardly cordial relationship because their ambitions required it. Still, Johnson would make sure Gore did not receive the choice committee assignments for several years. In response, Gore often went contrary to Johnson's wishes. The result was a strained working relationship that continued for many years.

As the Democrats savored their victory, there was unfinished business between November and December, including a resolution to censure Joseph McCarthy. In the summer of 1954, McCarthy had made the fateful decision to investigate Communist subversion in the military. In particular, he concentrated on Irving Peress, an army dentist suspected of Communist sympathies. During the process, McCarthy angered high military officials. In televised hearings carried by all the major networks, the army general counsel Joseph Welch exposed the senator as a bully and demagogue.[65]

Gore watched the hearings with great delight, admitting to one constituent that "I feel that the methods used by the senator from Wisconsin and which resulted in these hearings reflect adversely upon the dignity of the United States and are not in the best interest of the Nation." In addition, he wrote Senator John McClellan, ranking Democrat on the subcommittee, to praise him for his efforts, adding, "I hope the time comes when demagoguery will not be mistaken for statesmanship."[66]

The Senate initially responded with a resolution that tightened committee rules of presenting evidence, required verbatim transcripts, and limited cross examination. By the fall, the committee completed its investigation. Despite McCarthy's impassioned defense of himself, the committee recommended two counts of contempt and abuse with a censure sent to the Senate.

In early December, the motion went to the floor. Gore supported it, a position not uniformly popular among Tennesseans, many of whom viewed the attacks on McCarthy as part of the Communist conspiracy. A pastor wrote that "I want you to know that two years ago I cast my last vote for you. I am a Democrat but I do wish more Democrats would quit coddling the Communists." Another complained that it was disappointing to find Gore "increasingly aligned with the 'Pinko' element of the Democratic party."[67]

Despite such protests, Gore backed the efforts against McCarthy, even though he missed the first vote to attend an international trade conference. He wrote a friend afterward that "as to the McCarthy matter, I found the whole thing revolting . . . I would have gone even further than the censure resolution." Finally, in March, by a vote of 67–22, the Senate approved the committee findings.[68] While McCarthy remained in the Senate, his fifteen minutes of fame had passed and cancer claimed him in 1957.

Thus ended one of the darkest times in contemporary American history. McCarthy and his allies had victimized many people during their crusade. Most people had refused to speak out against the Wisconsin senator, but Gore and others had rallied to condemn him over time. This created a paradox for Gore, who wanted to portray himself as an anticommunist but saw the dangers inherent in McCarthyism. Even as the Red Scare dissipated momentarily, the issue would remain an important component of politics in the 1950s and 1960s.

As the McCarthy saga ended, a controversial issue from the previous year resurfaced in early 1955. As soon as Congress convened, the anti–Dixon-Yates forces regrouped. With the Democrats in control, they believed that they had a much better chance of success. In late January, Gore and Anderson presented a resolution questioning the legal validity of granting the waiver provision of the

Atomic Energy Act of 1954. Rep. Chet Holifield (D-CA) called on the entire AEC to resign as it was in a state of "demoralizing dissension."[69]

The turning point occurred in late spring 1955. New investigations uncovered that Wenzell of the First Boston Corporation had worked as a consultant to the Bureau of the Budget on the Dixon-Yates contract. The opponents of the contract smelled conflict of interest. Gore commented that such revelations went "a long way toward proving that the large financial houses of the country dictated the Dixon-Yates deal."[70]

The battle began in earnest in late June as Kefauver convened special committee hearings on the contract, calling Budget Director Rowland Hughes as the first witness. Several committee members grilled him about Wenzell's role, creating alarm in the White House. When Kefauver requested all pertinent papers, Eisenhower waffled, stating that no one should have the right to look at every file, thus "wrecking the entire filing system and paralyzing the processes of Government." At a legislative meeting with Republican leaders, he told them that he would make most papers available but that "no one could expect to be allowed to listen in on our every thought."[71]

For two weeks, the Kefauver committee probed. Wenzell testified that he had played a substantial role in formulating the contract, leading Gore to proclaim that "there is no question but we have the Administration on the run now." As the White House's position deteriorated, a compromise developed when Memphis mayor Frank Tobey began working with Gore and Clement to have Memphis develop its own power plant. After meeting in Gore's office on July 12, the mayor made the offer. Soon after, the administration accepted it, and Eisenhower ordered the contract canceled.[72]

The announcement set off a round of jubilant celebrations by public power advocates. Gore joined the group, announcing on the Senate floor that "the Dixon-Yates contract has become Eisenhower's Achilles heel. The contract was conceived in secrecy, nurtured in duplicity, and . . . terminated with the Administration in full flight." Nevertheless, he also cautioned that "we have suffered a serious loss . . . because we have witnessed the first major dismemberment of the TVA service area."[73]

The fight on the Dixon-Yates contract left the president very embittered. He told one friend that there had been nothing to cover up and that "as far as I know, the only mistake made was that one or two individuals, apparently believing that all preliminary conversations were in the class of privileged communications, mistakenly declined to testify on certain features until they had been advised to do so." He chafed at charges of dishonesty, lamenting that people believed "that only demagogues are honest. Actually there have been more falsehoods and innuendos uttered about the matter than on almost anything else I know."[74]

The affair left the junior Tennessee senator in a stronger political position. As one observer correctly noted, "Gore's role in Dixon-Yates paid off well, for he had achieved a degree of prominence rare in so short a Senate membership . . . Gore cannot be accused of 'making' an issue in order to gain prominence, but only of breaking Senate folkways and taking part in a controversy vital to him, his constituency, and the nation."[75] In the Senate for only two years, Gore had helped win a major victory and established himself as a rising star among the Democrats.

The battles over Dixon-Yates certainly enhanced Gore's national stature, and more papers began carrying stories on him. In September 1955, the *Orlando Sentinel* ran a piece entitled, "Gore Keeps Fit by Readying Cattle for Auction Sale at Carthage Farm." The author portrayed the Tennessean as a hard-working man who rose at 5 A.M. to complete chores on the farm and then went to the office at 8:30 to work with two secretaries, signing each piece of mail. According to the author, he was a man who "dons coveralls and sun helmet, heads for the cattle barn, picks up a brush and helps his farm hands get the animals in shape for the auction." He also told how Gore and his seven-year-old son, Al, would jump into the Caney Fork River after work, in " 'nature boy' style (no swim suits)."[76]

Even though the Tennessean never employed a public relations person, he always found his way into the national spotlight. Gore had his sights set on higher office, and he believed that 1956 might provide him a chance to make a splash. At this point, he worked hard in the Senate, admitting that he had become part of the "Senate club" as a result of his willingness to do the "day-to-day" chores such as attending Senate meetings and participating in floor debates. While recognizing that "I don't think I was ever a full member of the inner club," he had made the necessary connections to validate his national ambitions.[77]

Gore's goals seemed limited when contrasted with those of Kefauver, who had sought out the presidency in the 1952 primaries. Along with Johnson and others, Gore shared the belief that no southerner could win a national election. No one from the region had been even close to winning the presidency since before the Civil War, with the exception of Woodrow Wilson, who had more northern credentials than southern when he won. The civil rights issue and regional bias against the South undermined aspirations, and Gore believed that it would take someone starting as vice president and moving to the top of the ticket to break the trend.

In early 1956 Gore found himself embroiled in another controversy. Since the *Brown* decision in 1954, southern segregationists had grown increasingly hostile. Throughout the region, racists mobilized to prevent desegregation. One of the most prominent groups was the Citizens' Councils. These differed from the Klan in that they drew membership from professionals including doctors and lawyers. Instead of violence, they relied on political methods and economic coercion to force conformity among the white population. The ultimate goal was to create a unified wall of obstruction to block change.[78]

Many white politicians jumped on the bandwagon opposing desegregation, especially Senator Harry Byrd (D-VA). During his long career, he had demonstrated a penchant for opposition to almost everything. A relentless critic of the New Deal, Byrd consistently had pushed states' rights and criticized the expanding power of the federal government as threatening traditional values. This contrariness extended into race relations. After the *Brown* decision, he emerged as a leading spokesman for those that characterized it as "unconstitutional." In response, he called for southerners to renew their efforts to prevent the rise of the "totalitarian state" and called southerners to prepare for "massive resistance."[79]

As part of the strategy of massive resistance, prominent southern leaders called on their citizens to contest the Supreme Court decision in documents such as the "Declaration of Constitutional Principles." Formulated in early 1956, it was the work of Dixiecrat presidential candidate Strom Thurmond (D-SC), although Senator Sam Ervin (D-NC) wrote a less objectionable draft that became known as the "Southern Manifesto." Ervin argued that the *Brown* case ignored precedents in *Plessy v. Ferguson* (1896) and *Lum v. Rice* (1927) and therefore lacked validity. The manifesto encouraged southerners to defy desegregation, particularly orders issued by federal courts. It also warned other political leaders in the West and Southwest that they could become victims of "judicial encroachment."[80]

Only a few southern members in the House refused to sign the Southern Manifesto. Gore, Kefauver, and Johnson were the only senators who did not sign, although Richard Russell and others never asked Johnson because of his position as Senate majority leader.[81] Kefauver refused, in part because of his national ambitions. Gore characterized the document as "a bit of low doggerel which hardly lived up to its high-flown title." He regarded the manifesto as "utterly incomprehensible and unsupportable" and bordering on an act of secession. He recalled that "I wasn't prepared to have another Civil War, that both of my grandfathers had engaged in that conflict quite unsuccessfully and I was not prepared to do so."[82]

Because Gore had not been vocal publicly on the *Brown* decision, Thurmond and Ervin had hoped to get his signature. Fulbright had already caved in, as well as several moderates including Lister Hill (D-AL).[83] Thurmond—whom Gore characterized later as "not a man of a great deal of stature in the Senate (then or ever)"—tried to ambush Gore on the Senate floor. He had even alerted southern journalists to be on hand in the gallery, but when the South Carolina senator came up to Gore with the document and said, "Albert, we'd like you to sign the Southern Manifesto with the rest of us," Gore looked at him and threw it back with an emphatic: "Hell no!"[84]

Gore's refusal to sign made the regional newspapers and other media. It outraged white segregationists in Tennessee. A constituent from Chattanooga wrote, "I don't believe you can face one of your own people of the South and I suggest that you move to Harlem as you no doubt will be shunned in Tennessee." The mayor, board of aldermen, and chief of police of Brownsville castigated Gore for not supporting "efforts to preserve that which is most sacred and dear to all true Southerners." Another constituent simply wrote: "Et tu, Brute?"[85]

While not everyone condemned Gore's position, he worried about the manifesto and what it said about the future of his beloved South. He told Ralph McGill of the *Atlanta Constitution* that he was tremendously concerned "because of the intransigent attitudes on race by so many southern leaders." Both agreed that the segregationists were blind to what McGill characterized as "the great historical forces which are at work."[86]

Gore's stance on the Southern Manifesto was one of the high points of his career. Recognizing the danger that he would face from segregationists, he stood firm in the face of extreme pressure. The easy path would have been to go along with the crowd at home and in the Senate, but he refused. For this, he lost support at home and in the Senate, where the southern congressional caucus expelled him. It was a costly but courageous act. Brooks Hays, who also refused to sign, has been described as "a political moderate in a time of extremists . . . a courageous giant in a world of moral pygmies."[87] The same could be said of Gore, whose stand signaled to many other moderate white southerners that it was significant to do the right thing and be counted.

One of Gore's most lasting contributions to America's infrastructure developed around the same time as the manifesto controversy. Americans increasingly relied on the automobile for transportation, and better roads were a priority. Gore, Eisenhower, and others had seen the German autobahn and agreed with General Lucius Clay, the chairman of the President's Advisory Committee on a National Highway, that "a safe and efficient highway network is essential to America's military and civil defense."[88] There was also an economic component, as the road system would link major cities and open up new areas for production. Gore sensed this benefit especially. For many years, people in the Upper Cumberland had sought better roads to ensure markets and access to cheaper goods, and he merely continued that tradition.

The opening debates began in February 1955 after President Eisenhower forwarded a message to Congress that stressed "our unity as a nation is sustained by free communication of thought and by easy transportation of people and goods." He believed that the proposed system would combat the 36,000 highway deaths and millions of injuries and aid cities in a quick evacuation in event of a nuclear attack.[89]

Gore championed the cause for the Democrats, and his position on the typically lowly Public Works Committee had its advantages in this battle. The Democratic leadership selected him as chairman of a subcommittee to decide how many miles of new roads to build and how to pay for them. *U.S. News and World Report* noted that "highway building is one of the things to which the Democratic majority in Congress hopes to attach its party label so that it can be boasted of in the 1956 election campaign."[90]

Gore and other Democrats differed with Eisenhower mostly on how to fund the system. The Republicans wanted a $101 billion, ten-year program, mostly financed by bonds, with the local and state areas paying more than 70 percent of the cost. Gore feared placing too great of a burden on states, especially poorer ones. Instead, he favored a direct appropriation from the U.S. Treasury of $17.9 billion over five years, with the balance paid for by increased gasoline taxes and levies on right-of-way purchases by gasoline stations and motels. Unlike the Eisenhower plan, the federal government would pay nearly 70 percent. Republicans accused Gore of overspending, with Senator Bush complaining that the Gore measure "scatters billions of politically guided Federal dollars over the country in the next five years as though they were shot from a blunderbuss."[91]

Gore defended his program. At a speech at the National Governors' Forum, he told the audience that Americans relied heavily on highways and that the current system was inadequate. He complained that Eisenhower's plan lacked necessary funding and reflected the Republicans' unwillingness to spend money "to alleviate the human and material problems of our country" and that the administration had been forced to employ a publicity agency to promote its "unsound proposals."[92]

The debate continued throughout the spring of 1955, with Gore and his allies winning most of the battles. Johnson threw his full weight behind Gore's proposal, accusing the administration of using "sleight-of-hand" measures to add to the federal debt and turn too much power over to an executive federal agency. On May 22, the Senate rejected the administration's plan and accepted Gore's proposal.[93] However, it required many more steps to avoid a veto and pass the House.

Within a year, Congress finished the federal interstate highway bill. The Senate and House created a Highway Trust Fund that would use a "pay-as-you-go" system from special taxes on gasoline, diesel, tires, and truck registrations. On June 29, 1956, President Eisenhower signed the Federal Aid Highway Act in a hospital bed at Walter Reed Medical Center. No public ceremony occurred because the president feared showing any sign of health problems. However, he made sure that Gore received one of the two pens that he used.[94]

The final product was a monumental undertaking, one of the largest federal public works programs in American history. In final form, it was a $25 billion, twelve-year appropriation to start building a federal interstate highway system. Almost everyone greeted it favorably, including motorists, state and local officials, construction companies, and automobile manufacturers. One observer believed that "Congress had voted to enact nothing less than a fundamental change in American life."[95]

The new federal highway system guaranteed an unparalleled mobility to that point for Americans by dramatically increasing the number of drivers and cars and opening up many areas to development. At the same time, there were numerous unexpected consequences. Highways intensified the process of suburbanization. In many areas, pollution increased dramatically, especially smog. Some towns not on the highway grid faced depopulation and demise. As is often the case in American politics, this was a zero-sum game where there were many winners and losers.

Gore later drew criticism for his role in creating the highway system, and one detractor even characterized him as a member of the "Road Gang" whose members "looked after their own." Criticism escalated when Gore joined the Occidental Petroleum Corporation in 1972.[96] However, in 1956 he had no ties to the industry and had often battled the petroleum groups on issues such as oil depletion allowances. He was driven by no personal ambition regarding the highway bill, other than seeking the national spotlight. His beloved Carthage was not even on the interstate system, being bypassed by several miles with the construction of Interstate 40 to Knoxville to Nashville. Like many of his predecessors and colleagues, he believed the strength of the highway system to open markets to farmers and other Tennesseans clearly offset its negative consequences.

Even with the victory, Gore struggled to win greater power in the Senate. In May 1956, he requested an appointment to the Finance and Senate Foreign Relations Committees to fill the vacancy created by the death of Senator Alben Barkley (D-KY). "Please permit me to remind you that I am the only Democratic Senator of my class who has not been given a major Committee assignment," he wrote Johnson. Despite his pleas, Johnson denied the request and made sure that his rival had limited abilities to steal his spotlight.[97]

Despite such setbacks, he continued seeking national attention. He made a keynote speech to the Connecticut Democratic Convention in early July. Already in full campaign mode, he hammered the opposition. "If the Republican nominees are Mr. Eisenhower and Mr. Nixon then I say to you, with the deepest of conviction that neither of them has the qualifications to assure the United States of adequate leadership for the next four years." Gore complained that behind the claims of altruism, there had been "more tax loopholes opened in the guise of tax reform, more benefits granted to the large special interests than during any administration in our history." He compared Treasury Secretary Humphrey to a "modern-day Andrew Mellon" and stressed that like Humpty Dumpty, he and his cohort were "headed for a fall/and all the favors and money kingpins/Can never put George in the Treasury again."[98]

The campaigning reached a fever pitch in mid-August when the Democrats convened in Chicago. From the start, it was apparent that Stevenson was the party's choice, so the major question revolved around the number-two person. Several names circulated, including Kennedy, Kefauver, Gore, Hubert Humphrey, and Clement, with Rayburn remarking that "Clement is a bright boy. Gore is brilliant." By the second day of the convention, the *New York Times* disclosed that "Gore Is Reported Stevenson Choice."[99] Stevenson wanted desperately to balance his ticket, especially with a southerner or Catholic. Numerous debates developed within Stevenson's camp, but no one, including the candidate, could make the choice.

After much wrangling, Stevenson decided to open the process to the convention. Gore desperately wanted the job and set about forging alliances. Within a short period, he won the support of Oklahoma and several other delegations. Then he turned his efforts to Texas and its leaders. One of Johnson's confidants, George Reedy, reported that "a man came running up to us, his face absolutely distorted. Neither Jim [Rowe] nor I recognized him. His eyes were glittering." "Where is Lyndon?" the man asked. "Adlai's thrown this open, and I think I've got a chance for it if I can only get Texas." After a moment, Reedy noted, "Suddenly we realized we were talking with Senator Albert Gore of Tennessee, who both Jim and I had known well for at least twenty years and we didn't recognize him." Reedy concluded that "I have never seen before or since such a complete, total example of a man so completely wild with ambition, it had literally changed his features."[100]

After some discussions, Gore gained the Texas delegation's support. He had several positive forces working in his favor. First, many people did not like Kefauver, including Kentuckian Earle Clements, who characterized him as uncooperative and observed, "There was never much strength in the political alliance that Kefauver wanted to have with the party." On the other hand, the other major contender, John Kennedy, posed problems for most southerners and westerners. When pushed to support the Massachusetts senator, an Oklahoma delegate responded: "He's not our kind of folks." Another told Johnson, "My God, man, have you lost your mind? Kennedy, with his terrible farm record, and he is Catholic! The answer is no!"[101]

As the process unfolded, Gore genuinely thought he had a chance. With southern support and some western backing, he could perhaps squeeze ahead of Kennedy and Kefauver. On the first ballot, he ran a strong third to Kefauver and Kennedy with the support of Texas, Oklahoma, and several other states. At this point, several contenders including Humphrey dropped out. It appeared that he would have a chance.

However, on the second ballot, his candidacy unraveled. One of the first states, Arkansas, switched from Gore to Kennedy to avert a Kefauver victory. The defining moment came when Texas cast its votes. Right before, Gore looked at Johnson, who shook his head negatively, and the Texans went to Kennedy. At that point, according to Gore, the crowd went berserk; it appeared that Kennedy would win.[102]

While Gore liked Kennedy, he had to make a critical decision. He was under pressure from some pro-Kefauver delegates from his state delegation and others including *Tennessean* publisher Sillman Evans Jr., who reportedly told him "that the *Tennessean* wouldn't support him for dog catcher if he didn't get out of the race. The *Tennessean* will beat you if it takes a thousand years."[103] He also had his reputation at home to consider. To allow a New Englander, one that was

Catholic, to defeat a home-grown boy would have been political suicide, despite the fact that many of the Clement people did not like Kefauver.

With those considerations pushing him, Gore made his decision. He climbed on a chair and asked for recognition. Then, he took the microphone and bellowed: "With gratitude for the consideration and support of this great Democratic National Convention, I respectfully withdraw my name and support my distinguished colleague, Estes Kefauver." Immediately, the entire dynamic changed. Oklahoma switched and several other states followed. By the end, Kefauver had emerged victorious by a small margin. This left Theodore Sorenson to remember that Kennedy "had a few caustic comments for supposed friends who had let him down."[104]

It had been an exciting battle, one that left a taste in the mouth for the position that Gore relished for another four years. He sent letters to various delegates, including Fulbright, Rayburn, and Johnson, thanking them for their support. He wrote John Sparkman (D-AL) that "I am so grateful for your support of my candidacy for the vice-presidential nomination. Though I did not win, I felt proud to have made a respectable showing . . . with only a few hours work." Johnson responded that "I was delighted to cast my vote for you in Chicago and if I had thought there would be more than two ballots, I would have cast the votes again."[105]

The quest to become the number-two man became especially poignant over three decades later when young Al became Bill Clinton's vice president. Vice President Gore later remembered that his father always said that "the lure of the presidency never really overwhelmed me, though there were times when the vice presidency seemed extremely attractive." The younger Gore often joked, "Now, that's humility."[106] His son excitedly had watched the television as his father chased the vice presidency with such zeal in 1956, recalling his father standing on the chair and ultimately swinging his votes to Kefauver. In the long run, Senator Gore's choices obviously influenced his son's future decisions.

As the campaign unfolded, Gore concentrated primarily on limiting atomic testing. Increasingly, scientific information became available on the dangers of radioactive fallout to the atmosphere, water tables, and human fetuses. The Democratic Party, led by nominee Stevenson, had called for ending the tests. He wanted to seize the "moral initiative" and step onto the world stage with a successful campaign.[107]

The party called on Gore to assume leadership of the effort. Despite his initial infatuation with atomic power and energy, Gore studied the issues and grew increasingly concerned about the ramifications. The debate over atomic testing also reflected growing concern for the escalation in the Cold War, and the obsession of U.S. politicians with pursuing the goals of containing communism at any cost. He branded the failure to restrict atmospheric testing a "menace to mankind" and strongly supported Stevenson's call to end tests. He traveled across the country to discuss the issue, including a visit to Austin where Johnson arranged a national television appearance. There, he blasted the administration for its failure to seize the initiative on this worldwide danger.[108]

The speech was not the only memorable aspect of the trip. After it, Pauline and Albert traveled with Lady Bird and Lyndon to their ranch in the Texas Hill Country. Gore later complained that "one minute he would be driving seventy or eighty miles per hour (during a break in the conversation or while I was talking) and then Lyndon would slow to a perking rate, with first one hand and then the other on the steering wheel as he talked and gesticulated to add emphasis to his points." Gore remembered that "we had settled most of the country's problems by the time we reached the ranch[;] the four of us tarried besides the pool for a few moments and mourned the election outlook for the Democratic Party."[109]

Despite the pessimism, the family campaigned hard, including Pauline who hit the speaking circuit. Her abilities made her a popular choice, especially since most people recognized her as a powerful influence on her up-and-coming husband. Others requested her for other reasons, such as a Minnesota group that wanted "someone with a Southern accent because they are so crazy about Kefauver." Within a few weeks, she traveled to New Jersey, Ohio, Illinois, and Florida before finally returning home for two speeches in Nashville. At each place, she received warm welcomes including one engagement where a hundred more people showed than were expected.[110]

The campaigning and frequent travel with Albert created some problems for Pauline as she endured the challenges of balancing political and family roles. When Nancy was young, Pauline had had limited opportunities to speak and travel, but as the wife of a senator, engagements multiplied. Unlike many elite Washington families who shipped their children off to boarding schools, the Gore family made sure that the children stayed close. Al was now eight and needed a lot of attention, especially since the family lived in a hotel with limited places to play. With the senator continually at work, Pauline had the primary child care duties, which created many problems when she hit the road. Friends filled in during short periods of time, but longer stretches required more formal arrangements. During one campaign swing, she asked the widow of a one-time Tennessee congressman to travel to Washington to babysit Al, who had just started the prestigious prep school St. Alban's.[111]

Such decisions clearly tore at her. Years later, she confessed to a friend that "Albert and I were away so much." When her son became a politician, journalists challenged her about her absences. After she read one particular story, she remarked that "I cried my eyes out. I said, 'Here I have been, all of my motherhood, trying to keep from being a smother mother, and then have this confront me.'" In her defense, she stressed that she typically only stayed away for short times and that her longest absence was two weeks.[112]

Gore's most important work during the election cycle involved a subcommittee on elections. In February, he had landed the unenviable task of heading an investigation into campaign contributions and lobbying influences in Washington. The subcommittee's members included McClellan, Anderson, Kennedy, and Republicans Styles Bridges of New Hampshire and Barry Goldwater of Arizona. "The unfortunate trend toward mass interstate movement of campaign money to subvert the will of the people, particularly in smaller states," disturbed Gore. He promised to "bring the facts to the attention of the American people" and guaranteed to include labor unions and corporations within his inquiry into campaign spending. He assured his colleagues that "it is my earnest hope that the principal purpose and aim of the study will be corrective rather than punitive."[113]

Gore's selection as chairman created a controversy. At the initial meeting, he laid out a fairly ambitious plan, leading the Republicans to call for a new chairman or dramatically reduced powers for Gore and the selection of a Republican as chief counsel. Gore and Bridges fought for two weeks, during which the Republicans tried winning more equal footing. The Republicans ultimately won out; Gore stayed on the committee, but the more conservative and less partisan McClellan took over as chairman.[114] The Tennessee senator pushed for a careful look at campaign finances but had to accept a much slower pace than he wanted.

However, by the fall, Gore had regained the chair and added Senator Mike Mansfield to the committee. As soon as the conventions ended, he forwarded letters to all organizations, lobbyists, and official party groups and requested that they provide financial disclosures by September 1. After that point, Gore planned to ask for periodic reports, including receipts and disbursements, until the conclusion of the investigation in early 1957. He reported to Johnson that "it would not be my purpose to use this information politically, but rather to make it available to the press and the people, thereby bringing about 'disclosure' of the financial conduct of this campaign during its progress, not after its conclusion."[115]

The subcommittee followed through on its plans. *U.S. News and World Report* published Gore's picture with the caption "CAMPAIGN FUND WATCHER." The story reported that Gore had been looking into campaign funding and that he believed the investigation was having results: "Both parties complain that some large donations that were expected have 'dried up.' Mr. Gore feels that this is good. He wants to see the money come in from many small donors instead."[116]

The process proved extremely difficult. Gore employed John Moore, an attorney from Maryland, and asked Dr. Alexander Heard, a political science professor from the University of North Carolina, to serve as chief consultant. He antagonized his fellow Democrats by first focusing on their efforts. He requested records from Pennsylvania Democrats who had hosted a $25-a-plate dinner for Stevenson. According to Gore, "my fellow Democrats were not amused and reaction was somewhat greater than I had anticipated."[117] Still, the Republicans accused him of partisanship, and some called the investigation a "witch hunt."

Criticism also came from others who accused him of lacking diligence. Columnist Drew Pearson of the *Washington Post* wrote a scathing article, questioning Gore's travel to Bangkok for a meeting of the Interparliamentary Union at the height of the campaign. "Senator Gore's trip to Bangkok was as necessary as it is for me to go to the market with my wife to bring home the groceries," he wrote one person. He complained to another that "an election investigation comes only once in a lifetime, as far as that election is concerned. Once the evidence is destroyed in an election investigation, once people forget for a week or two it is too late to do anything about it."[118] Despite such criticisms, Gore plowed ahead, stepping on many toes in the process.

Throughout the fall, Gore campaigned for Stevenson. Despite many Democrats' best efforts, Stevenson could not compete against Eisenhower, given the economic prosperity of his first term and continuous positive job approval ratings. The Democrat had little to offer other than the nuclear test ban issue, and Eisenhower's low-key campaign played to the incumbent's advantage. By early October, the president told his son John, "This fellow's licked and what's more he knows it."[119]

When the election's results were tallied in November, Ike won by more than 9 million votes and took 457 to Stevenson's 73 electoral votes. Even Louisiana went to Ike and became the first Deep South state to vote Republican since Reconstruction. Tennessee also went to Eisenhower by a small margin. Still, there was a silver lining for Gore's party. Democrats held on to their margin in the Senate, 49–47, and increased their majority in the House to thirty-three seats. This led Eisenhower to lament, "If I'd known what the outcome would be, I would probably have refused to run."[120]

As the first Eisenhower term ended and another began, Gore's power would continue to increase at the state and national levels. Dixon-Yates, the interstate highway bill, the campaign finance probe, and his stands on civil rights enhanced his political profile in Washington and Tennessee. The near miss in Chicago was probably a blessing since Eisenhower crushed Stevenson. He continued to dream of a vice presidency that would serve as a springboard to the presidency. For the moment, he was content to be the junior senator from Tennessee and looking for new challenges.

# 5   A TIME OF PERIL ON MANY FRONTS

"EISENHOWER'S FINAL ACT, perhaps his most lasting contribution," Gore wrote, "was his warning to his countrymen of the dangers inherent in the burgeoning 'military-industrial complex' . . . One will never know, but historians can meditate upon the knowledge and possibly the anxieties which prompted this good and simple man of military renown to conclude his service with that prophetic valedictory warning."[1] During Eisenhower's second term, Gore would concentrate on foreign relations and military issues. At the same time, he continued his climb to power by focusing on domestic issues such as atomic energy, taxes, and interest rates. He gained significant power and was elevated to several prestigious committee assignments. He also survived a spirited challenge from a Democratic rival in 1958 and campaigned for the vice presidential nomination in 1960. By the time Eisenhower left the White House, a more polished and powerful Tennessee senator appeared poised to assume national leadership.

In February 1957, as the new session was just getting started, Gore again found himself embroiled in a controversy over civil rights. That month, the Memphis papers announced Gore's ten candidates for the Air Force Academy, including two African Americans. The news prompted an immediate outpouring of anger from across the state. One constituent asked, "I wonder if you have the mistaken idea that the negro's [sic] put you in office . . . I can see Kefauver is not the only one from Tenn. that has been brain washed by the N.A.A.C.P." A friend from Nashville, Sims Crownover, complained that "I just can not understand how you failed to know that they were Negroes. It appears that some of your staff must have slipped up very badly to make such a mistake." He also chastised Gore for failing to sign the Southern Manifesto and warned, "Albert, I have been your friend for a long time and I feel that you should listen to the people back home, I am afraid that you will be badly beaten in the next election if you do not reverse your stand on integration."[2]

Gore was unrepentant and responded to his constituents that he had personally examined the files and records of each applicant. "It is my understanding that it is not the practice of the local Selective Service Boards to apply either racial preference or racial discrimination in the administration of the draft program," he stated. "It had not occurred to me that I should do so in the case of those who voluntarily apply for training or service in the Air Force." While he expressed appreciation for the letters, he refused to consider any further action on the matter.[3]

In 1957, it was volatile to take such a position. The segregationists saw the elevation of any African American as an attack on their way of life. With an election approaching in 1958, the smart thing to do politically would have been to avoid the controversy. Most likely, Gore recognized the addresses and schools that each attended and knew, despite some of his denials, that the two men were African American.[4] Instead, he went forward. Was it for the support of the African Americans in Shelby County? That may have played a role, but clearly it cost him much more than he gained. Fundamentally, it was a hard choice but the right thing to do, and Gore continued to believe that such acts chipped away at the prevailing racism.

In early February, the election subcommittee produced a report that listed more than $33 million in campaign spending, although it noted that the outlays "far exceeded" the figure because of faulty reporting procedures. The figures were $20,685,387 for Republican candidates and $10,977,700 for Democrats, with the latter receiving substantial funds from organized labor, while corporations and wealthy families overwhelmingly gave to the Republicans. The committee also concentrated on practices of "questionable legality and desirability." These included loans by banks to political candidates and the "educational" activities of labor organizations and "institutional" and "public service" advertising by some large corporations. The report also questioned the regulation that individuals could provide no more than $5,000 annually to a candidate or political committee but that there was no limit on the number of candidates to whom an individual could contribute. Candidates also circumvented the $3 million limit by establishing committees for individuals and parties which were used to funnel funds. Gore and Mike Mansfield stressed that there was "imperative and immediate" need for full disclosure laws and "enforceable and realistic limits" on spending.[5]

The Republicans on the committee howled that the report was incomplete. Senators Carl T. Curtis of Nebraska and Barry Goldwater of Arizona argued that the committee had undercounted labor contributions. If included, Curtis believed that the spending of the two parties "probably would have been about the same." Others accused the Democrats of inciting class warfare by focusing on contributions to the Republicans from the wealthy and corporations.[6] In response to the report, Gore pushed to strengthen the Corrupt Practices Act.

Proposed changes included limits of $1,000 a year to all candidates for office, with only $250 allowed to candidates outside of the contributor's home state. The requirements on public disclosure of those who gave more than $500 a year would be strengthened, and the candidate would bear the responsibility for reporting all funds received. For the presidential contest, spending would be capped at twenty cents for every vote cast in the previous election. The *Baltimore Sun* acknowledged that "the thoughtful public has long disliked the acrid dollar smell that has carried away from many an individual election fight. Senator Gore may not get all he wants but he ought to get something."[7]

While embroiled in the generally losing fight over campaign finance reform, Gore found himself like many other senators in the last year or so of their term, thinking about reelection. In the summer of 1956, Wilma Dykeman, an astute observer, had already noted the overabundance of talent in Tennessee. The potential for the party to "be torn apart in the resulting scrap" between Clement and either Gore or Kefauver led her to observe: "These worries are real enough, because there is no place for Governor Clement to go—except after one of the Senate seats now held by Kefauver and Gore. In either case, the fight would be rough, interesting, and unpredictable." She noted that the politics of all three were similar and the race could digress into a choice of personalities, leading to a bitter conflict.[8]

By the middle of 1957, more people began looking to a possible fight between Gore and Clement. The governor had won points for opposing the Dixon-Yates contract and supporting reform in Tennessee. His keynote address at the 1956 Democratic convention, however, had gone badly—it went too long, and he appeared nervous and perturbed. Nonetheless, on the home front he appeared strong, and members of Gore's family issued warnings. "I agree with you that as of right now it appears that I may be able to get by without a serious fight next year," Gore responded optimistically. "I have often heard that the least politics is the best politics. I have stayed steadily on the job and have refrained from messing around in the internal affairs of Tennessee. In fact, I may have carried this a little too far by staying in Washington too closely. In any event, I am rectifying that now by accepting a number of engagements in Tennessee."[9]

Tennesseans also began seeing Pauline more often. In mid-May, Louis Davis did a piece in the *Nashville Tennessean Magazine* entitled, "Pancakes and Protocol: Vivacious Mrs. Albert Gore Thrives on the Washington Whirl." It outlined how she arose at seven o'clock and spent the first hour preparing pancakes while Al and Albert horseplayed. The story noted that she participated in the Democratic Congressional Wives Forum and at a club house on New Hampshire Avenue, all the while raising money for various groups, including the Home for the Blind in Washington. "[For] a lady lawyer who gave up her profession for a lifelong partnership, she plunges into her Washington tests with the zest of a school girl on an exciting vacation. But beneath all the gaiety is a time saving strategy that would keep any court docket clear."[10]

Despite all the politicking, Gore still found time for friendly banter with his compatriots, even on the Senate floor. During a debate on airline competition, he and Wayne Morse digressed into an argument about the merits of the Aberdeen Angus and Devon breed. Morse joked that "as Senators know, the Senator from Tennessee and I believe in the competitive system, because as the breeder of 2 competing blood lines or breeds of cattle, I think we have demonstrated our belief in the competitive system." Gore retorted: "The Senator from Oregon now has touched upon a different kind of stock, about which he exercises an amazing lack of good judgment. But I will not disparage the breed of cattle which he owns. I shall simply invite him to join with me in treating our Democratic colleagues to the products thereof." Gore promised to provide his colleagues with steaks if Morse would do the same for Devon meat for stew. To this, Morse responded that he knew that his colleagues would like the stew over steaks.[11]

Gore also established a good working relationship with a fellow cattleman when he received a prestigious appointment to the Senate Finance Committee in the new session. The new position brought Gore into closer contact with Robert Kerr (D-OK), who became one of his closer associates in the Senate. The oilman had been elected in 1948 and ultimately won the title of the "uncrowned King of the Senate." He was a well-known debater who according to one observer "valued facts and was an avid note-taker." Gore recalled that Kerr could "take the least amount of information and look and act more authoritative than any man in the world." At times, Kerr went for his opponent's jugular, once calling Homer Capehart (R-IN) a "rancid tub of ignorance."[12]

Kerr and Gore developed a good relationship that contained much good-natured kidding. According to Gore, Kerr had a "wit as quick and sharp as those of any man I ever knew and it was extremely difficult to cope with him in light banter." Nevertheless, he would try. On one occasion, Gore arrived at a committee hearing and commented to Kerr: "Bob, I passed the statue of Benjamin Franklin, and even he was smiling at you, and I wanted to tell you he was smiling at you." Quickly, Kerr responded, "Albert, you go back and take another look at that statue and you will see that he wasn't smiling at me, he was laughing at you." On another occasion, Gore, who liked to use big words to try to impress people, used a particularly obscure one, leading Kerr to stop the meeting they were attending and ask, "Wait a minute, Albert, what did you say?" When Gore repeated the word, Kerr instructed a staff member to "get me a dictionary!" He made Gore wait until he looked it up and satisfied himself to the meaning.[13] Their relationship would remain strong until Kerr's death in 1963.

His appointment to the Senate Finance Committee also provided Gore a better forum to press his economic views. As the session opened, Gore delivered a scathing attack on George Humphrey in a speech titled, "The Secretary of the Treasury: A Study of the Use of Public for Private Advancement." In it, Gore focused on Humphrey's failure to divest himself of private investments in companies doing business with the government. He complained that since taking office, Humphrey had "never overlooked an opportunity to lend the immense influence of his official position to the securing of business for his private companies, in Brazil, Canada, and Europe, as well as the United States." He also had helped place close business associates in the Federal Reserve bank in Cleveland.[14]

Humphrey had been one of Gore's favorite targets since Eisenhower appointed him in 1953. The son of a wealthy Michigan lawyer, Humphrey had risen to head the Cleveland-based M.A. Hanna Company (founded by McKinley's handler Mark Hanna, archenemy of William Jennings Bryan), a business with vast interests in plastics, petroleum, banks, and shipping. Several historians have characterized him as knowing "little about economic theory— only enough to pronounce it useless . . . Instead he relied on his business experience, which sustained his faith in the old-time Republican orthodoxy that what was good for business was good for the economy." Eisenhower regarded him as a guardian of "the welfare of the United States and all the people that compose it."[15]

Gore's attacks on Humphrey and his policies continued into the summer of 1957. In July of that year, he testified before the Senate Finance Committee and blasted the secretary's support of "high interest rates," which "diminished the possibility of competition" and encouraged "big business concerns to finance their capital expansion and improvement in large part from inflated prices and consequent swollen profits." He condemned reduced corporate tax rates, and artificially higher interest rates that benefited not just corporations but the banks charging them. "The result is to make the big bigger, the rich richer, and to threaten the existence of a climate truly favorable to individual enterprise and equality of opportunity . . . [I]n these ways, and in many others, Mr. Chairman, our Government is favoring material values over human values. This I challenge. I challenge it in whole and in part."[16]

With his populist sensibilities intact, Gore attacked the idea that if big business flourished, then the proceeds would flow to all Americans. In a classic zero-sum game, according to Gore, the wealthy took a disproportionate share of the profits and benefited from higher interest rates at the expense of the average American who relied on credit for everything from home mortgages to short-term loans for cars and home improvement. It made no sense to Gore that the government should favor those that had so much over those that struggled daily. He considered it a sure way to ensure a slowdown in the economy because it allowed the majority only limited purchasing power. His predictions about the shortsightedness of Humphrey's policy would soon come true.

As he continued battling the Eisenhower administration on economic matters, Gore faced a serious civil rights issue. During the election cycle, President Eisenhower had pushed for new federal civil rights legislation, partly to court the votes of northern liberals and African Americans. As proposed, the bill reintroduced in 1957 granted stronger powers to utilize the courts against discrimination and expanded the power of the attorney general to enforce the right to vote. Gore supported upholding the constitutional guarantees regarding suffrage because the Fifteenth Amendment guaranteed all people the right to vote regardless of race. He consistently backed efforts to ensure voting privileges, although he sometimes disagreed with the procedures for implementation and enforcement.

Gore's constituents uniformly opposed the legislation. They believed that it was the first step toward more radical civil rights legislation, which they often linked to the international Communist conspiracy. One constituent wrote that the civil rights bill "would put the South to the torch, sword and other horrors that you may have forgotten." Others attacked specific elements of the legislation, arguing that Gore should battle to limit the power of the attorney general and support amendments to prevent further usurpation of states' rights by the Supreme Court.[17]

Despite the protests, Gore backed the basic thrust of the legislation, telling constituents that he would "be willing to support a bill which genuinely undertakes to protect the right to vote . . . I have always felt that the right to vote is one that should not be denied to any qualified citizen." Nevertheless, he expressed some reservations, writing Frank Ahlgren that he supported either a bill or a constitutional amendment eliminating the poll tax and would back legislation that created a special assistant attorney general to concentrate on civil rights. He worried, however, that these actions were one thing, while "enactment of a law subjecting people to civil and criminal prosecution for some act which they are allegedly 'about to' take is of another."[18]

During the debates, Gore continued to express reservations. He characterized the original bill as not safeguarding trial by jury and conferring too much power on certain individuals. Gore favored amendments to limit the authority of the attorney general, a position some northerners, including Kennedy, supported. When Gore voted for the amended bill, he found that he pleased neither his southern colleagues nor many civil rights advocates, although moderates backed the bill. Roy Wilkins of the NAACP noted that "if you are digging a ditch with a teaspoon and a man comes along and offers you a spade, there is something wrong with your head if you don't take it because he didn't offer you a bulldozer."[19]

Gore's position on the 1957 Civil Rights Act was consistent with his views on civil rights. In general, he believed that the "badge of citizenship is the franchise. Its intelligent exercise is the citizen's one best hope for progress." He understood that the "law can remove barriers and provide opportunities. And reasonable administration of law can set a moral tone and foster an atmosphere conducive to general social progress." However, he did not like the expanded governmental jurisdictions and worried that "the price of excessive dependence on governmental power (now for a good cause, perhaps subsequently for a bad cause) may simply be to dangerously expand the coercive powers of government."[20]

Gore's response to the act reflected a go-slow approach to solving the problem of segregation. He admitted that he was not a "white knight for civil rights." "I wasn't anything more," he wrote, "than a moderate who believed in the Constitution, who respected and supported duly constituted courts of the land, and who had compassion for oppressed fellow Americans." Gore acknowledged that government regulations would not automatically overturn ingrained attitudes, although he differentiated between the ballot box and everyday life, fully supporting the former. "Law cannot per se create higher moral standards, cannot correct deeply held prejudices, cannot engender the spirit of neighborliness," Gore emphasized. He criticized some civil rights activists for having "no appreciation of the education in sensibility which must precede and accompany any vast social reform." To the former schoolteacher, education, along with the "establishment of a proper moral climate" and "a concerned and humane tone throughout society," provided the solution to racism.[21] He correctly predicted that extreme resistance would result if people forced radical answers down the throats of white southerners.

He already had seen the effects of education in his own family. From the start, he and Pauline had criticized racial prejudice and discrimination. Pauline had Nancy and her friend Nancy Fleming read Harper Lee's *To Kill a Mockingbird* until they knew its themes by heart. The story of a southern lawyer who supported justice and truth in the face of prejudice clearly affected Nancy's view of the world. According to Fleming, Pauline truly believed that the story "really hit at the heart of the whole matter." Later, Nancy would support civil rights, even when living in racist and segregated Mississippi in the 1960s and 1970s.[22] There would be many other demonstrations of Pauline's attitude, including her speaking to African Americans in public, in both Carthage and Washington, often to the dismay of her southern friends and husband's colleagues.

Albert often handled Al's education. In one lesson, he took Al to an open house at the Cullum Mansion in Carthage, just up the street from their home on Fisher Avenue. Instead of focusing on the splendor of the home, the senator took his seven-year-old son down to the basement where he pointed out the shackles hanging from the ceiling which had been used to hold slaves. The younger Gore admitted later that the whole event had a significant impact on him and led him to understand the "undeniable and palpable presence of evil" that had existed in his hometown.[23]

In 1958, Gore continued to focus on national issues with local implications. In February, he proposed a "full employment bill" to head off an economic calamity. He became concerned by "having seen thousands of my fellow Tennesseans standing for hours in the cold and rain to obtain small allotments of surplus food."[24] The idea of full employment had floated around since Truman, and with the economic slowdown, Gore began pushing the concept once more as a way to combat the economic stagnation.

His proposal led to criticisms. John Knight of the *Detroit Free Press* chastised him for "demagoging," to which Gore replied, "I believe that every available able-bodied man should earn his living, but I also believe that he is entitled to an opportunity." When critics argued that such a program would ensure inflation, Gore responded, "It is difficult for me to see how it is any more inflationary to provide a man with employment at minimum wages than give him something for nothing . . . [I]t seems to me that insofar as able-bodied men and women, who are destitute and unemployed, are concerned the choice is between making gainful employment available or making surplus food available. I prefer, and think they prefer, work instead of the dole."[25]

Gore had correctly predicted an economic downturn that struck the country. In addition to the full employment bill, he also pushed a tax reduction proposal for everyone but especially those who needed it most. He called for raising the personal exemption from $600 to $800 and paying for it by eliminating tax shelters such as the dividend credit and reducing the oil depletion allowance. He also wanted more public works programs to keep people employed and stimulate the economy while building necessary roads, buildings, and parks. He wrote John Spence of the *Memphis Press-Scimitar:* "I think the depletion of Federal revenues would be greater as a result of a depression than the added budgetary cost of preventing one. To put it bluntly, I think it is cheaper to prevent a depression than have one."[26]

His positions won national recognition as an editorial in the *Akron Beacon Journal* reported that "many of those who heard Gore belittle and berate the Eisenhower administration are ready to support him for President." "And don't think the handsome, personable senator isn't anxious to move into the White House," the writer, Clyde Mann, stressed. "How do I know? Al told me so." The editorial prompted a quick response from Gore. "You may be sure that I had no intention of saying to you, or anyone, by nod or otherwise, that I was a candidate for President, Vice President, or anything else." However, he added coyly that "this is not to say that I, as well as several of my colleagues, do not find pleasing and flattering an occasional suggestion of availability, human nature, particularly that of political figures, being what it is."[27]

Gore was not truthful with Mann; he did covet higher office. It appeared his Senate seat was secure since Clement appeared unlikely to pursue it. Throughout the country, he and his family continued to gain publicity. The *St. Petersburg Times* published a story, "The Gores of Tennessee are Fine Political Team." It highlighted that Pauline held a prominent place in her husband's life and noted her ability to catch an eight-foot sailfish. Papers also featured a story about Nancy and her work at the Brussels World Fair, where "a quartet of Russians . . . have learned that it isn't easy to play wise guy with a U.S. Senator's daughter." According to the writer, she had outsmarted the young Russians while working at a U.S. booth housing a historical machine; she was able to use the machine to answer a difficult question.[28]

In June, William White wrote a series in the *Washington Star* that featured possible presidential contenders, including "Gore a Serious Worker: Presidency Bid Seen Just a Possibility If He Could End South's Sectionalism." White highlighted that the Tennessean was a "non-cussin', non-smokin', non-drinkin' politician" and "looks like a Collar ad." Still, "he is about ten times as tough as he looks." "Though there is nothing self-righteous to him . . . Senator Gore nevertheless is a little like the small boy remembered from grammar school who was the brightest and best behaved in the room—and who invariably suffered from this among his classmates." White believed that Gore possessed political skills "but is rather short of that intuitively casual touch with his associates that is so helpful in his trade." To him, Gore was a southern liberal who could help the South become a positive influence on the Democratic Party. "For such a border State candidate—Senator Gore specifically in the present discussion—would never be gladly backed by the deep Southerners . . . They might take him as a matter of expediency; but he could never really reflect their views."[29]

While Gore focused on the national scene, an unexpected challenge developed in Tennessee during the spring. Several wealthy Tennessee industrialists angered by Gore's support of reciprocal trade and his positions on taxes allied with Republicans to unseat him. They were assisted by some outside interests, including some well-placed insurance company executives who had not forgiven Gore for leading the opposition to forgiving an estimated $124 million in taxes in 1957.[30] The group looked for a candidate with enough name recognition to challenge Gore. With Clement out of the picture, they found a willing candidate in ex-governor Prentice Cooper. Born in 1895, he was a native of Shelbyville in Bedford County and had served as governor of Tennessee from 1939 to 1945 and was later U.S. ambassador to Peru. While friendly with Kefauver, he was a well-known conservative who once told a delegate to the state constitutional convention in 1953 that "I do not want college professors around. They believe in the greatest good for the greatest number, and I do not believe in that."[31] A devoted segregationist, he had strongly criticized every effort to destroy white supremacy. For conservative Tennesseans, he was a perfect pick to challenge Gore.

The race issue emerged as the most volatile one in the campaign. Cooper immediately promised to defend segregation. Everywhere he went, a band or a loudspeaker played "Dixie." Don Oberdorfer, covering the race for the *Charlotte Observer*, remembered that on the campaign bus, Cooper liked to brag about his Ivy League education and his more cosmopolitan view of the world. Still, as soon as he left the bus to speak at a courthouse square, he immediately declared, "I'm Prentice Cooper. I'm going to keep the niggers out of the schools." Everywhere Cooper went, he would charge that Gore had sold out Dixie to advance his national political ambitions. Soon billboards sprang up reading, "Tennessee needs a Senator FOR, not FROM Tennessee." Cooper promised that once elected he would immediately sign the Southern Manifesto. According to Gore, the *Tennessean* dispatched a reporter to find a copy so that Cooper could fulfill his promise. Yet it was nowhere to be found, leading Gore to crack that it was like the "Holy Grail." He mused that "perhaps Strom Thurmond is saving it for his Presidential Library in Aiken, South Carolina."[32]

Cooper had a potentially explosive issue to exploit. In August 1956 there had been a tense confrontation in Clinton when twelve African American students entered the high school rather than being bused fifteen miles away to a school in Knoxville. Agitators rallied more than a thousand angry whites. When the mob appeared likely to overwhelm the small Clinton police force, Clement, with the support of Gore and Kefauver, ordered in the Tennessee Highway Patrol and National Guard to restore order. Tensions defused temporarily, although the action aggravated segregationists in Tennessee and throughout the South.[33]

A far more serious confrontation developed the following year in Little Rock. Efforts to desegregate Central High School encountered significant obstacles. When African American students tried entering the school, Arkansas governor Orval Faubus ordered the Arkansas National Guard to stop it. After prolonged debates and much foot dragging, the Eisenhower administration finally ordered in U.S. troops and federalized the National Guard, which effectively ended the confrontation. While more whites began to accept that desegregation was inevitable, there remained a very dedicated band of extremists committed to preventing any such action. Cooper and others wanted to exploit this and believed that the issue could be Gore's Achilles heel.[34]

Cooper and his allies attacked Gore on other fronts. The former governor called Gore an "ideal Senator of the Russian Dictator Khrushchev," and his supporters portrayed Gore as a representative of foreign interests and socialist governments. A .G. Heinshohn and the Tennessee Independents bought a full-page ad in several papers in early July that contained a cartoon of a bull with horns chasing a Tennessee businessman and worker and under it the line read: "Time to act . . . or be 'GORED' TO DEATH! WE CAN BEAT GORE the man who has betrayed his state. WE CAN BEAT GORE the man WHO 'sold us down the river.'" The article stressed that "the long-time record of socialistic 'World Thinker' Gore is ridiculous, absurd—and criminal for his arrogant disregard for the rights of American citizens."[35]

Gore lacked the campaign war chest and polarizing issues of his opponent. Instead, he actively campaigned on his record, highlighting his role in the defeat of the Dixon-Yates contract and his support for the National Interstate Highway Bill, TVA, atomic testing, and tax equity. To combat charges he betrayed his state, Gore told a Knoxville audience that "I know how to work effectively for Tennessee. The job can't be done effectively if you go and take a seat by yourself and say, 'I'm for Tennessee alone.'" He also fought back by associating Cooper with the Republicans. At a big rally in East Tennessee, Gore told the audience that if "Republicans want to run a candidate against me, why don't they have the courage to call Prentice what he is and run as a Republican in the general election?"[36] It was a smart tactic, linking Cooper to the other party in such a partisan state.

Outsiders became particularly interested in the Tennessee Democratic primary. William S. White called it a case of "moderation vs. racism." "The result will tell whether a moderately liberal and forward Southern political view can survive in the backwash of the racial crisis of Little Rock and elsewhere. And if this view cannot live in Tennessee . . . it can hardly live anywhere in the South." He added that Gore was "feeling the whip of the Southern right wing for having gone too far on civil rights," while a year earlier southern moderates "were under the lash of the Democratic liberal wing, and of Northerners in general, for not being willing to go far enough." A victory would demonstrate that moderate southerners could promote compromise and remain prominent in the Democratic Party.[37]

Cooper's significant financial advantage worried the Gore family and its supporters. Thousands of billboards appeared, and Cooper bought large blocs of radio and television time. Nancy tried to scrape together money to return home from a temporary job at the World's Fair in Belgium to hit the campaign trail, although Pauline reported that "it took dire threats to keep her over there." Al became so concerned that he caught a ride to a nearby town to hear his father speak. He brought $5 he had earned while hoeing tobacco and offered it so that his father could buy some radio advertisements. Later, Pauline noted, "and his father did, too. It was Albert Jr.'s $5 and others like it and the vote of the people who didn't have $5 that won for us."[38]

Albert and Pauline criss-crossed the state, making as many as four speeches a day. They often gathered with people on the courthouse lawn, where both of them would speak. While deadly serious about the major issues, they had some light moments. In Cleveland, Gore found that the public address system had failed. Undeterred, he found a preacher holding services who had a very good sound system. He made a donation and the pastor allowed him the use of his equipment and even threw in a prayer for the senator at no charge. On another occasion, Gore was speaking on the steps of a courthouse when suddenly one of the inmates from the county jail yelled out the window, "Vote for Gore." The senator smiled and responded, "I'm grateful for all support but I wonder if he'll be out in time to vote."[39]

The Democrats held their primary in early August. Orval Faubus, the pro-segregationist governor of Arkansas, had won nomination for his third term a few days before the Tennessee primary. In response, the *Arkansas Gazette* wrote that "the moderate position formerly espoused by many Southern political leaders, and by this newspaper as a matter of principle, has been rejected by the mass of voters in this upper Southern state and is now clearly untenable by many in public life anywhere in the region." Despite such predictions of doom, Gore won easily. He took 60 percent of the vote, 362,271 to 239,316, carrying most of the state with the exception of some western Tennessee counties. After winning, Gore announced that "this shows that you can still take a position and decency and morality if you're willing to stick to it." The senator wrote a friend that the campaign was hard but he was proud that the people of Tennessee had focused on the issues and ignored the hot-button, emotional topics.[40]

On the surface, it appeared a victory for southern moderates. A *Washington Post* writer stressed that "Southern 'moderates' at the Capitol breathed easier last night in the wake of Sen. Albert Gore's impressive victory over former Gov. Prentice Cooper." A *U.S. News and World Report* columnist observed that at first glance "the Tennessee primary looked like a victory for those who favor a 'moderate' approach to the school-integration issue. This, however, now turns out not to be the case." Buford Ellington, the Democratic nominee for governor, and noted segregationists would control the state's internal affairs while "Gore will be off in Washington." The reporter noted that the two segregationist candidates in the gubernatorial race had won 414,437 votes while the two moderates garnered 259,332.[41]

While Gore had won more than 60 percent of the vote, the Cooper challenge pointed to future problems for the senator. The race issue in particular began to stick with white segregationists. Gore recognized that "the potency of the race issue—symbolized by the code words, 'Southern Manifesto,' 'anti-South' and 'non-Tennessee'—had its effect, particularly in west Tennessee, where Cooper ran strongly and where . . . the labels left lasting scars on me." Still other problems developed as his supporters and opponents alike agreed that the senator had been putting more effort into his national aspirations than into taking care of business at home. Gore spent most of his summers on the farm, but he had grown more tied to the Washington scene in terms of friends and political alliances. Eventually, he would become less tuned to the pulse of his home state.

With the Democratic nomination sewn up, Gore focused on other matters. Since the presidential election, Gore had criticized the administration for failing to move forward on an atmospheric nuclear testing ban. He argued that although no consensus existed in the scientific community, "so far as I know, no reputable scientist will . . . flatly assert there is no danger to the human race arising from the radioactive fallout." The poisons absorbed into plants and animals and deposited into bones led many to believe that levels of tolerance among humans were sufficiently low to warrant concern. "I am not one to say that peace and security can be obtained without risk. If I felt that continued testing of hydrogen bombs would contribute materially to peace, then I would be prepared to accept such degree of risk as may be present. But do we advance the cause of peace by hydrogen bomb testing?"[42]

Under pressure from the scientific community, as well as from Democrats like Gore, the Eisenhower administration reexamined its position and moved forward on discussions of the matter with the Soviets. The president wrote Bernard Baruch, who had allied with Gore on the issue, that "your comment that proposals to limit testing must prove illusory if the threat of atomic destruction remains uncontrolled is one which I fully support."[43]

To strengthen his calls for a change in U.S. policy, Gore headed a congressional delegation that went to Geneva in late 1958. There, he proposed a three-year suspension of above-ground testing in an effort to break the impasse. "Our successful major first step might well lead to others," he told reporters. "The United States could show that it is willing to stop, that it will stop contaminating the world atmosphere. Any other nation that refuses to do so must bear the full blame for her attack." The *Memphis Commercial Appeal* editorialized that Gore's plan "deserves the Administration's most careful consideration with the humanities the major approach factor."[44]

Following the conference, Gore took his message directly to Eisenhower. At a White House meeting, he "urged the President to approve a unilateral cessation of aerial atomic explosions for at least three years in order to force the Soviet Union on the propaganda defensive in the world." While acknowledging that underground and stratospheric testing remained viable, he encouraged Eisenhower to "seize the propaganda initiative by timing the stopping of the aerial explosions at the point when the Soviets finally decide to reject any dependable agreement on stopping tests."[45]

As he focused on the test ban, Gore also continued campaigning for his fellow Democrats. He traveled around the country making speeches, hammering Republican ties to economic elites. He told a Michigan audience that "if the

Republican Party was ever reincarnated into a homing pigeon, no matter from where it was released in the universe, whether from a jet plane or in outer space, it would go directly home to Wall Street without a flutter of the wing."[46] Such characterizations helped the Democrats, and they emerged victorious from the November elections, extending their Senate majority to 64–34 and dominating the House 282–154. The huge turnover can be attributed to the quality slate of candidates the Democrats offered and the apparent stagnation of the economy. While most people continued to look favorably on Eisenhower, concern about the country's future direction was growing.[47]

Democrats continued to hold strong in Tennessee as well. One of the disturbing aspects of the state campaign was Gore's willingness to support the Democratic gubernatorial candidate, Buford Ellington, who faced a strong challenge from former Democratic governor James Nance McCord, who ran as an independent. Ellington was extremely conservative and in 1958 labeled himself an "old-fashioned segregationist." Gore later explained that "I had always been intensely loyal to the Democratic Party. So, I promptly endorsed Ellington." He also wanted his support at the 1960 Democratic convention, winning an "I'm for that" from him. During the campaign, the two made joint appearances throughout the state.[48]

Gore's support for Ellington made a black mark on the senator's record and sent a confusing message to Tennesseans and other southern moderates. He recognized Ellington's conservatism but endorsed him anyway. Although he took courageous stands on civil rights with the Southern Manifesto and the Air Force Academy applicants, African Americans could see him criss-crossing the state with an avowed segregationist. This willingness to subordinate his principles to his ambitions and partisan politics disappointed some people, although others characterized it as politically prudent, for once demonstrating a political aptitude that he often failed to display. Nevertheless, it was the wrong message at the wrong time for him to send, especially with the conservative reaction gaining momentum in the state and region.

As the new session opened in 1959, Gore finally obtained a prized assignment, an appointment to the Senate Foreign Relations Committee chaired by J. William Fulbright. His efforts on the atmospheric test ban and reciprocal trade had helped pave the way for his nomination to the committee. This prestigious appointment, however, placed him in the middle of numerous contentious issues that would provoke clashes with many of his constituents, especially on the matters of Vietnam and family planning. This step up the national ladder fit well with his career ambitions, despite its potential pitfalls.

In the first session of 1959, the economy and foreign relations consumed Gore's attention. He continued complaining about the tight money policy, wondering if there were "too many dollars chasing too few yachts." He attended presentations on the cold war by George Kennan and Dean Acheson and made a speech at the prestigious Gridiron Dinner. In between engagements, he found time to take care of his Tennessee constituents. For example, his office worked with the Department of Health, Education, and Welfare (HEW) to help Murfreesboro secure $68,160 for building new elementary classrooms.[49]

Also during the spring, Gore fought off an attack from columnist Drew Pearson after he failed to support the journalist's plan to have children contribute a nickel each to help rebuild the school in Clinton, Tennessee, after terrorists destroyed it in October 1958.[50] Pearson retaliated by charging Gore with nepotism, citing Christine Coggins, a niece who worked in his office, and other family members employed in the Senate Post Office. He also speculated about Nancy's service as a guide in the U.S. pavilion at the World's Fair, implying that the senator's position ensured her job and paycheck.[51]

Gore refused to answer Pearson's charges directly, but he wrote Creed Black, executive editor of the *Tennessean*, to clarify "inaccurate" references. Nancy had earned her position in Brussels and received only $150 a month, and he offered to provide the canceled check of $3,200 to show that the family had paid for the bulk of the trip. He admitted he had his niece on his staff, but remarked that she drew a modest salary and was an excellent employee who previously had worked for Kefauver. "I have neither written nor spoken to Mr. Pearson about his outrageous treatment of my public record. I have resented it, of course, but I suppose this is the kind of cross that a man in public life must be prepared to bear upon occasion."[52]

The controversy soon quieted, freeing Gore to deal with other things. In June, a fund raiser approached him and asked him to join the 750 Club, which included Kefauver and Johnson. Participation guaranteed two tickets to the 1960 Democratic National Convention in Los Angeles and preferential treatment there. Gore responded that "membership in the 750 Club is, of course, quite beyond my modest means. Whether I can interest someone else in the membership, I have not yet determined. As a general proposition, a great majority of my friends who are well fixed financially are inclined to be Republicans."[53]

As the election cycle began, Gore increasingly focused on the economy. In particular, he tied the administration's tight money policy to the recent economic downturn. At one event, he observed with true populist flair that the current battle over interest rates dated back to the days of Jackson. "Traditionally the Democratic Party has been on the side of those who wanted an adequate supply of money. The Republican Party, since its inception, has been the chief spokesman for those who wanted tight money and high interest rates . . . I want the government to get off the back of the little man and place some of the necessary burden of government and national defense on the back of the big rich."[54]

For his efforts on economic policy, Gore received praise from several quarters. Truman encouraged him to keep up the fight, while Johnson wrote that "I often envy your grasp of the most difficult economic problems of our times." He also thanked him for a recent gift. "That big, beautiful pig is causing such a stir down in Johnson City that I wanted to say once again how very grateful I am to you . . . I hope that one day my stock will compare favorably even with yours and if so, it will be because you started me off in such a fine fashion."[55]

While involved in economic issues, Gore found himself increasingly engaged in foreign affairs. In November and December 1959, he traveled with Senator Gale McGee (D-WY) to Germany, Egypt, Israel, Vietnam, and Japan. As was often the case, Pauline accompanied her husband, although the family paid for her expenses. Later she advised her daughter-in-law and granddaughter that it was important to share interests with their mate, including foreign affairs. She also believed that there were many unscrupulous women in the world attracted to men in power. Her being at Albert's side reduced any potential for, or rumors of, inappropriate behavior. At the same time, she enjoyed learning about the world for herself.[56]

Two areas of foreign affairs in particular disturbed Gore. The first was the Palestinian refugee camps in Jordan. The poverty, despair, and anguish of those in the camps concerned him, and he and McGee issued a joint statement calling the refugee program "immoral, dishonest and unfair." They highlighted the exchange of 150,000 ration cards on the black market, with no oversight by the Jordanian government, which "[breeds] contempt of law and order, promotes and rewards dishonesty." The two senators called for fundamental changes, including reorganization of the program and public works projects such as reforestation, reclamation, and road construction.[57]

While Gore and McGee agreed on the refugee issue, they found themselves at odds over South Vietnam. They stopped there partly in response to a series of articles written by Albert M. Colegrove, a correspondent for Scripps-Howard. He had remarked that Washington had kept Vietnam from Communist conquest, "but at what a cost! We have wasted many millions of dollars, and still are. Washington has sent some prime human jackasses to this country billed as American 'experts.' Their stupidity and stuffiness have seriously hurt U.S.

prestige." He complained that these experts lived rent free in comfortable villas and skimmed money from inflated expense accounts. He also spotlighted the corruption of Vietnamese officials and their failure to try to create a sustainable economy, lamenting, "They get from America the millions necessary to buy what they want but can't afford."[58]

Gore and McGee stayed for five days in South Vietnam, visiting various sites and meeting with U.S. military advisers and civilian heads of the economic and assistance programs. The two senators also spent time with various Vietnamese officials, including a three-hour discussion with President Ngo Dinh Diem.[59] The short stay left an indelible mark on Gore.

After returning home, Gore voiced concerns about U.S. policy in South Vietnam, calling the foreign aid program an "economic monstrosity" and pointing out that clearing land at a French plantation cost $40 per acre whereas the U.S. program ran $130 per acre. He complained that the programs failed to adequately include the Vietnamese people, "the country's greatest single asset."[60] While acknowledging some successes, he stressed that Washington needed to reevaluate its approach and set reasonable long-term goals.[61]

One of Gore's major problems with the U.S. policy in South Vietnam was its support of Diem. "President Diem is a forceful, determined and dedicated leader for whom I hold respect and admiration," he told reporters, "but whose authoritarian policies seem to be growing instead of diminishing, a fact which I find disturbing."[62] He also complained about government corruption, noting that the United States had requested six times to audit the Vietnamese government's international funding distribution system but had been repeatedly denied. Diem had made little progress toward democratic rule, and attainment of substantial gains seemed far in the future.[63]

Not everyone, including McGee, agreed with Gore's appraisal of Vietnam or even cared about the issue of supporting authoritarian regimes as long as they were pro-American.[64] The government backed dictators such as Diem, Syngman Rhee, Fulgencio Batista, and Shah Reza Pahlavi Mohammad. However, some in Congress, including Wayne Morse, Joseph Clark (D-PA), and Ernest Gruening (D-AK), had begun to question whether a democratic nation could uphold its values and international leadership while supporting authoritarian regimes. They began issuing warnings and predicting dire consequences if support continued.[65]

Gore echoed these ideas and increasingly called into question in executive sessions of the SFRC the wisdom of U.S. policy, particularly in South Vietnam and Cuba, where Fidel Castro soon would seize power. The questioning was part of the continuing evolution of his thinking on the basic ideas of cold war strategy. While he backed U.S. intervention in Vietnam and engagement elsewhere, he believed that the United States could not support authoritarian regimes and maintain its moral leadership in the international community. He also thought that the simplistic explanation of Moscow-inspired conspiracies increasingly overlooked the numerous causes of local unrest. Still, he did not argue for withdrawal but for upholding U.S. ideals and doing a better job of dealing with people in the third world.

Gore also started another controversy on returning home. After discussions with Prime Minister Jawaharlal Nehru in New Delhi, he concluded that the United States should expand its efforts to fund birth control programs in the developing world. "My personal feeling after seeing teeming thousands of hungry children in the arms of their haggard mothers, already pregnant again," he told reporters, "is that we could not think of a more merciful thing or one more conducive to peace and stability than such a program." At a speech at Princeton he commented that "to further this great humanitarian end, the United States should respond in any way it properly can—either through Government agencies or through private organizations. What is now being done to meet this problem quite obviously is inadequate."[66]

Gore met a great deal of opposition to his proposal to increase funding for family planning programs. The Eisenhower administration had promised not to provide any artificial forms of birth control, stating that it was outside the U.S. role.[67] One constituent took Gore to task for his proposal. "Your usurpation of Almighty God's omniscience and providence is truly diabolical . . . The fact that he, in his infinite wisdom, has co-operated in bringing forth persons a 'little less than the angels' is lost on you. You would rob mothers' wombs, thereby preventing the procreation of creatures who would have the opportunity of serving God . . . [Y]our stand is typical of the amorality of our times. Aloof in smug respectability, you would avoid the helping hand . . . ultimately, we, the American People, must pay the price of birth control preachments [sic] and its practice. The justice of almighty God cannot be mocked forever."[68]

The issue of birth control and Gore's subsequent lack of attention to the topic reflected a man with an inquiring mind that sometimes lacked the ability to concentrate and follow up. Frank Valeo, who had worked on the SFRC staff and later as assistant to Majority Leader Mike Mansfield, recalled that Gore "had his own way of getting interested for a brief period of time, and posing and displaying great erudition in regard to the problem, and then kind of dropping and leaving it."[69] His mind constantly worked on many different levels, oftentimes leapfrogging from one interesting topic to another. There was so much to learn, and world population really would not become a significant issue until the 1970s.

Gore's focus on foreign relations reflected his desire to solidify his credentials in this area to further his national ambitions. He remained pessimistic about his chances for the presidency for many reasons. Apparently concurring was National Democratic Party chairman Paul Butler, who apologized for saying that "it was not in the cards for a Southerner to be nominated in 1960." Still, Butler admitted that "I don't see anything in the cards that indicates that I was wrong."[70]

Gore agreed with Butler. He wrote to one person that "though with some fortune it may have been possible for me to have been in strong contention, the chances of the Party selecting its candidate from south of the Mason-Dixon Line appeared too remote. There I took the position a long time ago which is still my position: 'I am not a candidate and do not expect to be.'" However, he complained that he resented "both sectional and religious prejudice in our national politics. But, as you know, the Democratic Party has not nominated a Southerner for President since the Civil War. This is unjustified and some day it will be broken, the sooner the better, but I concluded that it was now most unlikely."[71]

The major obstacle to a southern presidential nomination remained civil rights. Events on several fronts in 1960 refocused attention on the issue. Following highly publicized sit-down strikes in several southern cities, civil rights proponents in Congress led by Senator Paul Douglas introduced new legislation that included new criminal penalties for obstruction of federal court orders and required that officials record federal election returns for use by the U.S. attorney general. Other provisions included the right of federal judges to appoint special referees to register black voters in areas where the government had certified the existence of a pattern of discrimination.[72]

As before, a vocal group of Gore's constituents opposed the bill. In February 1960, a constituent told Gore that "the Liberal national attitude of yourself and Senator Kefauver is a great disappointment to most of the white people of Tennessee . . . We hold you and others like you responsible for the present racial strife created by the lunch counter sit down strike by the Negroes." Despite such vehement denunciations, Gore took a similar stance as in 1957 by promising to eliminate objectionable provisions while supporting the thrust of the bill.[73]

In the Senate debate, Gore supported reducing direct references to segregation by backing language that imposed criminal penalties on obstruction or interference with any court order. He opposed larger grants of punitive powers to the attorney general and wanted to restrict the power of the president to appoint federal voter enrollment officers. However, he agreed that "using, importing, or transporting" explosives for the destruction of any building or vehicle should be a federal offense. He also vigorously defended efforts to protect voting rights and backed the idea of extending the voting record maintenance to primaries and special elections rather than only federal ones.[74] After 400 hours of debate in the Senate, which included an uninterrupted 125-hour filibuster, a compromise bill developed that Gore supported. While accepting several of the major parts of the legislation, the final bill removed explicit focus on southern states and segregationist crimes. Proponents of civil rights attacked the final bill as "a victory for the old South," and Thurgood Marshall, NAACP counsel, called the act "not worth the paper it was printed on."[75]

His moderate position on civil rights kept Gore's name in the news as a possible Democratic candidate as the campaign cycle began. Russell Baker wrote an article about Gore's ambitions for the vice presidency. "As the junior Senator from Tennessee, Gore, a not-too-Southern liberal who is not too liberal for the South, has been systematically toiling to remind the Democratic kingmakers that besides being acceptable all around he is capable of bringing considerable distinction to the ticket." He talked about the self-described "combative hillbilly" who was "an activist who is easily irritated by appeals to settle for little rather than risk losing all in a cloud of gunsmoke." "Some say he has a talent for picking colorless or profitless causes" and that he lacks one important quality for reaching the "political pinnacle—sheer dumb luck." Still, Baker made it clear that this was a man to watch.[76]

Gore denied Baker's claim, but he remained a Democratic trooper. He spoke in early May at the National Democratic Club in New York City. "Out of concern for our two party system, I suggest at Chicago in July the Republicans have a trial run between the 'old' Nixon and the 'new' Nixon." He also argued that the Republican Party "holds that those who have, by one means or another, amassed economic power, are best qualified to say what is best for the rest of the people." Democrats needed to offer alternatives to the selfishness and unbridled greed.[77]

He also visited other important Democratic constituencies. In early June, he spoke to the United Jewish Appeal in Chicago and argued that a settlement of the Arab-Israeli controversy was possible if the Arab states renounced their vow to drive the Jews into the ocean. He highlighted his meetings with Israeli prime minister David Ben Guirion and Egyptian president Gamal Nasser during visits to the region which helped him "realize that the resolution of the Arab-Israeli dispute, now so bitter as to constitute a continuing life or death struggle, would be in the interest of both sides and, indeed, that such a settlement is essential if the economic potential of the area is to be realized and if there is to be any real hope for enduring political stability." He acknowledged it would require time and good-faith negotiations to achieve peace and guarantee that Israel remained "a shining example of the concept of democracy and individual freedom."[78]

Gore's best efforts to position himself for the vice presidency were for naught. When the convention opened in Los Angeles in July, the party solidified behind Senator John F. Kennedy. While talk of Gore joining the ticket persisted, Kennedy ultimately settled on Johnson. He made a very calculated decision, hoping to win the border states with a choice who had a good reputation as a centrist and ample name recognition.[79] In contrast, Gore lacked the national recognition and had a maverick and populist streak. With Johnson, the ticket was solid, and Gore wholeheartedly backed it.

The Tennessean immediately went to work for Kennedy. They liked each other, although Kennedy had been angry over Gore's role in Kefauver's nomination for vice president in 1956. Gore admired Kennedy and considered him an intelligent, charismatic centrist who could lead the country. The Massachusetts senator respected Gore and his willingness to tackle difficult and complex issues of national interest. While they had not been great friends during their time in the Senate, mutual respect and shared common values brought them together. Differences developed over specific issues during Kennedy's presidency, but Gore remained an ally on many occasions.

Almost immediately, Kennedy asked Gore to serve on a special election committee consisting of Fulbright, Clark Clifford, Dick Bolling, and Fred Button. They were to examine the issues, submit speeches, and make recommendations regarding Nixon's moves. Each had his specialties, such as Fulbright on foreign policy or Gore on economic and nuclear issues.[80] They set about gathering materials and making them available to the Democratic nominee.

Some speculated that such efforts would propel Gore forward in the party leadership, and some Democrats believed he would make a good replacement for Johnson as Senate majority leader. Gore was not so sure, writing a friend: "This is one job . . . which I would not want. I do not have the faculty for easy compromise, which appears necessary for a good majority leader."[81] He was right, and the push never gained much momentum.

On the campaign trail, Gore defended the Democrats' choice of Kennedy in the face of constituent opposition. One wrote that "you and Mr. Kefauver deserted your section of the country . . . by aiding and abetting those who intend to integrate Negroes . . . and now you would desert your religion and that of the majority of the people of your state and endorse integration of church and state by standing up for Mr. Kennedy." She promised to vote Republican for the first time because "I hold honor, my country and God far above a mere political party."[82]

Gore responded quickly to such criticisms. "I have served with Senator Kennedy and Senator Johnson. They are outstanding men, fully capable of providing the necessary leadership we need in the critical years ahead." When a Nashville Baptist minister attacked Kennedy's Catholicism, Gore replied that "upon a number of occasions, Senator Kennedy has stated clearly and emphatically that, if elected President, his decisions will be based solely upon what is in the best interest of the United States and that he will in no sense be dictated to or otherwise influenced by, the hierarchy of his church." He went on to argue that no person should be denied the ability to hold public office because of his religious affiliation. Still, Gore recognized the potential of the religious question. "A goodly number of people may well be influenced in their votes because of this religious question," he told reporters. "I hope it will not be a major fact, but in some areas it will."[83]

Gore had difficulty understanding his constituents' opposition to Kennedy, whom he characterized as "intelligent, witty, gracious, handsome and eloquent." Nixon, by contrast, was "deficient in grace or charm, unprepossessing in appearance, plebeian in intellect, and painfully humorless." He recognized, however, that Nixon "had a certain chauvinistic energy, a cunning shrewdness, an instinct for the narrow prejudice" that would appeal to the "rough-and-ready element, the social conservatives, and the economic royalists." This also meant that he would have influence with the religious fundamentalists and the segregationists in the South.[84]

Many shared his view of Nixon, including Sam Rayburn, who stressed that "he has a hateful face, the worst face of anyone I ever served with." During the campaign, he complained about Nixon on television. "Look at what they're doing, putting someone like him on that machine. It's all going to be like that Checkers speech, trying to trick people into electing him. They're going to try and trick people into making him President."[85]

Gore remained optimistic as he wrote Gene Graham at the *Tennessean* that "the image of Jack Kennedy as a fighter for the right things seems to be shining through," contrasting it with the Republican record of obstructionism. Yet he had some worries. "Our situation in Tennessee disturbs me quite much. You know about a lot of foot-dragging in the last two campaigns when the Republicans carried the state. I hope there will be no repetition of this. We need the right leadership for the campaign."[86]

Gore labored tirelessly to help carry Tennessee for the Democratic ticket, planning speaking engagements in key areas of the state for Kennedy and Johnson and helping prep Kennedy for the debates. He hammered Nixon whenever and wherever possible. In mid-October, he wrote Kennedy: "You are ahead and on the ascendancy. Public welfare requires your victory," and encouraged Kennedy to brand Nixon as "rash, reckless," especially under pressure. Gore also urged the nominee to "increase emphasis on jobs, minimum wages, . . . high interest rates and cost of living," as well as "price rises by monopolists which result in exorbitant profits and unjustified internal financing."[87]

On election day in November, the hard work paid dividends. Kennedy won by a narrow margin in the popular vote and 303 to 219 in the electoral college. Again, Tennessee went to the Republicans by a slim majority, but Gore and others rejoiced in the national victory. "Congratulations. I am confident that your administration will be successful and great. If I can contribute in any small way, command me," Gore wrote the president-elect immediately after the victory.[88]

Gore's service during Eisenhower's second term had been eventful. Several times he found himself involved directly in the battle over civil rights, which in large part led to a spirited contest with Cooper for the nomination in 1958. Increasingly, he became involved in matters of taxes, interest rates, and the economy through his service on the Senate Finance Committee. He achieved his goal of winning a seat on the Senate Foreign Relations Committee, throwing him into a prestigious circle of policymakers. While his ambitions fell flat in his quest for the vice presidency, he had accumulated a substantial amount of power in a relatively short time. With the Democrats returning to the White House and controlling Congress, the upcoming session appeared a very bright one for progressives and liberals in the Democratic Party.

# 6  LIVING IN CAMELOT

"I HAD BEEN galled by the laissez-faire politics of President Eisenhower, and I enjoyed thinking that by my fights in the Senate I had forged the economic issues on which my friend Kennedy had largely been elected," Gore wrote. "With my friend in the White House, I was brimming with enthusiasm to get to work in the Senate."[1] Throughout the country, others shared his optimism that the young, vibrant, charismatic John F. Kennedy, with his charming wife and influential family, would make a difference in their lives.

Gore and other progressive and liberal Democrats believed that the new president would reverse many of the Eisenhower administration's policies on civil rights, taxes, interest rates, and foreign relations. For three years, Gore found himself in the middle of numerous battles, more times than not as a supporter of the president. He continued to gain stature as a Democratic spokesperson, although his maverick personality became more dominant as his ambitions for higher office faded. However, by 1963, that optimism had wilted in the face of Kennedy's assassination and growing unrest in the United States and on the front lines of the cold war in places like Vietnam.

Despite his cooperation with Kennedy during the election, Gore initially found himself in conflict with the president-elect. John Kenneth Galbraith and other prominent advisers had pushed for Gore to be appointed Treasury secretary. Gore admitted being flattered but said he loved the Senate and wanted to stay. Instead, he pressed for a good Democrat who backed tax reform and lower interest rates.[2] In Gore's opinion, Kennedy made a terrible choice when he promoted Eisenhower's undersecretary of state, Douglas Dillon, to head the Treasury Department. The Republican financier had strong ties to Wall Street and large business interests. According to Theodore Sorenson, Kennedy's choice "reassured many leaders of finance" but "annoyed many leaders of both parties." Gore protested that Dillon was an "affable easy goer" at a time the country needed a visionary.[3]

Gore's disagreement created tensions with Kennedy and his advisers. The Tennessean speculated later that Kennedy chose Dillon because he "had an awesome regard or a kind of mythical respect for the financier and big businessman," partly due to the enormous influence of his father, Joseph Kennedy.[4]

More likely, Kennedy made the choice because he also had close ties to Wall Street and the Boston financial empires. As a result, his economic policies often resembled Republican orthodoxy more than those of the liberal and progressive wing of the Democratic Party.

Gore's disagreement with Kennedy did not compare to one brewing between Gore and Johnson. In January 1961, the newly elected Senate majority leader, Mike Mansfield, proposed allowing Johnson to preside over the Senate Democratic Caucus meetings. Several senators, led by Paul Douglas (D-IL) and Joe Clark (D-PA), denounced the power grab. Gore joined the chorus by telling Johnson that "this caucus is not open to former senators." A heated exchange followed, and numerous accusations and barbs flew, with Gore throwing his share at Johnson. Mansfield assistant Frank Valeo recalled that Gore's "face was flushed with indignation beneath the neat and orderly waves of gray hair, and his speech was slow and deliberate as he released his words in a prolonged drawl, intensifying the agony that they seemed intended to inflict on Lyndon Johnson." Despite Gore's protests, the proposal passed 46–17. Still, Gore noted that "you could feel the heavy animosity in the room, even from many who voted for Lyndon."[5]

Afterward, an infuriated Johnson told one person that "I now know the difference between a caucus and a cactus. In a cactus all the pricks are on the outside." While Johnson had won, he recognized it as a hollow victory, and he never tried to exercise even nominal control over the caucus. Kennedy, however, called Gore the next day to congratulate him for doing the right thing. Gore believed that "obviously, he would not wish to have to approach the Senate through Johnson."[6]

While the bureaucratic battles continued and the new administration matured, Gore returned to taxes and reining in the power of big business. There were several clashes, but one of the more memorable developed when Gore went after the business hierarchy in early 1961. He concentrated on corporations' widespread use of stock options to compensate chief executives, a tactic designed to avoid paying income taxes in favor of the lower capital gains taxes. He targeted Thomas J. Watson Jr. of IBM, who had received $4 million in restricted stock options since 1956. While acknowledging that some people said it was impossible to become a millionaire under the current tax system, Gore retorted: "How wrong they are. There are many beaten paths to virtually overnight multi-million-dollar fortunes for the insiders of our large corporations. A restricted stock option requires neither capital nor risk, nor taxes; it is a free ride." In response, he proposed S.1625, which called for amendment of the Internal Revenue Code of 1954 to "terminate the special tax treatment now accorded certain employee stock options."[7]

Gore's efforts prompted a quick response from many, including New York governor Nelson Rockefeller. In a speech to an IBM group, he commented that he had read "that a certain southern Senator is advising us in New York State what we ought to do. Maybe he is a little worried about the competition up here." Despite the criticisms, Gore remained steadfast. In a speech to the Tax Executives Institute in late May, he battled back by emphasizing that the United States needed "a proper distribution of the fruits of economy, for political democracy and the non-stratification of society will hardly survive without it." To illustrate his point, he quoted Adam Smith: "The subjects of every state ought to contribute toward the support of the government, as nearly as possible, in proportion to their respective abilities; that is, in proportion to the revenue which they respectively enjoy under the protection of the state."[8]

Not long after, Gore took on an industrial giant regarding taxes. He created a controversy when he challenged a tax bill designed by Delaware's congressional delegation. The Delaware congressmen had constructed a bill allowing tax relief for DuPont after a federal court judge ordered the corporation to divest some stocks in an antitrust case involving General Motors.[9] Gore attacked the plan as the "duPont tax relief bill" and stressed that the bill would not protect the small stockholder but mainly the members of the family and corporate executives, all the while denying the Treasury hundreds of millions of dollars. He asked if it was ethical for Congress to influence the outcome of a case, worrying aloud that it could repeat such actions in suits involving civil rights, bankruptcies, and consumer protection.[10]

As Gore led the charge, the DuPont Corporation counterattacked by orchestrating a letter-writing campaign that asked: "Why do you want to unjustly tax thousands of innocent investors in Dupont and General Motors Company?" One of Gore's constituents complained that Tennessee had seven DuPont plants that poured more than $61.5 million into the state. "I find it hard to believe that you want to penalize the very same stockholders who have invested millions of dollars in this state," he chastised. Despite the pressure, Gore stood firm. He took the offensive on the Senate floor, telling his colleagues that "I believe that the pressure for the passage of the bill does not come from taxpayers in the 20-percent bracket, or the zero bracket retired workers, widows, or orphans, unless they have been misled, but comes from the corporation officials and the high tax bracket stockholders."[11] He noted that even those taxed in the 30 percent bracket would pay less than $50 in taxes under the settlement.

As with many previous tax battles against special interests, Gore lost. As the bill reached the White House, Gore urged Kennedy to veto it, but to no avail. He wrote a constituent afterward: "Though the battle on the DuPont tax relief bill was lost, I believe that as time passes my position will be vindicated. I shall continue my efforts to eliminate the loopholes of tax favoritism."[12]

Gore rarely won battles to close the loopholes or prevent massive government handouts to corporations such as DuPont. So why would he continue to challenge the large vested interests? Mainly because deep down he was an idealist who believed that if he fought the powerful, ultimately there would be victories like those that had been won by the progressive reformers of the early twentieth century. What he failed to realize was that the many so-called liberals leading the Democratic Party wanted to avoid class conflict and had significant ties of their own to big business. They wanted to create a bigger pie rather than divide the existing portions more equitably. Politically, this was a more attractive course and allowed men such as Robert McNamara or Dillon to work easily within the administration. Yet Gore continued to believe that he eventually would change the minds of enough Americans and their representatives to secure victory. At the least, he thought that by battling big business elites he was doing the right thing, and that mattered as much as victory.

While tax battles drained his energy, Gore was drawn quickly into President Kennedy's efforts to change U.S. foreign policy. One of Kennedy's first reforms was the creation of the Peace Corps, an organization he envisioned as populated by idealistic, educated Americans taking their knowledge and expertise to the nonindustrialized world to showcase American ideals. Building on the critiques William Lederer and Eugene Burdick had made in their book *The Ugly American* (1958), Kennedy had complained that the U.S. diplomatic service was "ill-chosen, ill-equipped, and ill-briefed" while the Russians sent out doctors, teachers, and others to places in need. With the Peace Corps, Kennedy hoped to counter the image of the "ugly American." Volunteers would become front-line soldiers in the struggle for the hearts and minds of the people of the third world.[13]

Once in office, Kennedy selected his brother-in-law, Sargent Shriver, to lead the crusade. To circumvent congressional battles over the issue, the president signed an executive order in early March that created the Peace Corps and gave the organization a start-up budget of $1.5 million from his discretionary funds and office space in the Maiatico Office Building. Shriver recruited experts on organization-building, including Franklin Williams (California's first African American assistant attorney general) and Bill Moyers, one of Johnson's assistants. Soon, they began setting up standards and goals for the Peace Corps.[14]

Gore and his family became thoroughly intertwined with the Peace Corps as his daughter Nancy became one of the first twelve staff members. She fit the mold of the prototypical Peace Corps volunteer, a well-educated, bright, idealistic, dedicated, and enthusiastic person with a keen understanding of politics. She joined the group without asking about the salary and eventually became Moyers's chief assistant. Over time, she became an integral part of the institution, leading one observer to describe her as the "Peace Corps' resident Scarlett O'Hara and female political sage."[15]

Shriver went to great lengths to win Gore's support, especially since he was a member of the Senate Foreign Relations Committee. The permanent appropriations battle for the organization developed in the late spring, and Hubert Humphrey encouraged Shriver to reach out to Gore. "Albert's a fine senator, very distinguished, hard-working," he observed, "but Albert's a loner; Albert's a maverick. So he'll need a little loving." He instructed: "I want all of you at the Peace Corps to love Albert. Go to his office. Sit down dutifully. Take notes on what he's saying. As soon as you get back to your office, call him and thank him for the points he made—A, B, and C—about how to get the Peace Corps legislation through . . . I don't care if his darling daughter does work at the Peace Corps. Albert's very independent and this is what you'll have to do to make sure of his vote."[16]

It was an easy sale; Gore had tired of a U.S. policy that relied heavily on military efforts that sowed the seeds of repression. He genuinely believed in the nobility of the Peace Corps. When asked whether he would support making the Peace Corps permanent, Gore responded affirmatively that "with careful planning and determination, the Peace Corps can complement our foreign aid program." As a result, he cosponsored the legislation that created a lasting agency in June 1961.[17] The appropriations bill passed easily, and the Peace Corps became a very popular organization.

In another area of foreign relations, Gore found himself in the middle of a major controversy. Relations between the United States and Cuba had deteriorated since Fidel Castro seized power in 1959 and expelled the U.S. military mission, executed hundreds of former Batista supporters, implemented land reform, and limited the profits of American-dominated electric and telephone companies. He also began negotiating with the Venezuelans and the Soviets for aid to end Cuba's dependence on the United States. By January 1960, Eisenhower called Castro a "mad man . . . who is going wild and harming the whole

American structure." Soon after, the president gave the CIA a green light to start training Cuban exiles to overthrow Castro.[18]

Kennedy had inherited the Eisenhower administration's plan to overthrow Castro. On April 17, 1961, more than a thousand Cuban exiles landed at the Bay of Pigs and tried to establish a beachhead to await a massive uprising that would overthrow Castro. From the start, the invasion went badly; poor choices of location and bad luck pinned down the rebels. After a short time, Castro's army and air force crushed the uprising, thoroughly embarrassing the Kennedy administration once its complicity became apparent.[19]

The day after the failed operation, Gore visited Kennedy at the White House, recounting that "his hair was disheveled, his tie askew, and his eyes sleepy; I had never seen him like that. He seemed relieved to have a friend to talk to, and he told me the fantastic story." The report surprised the senator, but he listened as Kennedy intensely criticized General Lyman Lemnitzer, chairman of the Joint Chiefs of Staff (JCS), who had advised that the plan was feasible without U.S. air cover. Once the Cubans disembarked, the general reported that the mission would fail unless Kennedy provided air support. The president believed that Lemnitzer and other JCS members had hoped to paint him into a corner to ensure U.S. military intervention. Gore reported that "with colorful language, he said he would never again rely on Lemnitzer's advice." Later, the president told Sorenson: "All my life I've known better than to depend on the experts. How could I have been so stupid to let them go ahead?"[20]

Gore went to the defense of the president in the aftermath of the debacle. Kennedy convened a special commission headed by General Maxwell Taylor while Fulbright called for an SFRC inquiry. In one of the first meetings of the committee in early May, Gore questioned Richard Bissell, one of the chief CIA operatives involved in the operation. During an exchange, Gore emphasized that the "Communists played a very shrewd and effective game" in Latin America, "capitalizing upon the poverty of the masses, and it is horrible."[21] But he maintained that there was much more to solving the problem than merely plotting an invasion by Cuban exiles.

As Lemnitzer testified, Gore asked if the general had advised President Kennedy that the Bay of Pigs invasion was "a feasible military operation without U.S. planes." Lemnitzer initially denied the charge, but Fulbright reminded him, "General, I was there and heard you say it." At that point, the general admitted it, although he denied supporting the plan that the CIA had implemented.[22] As Gore walked out for a lunch recess, he commented to a reporter:

"I have reached the conclusion of my own that we definitely need a new chairman of the Joint Chiefs of Staff and new members."[23]

A political firestorm immediately erupted as headlines blared, "Gore Demands Lemnitzer Be Fired." The JCS and its allies responded quickly, denouncing Gore for undermining the country's confidence in the military. Senators such as Homer Capehart (R-IN) defended the JCS, although Senator Frank Church (D-ID) argued that the Pentagon and CIA shared the blame for advising that "the plan was feasible." Gore refused to retreat, emphasizing that "I had reserved judgment until I heard from the chairman himself."[24]

The most vocal criticism came from within the Pentagon. Secretary of Defense Robert McNamara sent Gore a curt note claiming: "I am responsible for the operations of the Department and for the actions of all of the military and civilian personnel assigned to the Department . . . Any errors are my errors, whatever deficiencies are charged to the Department should be charged to me and no one else . . . The Joint Chiefs are intelligent, experienced, dedicated men. I have confidence in their abilities and consider it an honor to serve with them."[25]

Some Tennessee constituents also hammered Gore. One accused him of trying "to curry favor with the Kennedy administration by blaming Joint Chiefs of Staff instead of the true culprits, the liberals and Stevenson." Gore responded that after hearing the JCS testimony he concluded the advice was poor: "Confidence in the military leadership of this country is essential but this confidence must be earned."[26]

Ultimately, his loyalty to Kennedy required Gore to take one for the team. General Curtis LeMay and several other high-ranking officers threatened to resign unless Kennedy made a public statement that contradicted Gore's assessment. The Tennessean knew he had Lemnitzer's admission and Kennedy's assessment on his side, but the former was classified and he refused to put the president on the spot. He told the president that he understood and that "I'll take it." Kennedy, appreciating the gesture, had McNamara investigate some overspending by the Pentagon. It was a bitter pill to swallow, but Gore did it.

Despite the setback, Gore remained unrepentant in other ways. When Kennedy appointed Taylor to act as a special military representative to the president, Gore gloated. He wrote an editor in Paris, Tennessee: "Incidentally, the President's appointment of General Maxwell Taylor yesterday tended to confirm my assessment of the quality of military advice that he has received from the Chiefs of Staff, not only in the unfortunate Cuban affair, but in other instances about which I know."[27]

Although he lodged some criticisms against Kennedy over Cuba, primarily regarding the exchange of agricultural goods for prisoners, Gore typically supported the president on foreign policy. They agreed on efforts in Laos, foreign aid, the "Food for Peace Program," nuclear testing, and the Alliance for Progress, although Gore feared the latter might "widen the gap between the very rich very few."[28] He supported the president in full during the Berlin crisis of early June 1961. Soviet president Nikita Khrushchev had informed Kennedy that he intended to turn over control of access points to Berlin to the East Germans and effectively quarantine the city unless the Western powers relinquished control of their sectors of the city. Administration officials characterized the action as a "simple conflict of wills," and Kennedy announced that Berlin was "not an isolated problem. The threat is worldwide . . . [in] our own hemisphere . . . [or] wherever else the freedom of human beings is at stake."[29]

Throughout the crisis, Gore backed Kennedy. He wrote one constituent that "we will not abandon them as an island in a communist sea. The maintenance of freedom in Berlin is thus symbolic of the struggle for freedom everywhere." To another who had criticized Kennedy's defeatist attitude, he responded that "we have, among other things, taken action to strengthen our military forces and have announced forthrightly our position of firmness with respect to Berlin."[30] In almost every area, Gore supported the president's decisions until the crisis subsided at the end of 1961.

Despite agreement over standing steadfast against the Russians in Berlin, tensions remained between Gore and the president over the third world. As chairman of the SFRC subcommittee on Africa, Gore visited the continent in September and October 1962. Traveling with Pauline, several senators, and Carl Marcy of the SFRC, Gore stopped in Libya, Sudan, Ethiopia, Kenya, Morocco, Rhodesia, Nigeria, and Liberia. On his return, he issued a statement for the committee that aid should be provided only to those respecting basic human rights and complained that "there are other states in Africa receiving United States assistance which do not, in our opinion, measure up to the minimum standards of free societies."[31]

The issue of Africa and Gore's interest in backing democracy brought him into conflict with Kennedy, his predecessor as chairman of the SFRC subcommittee on Africa. The administration supported building a huge dam on the Volta River in Ghana. Gore characterized the decision as "the wrong kind of aid and in the wrong place." He considered Ghana's government undemocratic and disliked its president, Kwame Nkrumah, who had visited Moscow and praised Khrushchev for supporting oppressed peoples. "[The] principal beneficiaries will be Nkrumah and his clique and the huge U.S. corporations (Kaiser and Reynolds) which have sponsored it. It will produce a million kilowatts of electricity in a country which now uses 40,000 kilowatts."[32]

Gore's opposition led to a confidential letter from Kennedy. "After the most careful consideration of this complicated problem, I have decided to go ahead with the project," the president wrote, arguing that if he opposed the project it "would take on anti-African rather than anti-Nkrumah overtones." Kennedy wanted to fortify moderates by demonstrating that the United States backed strengthening the ability of Africans to support themselves. He called the $25 million a modest investment to assure leverage in Ghana rather than "an endorsement of president Nkrumah." Gore remained skeptical, and he made one last plea in February 1962 to Kennedy to stop the plan, but the president ignored it.[33]

Gore and Kennedy united in the spring of 1962 to challenge the steel industry. A battle had been brewing for some time after the major steel companies announced their intention to raise prices in response to wage boosts. Gore worried about a serious inflationary effect on the economy because the increases would affect major industries including automobiles, farm equipment, and defense. He charged that the steel industry was a monopoly and that its leaders believed in "private enterprise, not free enterprise"; he even suggested that the "large steel companies can and should be broken up into smaller units so that true competition may be restored."[34]

Ultimately, the administration helped lower the demands of the labor unions in contract negotiations. In return, Kennedy believed he had received a promise from the industry not to raise prices. However, U.S. Steel chairman Roger Blough visited Kennedy on April 10, 1962, and told him that he was about to increase the price of a ton of steel by six dollars. Soon, the other companies followed his lead.[35] Kennedy was livid because he believed that Blough and his allies had reneged on the deal that promised no price increases and help for all efforts at price stabilization. One of his aides, Arthur Schlesinger Jr., described Kennedy's reaction as a "mixture of incredulity over what he saw as the selfishness and stupidity of the steel industry and anger over what he regarded as its premeditated deceit." The president remarked, "My father always told me that all businessmen were sons-of-bitches, but I never believed it till now."[36]

The White House went on the offensive. Kennedy ordered the Justice Department to investigate whether the action violated antitrust laws. At the same time, the Department of Defense and Agency for International Development began planning to purchase steel from domestic and foreign companies that had refused to follow the industry's lead. Within a short period of time, Kennedy gave a nationally televised news conference blasting the steel companies for endangering the economy and for not having "a higher sense of business responsibility for the welfare of their country."[37]

Part of the offensive required legislative action. The same night that Blough delivered his news, fourteen-year-old Al received a call from the White House. He contacted his parents at a reception and asked his father to return home to talk to the president. Once there, Gore recalled that the president was "unusually agitated, mad as hops." He told him about Blough's decision, stressing it would destroy his price stabilization program. "Now this **** undertakes on his own to undo it all," Kennedy complained. Then, he asked for Gore's help in organizing opposition in the Senate, which Gore was happy to provide. Young Al came up to his father after having listened to the conversation on an extension and exclaimed, "Whew! Dad, I didn't know a President talked like that!"[38]

Gore immediately sprang into action. This was his kind of fight, against greedy corporations trying to gouge the consumer and hurt the country. The next day he attended a White House reception where he located allies and asked them to make speeches criticizing the steel industry and its audacity for endangering national security. Most agreed, and many worked late into the night with the assistance of Gore and his assistant Bill Allen to prepare their addresses.[39]

On April 12, Gore and his allies rose to the Senate floor and unleashed a heavy barrage on the steel companies. He denounced the industry for working in collusion to increase prices. Gore went so far as to advocate regulation of steel prices in a manner similar to public utility prices. Others pushed for an "Emergency Steel Act of 1962" that would roll back prices to April 9 levels.[40]

Initially, the steel industry fought back. Blough denounced "retaliatory attacks" and claimed that "never before in the nation's history have so many forces of the Federal Government been marshaled against a single industry."[41] Ultimately, the White House and congressional pressure combined with strong public disapproval led Bethlehem Steel to rescind the price increase. The other companies followed soon after, and most of Gore's constituents applauded him for his efforts.

While some of his constituents may have liked his position on steel, Gore's next major stand in favor of the Kennedy administration's policies produced a loud outcry in Tennessee. In January 1961, the University of Mississippi denied admission to an African American veteran of the U.S. Air Force, James Meredith. With the encouragement of Medgar Evers of the Mississippi NAACP,

Meredith filed suit. Ultimately, the Fifth Circuit Court found that he had been rejected "solely because he was a Negro" and ordered his admission.[42]

In response, the segregationists planned massive resistance. Led by Mississippi governor Ross Barnett, they wanted to block Meredith entrance.[43] It would take Kennedy's efforts to ensure his enrollment. On September 26, Barnett and Kennedy reached an agreement whereby Barnett agreed to respect the court order but only after Kennedy promised to have a federal marshal pull his gun and point it at the governor to allow him a public show of resistance. However, when the time came, a bloody riot ensued as protestors attacked the administration building guarded by federal marshals and national guardsmen. Carrying rifles, bricks, and Molotov cocktails, they yelled, "Go to Cuba, nigger lovers," and "You nigger-lovers, go to hell!" Ultimately the troops fired tear gas; by dawn, two were dead and hundreds wounded.[44]

On October 1, 1962, Meredith entered classes to the taunts of "that blood is on your hands, nigger bastard." More than 23,000 federal troops descended on Oxford to keep order, leading to loud denunciations throughout the region of another military occupation of the South. Most blamed the violence on Meredith and some carefully orchestrated Communist plan to create the unrest. Many praised Barnett. Senator Russell told an audience in Birmingham that he supported "the great and courageous governor of Mississippi" and that "it is regretful that we have no one in the Supreme Court that recognizes the fundamentals of democracy."[45]

Many of Gore's constituents shared Russell's opinion. "In view of what happened at 'Ole Miss' at Oxford Miss.," one wrote, "I ask you to help and work for the impeachment of the Warren-Court, President John F. Kennedy, and Attorney General Robert Kennedy." "It is an outrage, in my opinion, an Irish upstart can threaten to shed the blood of honest citizens of the Sovereign State of Mississippi," she complained, adding, "Even liberals, ellected [sic] from southern states to the Senate should not condone the nefarious actions of the would be dictators."[46]

Despite overwhelming opposition at home, Gore publicly defended Kennedy. In response to letters, he wrote that "ours is a government of law rather than of men. We must keep it so. In the final analysis, it is incumbent upon all citizens to obey and respect the law and the decisions of our courts . . . Above all, officials of our government, whether Federal, state, or local, have the responsibility and duty to take whatever action may be necessary and appropriate to preserve law and order and to prevent violence, anarchy, and bloodshed."[47]

Most Americans, especially civil rights supporters, commended the use of federal troops at Oxford, and Gore later emphasized that "the incident at Oxford represented a turning point, signaling the end of the era in which the threat of mob violence and state interposition could actually prevent the enforcement of federal court orders." He praised Kennedy for his decisive action and blamed Barnett and his allies for causing the problems. To him, they confirmed every negative southern stereotype and provided a form of leadership that split the South, playing into the hands of the Bourbon elites who wanted to keep the classes divided. He recalled in 1972 that "given the paranoia of Mississippi's leaders . . . there was nothing that could be done to rescue the state, and it still remains America's South Africa."[48]

No sooner had the Ole Miss incident quieted than another serious crisis arose. On October 14, U-2 spy photographs revealed the presence of Russian nuclear missiles in Cuba. Two days later, when he received the information on the sites, Kennedy exclaimed that Khrushchev "can't do this to me." Soon after, his brother Robert added: "Oh shit! Shit! Shit! Those sons of bitches Russians."[49]

Kennedy immediately convened a meeting of the executive committee of the National Security Council (which became known as ExComm). The meetings took place in complete secrecy. On the first day, the options proposed included air strikes and an invasion. Others led by Adlai Stevenson and Robert Kennedy proposed a blockade. By October 22, Kennedy went on national television and announced a blockade to prevent any additional missiles from reaching the island. The nation waited and wondered how the Soviets would respond, while some anticipated Armageddon.

Throughout the confrontation, Gore supported the president. He wrote his constituents that the Communists controlled Cuba and threatened the United States. "The Congress, has, by resolution," he noted, "tendered its overwhelming support of whatever action, including military action, the President may deem necessary in the interest of national security." He proudly boasted, "I helped draft this resolution, and I supported it."[50]

For two weeks in October, the two countries hovered near war. Proposals flew back and forth between Moscow and Washington. Fortunately, moderates on both sides carried the day. In return for a pledge not to invade Cuba, Kennedy received Khrushchev's promise to remove the missiles. Secretly, the United States also agreed to remove its antiquated Jupiter missiles from Turkey. Robert Kennedy noted by October 28: "It looks like this is the first time I can go home feeling at ease, knowing that nothing bad can happen to my family."[51]

Hawkish Democrats and Republicans criticized Kennedy's response to the crisis. Senator Russell observed that Ho Chi Minh must have been encouraged by the fact that the United States had not bombed Cuba. He explained that a U.S. attack "would have had a very salutary effect all over the world; that would have influenced the course of events everywhere there's a contact between the free world and Communism." Gore disagreed and characterized the resolution as a victory for the United States, praising Kennedy for eliminating a military threat so close to American shores. "I think President Kennedy has acted with great courage and also with great restraint in his handling of the Cuban problem," he declared.[52]

While foreign policy issues remained important, Gore shifted his focus to taxes as 1962 ended. Since the summer, President Kennedy had been promoting a tax cut to stimulate the sluggish economy, one that proposed slashing all rates, including the highest ones, by 29 percent. Gore, of course, objected to the plan. Columnist Drew Pearson wrote that "Gore Rips Bonanza for 'Fat Cats,'" revealing that "the senator from Tennessee suggested instead that the low income groups should be given the biggest tax break. He pointed out that the fat cats would be more likely to salt their tax saving rather than spend it to stimulate the economy."[53]

Gore made his case for a different sort of tax cut. He lobbied Mansfield, arguing that "the graduated income tax is a hall-mark of a democratic society, one of the most important mechanisms by which the continuation of economic democracy, without which political democracy can hardly be expected to remain viable, is assured. That a Democratic Administration would seek to attack the graduated income tax by drastically lowering the top brackets and making the graduations less steep is unthinkable." Instead he urged that the personal exemption be increased and that the highest priority go to lowering the rate on the poor and working class.[54]

Gore battled the tax cut in other ways. Kennedy had commissioned a special blue ribbon panel of businessmen to support the measure, one headed by Henry Ford II, chairman of the board of Ford Motors. In a session of the Senate Finance Committee, Gore asked Ford whether he thought it was fair that a Ford employee making $4,000 would receive a reduction of $3 per week while an executive making $300,000 would take home an additional $50,000 a year. Ford answered, "If a man has worked his way up the organization, the reductions will be greater than for a fellow with lower pay." When pressed about the disparity, Ford told Gore that "there are always inequities in things and it's too bad, but that's the way things are."[55]

The exchange led Gore to question the foundation of the Kennedy plan. He remembered thinking: "As I studied [Ford], the thought occurred to me that except for the ingenuity and the fortune of one of his grandfathers this man might be a check-out clerk at a supermarket, or perhaps the manager of a small store after he had 'worked his way up' . . . Yet because of his gargantuan inheritance, from one of America's richest fortunes, permissible by our faulty tax laws, there he sat as chairman of one of the world's largest industrial combines, a frequent guest of the White House, prating on as if his financial position endowed him with a wisdom he must impart to Congress."[56]

Like many of Kennedy's initiatives in 1963, when his approval rating had fallen to very low levels, the tax plan temporarily stalled, leading to tensions between the president and Gore. Kennedy repeatedly called the Tennessean a "son of a bitch" at a meeting with economic advisers in late 1963 and complained bitterly that "if we get a good recession next summer, it's not going to do him much good, is it."[57] Still, as with other policies, his successor Lyndon Johnson would seize the idea and run with it after he took office in late 1963, setting the stage for a confrontation with Gore, who remained a committed foe of the plan.

The issues of taxes, civil rights, and Gore's support of Kennedy's foreign policy ensured a growing conservative backlash in Tennessee as an election neared. In late January 1963, Gore spoke at the Farragut Hotel in Knoxville as a small crowd of protestors lined the street to denounce him. The next day the editors of the conservative *Knoxville Journal* wrote about "The Two Faces of Gore." They noted that Gore knew he was in trouble and had made this trip to explain "to the public that the flaming liberal Gore in the capital is one and the same with Gore, the conservative representative of the majority of the citizens of Tennessee." They concluded that "Tennesseans are tired of electing a political Dr. Jekyll in Tennessee and then having him show up as Mr. Hyde in Washington."[58]

Even though critics at home tried to link him to the liberal establishment represented by the Kennedys, Gore made a special effort to invite the president to Tennessee to celebrate an anniversary of the TVA and the eightieth anniversary of Vanderbilt University. On May 18, Gore accompanied Kennedy as he visited several sites inaugurating new construction and then traveled to Nashville where people lined the motorcade route to Vanderbilt Stadium. Afterward, the president thanked Gore for the "generous hospitality."[59]

A real test awaited Gore when Kennedy returned to the White House. While the administration's civil rights policy had relied heavily on private initiatives and the courts in its first two years in office, the clashes at Birmingham in

1962 had led to increased calls for a federal response to combating segregation and defending voting rights. In the summer of 1963 the administration proposed the most encompassing civil rights legislation since Reconstruction. It attacked segregation by giving the attorney general the right to join civil rights suits filed by individuals and provided federal judges very broad injunctive powers and strengthened their ability to issue contempt orders against officials who interfered with desegregation.[60] A chorus of southern opposition arose immediately. The southern caucus organized "Teams of Southern Senators" with captains such as Lister Hill (D-AL), John McClellan (D-AR), and John Tower (R-TX) to develop tactics to stall the bill. They had staff coordinators to supervise each team and work to defeat the legislation. Noticeably absent were Gore and Estes Kefauver.[61]

The race issue remained relevant for Gore, especially with the 1964 Senate election approaching. One particularly angry Memphis constituent condemned Gore's recent public criticism of Alabama governor George C. Wallace for refusing to obey court orders regarding desegregation. She emphasized that Wallace was "one of your betters by far . . . the latchet of whose shoes you are not fit to tie." She complained about Kennedy's "socialist-communist advisers— Jews and negro" and added that "your attitude and your words prove your unfitness for the place you have, and also uncover the charlatan and hypocrite. We hang our heads in shame for what represents Tennessee."[62] There were growing numbers of Tennesseans, especially from the western part of the state, who shared her opinions.

As the battle on the civil rights act began, Gore tried to find some middle ground. He called the president's legislation a "strong" program but emphasized that he disagreed with several provisions, especially a section that allowed for the punishment of the whole state for the actions of one area. He realized that the resistance in Shelby County could endanger funding for the whole of Tennessee. When asked whether he would support the act, he stressed that in 1957 and 1960 "a reasonable bill emerged which I supported."[63] Civil rights legislation lost momentum as the administration focused on other issues, but it was never far below the surface.

Another controversy clearly important to Gore's Tennessee constituency developed in the summer 1963. In 1962, the Supreme Court had stopped New York's required practice of daily recitation of a prayer in school because justices argued it violated the separation-of-church-and-state clause of the First Amendment. It reaffirmed such a view when it overturned a Texas requirement for daily Bible reading and reciting the Lord's Prayer. The action set off a flurry of activity including calls for a constitutional amendment to overturn the Court's rulings and reintroduce school prayer and religious studies into the schools.[64]

Gore's constituents peppered his office with letters and telegrams condemning the Supreme Court. A Memphis woman argued that the Founding Fathers never intended such an interpretation. "Discouraging the teaching of religion to the younger generation" she believed was a Communist plot. "Surely our legislative body will not abrogate the principles on which our Constitution was based at the behest of an avowed atheist who is enjoying all the rights and privileges which stem from the very religious convictions she seeks to outlaw."[65]

Gore listened to the appeals to support a constitutional amendment reinstating school prayer as proposed by Senator Everett Dirksen (R-IL), but he refused. He responded that "as I understand it, the Court did not condemn religious activity; it simply held that government may not require a religious exercise in the public schools." He never questioned the Supreme Court's ruling and instead warned that "constitutional amendments affecting freedom of religion and separation of church and state should be approached with the greatest of caution."[66]

The school prayer issue was an opening salvo in the culture wars of the 1960s, which continued for many years. It was an especially volatile issue in Tennessee, whose Protestant evangelical majority had little understanding of or pity for the effects of school prayer on atheists and non-Christians. The supporters of school prayer could not understand how their senator would not jump at the chance to defend their traditional values, which for many included segregation and the right to bear arms. Gore, however, remained consistent in his respect for the highest court in the land and never really wavered.

During this time, Gore had to deal with personal issues. In late July, his mother passed away at the Smith County Hospital of an extended illness at the age of 84. When Kennedy expressed his sympathy on the passing of Gore's mother, Gore responded that "hers was a full, happy and useful life. Even so, there is sadness of parting and your message helped."[67]

Albert and Pauline devoted a lot of attention to their immediate family. They had helped Nancy grow into an independent and intelligent woman. She had attended Holton Arms in Washington and then Vanderbilt University, graduating in 1959. She was good at making friends, and her beauty and intelligence attracted many suitors. A friend, Jim Sasser, described her as a "free spirit" who had the "tenderest of hearts." His wife, Mary Sasser, who met Nancy as a freshman at Vanderbilt, characterized her as "a lot more sophisticated than the rest of us" because of her education and travels. Nevertheless, she called Nancy "a lot of fun" and "warm." Another college friend, Jane Holmes Dixon, called her "vivacious, entertaining."[68]

Most people who knew Nancy at Vanderbilt stressed that she was very different from the traditional southern belle who dominated the campus. She was an "individualist" who "made her own rules," Jim Sasser recalled. Another friend, Fred Graham, observed that "she had a very rebellious, smoky way about her." There were many examples of her challenging the norms, including her failure to wear the mandatory coat over shorts. She put off the required physical education requirements until near graduation, cramming them into her last summer term. On other occasions, she ignored conventions. One time, she took off to participate in the Maid of Cotton event in Chattanooga. On arriving, she exclaimed, "I'll be damned, I left my shoes in Carthage." Her escort, Bill Ray, stressed that it "didn't bother her one iota. She had on this long dress. She went across the stage barefoot."[69]

Nancy never worked very hard in the classroom, although she was a good student. She learned to speak French and loved history and government classes. Yet she showed little inclination to further her education after Vanderbilt. According to a friend, Gilbert Merritt, she "did not really like school." To him, she had an "inquiring mind" but showed little interest in studying law or seeking an advanced degree. Holmes Dixon stressed that as with most women of the time, and especially those in the South, society pushed her to get married and raise a family.[70] Like her mother, she would remain behind the scenes, helping but never venturing too far outside the established norms.

While Nancy dated a lot, she never settled down. Both in Washington and in Nashville, she believed that many of the men wanted to use her as access to her father. In 1959, however, Holmes Dixon introduced her to a fellow Mississippian, Frank Hunger, who had stopped in Nashville to say goodbye to Dixon as he headed for Taiwan as an Air Force pilot. When he saw Nancy, he was smitten. They became friends, although not until 1964 when he left the Air Force and entered Duke Law School. Their romance would blossom further, and they would marry soon after.[71]

Throughout her life, Nancy's relationship with her father was close. According to Sasser, she "worshiped her father," and Holmes Dixon observed that "he adored her." They were alike in many ways. She was a maverick who loved politics, which created a strong bond. Mary Sasser observed that Gore always treated Nancy as an equal, never talking down to her or discouraging her from choosing her own path. In fact, he often sought her counsel and asked her to run his 1964 campaign when she was only twenty-six.

There were many times when Nancy affected her father's decisions. In one instance, she helped her friend Gilbert Merritt. In 1965, the twenty-eight-year-old Vanderbilt law graduate wanted the job as U.S. district attorney for Nashville. When Merritt asked Gore for his support, the senator replied that he was "looking for someone with a little gray in their hair." Disappointed, Merritt thought he had lost the job. However, Nancy intervened and traveled to Carthage for dinner and worked in tandem with Pauline to push for Merritt. At the table, Pauline asked, "Albert, what were you doing when you were 28?" When he responded that he was the superintendent of schools, Pauline told him, "I think [Merritt] knows a lot more about being U.S. attorney than you knew about being superintendent of schools." "I know him. Nancy knows him," she added. The next day, Gore recommended Merritt for the job.[72]

Nancy did clash with her parents from time to time. They did not like her smoking, a habit she picked up in high school. To deter her, they tried suspending her car privileges and cutting her allowance, but she continued. Her drinking also bothered her parents. One night she got drunk at a Washington party. She retreated to a friend's house to sleep it off, telling her friend, "I can't go home. The Baptist [Albert] will be there!" The fear of disapproval and a normal rebelliousness influenced her relationship with her parents. She also had the added pressure of being the daughter of a well-known senator. Still, her friends emphasized that while sometimes rebellious, she carefully avoided doing anything to purposefully embarrass her parents, and the three remained close until her death in 1984.

Nancy was also extremely devoted to her brother, Al, whom she called Bo. While working at the Peace Corps she spent a lot of spare time with him. She regularly attended his football and basketball games, especially when her father and mother were out of town. One day when she took off from work, one of her co-workers questioned her dedication to the job. She did not argue and merely responded that "I have to go. St. Albans has a basketball game."[73]

Throughout her life, Al and Nancy stayed close, despite their age difference. One of Al's school friends remembered one day that Nancy showed up to talk with her brother at school. One thing that to him truly stood out about the relationship was "the warmth of it." One of Nancy's Peace Corps colleagues, Charles Peters, remarked: "She loved Al, and it was clear to me that she was filling a role."[74]

Although Nancy contributed to Al's everyday care, Pauline and Albert remained the main force in shaping their son. Instead of shipping him off to boarding school, they kept him at home. For his first three years of school, he attended an elementary school in Smith County. Starting in fourth grade, he became a student at the prestigious St. Alban's school in Washington. Pauline had selected St. Alban's because it was one of the first private schools in the area to integrate students and faculty. The choice of schools reflected an ambivalence in the Gore family. They wanted their son to know his roots, but they also sought to give him the advantages of a prestigious education. Both had high hopes for their son, whom almost everyone described as intelligent, mature, and ambitious. Mattie Lucy Payne, a housekeeper and nanny for the family, knew that "Mr. Albert had it in his mind that Al would be in the White House."[75]

Senator Gore was especially active in trying to give his son a range of experiences. As he grew up, Al frequented the Washington social scene, attending various dances and parties, but each summer Gore sent him to the farm in Tennessee to work. A friend, Hank Hillin, told one reporter that "Senator Gore was afraid he'd grow up without learning to work." Another friend whose family worked on the farm, Gordon Thompson, stressed that the senator "always told my dad if Al didn't work, he wanted to know about it."[76]

At the farm, Al awoke before dawn and began chores, which included hauling hay and feeding the animals. Several summers, he lived with the Thompson family in a house with no indoor plumbing or air conditioning. Senator Gore assigned especially arduous tasks such as clearing a hillside of brush by hand. Sometimes, there were disputes between Albert and Pauline over the treatment of their son. In one case, Gore made Al plow a steep hillside. Pauline feared that her son would be hurt and complained, "Yes, a boy could never be president if he couldn't plow with that damned hillside plow."[77] The senator remained steadfast and merely replied that it was necessary for building his character.

The discipline was often severe, and certain farmhands had permission to spank Al if he misbehaved. While Pauline never resorted to corporal punishment, choosing instead to reason with her son, the senator followed the traditions of his parents and would administer correction when he believed it necessary. To enhance the development of discipline, Al attended classes at the Castle Heights Military Academy in nearby Lebanon.[78] Senator Gore wanted to make sure his son did not become like so many of the spoiled and conceited members of the Washington and East Coast establishment.

Not everything about the summers was bad, and the future senator and vice president always spoke fondly of his time in Carthage. He was away from Washington and the pressures of being a senator's son. He raised his own cattle for sale, sometimes making a nice profit. In addition, after work, he went with friends to the Carthage swimming pool or jumped into the Caney Fork or a cow trough to cool off. He camped with friends, running electrical cords to the tent so that they could play cards until late at night. At other times, they hunted in the hills. As he matured, he hung out at the B & B Diner in Elmwood or water-skied with his friends. He also developed a close relationship with one of his friends' sisters, Donna Armistead, whom he dated through most of his time at St. Alban's.[79] The summers and vacations back home were hard, but he clearly enjoyed the life on the farm and his friends in Carthage.

Many outsiders found it difficult to understand why the senator was so hard on his son, a viewpoint shared by Pauline at various times. One person recalled that "it was horrendous," while one of his cousins from Washington who visited observed that "Al's father would just work the dickens out of him."[80] There are several explanations for why he would treat his son so harshly—in a way that many would characterize as sadistic. Senator Gore already had in mind a political career for his only son and believed that it was important for him to be able to connect with people in Tennessee and that laboring on the farm would help him understand them. At the same time, Gore wanted his son to have a good work ethic, and the farm provided an excellent way to instill it.

Gore also had been shaped by World War I, World War II, and the cold war. Many Americans believed that conflict with the Russians was inevitable. Accordingly, it was important to prepare young men for arduous military service, and Gore believed that manual labor and the accompanying discipline would help his son survive the perils that lay ahead. While this idea was less apparent, it had an influence on a whole generation of Americans and was reflected in Tennessee culture and its emphasis on sports such as football. Thus, Gore worked his son to prepare him for the future, in a manner not unlike the one that he had experienced.

Gore also made sure that he treated his son like an adult, even from the earliest stages. "His dad was always explaining stuff to him," a childhood friend observed, adding that "if Al asked a question, his dad would go into real detail. Where I would like an answer of about seven or eight words, he'd go on for fifteen minutes."[81] The conversations were typically not about sports, cars, or girls, but economics and foreign policy. The two would discuss the topics at length as Gore encouraged his son to think and learn about the world outside of the small realm of the apartment in the Fairfax Hotel or the farm in Carthage. The education went beyond conversations. Pauline recalled that "Al always listened to what his father was doing and how his father was doing it."[82] Few people had such a forum to learn about politics. It was a family business—

one that Al initially sought to avoid, although the pull into the family business ultimately proved too much.

Pauline also played a significant, although more subtle, role in her son's education. When the family had people over for dinner, she noted that "I selected guests for us; if it so happened there was a great guest who was a good conversationalist and the issue was proper for me and my son, then I would see if I could wedge Al in."[83] In many people's eyes, she appeared to be the one who pushed her son toward becoming a successful politician. She later commented to a reporter, "I always told Al that there was so much more room at the top than there was at the bottom or in the middle." One of Al's teachers, John Davis, recalled in the late 1990s that "she wanted to have her son exactly where he is now, and perhaps president."[84]

Al desired to please his parents. He was mature, and everyone around him remarked that he always wanted to try to perform well for his father and mother. The chaplain of St. Alban's described him as different from others who appeared "restless under discipline." Instead, he seemed to thrive on it, using it "for its main purpose, which is to get things done." Mattie Lucy Payne noted that "anything his daddy told him to do, he did. He was a child who always listened to his parents, never talked back to them." His mother stressed that "he never wanted to be the person to make an unhappy noise."[85] His parents imparted to him the foundations that served him in his political career, including self-discipline, the value of hard work, the importance of service, and commitment to family.

Family was important, but politics remained Gore's profession and passion. In the summer of 1963, the Nuclear Test Ban Treaty went to the Senate for approval. Since taking office, the Kennedy administration had built on Eisenhower's efforts and negotiated with the Soviet Union on the issue. Initially, Gore had played a substantial role in the matter, but Johnson, to get back at Gore over the Democratic caucus, helped orchestrate Gore's replacement by Humphrey as the chief Senate adviser on the ban.[86]

Despite the slight, Gore supported the treaty. When constituents complained that the Soviets would never respect any agreement, Gore called the ban vitally important to mankind and a step toward reducing tensions and conflict. "I think it offers hope for an end to radioactive contamination of the air all must breathe . . . it may deter the spread of nuclear weapons into the hands of other nations."[87] On the Senate floor and in the press, Gore, Fulbright, and others supported the treaty. It passed in late July 1963 by a large margin (only nineteen dissenting votes), thus putting into place significant limitations on nuclear tests in the atmosphere and underwater. Kennedy called it the first step toward "a more secure world," and he considered it one of his most important legislative victories to that point.[88]

While victorious on the Test Ban Treaty, Kennedy encountered stiff opposition from several senators, including Gore, over COMSAT, an effort to create a private corporation for a commercial satellite system. It was during this congressional battle that Gore and Tennessee suffered a major blow. While leading the resistance to COMSAT, Kefauver became ill on the Senate floor. The hard-drinking and heavy-smoking senator checked into Bethesda Naval Hospital. Doctors recommended open-heart surgery, but before it occurred, the ballooning wall of his aorta burst, and he died on August 10, just a few days past his sixtieth birthday.[89]

The loss of Kefauver was a profound one for Gore, who had visited him in the hospital. The two men had never been really close personally, although Al and Kefauver's daughter Diane had dated and were friends.[90] Gore knew about his numerous shortcomings regarding the bottle and women but never really let that influence how he related to the senior senator. Gore would miss Kefauver in many of the legislative battles, and over time it became apparent that his death had wounded Tennessee's Democratic Party, especially the progressive wing, allowing the Republicans led by Howard Baker to gain significant ground. While Kefauver's ultimate successor, Ross Bass, had much in common with Gore, he never had Kefauver's influence or political organization.

After Kefauver's death, Gore and others increasingly focused on problems in South Vietnam. Since taking office, Kennedy had tried to build up the Diem regime against intensifying attacks from the Viet Cong. The number of advisers increased from a few hundred to more than sixteen thousand. Many Americans had joined the fighting, including Special Forces troops and helicopter pilots. Despite the massive infusion of military and economic assistance, the situation continued to deteriorate.[91]

Gore issued numerous warnings to the administration about the weakness of the Diem regime and the need to develop alternative policies, including employing a model of negotiations similar to the one the superpowers had used in Laos in 1961. However, he only voiced his objections in SFRC executive sessions (which were closed to the public) or in private meetings with the president. He wanted to support the president publicly and feared aiding the enemy by demonstrating differences in Washington.

The crisis in South Vietnam intensified in fall 1963 when Buddhist leaders, tired of the nepotism and repression of the Diem regime, began protests. Violent clashes occurred in the streets and American newsmen caught many of them on tape. One of the most vivid images was the self-immolation of a Buddhist monk on a Saigon street. The act reinforced to many Americans that Diem lacked legitimacy and led to a call for a reevaluation of U.S. policy.[92]

During the Buddhist crisis, Gore became more vocal. In October, he told Secretary of Defense Robert McNamara in a session of the SFRC that he questioned the "enormous importance" the military placed on South Vietnam. "I know of no strategic material that it has, I know of nothing in surplus supply there except poor people and rice. It seems to me we have no need for either . . . Why must we suffer such great losses in money and lives for an area which seems to me unessential to our welfare, and to freedom, there being none there?"[93]

The crisis intensified when Ambassador Henry Cabot Lodge Jr. and other U.S. officials plotted with South Vietnamese army officers to overthrow Diem. The conspirators seized the president in a November 1 coup. Soon after, they executed him and set up a provisional government under the leadership of General Duong Van Minh.[94]

Gore responded to the new government by increasing his call for new policies. "I cannot speak too strongly my deep feeling that this constant and repetitive identity of the United States with military coups and repressive regimes will in the long run erode the image of the United States in many parts of the world," he told Secretary of State Dean Rusk in a November executive session of the SFRC. He emphasized that after so much effort in South Vietnam, "I am not sure we are not worse off now than we were before we supported them." However, he never went public with the suggestion, believing that he needed to support Kennedy.[95]

By November 1963, Gore's position had evolved. In 1959 when he visited South Vietnam, he thought that the problem was that the United States needed to administer its programs more effectively and push Diem toward democratic reforms. Within a relatively short period, he began to openly question, although in private, the basic principles guiding U.S. intervention in Southeast Asia and what policies might achieve success in war-torn Vietnam. In large part, this reflected his continued fear of another large U.S. military intervention close to China. His growing opposition to U.S. support of repressive military regimes drove him to ask increasingly tough questions. Furthermore, he had moved into a group of policymakers who argued that the United States had increasingly overextended itself in an effort to contain communism, weakening its commitment to vital areas of national security. His skepticism and fear of deeper U.S.

involvement would continue to grow as the new government in South Vietnam proved incapable of creating stability and order.

Gore and the nation received a shock right on the heels of the turmoil in South Vietnam. On November 22, 1963, Lee Harvey Oswald assassinated the president in Dallas. Gore, like most Americans, mourned the president's passing. When a Chattanooga resident complained about the government paying for Kennedy's funeral, he responded: "President Kennedy died in the service of his country, and I feel it is appropriate that this action be taken . . . It would be my fervent hope . . . that such a tragedy that befell president Kennedy will not strike again in our history."[96]

Grief-stricken, Gore made only one major public statement on the matter. Four days after the assassination, he rose on the Senate floor to address those who blamed all Americans for the tragedy. "I accept no blame for what that demented man did . . . I reject the mass guilt which many are trying to attribute to the entire country . . . National tragedy this has been and a national time of mourning. But a national sin? . . . No."[97]

What had begun three years earlier as a period of hope had deteriorated by November 1963 into one of despair. For the first time in six decades, violence had claimed the life of an American president. Some conservatives, especially segregationist ones, rejoiced, but Kennedy's death stunned and saddened most Americans. These included Gore, who had a good relationship with the president, albeit one marked by sharp disagreements at times. He had genuinely admired Kennedy and many of his ideas, and the president's sudden departure left a hole in the progressive and liberal wings of the Democratic Party. Into this void stepped Lyndon Johnson, which was a mixed blessing for Gore and the country.

# 7 IN THE MIDST OF THE GREAT SOCIETY AND BEYOND

DISILLUSIONMENT AND DESPAIR enveloped the country following Kennedy's assassination. Like so many of his countrymen, a distraught Gore worried about the nation and its future. He wrote Lyndon Johnson about his concern, telling him that "you have my prayers and best wishes. May God be with you and the Country through your leadership." The Texan soon responded that "nothing has meant more to me during these hours of sorrow after the death of President John Fitzgerald Kennedy than the messages from friends like you. I appreciated your thoughtfulness. I shall cherish your prayers in the days ahead."[1]

For the moment, the two men set aside their animosity. Over the next five years, Johnson and Gore's complex relationship continued to mature. They could cooperate on issues such as Medicare, voting rights, and economic development. Just as easily, however, they would clash over taxes, interest rates, and Vietnam. Still, both would agree that the events during the Johnson administration were among the most notable in American history. While the liberal and progressive agenda made substantial advances, especially during the first three years, by 1968 the coalition appeared in retreat in the face of a conservative backlash. By the end of Johnson's term, Gore found himself trying to stay ahead of the wave that would consume Johnson, Hubert Humphrey, and the Democratic Party and bring to the forefront his old nemesis, Richard Nixon.

Despite the cordial messages Johnson and Gore exchanged following Kennedy's death, almost immediately Gore took issue with the administration over the tax cut initially proposed by Kennedy. Gore's opposition to it frustrated the White House. Treasury officials complained that they had addressed his concerns on expense accounts, stock options, and foreign income; one stressed that "it is my opinion that Senator Gore will never be convinced of the merits of this bill. Even if he were convinced, he seems to have locked himself into a political posture in Tennessee that he cannot readily abandon."[2]

In response, Johnson told Treasury Secretary Douglas Dillon that he wanted to put the heat on Gore, encouraging him to inform Katherine Graham at the *Washington Post* about Gore's delaying actions. He wanted someone "for God's sake" to get up on Capitol Hill and "take pictures of Gore talking all morning. At least put a little heat there because he's going to keep it up if you don't."[3]

Most in the administration agreed that Gore was a lost cause even as Johnson launched a full court press to win approval. He told an audience of businessmen in Denver that "I need [the tax cut] now . . . I am the only President you have. If you would have me fail, then you fail, for this Nation of yours fails. If you would have me succeed, then you benefit, and the country benefits." Johnson prodded Senator Eugene McCarthy (D-MN), telling him to get the Democrats on the Finance Committee to "attend the meetings, make them keep their mouths shut, make them vote down amendments, and get me a bill out on the floor." Behind the scenes, he cajoled the powerful Harry Byrd (D-VA) to support his efforts with promises of fiscal responsibility. When the bill passed the Senate by a vote of 77–21, Johnson congratulated Byrd, telling him, "You're a gentleman, and scholar, and a producer, and I love you."[4]

While Gore and Johnson did not see eye to eye over taxes, they agreed on many new initiatives. In February 1964, Johnson proclaimed that his administration "here and now, declares an unconditional war on poverty in America . . . we shall not rest until the war is won." From this promise evolved many of the "Great Society" programs including Economic Opportunity and Aid for Families with Dependent Children, as well as the Elementary and Secondary Education Act, Food Stamp Act, Job Corps, and Appalachian Regional Development Act.[5] Gore supported most of Johnson's initial Great Society proposals as they paralleled his view of government's ability and responsibility to attack problems of poverty, inadequate health care, and limited educational opportunities for all Americans. He considered the programs "a model of liberal political craftsmanship." Johnson's job training and education programs drew special praise from Gore.[6]

To help the president promote his ideas, Gore traveled with Johnson to Ohio, Kentucky, and Tennessee in the spring of 1964. After visiting an Ohio university town and Lexington, Kentucky, Johnson complained, "When will we see some poverty?" On arriving in Knoxville, the president's limousine turned off Market Street onto Vine Avenue. On the block stood a dilapidated old home with a tin roof and a family of eight in front. Immediately, Johnson told the driver to pull over, and he jumped out to secure a photo opportunity with the family. As Gore watched, one of the policemen whispered to him, "That fella's the biggest bootlegger in town."[7]

The decision to support the new president and his ambitious program was not difficult for Gore, although he expected to incur the wrath of Tennessee conservatives. He also recognized that he needed the president's assistance in a tough election-year battle. A rumored challenge from Buford Ellington never materialized, but major changes taking place in the state threatened Gore's re-election bid. Most Republicans and many conservative Democrats lined up be-hind Arizona senator Barry Goldwater, a zealous anticommunist and states' rights advocate who had solid support in Tennessee. The Republican East began allying more with the anti–civil rights and anti-government groups in the West to create a powerful coalition. Gore's position on civil rights and school prayer and his support for Kennedy had alienated many lower- and middle-class white voters and weakened his political base of support. It appeared that the Republicans might be able to take advantage of the changes and unseat him.

Limited resources and an untried campaign staff led by his daughter Nancy complicated his campaign. Gore's attitude also made him vulnerable. Always one who wanted the record to speak for itself, he had not done a good job of keeping in touch with the home supporters and general public. Gore never hired a publicist, nor did he participate in rituals common to fellow politicians. Annually, Kefauver sent out fifty thousand Christmas cards and hired a staffer to read the newspapers for birthdays, death announcements, and anniversaries, and then to send cards with his good wishes. Furthermore, Gore's campaign style in 1964 remained much like that of 1938 as he traveled from place to place, making speeches and relying on a small staff to spread his message across the state. Unlike Pauline, who could name all the major players in a town or county, the senator rarely worked to curry the favor of the local leaders. Despite the national mood in favor of Johnson, it shaped up to be a difficult contest.

As the 1964 election approached, a significant battle over civil rights placed Gore in a very precarious position. After Kennedy's assassination, the Johnson administration had launched a full-scale effort to pass his legislation, often evoking his memory to promote it. "We have talked long enough in this country about equal rights," Johnson asserted on November 27, 1963. "We have for one hundred years or more. It is time now to write the next chapter, and write it in the books of law."[8] With renewed vigor, supporters of the civil rights bill pres-sured Congress to pass the legislation.

A huge quantity of mail descended on Gore's office, the majority encourag-ing the Tennessean to oppose Johnson's proposal. "One of the few remaining [rights]," a Memphis constituent stressed, "is the right of private property and freedom to choose our associations and who we shall sell to, buy from, employ and serve in a manner regardless of race or color." He added that discrimination would always exist and that "the President's law will not stop it in this country and would only give him more power over the private citizens and business, of which there is too much now." A Germantown constituent wrote that the civil rights activists were Communists whose slogan of civil rights was "an exact parallel to the slogan of 'agrarian reform' which they used in China." He argued that in reality southern blacks already lived better than the Soviets.[9] While there were a few voices of support, they paled in comparison to the opposition.

As in earlier battles over civil rights, Gore withheld his support of the original bill. He remained a moderate, supporting the basic thrust of the bill but seeking measures to restrain executive and bureaucratic power. In particular, he disagreed with Title VI (Non-Discrimination in Federally Assisted Programs), which empowered HEW to withhold funding from hospitals and schools on a statewide level. He despised discrimination but worried that administrators would act arbitrarily on the basis of yet unwritten guidelines, often punishing an entire state for the actions of a particular section. He stressed his belief that the action was an "undemocratic grant of power and with regard to the ethical principle of punishing the many for the (real or alleged) shortcomings of a few." Assurances that bureaucrats would not abuse their position left Gore unconvinced.[10]

When the debates on the legislation began in the Senate in June 1964, Gore joined hard-line segregationists in opposing certain sections of the bill. He was not active in the process, offering only one amendment on June 10, a failed attempt to strike Title VI. Strom Thurmond, Richard Russell, Sam Ervin, John Tower, and Russell Long (D-LA) proposed the bulk of amendments. Gore favored those that limited the power of the attorney general and federal employees to implement mandates and sought safeguards by requiring hearings dealing with Title VI to be conducted in conformity with the provisions of the Administrative Procedure Act. He also supported an amendment to require that Congress, rather than the president, approve the rules and regulations.[11]

He often disagreed with the hard-line segregationists' attempts to weaken the legislation. When pressed, he stood behind the extension of the Civil Rights Commission and expansion of the job training program. He opposed attempts to nullify the president's executive orders on ending discrimination in housing and voted against Russell's amendment to delay implementation of the bill until the country could hold a national referendum. Finally, he stood against attempts by some southern senators to utilize the bill to help break unions.[12]

After months of debate and attempts at compromise, Gore voted against the final bill, although he recognized the futility of the exercise. His decision reflected a fear of expanded federal power exercised by unelected, faceless bureaucrats and, according to his critics, the pressures of an intensive election campaign. He wanted to adopt a more moderate long-term program that ensured alterations in attitudes and actions, as well as laws.[13] In the end, he remained a gradualist who believed that time, education, and economic opportunities provided the most effective means of creating a New South.

Gore also had grown tired of the harping and hypocrisy of nonsoutherners who, he believed, totally disregarded the southern way of life. He wrote that the "intemperateness of language and attitude was by no means monopolized by Southerners. Many people from outside the South, including politicians, were not only extreme in their denunciations of the South, but increasingly hypocritical in their refusal to acknowledge, much less deal, with racial discrimination in their own constituencies." Such attitudes ensured that the "white South felt put upon and, not without justifications, became angered; instead of concentrating on correction, it entrenched and fought back." The Civil Rights Act of 1964, Gore complained, called for uniform application and enforcement in all fifty states, but its focus was on the South; he noted that a fellow senator correctly had accused other sections of the country of "monumental hypocrisy" for their failure to require equal enforcement of the legislation.[14] Race riots in the North, upper Midwest, and West Coast after 1965 illustrated the prevalence of racial discrimination across the nation.

Gore later admitted that the vote against the 1964 Civil Rights Act was one of his most colossal blunders as a legislator. Al and Nancy had badgered their father to support the bill, but he remained steadfast. Al recalled that at the time, though only a teenager, he "had strong feelings of my own that we needed to move forward on civil rights." The tall, lanky, dark-haired sixteen-year-old sat at the dinner table with his gray-haired father and argued at length about the matter. While recognizing that his father had made a "cogent and logical argument," he could not accept the conclusion. "It was the first time I can remember, one of the only times, feeling I was right and he was wrong on a matter of public importance."[15]

Gore's self-criticism and his son's judgment were correct. The senator succumbed to the pressure of the racists in an election cycle. More important, he recognized that his efforts to eliminate objectionable factors such as Title VI, while justified in defending a state such as Tennessee, were doomed. He should have voted for the measure and then worked to make sure that the government properly administered it. Instead, his hard-headedness and campaign posturing caused him to make a serious mistake and send the wrong message to his constituents in Tennessee. The racists already hated him and would never vote for him. He should have taken the moral high ground and made another courageous stand as he had done before and would do again.

In the aftermath of the civil rights battle, Gore concentrated on the election by spending more time in Tennessee, where a potent challenge from Republican Dan Kuykendall of Memphis was developing. While publicly exuding confidence, Gore knew he had a hard fight on his hands. He reported to a friend in early July that "Pauline and I got into the farm late last night after four days of campaigning in West Tennessee. My situation is in excellent shape over there but I found more Goldwater supporters than I expected to find." He faced additional problems in the west, as his vote on the Civil Rights Bill left African Americans disenchanted. A slogan even floated around the African American community telling people to "Ignore Gore in 64."[16]

In addition, Gore initially lacked strong backing from the White House. While publicly supportive, Johnson still held a grudge against Gore. The president liked pliable people, telling a confidante that "I want people around me who kiss my ass on a hot summer's day and say it smells like roses." During one conversation in August with George Smathers (D-FL), Johnson complained about Gore's actions during the 1961 Democratic Caucus. When Smathers reported that Gore had lamented that the president did not like him, Johnson instructed him to tell Gore that "I never saw the president show any indication but every time he had a caucus you used to get up and attack him and I wouldn't be surprised if he didn't appreciate it." Smathers complained about the Tennessee Democrats not being able to find someone who could beat Gore and take over. Johnson simply responded, "I don't know either."[17]

Despite the flurry of activity of campaigning, an international crisis developed as the election neared. On August 2, the USS Maddox, while supporting covert actions against North Vietnamese targets by South Vietnamese commandos, came under attack by North Vietnamese torpedo boats. In response, Johnson ordered the USS Turner Joy to the area and promised: "If they do it again, they'll get another sting." Two days later, in stormy weather, the two ships reported radar contacts and believed that they were under attack. This time, the administration wanted retaliatory strikes on the North Vietnamese, but Johnson sought some political cover before ordering further attacks.[18]

Working with Senators Fulbright, Russell, and Dirksen, the White House pushed the Tonkin Gulf Resolution that granted the president the right to take "all necessary measures to repel any armed attacks against the forces of the United States and to prevent further aggression." It immediately went to Congress where most senators responded by rallying around the flag, although several voiced concerns. Ernest Gruening called the action a "predated declaration of war." Wayne Morse complained that the United States had provoked the attacks by aiding the South Vietnamese commandos. Frank Church (D-ID) warned that the United States had failed to break the spirit of the North Koreans by bombing "every house, bridge, road until there was nothing left but rubble . . . [E]xpanding the war is not getting out, Mr. President. It is getting further in."[19]

Gore found himself in a quandary. In June 1964, he had expressed an opinion publicly that Johnson's policy toward Vietnam "mystifies me a bit" and acknowledged the fear that Johnson had turned over too many decisions to the military. He praised Church for raising his "reservations and doubts" and noted his history of questioning policy in Vietnam. Still, when it came time to debate the Tonkin Gulf Resolution, he argued that "when U.S. forces have been attacked repeatedly upon the high seas . . . whatever doubts one may have entertained are water over the dam . . . Aggression against our forces must be repulsed."[20]

Despite lingering skepticism among some senators, the administration won passage in the House by a unanimous vote and 88–2 in the Senate, with only Gruening and Morse dissenting. McGovern emphasized later that there was a "feeling in the country that we had to close ranks," especially after Kennedy's death, and that "Johnson was too shrewd to get involved." In addition, Fulbright had assuaged many of the fears of his colleagues by promising that Johnson could be trusted to wisely utilize the power.[21]

Within a short time, Johnson proved Fulbright wrong. Most senators including Gore believed that the Tonkin Gulf Resolution was a limited grant of power. The Johnson administration interpreted the document otherwise. America struck back hard in 1964 and once the election ended, Johnson dramatically escalated the bombing campaign, which led to new requirements for troops to protect the air bases. Within a year and a half, the American commitment to Vietnam had grown to several hundred thousand troops and billions of dollars. Over time, it became apparent that the second attack had not occurred, a point reinforced by the recent release of North Vietnamese documents.[22] Johnson and his military advisers wanted an excuse to strike back, and though they may not have knowingly misled the Congress, they never rectified the mistake.

Gore regretted his vote for many years. He wrote that Congress had failed in its duties and that he "erroneously" voted for the resolution. At the time, he believed there had been an "unprovoked attack" on a U.S. warship in international waters. When he uncovered the misinformation, he noted raising "critical questions about the war—its legality, its morality, its wisdom and its justification."[23] Once Johnson had the power, he refused to relinquish it, and a divided Congress could not wrest back the authority it ceded.

The Democrats' attention shifted to Atlantic City and the national convention in mid-August. Johnson's nomination was a foregone conclusion, so the party focused more on the vice-presidential nomination and the platform. In particular, Medicare and Social Security commanded Gore's attention. He pushed a $7 increase in Social Security checks, hoping to offset his opposition to the tax cut among the 400,000 Social Security beneficiaries in his state.[24]

Gore also encouraged the Democrats to support Medicare, a system for health care for older Americans. He continued to criticize the efforts of Rep. Wilbur Mills (D-AR) to increase Social Security payments to cover some of the costs of medical insurance. Gore believed that this limited approach would not help those already struggling with choices between housing, food, and health care. Shortly before the convention, Gore had offered the Medicare proposal that created a health insurance program in the Senate Finance Committee. Without administration support, his proposal lost eleven to six.

When the convention began, Gore and others set out to include a vigorous commitment to Medicare in the Democratic platform. However, the original proposal was weak because Johnson and others feared inciting strong opposition from the conservatives and the American Medical Association (AMA). Already, conservative spokesman and future California governor Ronald Reagan had branded Medicare the advance wave of socialism that threatened to "invade every area of freedom in this country." He predicted that his fellow citizens would spend their "sunset years telling our children and our children's children what it was like in America when men were free."[25] While Johnson privately supported Medicare, he wanted to avoid a battle before the election.

Once in Atlantic City, Gore confronted Johnson's choice for vice president, Hubert Humphrey, on the matter. Gore threatened to take the microphone and echo Truman's sentiments on the merits of Medicare. With Humphrey vigorously scribbling notes, the Tennessean blasted the platform statement on the issue as "mamby-pamby" and asked whether this was a meeting of the AMA or Democrats. As Humphrey exited with notes in hand, Gore believed that he had made his point. Johnson wanted to avoid any appearance of aggravating the liberals, especially with Robert Kennedy in the wings. The platform rewrite soon contained a stronger endorsement: "We will continue to fight until we have succeeded in including hospital care for older Americans in the social-security program."[26]

Following the convention, Gore and Johnson had a telephone conversation about Medicare. Gore told the president: "What this bill will do is provide pre-paid medical care for the great body of our self-supporting, self-respecting, proud people who want to remain so even after they are 65." He also encouraged Johnson to push Lister Hill for help since he was the son of a doctor. Later, he told the White House that he would kill any legislation that did not contain a strong Medicare plan.[27]

As the election approached, Gore and Johnson put aside any public differences. In national polls, Johnson had a huge lead, but he wanted to take no chances and worked feverishly to win by a huge margin.[28] As his own race with Kuykendall tightened, Gore realized he needed the president's support and wrote Johnson in early September that "though I must largely confine my campaigning to Tennessee, I wish to enlist in the battle for your election." Johnson responded, "This is to let you know that I am grateful for your friendship and support—and for the good Democrats in Tennessee."[29]

While he never conducted polls, Gore knew that the campaign was tight. The racists and John Birchers combined with the mainstream Republicans in the East to make significant inroads against him because of his record on civil rights, taxes, and Vietnam. Even some in the Catholic hierarchy lined up against the Democrats. Father Edward J. Cleary, who headed a parish in suburban Memphis and had edited the *Tennessee Register*, the official paper of the Tennessee diocese, denounced the Democrats and urged his parishioners to join the John Birch Society. "Too many Catholics accept JFK and his policies for the simple reason that he is a Catholic." He warned that the civil rights movement was a "criminal organization . . . under a central direction not located in our country." In October 1963, he had called for a "truly conservative Christian revival," which would "bring about an intellectual counterrevolution against the inroads and encroachments of Marxism, usually described as liberalism."[30]

Such pronouncements worried Gore and Johnson. The president phoned Gore on October 2 and expressed his worries about the Senate races and his campaign in Tennessee, recognizing that his push on civil rights had hurt. He had already told Bill Moyers that signing the 1964 Civil Rights Act had "delivered the South to the Republican Party for a long time to come."[31] In their conversation, Gore and Johnson lamented the rising white registration and expected low African American turnout, leading Gore to report that "I think it is a real tough battle now. My suitcase is packed and I'm leaving here within an hour and I'm giving it everything I have." Johnson told him, "You let me know what else, Albert, I ought to be doing and keep me in touch because there's not anybody else that I am more interested in than myself than you." Gore said that he enjoyed "being on the team," and Johnson answered, "I know it . . . I am glad we got all that underbrush cut out and we'll just fight it out and on to victory."[32]

To help Gore and other Tennesseans and shore up his own position, Johnson visited Nashville a week later. "I want to salute my friend," he told an audience, "one of the most courageous and one of the ablest members of the United States Senate, Albert Gore." The president bragged that Gore's voice was one of the most influential in the nation, and "the only one that I know that fights harder and may have better judgment than Albert is his wife Pauline." During the same visit, Frank Alhgren talked with Johnson on the phone. The editor warned that "Gore and Bass are in trouble here. They won't tell you that. And it is going to take a visit from you to pull this thing out." Johnson responded that "we're in trouble everywhere . . . We got to work at this thing." Using football analogies about rolling over the opponents during the fourth quarter, Johnson said, "We got to hit every day and we got to give them the works."[33]

Both candidates continued their work. Throughout October, Gore hammered home his record on atomic energy, the TVA, public works, Social Security, and education. When the final vote took place, he won by a fifty-thousand-vote margin. Immediately, he announced his great joy at reelection and the end of the campaign. He told a crowd that his only immediate goal was to have some family time by watching his son play football at the upcoming homecoming game.[34]

The bittersweet victory was a harbinger of things to come. A relative unknown had come fairly close to defeating the incumbent senator. Gore had utilized a small, inexperienced staff and a budget of around $50,000 for the entire campaign. His comparatively narrow victory signaled changes underway in Tennessee even in the face of Johnson's victory in the state and landslide in the national election.[35] The racists and conservatives were gaining momentum as Thurmond and others defected to the Republican Party after 1964, and Tennessee's Republican Party had for the first time sent an all-white delegation to the national convention. Working-class whites, especially in middle and western Tennessee, had become more angry with the Democrats. A new ingredient, George Wallace, was about to enter the mix, and he helped move the traditionally Democratic state to a Republican one. Gore was safe for six years, but the 1964 election suggested that his days might be numbered.

Following the grueling campaign, Gore found his relationship with Johnson sour again as the two clashed over Vietnam. During the election, Gore had held his tongue, but in late December 1964 he spoke on the topic in Miami, calling for a negotiated settlement to the conflict. His recommendation sparked a walk-out by some of the audience. The story made the national news, angering Johnson and his advisers. The president demonstrated no animosity in public, merely telling Gore a few days later: "You looked good on TV."[36] Nevertheless, Gore recognized Johnson's unhappiness, and existing tensions that had subsided during the election resurfaced.

Gore chose to go public with his views because his election victory and his ambivalent relationship with Johnson now freed him to take the more controversial position, despite the wishes of the majority of his constituents. Furthermore, it had become apparent that Johnson had lied about the attacks on the U.S. ships in the Gulf of Tonkin, which infuriated Gore and many others. Finally, he believed that the Johnson administration's liberal interpretation of the resolution threatened to carry the United States into nuclear conflict at the worst, and a quagmire at the best.[37] It was time to step up and lead.

The Miami speech caused problems for Gore as the conservative *Nashville Banner* ran a column by syndicated writer Holmes Alexander denouncing the "peace party" in the Senate, including Gore. "Most of the senators who fall in line for hauling down the Stars and Stripes," he complained, "are financially supported by peace-mongering groups . . . I don't suppose there's a weaker chink anywhere in the Free World armor than this pacifist clique within our own Congress." Afterward, one constituent wrote that negotiations signaled retreat: "I don't think this is the proper policy stand for a Representative of the 'Volunteer' State."[38]

Despite the criticism, Gore pushed for negotiations to end the fighting, telling one constituent that "I simply do not believe that there is a military victory to be won in Vietnam." He highlighted how the French had wasted thousands of lives in a country where factors such as race and religion created an unstable situation. "I do not accept the so-called domino theory as being valid in every respect," he wrote. "The people of Vietnam do not fully support our intervention, and as long as this is so, political stability in the area will not be forthcoming."[39]

Gore and Johnson also clashed on economic issues. When Dillon resigned, Johnson chose Henry Fowler to succeed him as secretary of the Treasury. In a telephone conversation with the president, Gore called Fowler a "damn poor choice . . . a turncoat" who "paraded as a true liberal and true friend of the people, and Dillon let him go to his spa in Florida for a time or two and he became a patsy for big money." Johnson defended Fowler, arguing he was a good man who would keep interest rates low. Gore warned the president to "keep your eyes open."[40]

While at odds over Vietnam and the economy, Gore and the president teamed up on civil rights. Following the confrontations in Selma, Alabama, in early 1965, Congress began debates on a new law to strengthen the Fifteenth Amendment.[41] The resulting Voting Rights Act of 1965 "guaranteed all citizens their right to register and vote free of discrimination." The legislation suspended literacy tests and other devices to minimize minority voter registration, allowed the appointment of examiners when the attorney general certified racial discrimination existed, and created stronger punishments such as jail time and fines for interference in the process.[42]

Despite his no vote on the Civil Rights Act, Gore strongly supported the new bill. When constituents voiced opposition, he wrote that "I believe the right of qualified citizens freely to exercise the franchise is clearly guaranteed in the United States Constitution." He noted that there were areas where this fundamental right had been denied and argued that "this cannot be tolerated. Freedom of the ballot box is the very essence of democracy."[43] During the voting on amendments to the legislation, Gore supported attempts to strengthen the bill, including measures that further limited state-imposed voting restrictions and assigned additional monitors to districts with poor voting records among African Americans. At the same time, he opposed most attempts to weaken it, such as amendments that sabotaged triggering mechanisms and called for examiners to administer literacy tests. The bill passed easily, 77–19.[44]

Passage of the Voting Rights Act marked the apex of congressional activism in civil rights. When combined with the Civil Rights Act, it gave most power to the courts and the executive agencies charged with enforcing the legislation. Over time, Vietnam and new social programs became the centerpieces of the Johnson administration's policy, diverting time and energy from civil rights. The movement also lost momentum in Congress because the major issues such as voting rights and segregation had been addressed. For the next five years, Congress continued to tinker with the laws, although nothing evolved approximating the broad range of programs created in 1964–65.

During the rapid expansion of Great Society programs, as well as the Vietnam War, Gore continued focusing on how to pay for the programs without creating huge deficits, inflation, and higher interest rates. He continued to make the case that wealthier Americans needed to pay their fair share and stop dodging their responsibilities. In a *New York Times Magazine* article, "How to Be Rich without Paying Taxes," he revealed that seventeen millionaires recently had avoided paying any income tax. While their accounting was legal, Gore stressed that America needed "taxation based on ability to pay," not a system that relied on who had the best lobbyists and lawyers to create loopholes.[45]

In particular, he attacked oil depletion allowances, self-serving foundations, hidden income in stock options, and exclusions from foreign income. "Tax loopholes are often made quite innocently," he observed, "but once the rich and powerful seize upon a loosely drawn section of tax law, it becomes difficult to change it." Tax reform was impossible without limiting the lobbies that undermined true reform. To achieve dramatic changes, Gore believed that a committed Congress, secretary of the Treasury, and president would have to be "willing to take on all comers in an all-out battle for a tax policy that is fair and equitable."[46]

The story reinforced his Populist credentials, which George McGovern noted as one of the characteristics that made Gore stand out from other liberals. A professor from Compton College in California asked Johnson whether he had read the article. "WHAT ARE YOU GOING TO DO ABOUT THIS IF ALBERT GORE IS RIGHT? And if he is right, the situation—pardon my expression—STINKS."[47]

The biggest legislative battle of mid-1965 developed not over taxes but Medicare. Even those who opposed the measure believed the legislation would pass. In December 1964, Russell wrote his constituents that "because the President is committed to a Medicare bill and the liberals greatly increased their majority in the Congress in the last election, there is little doubt that a Medicare bill will be passed in the next Congress." Even Mills responded that his committee "would be able to work something out."[48]

Despite criticisms from some constituents regarding the bill, Gore wholeheartedly supported the legislation when the Senate started debates in July.[49] He backed a plan that created a tax to fund the program, which provided for medical care for the elderly and an insurance program for the less fortunate. Johnson threw the full weight of the White House behind the bill, stressing that too many older Americans had chronic problems and more than half lacked health insurance. He asked for modest investments by working people to prevent catastrophic health care disasters for them and their loved ones.[50]

An unlikely challenge arose from those who wanted unlimited care. On this point, Gore sparred with Kennedy's former HEW secretary, Senator Abraham Ribicoff (D-CT). During floor debates, he argued that under the current plan "virtually every case of catastrophic health costs would fall within the durational limits provided in the bill." He pushed starting "prudently" and working to create a system based on experience to sustain an effective program.[51]

As expected, Congress approved the Medicare plan. To celebrate the victory, Johnson and many of the cosponsors of the bill including Gore flew to Independence, Missouri. In a public ceremony, Johnson had former President Truman witness the signing of the bill into law to celebrate his contribution to promoting comprehensive health care. Johnson praised Truman "not because he gave them hell—but because he gave them hope."[52]

One writer has characterized the Medicare/Medicaid plan as a "jewel in the crown" in Johnson's agenda.[53] Problems developed with skyrocketing costs as doctors, hospitals, and pharmaceutical companies raised prices to "reasonable costs." Still, it was a major victory for many elderly Americans. The numbers of uninsured fell dramatically, and the threat of bankruptcy created by illness was reduced dramatically. Improved health care ensured longer and better lives. Gore's vision of government as having a role in protecting the less fortunate clearly shone through in the Medicare victory.

The success of the Medicare bill marked the high point of the session and of liberal and progressive activism in the 1960s. Following the first nine months of near record-breaking passage of legislation, the pace slowed dramatically in fall 1965 as the country digested the changes and grappled with the upheaval of the summer of 1965. Race riots in Watts and elsewhere had wracked the country and shaken the confidence of those pushing change, confirming conservative fears that government efforts would accomplish little and only upset race relations in the country.[54]

The new year began with significant debates on Vietnam, the issue destined to tear apart the liberal and progressive coalition that had pushed through the majority of the Great Society programs. The continuing military buildup failed to satisfy some senators, such as Richard Russell, who wanted to let the North Vietnamese "know they are in a war." Others such as Senator John Stennis (D-MS), a high-ranking member of the Armed Services Committee, told the Mississippi legislature that ultimately the war would require stationing more than 680,000 troops in Vietnam and the possible use of nuclear weapons if China intervened.[55]

However, dissenting views existed. Mike Mansfield, recently returned from a presidential fact-finding tour in Vietnam, informed Johnson that the "best chance of getting to the peace table is to minimize our military action." Fulbright also pushed negotiation and asked, "If we win what do we do? Do we stay there forever?"[56] By the end of January, a major confrontation developed between the "doves" on the SFRC and the White House, centering on a $415 million supplemental foreign aid bill. In response to the military buildup and intensified bombing campaign, Fulbright opened the meetings to the public and arranged for the major networks to televise them. The powerful chairman had set the stage for the first major public debate on the war.

On the first day of the hearings, January 28, Gore made his position clear. He grilled Secretary of State Dean Rusk, telling him, "Many people do not believe, many members of Congress do not believe, that the costs, the risk of nuclear war, the dangers of war with China or perhaps both China and Russia, are worth the endeavor." Next, he attacked Rusk over the administration's liberal interpretation of the Gulf of Tonkin Resolution. "I certainly want to disassociate myself [from] any interpretation that this was a declaration of war . . . Or that it authorized the Administration to take any and all steps toward an all-out war."[57]

For more than two weeks, Gore and the other doves on the SFRC, including Fulbright and Morse, continued challenging the administration. The *Nashville Tennessean* ran the headline "Gore Calls War 'A Serious Mistake.'" Fulbright and his staff called sympathetic witnesses, including the primary architect of the containment policy, George Kennan, who argued against escalation. At one point, Gore interjected that he agreed it was important to stop the conflict from escalating "and most of all to prevent it from becoming a war between the United States and China."[58]

The event was the most important televised spectacle in Congress since the McCarthy hearings. The White House tried to upstage the hearings by pressuring the major networks not to carry coverage and even orchestrating an impromptu meeting in Honolulu between South Vietnamese leader General Nguyen Cao Ky and Johnson to shift attention from the SFRC. A Johnson aide, Mike Manatos, bitterly complained that the senators were providing aid and comfort to the Viet Cong.[59] By February 19, Johnson ordered the FBI to investigate "whether Senator Fulbright and other Senators were receiving information from Communists."[60] Throughout the government, "hawks" denounced Fulbright, Gore, and the other doves for being Communist dupes.

An estimated 22 million Americans watched the hearings. At one point, Gore told a story about a journalist who went home and found his wife transfixed on the hearings. She met her husband at the door with the greeting: "You have an unclean house but a highly informed wife." Pat Holt, one of the SFRC staff members, stressed that the hearings were important because "they contributed to . . . the erosion of support for the Johnson policy in the Senate." He added that they also made public dissent more acceptable because the opponents were not "a bunch of crazy college kids invading deans' offices . . . they were people of substance."[61]

In his own family, Senator Gore won much support. Al skipped classes at Harvard to watch his father on television. He wrote his girlfriend Tipper that he had talked with his father and "he was so pleased when I told him I missed two or three days of classes to watch him on television. He tried not to show it and said I shouldn't have missed classes, but he was awfully pleased." His father's efforts against LBJ "made me swell with pride," he remembered.[62]

The increased involvement in Vietnam caused another tussle between the Johnson administration and Gore, this time over taxes. In March 1966, the administration proposed stopping decreases in excise taxes, leading to vigorous denunciations by Gore, who noted, "I wanted, and still want to get rid of these burdensome, regressive, and unfair taxes." He called it "particularly galling that, while we gave the greatest tax reduction to people in high income brackets—to be specific, men like Henry Ford—when we find it necessary to increase revenue, we lay the burden upon the people who must buy the automobiles and who must use telephones." He called the entire process "undemocratic and inequitable."[63]

In response, Gore called for a coherent tax plan that increased revenues by closing corporate and personal loopholes. He warned that inflation and program cuts were imminent if the administration continued its current path and continued to fight a costly war in Vietnam. He also ruled out borrowing, fearing it would guarantee higher interest rates.[64] While Vietnam lacked the scale of World War II, he considered the issues comparable and that only innovative and quick actions could prevent an economic meltdown.

Gore also remained deeply involved in other foreign policy issues, including nuclear proliferation. The issue took on a new urgency after the Chinese exploded a nuclear device in October 1964. At this point, the Russians and the Americans began more serious talks to prevent the spread of the technology.[65] As chairman of the SFRC subcommittee on disarmament, Gore grappled with several contentious points, including official recognition of the Communist government in China. In May 1965, Gore wrote that "we might not be able to indefinitely maintain the fiction that the Chiang Kai-shek group represents the people of China at the United Nations." In early January 1966, when asked if China needed to be at the bargaining table regarding the nonproliferation agreement, he responded yes.[66]

Gore's statements on the matter were controversial. The powerful anti–

Communist China lobby saw any negotiation with Red China as betraying the Nationalists on Taiwan and opening the door to cooperation with the Communists. They believed any step toward conciliation undermined the inevitable return of the Nationalists to the mainland and compared those who proposed negotiation to those who had lost China in 1949.[67]

Despite criticisms, Gore understood the complexities and volatility of the subject. The United States needed China to sign the Nuclear Test Ban Treaty of 1963 to prevent massive atmospheric contamination, so he proposed in June 1966 that the United States should enter "into a 'no-first' use-of-nuclear-weapons treaty if China would adhere to the existing nuclear test-ban treaty."[68] The United States also needed to discuss the issue of nuclear arms with Beijing to prevent the conflict in Southeast Asia from becoming Armageddon, and only steps toward normalization would allow the process to go forward. International realities required the United States to deal with Communist China. This pragmatic, although unpopular, stance angered those who already accused the senator of being soft on communism.

Others criticized Gore and his allies for advocating negotiation with the Soviet Union over nuclear arms. They deemed the Soviets as untrustworthy, especially the new leader, Leonid Brezhnev. Nevertheless, Gore supported the nonproliferation treaty in January 1966, arguing, "It is eminently in the interests of the United States and other nuclear powers. But also in the interests of humanity as a whole, because it lessens the danger of a nuclear outbreak."[69] For the moment, the issue quieted, not resurfacing for more than nine months as the two sides disagreed over arming the NATO and Warsaw Pact nations.

As the autumn began, Gore saw some of his work mature. He flew back from Washington to Nashville. After getting his car, he headed toward Carthage on Interstate 40, which had been under construction for years and previously only reached as far east as Lebanon. However, when he reached the turn-off that day, construction workers informed him that the road was open past Carthage. Happily, he continued on the newly opened stretch of road, not passing far from Possum Hollow. "I pulled off on the shoulder and looked and looked and looked. There was Possum Hollow and here was this new road . . . I was so proud that I was useful in bringing about this kind of development. I just sat there in my car and looked at my old home, up the creek, and cried like a baby."[70]

During the congressional session, Gore began focusing more on one of his favorite topics, high interest rates. He denounced Johnson for creating a phony balanced budget, complaining about the sleight-of-hand tactics such as selling

FHA and VA mortgages and using the receipts as current income. On the Senate floor, he claimed that such policies had resulted in interest rates "now higher than the Hoover rates." Gore urged Johnson to change the trend because he would not "wish history to record him as one whose policies robbed the Democratic Party of its heritage of being the party of the people."[71]

Gore saved a lot of his venom for the bankers, arguing that the Federal Reserve system's board of governors was "banker oriented" and "always seem[s] happy to find an excuse to run up [interest] rates."[72] He called the 6 percent prime rate "shameful" and complained that the high rates merely shifted more income into the hands of those who had been sufficiently lucky to inherit or accumulate wealth, ensuring less for those "productive elements of society, both business and labor."[73]

Gore's constant harping had some effect. He met with White House officials Walter Heller and Jon Fowler. Afterward, Heller noted that "one thing on which all three of us agree is that a firm commitment to raise taxes is one of the most effective things you [Johnson] can do to take the pressure off of interest rates." Gore suggested imposing higher rates on the wealthiest and closing loopholes, a "national usury rate" ceiling of 6 percent on mortgages, and laws to prevent the export of money into foreign bank accounts in the event of a tax increase. Calling Gore's measures "extreme," Heller conceded that it would make sense for the administration to emphasize the $4 billion that had been put at the disposal of the Federal National Mortgage Association (FNMA) to ease the mortgage market.[74]

Higher interest rates and taxes and the stalemate developing in Vietnam alarmed Gore and many other Tennessee Democrats. For the first time in years, a Republican Senate nominee appeared to have a good chance to unseat a Democrat. The incumbent, Ross Bass, had won the special election in 1964 to fill Estes Kefauver's vacated seat. A former congressman, Bass was a progressive and described by Senator Christopher Dodd (D-CT) as a person with "an inherent dislike for the large, the impersonal, and the selfish."[75]

Gore and Bass worked well together on many issues, including Medicare, federal aid to education, the TVA, and the war on poverty. Bass had supported the Civil Rights Act of 1964 and the Voting Rights Act of 1965, despite having signed the Southern Manifesto and voting against civil rights legislation in 1957 and 1960. The only measurable difference between the two was Bass's support of Johnson's Vietnam policy.[76]

As before, Gore avoided taking sides in the primary election in 1966. Frank Clement had decided to challenge Bass for the Democratic nomination, blasting him for being a "rubber stamp" for Johnson. The governor promised to represent the state, not the president. Bass defended his record, but his position worsened with the growing disillusionment with the war, race relations, and increased government spending. Clement received assistance from Howard Baker and other Republicans who began bashing Bass early, promising to help the people overcome "the threat of federal dictatorship."[77]

In the August primary, Clement won by a small margin. According to Gore and many others, the Republicans shaped the outcome because they fielded no real gubernatorial candidate or opponent for Baker. This allowed many Republicans to cross over in the primary and vote for Clement. Many of them believed that he provided a better target because of his tax rate hike as governor and progressivism on civil rights, including the appointment of Benjamin Hooks to the criminal court in Shelby County, the first African American state judge since Reconstruction.[78] As a result, Clement won a small majority by carrying Republican areas by large margins.

The Democrats recognized the threat from Baker. They knew that most Republicans were content with the conservative Ellington in the governor's mansion, so they focused on the Senate race. Gore strongly supported Clement, making speeches throughout Middle Tennessee and other areas where he was popular. However, Ellington reportedly met secretly with Baker and promised not to work for Clement.[79] Baker already had other advantages including a large campaign chest and ties to prominent national leaders, including his father-in-law, Everett Dirksen. Clearly, he had a good chance of winning.

As the campaign unfolded, Baker attacked the Democrats for infringing on states' rights and called for more federal revenue sharing. He denounced the Johnson administration's handling of the war in Vietnam, calling for more forceful measures to end the stalemate. Clement, by contrast, lacked good issues on which to run and constantly had to distance himself from the national party. When the final tally came on November 8, Baker won by 100,000 votes, making him the first Tennessee Republican in the Senate in nearly a century.[80]

Baker's victory was a harbinger of things to come.[81] He took East Tennessee as expected but also most of West Tennessee, including Shelby County. The Republicans successfully tarred the Democrats as the "tax and spend" party that undermined individual liberties. The ongoing shift of the white Democrats into the folds of the Republican Party intensified. Issues such as school prayer and gun control further strengthened the position of the Republicans as the defenders of the average citizen in the face of a tyrannical federal government.[82]

Clement's defeat highlighted the change taking place in Tennessee and elsewhere in the South.

While the signs were ominous in Tennessee in 1966, as the new congressional session opened in 1967 Gore refused to avoid controversy. He soon found himself again embroiled in the contentious issue of school prayer. Senate minority leader Everett Dirksen had reintroduced a constitutional amendment to allow voluntary school prayer, telling one group that "organized atheists in our society today are striving for supremacy and as a minority are forcing their opinions on the majority." The Illinois senator also wrote in *Human Events* that "I would hate to have it said that our attitude toward prayer begins to approximate the lack of respect for prayer and its spiritual refreshment which appears to be the attitude of the Soviet Union."[83]

The pro–school-prayer forces were well organized, flooding Gore's office with duplicate postcards containing the text of Dirksen's proposal (S.J. Res. 1). People signed it, urging Gore to back Dirksen's amendment. In predominantly conservative evangelical Protestant Tennessee, there was a lot of support for it. Many people blamed the civil disorders, increase in divorces, and other problems on those who had removed prayer from the schools. The explanations found a receptive audience among cultural conservatives.

Despite such pressure, Gore refused to support Dirksen's amendment. Over and over he reiterated that he believed in the separation of church and state and that people should move cautiously in this area of law.[84] This position was unpopular and hurt him, especially with white middle- and working-class voters who remained Democrats because of economic issues. However, they were already angry over his position on Vietnam and civil rights, and his failure to support the amendment further fueled their willingness to support Republicans.

While battling on the cultural front, Gore spent most of his energy in the spring and early summer defeating a campaign finance bill proposed by Russell Long (D-LA). His plan centered on allowing a $1 contribution from tax returns with the money funneled into the parties to support presidential campaigns if they promised to limit their private spending. Despite Gore's protests, a preliminary proposal had passed in 1966, but the issue remained hotly contested. When debates resurfaced in March 1967, Gore immediately denounced the effort by criticizing the lack of restrictions on spending the money and the absence of safeguards against corrupt practices. He also worried that there were constitutional questions involved, primarily over whether taxpayers could designate how to spend their tax monies.[85]

Throughout April and May, Gore battled Long on the Senate floor. With his long-time assistant Bill Allen often at his side and Pauline in the gallery passing down notes, he stood firm against the Long proposal. He criticized it for interfering with the political development of alternative parties because only the Democrats and Republicans would receive funding. At another point, he stressed that the act merely allowed public money to commingle with private money without much oversight. "Let us be candid and acknowledge that there is a danger to our system of self-government," he warned, "through the undue influence of money in elections." In response, he called for "some real reform to protect the right of an ordinary citizen to cast one vote and have that vote equal to the vote of another."[86]

His tireless work succeeded. The *Washington Post* reported that the vote to shelve Long's proposal was "a particularly sweet victory for Albert Gore, a man long regarded as the champion of lost causes." The reporter observed that in the frequent floor exchanges, a striking contrast developed between Long, the "balding, plumpish type who dresses indifferently, can stutter and grope for words under pressure," and Gore, who "never loses his icy composure or is at a loss for words." In victory, Gore stated that "after butting one's head against a brick wall for so many weeks, to finally find a passage is, to say the least, exhilarating."[87]

Immediately afterward, Gore introduced his own campaign finance plan, telling his colleagues that "current campaign financing practices gnaw like a cancer at the most vital function of our self-government processes." His bill concentrated on limits on individual giving, timely disclosure of gifts in primaries and general elections, and the public financing of presidential and congressional elections of legitimate candidates. He also wanted the Federal Communications Commission (FCC) to institute regulations that required radio and television stations to provide equitable and free broadcast time. Gore wrote a constituent that "in my view, successful candidates should be beholden to no one other than the public generally. This is the objective I seek."[88]

Many critics protested, including Senator Hugh Scott (R-PA), who complained that candidates would avoid running on private contributions because of the appearance that "big contributors were buying a piece of me." The Tennessee Association of Broadcasters complained that it already followed guidelines giving candidates equal time at low cost.[89] In the face of such opposition, including that from many senators who believed that the current system benefited the incumbent, the bill languished in committee.

A far more potentially explosive issue seized the headlines in the early summer 1967. For years, problems had fermented in the Middle East as Egypt,

Syria, and Jordan remained bitter over Israel's military victories in 1948 and 1956. In response, they purchased U.S. and Soviet military equipment while Washington funneled billions to Israel to maintain the balance. In 1964, the Arabs helped found the Palestine Liberation Organization (PLO), and a wave of terrorist attacks on Israel began. Egyptian president Gamal Abdel Nasser demanded that the UN withdraw its peacekeeping forces in the Sinai Peninsula and ordered troops to seize the outpost of Sharm el-Sheikh.[90] When Egypt and Jordan signed a military pact in early June, each side mobilized.

Diplomats from the United States, Soviet Union, and UN tried, but failed, to defuse tensions. On June 6, the Israeli air force suddenly swooped down and destroyed most of Egypt's planes on the ground. Within a couple of hours, its tanks rumbled toward the Suez Canal. In response, the Syrians and Jordanians attacked, only to be routed. Within six days, the Israelis had occupied the West Bank, the Golan Heights, and the Sinai. A truce followed, although it took months to hammer out a peace agreement.[91]

Like most Americans, Gore supported the Israelis. Since 1948 he had backed Israel, and he disliked Nasser and other Arab nationalists who promoted neutrality in the cold war. Still, the Palestinian refugee problem concerned him. In early July, he made a fact-finding tour of Israel and the refugee camps. He found that most refugees had fled to Jordan. During his meetings with Israeli foreign minister Abba Eban, he focused on the repatriation of the refugees. "I have stressed . . . that the whole world will be watching anxiously for good faith in performance of the pledge to allow innocent refugees to return in an orderly, humane manner," he told reporters. "Perhaps compassionate treatment of these victims of conflict could smooth the path to conditions of peaceful coexistence in this distraught area."[92]

After returning home, Gore reported to the president on the matter. "I know your long-standing interest in alleviating the plight of these unfortunate victims of two wars in the last two decades," Johnson wrote in reply. "Your first-hand report is a help to me and I want to thank you for the speed with which you have prepared and transmitted it." The president responded that the U.S. government had airlifted five thousand tents, fifty thousand blankets, and other materials to Jordan for the displaced refugees and provided $5 million for UN and Red Cross relief efforts.[93]

On the Senate floor, Gore also emphasized the relevance of the refugee problem to the negotiation process. "I am convinced by my experience and talks on this trip that the Arabs are as of now emotionally and politically incapable of a formalized peace agreement with Israel." He also noted that the Israelis would not relent for fear of endangering their security. To him, the problem of the refugees lay at the heart of the conflict. Their plight provided hard-liners with anti-Israeli propaganda while for moderates it represented a question of good faith in negotiation. "The rights and the plight of the refugees symbolize a surging quest through the Arab world for not only justice for the refugees but for dignity and respect for the Arabs," he told his colleagues.[94] He knew that the conflict was multidimensional but that solving this issue was an important starting point.

Gore also understood that the United States needed to balance its policies in the Middle East to create some stability. "One of the most important services the United States can render Israel is to prevent the adoption by the Arab Nations of a hardline united front against Israel," he wrote the Jewish Community Relations Council in Memphis. "At the present time there are various divergences of views among Arab leaders, and certain policies of the United States government are aimed at maintaining and widening these divergences."[95]

One of the administration's efforts in this area provoked Gore and others in late August 1967. Throughout the summer, there had been an investigation into arms sales to the third world. Senator Church and others asked why millions of dollars of taxpayers' money went to fund the purchase of sophisticated weaponry by countries not needing it, and they questioned the administration's failure to disclose the sales. On the Senate floor, Gore remarked, "If this country is to be called upon by the U.S. Government or the U.S. Congress to be the greatest merchants of death in all history, then Congress should be fully aware of what is to be done before it happens."[96]

In the process of investigation, Gore helped uncover that the United States had provided secret loans to several Arab countries to purchase weapons. Columnist Eliot Janeway praised Gore, writing that "when the can of worms was opened, Sen. Albert Gore . . . who manned the can-opener, brought out the damning disclosure that secret arms loans were made, without the knowledge of Congress, to countries dedicated to the destruction of Israel." He praised Gore for punching a serious hole in the administration's argument that it needed to remain in the arms business to protect Israel.[97]

The problem of the Middle East perplexed everyone. The attempts at negotiations through the United Nations and individual efforts for a lasting peace went nowhere. U.S. officials could not even secure an Israeli promise not to use weapons of mass destruction to defeat its enemies. The festering problems of the refugees, disputed lands, and others made many Americans throw up their hands in frustration. The lingering issues unsolved in 1967 continue to plague U.S. policymakers.

While the Middle East diverted attentions temporarily, Vietnam remained the primary international focus of the United States. Throughout 1967, the Johnson administration had continued to build up its forces. Nightly, Americans watched on television as U.S. troops waded across the rice paddies in search of an elusive enemy and listened to reports of the large number of enemy killed or captured. Many believed President Johnson and General William Westmoreland, who promised that victory was near.

Despite the optimistic predictions, others remained skeptical, including Gore, who continued to speak out on the issue. He told his colleagues in late October that the United States must find a way to "extricate ourselves as honorably and cleanly, and as gracefully as possible" from Vietnam. He questioned the validity of claims that the Vietnamese were puppets of the Chinese, pointing out the historical animosity between the two states and comparing them to the Irish and English. He also argued that the Soviets did not want an emasculated America in Asia. Moscow's conflict with the Chinese since the late 1950s made the Soviets want to prevent a power vacuum that only served Beijing.[98]

Gore's foreign relations philosophy reflected the ideas of George Kennan and other realists of the times. "We cannot police the world," the Tennessean declared. "To attempt to do so, outside of our truly 'vital' areas, is to court national disaster." He believed Vietnam drained American resources and energy, weakening U.S. resolve in areas of essential interest including Western Europe and Japan. "But when any nation's leadership has a false conception of what is the true, vital, national interest, the nation is in trouble. [T]his is the case now. We are in trouble. We are a deeply troubled people—a deeply divided people."[99]

For Gore, bringing everyone to the bargaining table represented the only possible solution to the Vietnam quagmire.[100] Vice President Humphrey complained that Gore had misrepresented the administration's position on neutralization, an idea he argued the president supported. Gore responded that the administration's goal was "a Vietnam that is neutral in name only . . . one that is in reality pro-U.S. in its policy and institutions." This stance crippled any efforts at negotiation. Although Gore desired to see pro-U.S. democratic nations in power, he expressed doubts that using force could accomplish the goal.[101]

Gore's opposition to Vietnam increasingly had negative consequences at home. Many Tennesseans agreed with George Wallace's statement that "we ought to take the Viet Cong supporters in the United States before grand juries and indict them. They are nothing but traitors." The editors of the *Memphis Commercial Appeal* blasted Gore in late October 1967, telling him to quit complaining and respect American goals of a government free of Communist domination: "If Ho wants peace, let him show it by a sincere gesture." Other constituents forwarded more extreme criticisms, encouraging Gore to push Johnson to use atomic weapons against the North Vietnamese.[102]

The entire debate was gut-wrenching for many Americans. A Memphis constituent wrote the senator that he was near graduation from Brown University, and it appeared likely that he would be drafted into what he characterized as a "morally wrong and politically unwise" war. He had concluded that he could not kill the Vietnamese, whom he believed were fighting justifiably to end foreign domination. However, he opposed dodging the draft, stressing that he was a "loyal American." He pleaded for advice. Gore's response came within four days. The senator admitted that he opposed the war, but "I certainly could not advise or condone shirking one's duty to his country." He underscored the country's commitment to majority rule and that "the individual citizen may not decide for himself whether or not he will do what he is legally called upon to do. This applies to the payment of taxes, service in the armed forces or other similar requirements." He concluded that if a citizen could not accept the policies, "he must face the consequences."[103]

As Gore wrestled with the complexities of Vietnam in late 1967, another divisive issue arose in Congress. For many years, the courts had prodded southerners to accept school desegregation orders. They met strong resistance as evidenced in Prince Edward County, Virginia, where local leaders closed the schools and gave vouchers to whites to attend private schools. In other areas, segregation of the teachers maintained the status quo, a point highlighted in the *Bradley v. Richmond School Board* case. In addition, freedom of choice alternatives undermined attempts to cross lines from established patterns and ensured the *Green v. County School Board* case that overturned the policy.[104]

In response to the resistance, the Warren Court and federal judges began requiring busing to ensure school desegregation. Because segregation had guaranteed that whites and blacks often lived in different areas, the judges argued that blacks and whites would have to travel across neighborhoods to attend school together. Only then would funds be allotted more equitably, equality of education secured, and segregation ended.[105]

From the start, Gore opposed school busing and denounced the use of federal funds to pay for it. On the Senate floor, he asked whether it was "wise, fair, and advisable to use U.S. Government funds . . . to require a child to undergo the hardship and hazard of daily bus travel to some designated neighborhood outside of his own for some purpose . . . would it be equally fair, wise, and advisable, and within the police power, to require the parents of such child to move to such neighborhood?"[106] Gore made many other public declarations against busing. He believed that community-based schools were the best form of education. The threats of violence and the potential for white flight to the suburbs, and subsequent deterioration of the tax base, distressed him. When his constituents called for "freedom of choice," nevertheless, Gore responded that he lacked any real power in the matter and that it was up to the courts to settle it.[107]

The issue of busing perplexed many Democrats who supported civil rights, including McGovern, who admitted that busing made "liberals uncomfortable." He was not, in his own words, "uproarious" in his support of it, but like Gore he believed that the federal courts interpreted the laws and it was therefore the duty of Congress and the executive branch to enforce the statutes.[108] Still, the issue was not volatile for McGovern, whose state lacked any significant African American community, as it was for Gore.

While Gore opposed "making the schools bear the brunt of the struggle for racial equality," he supported other programs that attacked discrimination and de facto segregation. He believed that legal barriers existed and that the federal government could correct them by supporting special job training, education funding, and programs to compensate for past discrimination, although he warned against the adaptation of strict quotas because they would "exacerbate rather than ameliorate relationships." To him, strong leadership would encourage a change in attitudes, especially in the South where many elites relied on racial divisiveness to maintain their position. Continued attempts to legislate "personal acceptance," Gore warned, would prove counterproductive, and he maintained his belief that reversing age-old attitudes would take many years.[109]

The year 1968 opened with a series of foreign policy crises including North Korea's seizure of the U.S. intelligence ship the *Pueblo* and its crew.[110] However, by far the most serious foreign policy issue developed when the Viet Cong and North Vietnamese Army (NVA) launched the Tet offensive in late January. It caught the Army of the Republic of Viet Nam (ARVN) and U.S. forces off guard. In horror, Americans watched as U.S. troops fought the Viet Cong in the compound of the U.S. embassy in Saigon and as the enemy troops captured Hue. While U.S. and ARVN forces inflicted heavy casualties during the counteroffensive, Johnson's credibility suffered a major blow. In many people's minds, including those who had supported U.S. involvement, the Tet offensive demonstrated that promises of an impending victory were not realistic.[111]

Several weeks after Tet, Gore spoke out about Vietnam at the University of Idaho's Borah Foundation. With the assistance of Jim Lowenstein of the SFRC staff, he delivered a blistering critique of Johnson's policy. He warned against tying the need for a pro-Western government in South Vietnam to national security. "We are destroying the country we profess to be saving," he told the crowd, and worried aloud about the dangers of an expanded conflict with the Soviet Union and China. "The further tragedy is that we are also seriously damaging—if we are not in danger of destroying, ourselves." Gore received loads of negative constituent mail regarding his Idaho speech, although many from outside Tennessee praised him. In response, he wrote that "we must learn, as other powerful countries in the past have had to learn, that we cannot impose our will on the world by force." To create a world order that benefited everyone, the United States needed to "regain the high 'moral' position we enjoyed in the world a few years ago."[112]

Soon after the Idaho speech, the SFRC publicly grilled Rusk.[113] Gore welcomed the hearings as a way to prepare the public to accept concessions necessary for withdrawal. He noted that the French in Vietnam and Algeria and the British in India and Rhodesia had developed formulas to extricate themselves. "In this distraught situation, the national interest requires all of our people, whatever the consequences, to guard their vanities and to suppress their ambitions, and to take and support such action as appears in the long-term best interest of our country."[114]

The pressure from the SFRC and war protestors had an effect. When the JCS requested 206,000 additional men, Johnson asked his new secretary of defense, Clark Clifford, to create a task force to make recommendations on it. In early March, Clifford had responded that "I see more and more fighting with more and more casualties on the U.S. side and no end in sight to the action." Instead, he proposed sending 22,000 troops and pushing President Nguyen Van Thieu and Ky to force the ARVN to take a more substantial role in the fighting.[115]

A political bombshell followed on the heels of the rejection of the JCS request. In mid-March, Senator Eugene McCarthy challenged Johnson in the New Hampshire primary and garnered 43 percent of the vote. Johnson interpreted this as support for McCarthy's dovish position, although later studies showed it was more in response to the sagging economy and Johnson's timid conduct of the war. Soon after, Robert Kennedy announced his plan to seek the nomination. Facing these new challengers, Johnson made a fateful decision. On March 31, in a nationally televised speech, he told the audience that throughout his public career he had "put the unity of the people first . . . ahead of any divisive partisanship." Then with a dramatic flair, he stated: "Accordingly, I shall not seek and I will not accept, the nomination of my party for another term as your president."[116]

The president's decision shocked almost everyone. Despite their differences, Gore praised Johnson on the Senate floor. "Unquestionably, in my mind, the hearts of millions of people reached out to our President as he dramatically and eloquently placed peace, unity, and the interest of his country ahead of all else." Exploiting the moment, Gore stressed that the president's decision reflected his belief in unity, which Americans needed to pursue peace. To him, whoever succeeded Johnson should promote peace and end "a tragedy which has brought bloodshed, heartache, and trouble to our people."[117]

Johnson remained committed to several issues including the 1968 civil rights bill, which concentrated on fair housing. The president told the country that "minorities have been artificially compressed into ghettoes . . . where human tragedies and crime abound." He added that federal laws were "essential if we are to relieve the crisis in our cities." This was Gore's last major legislative battle over civil rights. As before, constituents criticized the bill, but Gore remained steadfast in his support. He simply noted that discrimination in housing was morally wrong and unconstitutional and that ending the practice "is a much better way to achieve true integration of our society than to rely on such disruptive expedients as the improvident transportation of school children."[118]

The Senate victory occurred fairly easily when contrasted to preceding battles. Attorney General Ramsey Clark and the Leadership Conference on Civil Rights headed by Roy Wilkins congratulated Gore for supporting cloture and passage of the final bill.[119] However, it would take the assassination of Martin Luther King Jr. in Memphis to push the House to pass the bill into law in April 1968.

King's assassination also sparked controversies that affected Gore. Johnson had ordered the flags on federal grounds lowered to half mast. Some Tennesseans opposed honoring the fallen civil rights leader. One complained: "Lower the flag to half mast, pay homage to this man of peace. His actions were supposed to have been directed through a love that would last, but wherever he went there was always chaos left along our streets." Gore merely responded that the president had the right as commander-in-chief to lower the flag, and that he supported the decision.[120]

King's death tore apart the country. Riots erupted in more than 150 cities with the bulk of the destruction in the major metropolitan areas of Chicago and Baltimore. African Americans also took to the streets in Washington, D.C., where, at the riot's height, Al had to drive to pick up his mother from a store when looting broke out in the area.[121] As the fighting and mayhem continued, it polarized black and white radicals and further isolated moderates like Gore.

In response to the rioting, more law-and-order legislation made its way through Congress. In June the Senate approved the McClellan Crime Bill, which included new laws on wiretapping and admissibility of evidence. By far, the most controversial aspect of the bill, at least to Tennesseans, was its gun control measures. Gore found himself voting for limitations on the age of buyers and some types of weapons, going against previous stands in which he had been very hesitant to support any restrictions. Gore's vote was very unpopular with constituents who opposed any gun control provisions as hundreds of letters flooded his office, some with multiple signatures. One constituent complained, "We know that gun registration would do nothing to stop crime. You must punish the offenders that use guns in crimes. Taking our guns, which is the ultimate goal of the communists and fanatics, would be all the gun laws do. The next thing after registration is confinscation [sic]."[122]

The issue of gun control became infinitely more contentious by the late 1960s and put Gore in a terrible predicament at home. Many of his constituents believed conservative propaganda that Communist agents wanted to take away their guns so that they could not resist a takeover. At the same time, there was a longstanding racial component of gun ownership going back to the days of slavery and the fear of a slave revolt. With the rioting in the cities, many whites wanted to make sure they had guns to protect themselves from the hoards of rampaging African Americans that they watched on television. While Gore's stances reflected relatively limited support for gun control, the National Rifle Association and other gun rights' advocates skewered any efforts to limit gun ownership as un-American. Their message was popular in Tennessee, where gun ownership was high and many people believed it was an inalienable right to own one.

Gore further incensed conservative Tennesseans with his response to the Poor People's March. King had planned the march before his death, intending to draw poor people from all over the country to the Capitol to demand new antipoverty programs. His successor, Rev. Ralph Abernathy, pushed forward with the plan in May. Soon the marchers built a camp city in the West Potomac Park called Resurrection City, much to the dismay of Washington officials and tourists. The participants in the camps, which Attorney General Clark described as "pitiful poor people with their ugliness and misery sprawled on the monument grounds," led to many denunciations of the march. Rep. Bill Brock (R-TN) criticized HEW for forwarding the welfare checks to a central office for distribution. "I'm not sure we should be paying them to come here to tent city and demonstrate. If they're physically able to travel hundreds of miles and endure the discomforts of that shantytown, they're able to get a job," Brock told reporters.[123]

Many people shared Brock's view of the marchers, but not Gore, who reached out to them. When people complained about the participants, he responded that "the right of petition, specifically guaranteed by the Constitution, must be respected." When he missed a delegation of marchers at his office, he entered into the *Congressional Record* a promise to make himself and his staffers available to them. He set aside several hours specifically to talk with any of them who wanted to discuss the issues.[124]

Gore took another controversial position when he backed Johnson's nomination of Abe Fortas as chief justice of the Supreme Court. Warren Burger had decided to retire, wanting to allow Johnson to name his successor because he feared Richard Nixon's victory in November. Fortas, a Memphis native and respected jurist, had a close relationship with Johnson, dating back to 1948. Since his appointment to the Supreme Court, the associate justice often had crossed ethical lines to provide Johnson information on Court proceedings. The president wanted Fortas in place to protect his legacy and planned to use his vacancy to appoint a fellow Texan, Homer Thornberry, to pacify southerners such as Russell.[125]

Republicans and conservative Democrats lined up quickly to oppose Fortas's nomination. Senator Robert Griffin (R-MI) argued that the next president should appoint the chief justice, while southerners led by Thurmond and Eastland denounced Fortas's liberalism and ties to Johnson. John McClellan encouraged his colleagues to allow the nomination to go forward because he wanted "that SOB formally submitted to the Senate" so he could help defeat it.[126]

The majority of Gore's constituents opposed Fortas's nomination. Some criticized him for being too lenient on criminals and pornography, while others focused on his opposition to school prayer. One group from Memphis gathered more than a hundred signatures to emphasize that "we feel that his association and contacts with known communist front organizations, and known Communists, make him totally unfit to preside over the highest court in our land." Regardless, Gore backed Fortas, knowing that many of his critics were anti-

Semites. He introduced Fortas to the Judiciary Committee during the confirmation hearings and soon after released a statement stressing that Fortas would be the first Tennessean appointed to the nation's highest judicial position. "Justice Fortas is an able lawyer, an eminent jurist, and dedicated to the welfare of the country," he declared. "I came to admire him as a person and to respect his ability as a lawyer and as a judge."[127]

Bitter debates developed in the Judiciary Committee, but it approved the nomination 11–8. However, when the nomination hit the Senate floor, Griffin and others began a filibuster to kill it. Gore criticized the opposition, underscoring that the most eminent jurists in the nation had called for a vote on Fortas and Thornberry. "Thus, I join the committee of lawyers in urging the Senate to act promptly and fairly to fulfill its constitutional responsibilities." He added that Fortas had been considered a worthy nominee in 1965 and that senators should not use legislative maneuvers to block the president's prerogatives on judicial nominations.[128]

A tenuous situation went from bad to worse. A new controversy developed when investigators uncovered a $15,000 payment to Fortas by wealthy benefactors for teaching a course at American University. Gore defended him, accusing critics of character assassination, calling the compensation fair and reasonable, and highlighting the public service rendered the students.[129]

Despite the efforts of Gore and others, the nomination went nowhere. When the vote for cloture on the filibuster failed by a wide margin, Fortas requested the withdrawal of his nomination. The president accepted reluctantly. Over time, further revelations about Fortas's business deals and pressure from Nixon's attorney general, John Mitchell, ultimately led to his resignation from the Supreme Court in 1969, leaving a great deal of bitterness on all sides.[130]

Gore's positions on Fortas, Vietnam, civil rights, and other issues had an impact on his and his party's popularity in Tennessee. By the summer of 1968, the Democratic Party was on the defensive. The "solid South" was swiftly eroding because of the party's civil rights policies. In 1963, Alabama governor George C. Wallace had moved to the forefront of the states' rights and segregationist movements with his inaugural statement, "Segregation now . . . segregation tomorrow . . . segregation forever." He followed this with the famous standoff at the door of the University of Alabama registrar's office trying to prevent integration. Overnight, he became a hero to millions of whites throughout the South as the true defender of the faith. He followed the effort with a short-lived challenge to Lyndon Johnson in the presidential primaries in 1964 and built on the efforts by Goldwater in the Deep South to rise to national prominence through his showmanship and unrelenting defense of issues important to conservative whites nationwide.[131]

The pugnacious and charismatic Wallace gained more fame after 1964 by virulently denouncing the increasing power of the federal government and especially the Great Society programs. With the backing of conservative organizations such as the John Birch Society, Twentieth Century Reformation, and Americans for Constitutional Action, as well as leading Christian fundamentalists like Billy James Hargis, Wallace made significant inroads as the well-organized groups distributed his statements via computer-generated mass mailings. He attacked the "liberal newspaper editors" who encouraged mob violence that resulted in "guerrilla bands" burning and looting the cities. Also, he blamed the decline of American society on the hippies, beatniks, drug pushers, civil rights agitators, and "queers" who promoted a promiscuous lifestyle that a Communist conspiracy had designed to destroy the United States from within. Wallace hammered away at these themes, telling one audience in Los Angeles in November 1967 that "you people work hard, you save your money, you teach your children to respect the law" but that when riots occurred the "pseudo-intellectuals explain it away by saying the killer didn't get any watermelon to eat when he was 10 years old."[132]

Wallace's message resonated with many white Americans. Ronald Reagan had found the same type of rhetoric effective as governor of California, and conservatives of both parties began echoing his positions.[133] The media also liked Wallace because of his flamboyant style and controversial positions, which sold copy; he therefore had access to key markets. The death of his wife, Lurlene, from cancer in May 1968 made him even more sympathetic. By the summer of 1968, he was a viable presidential candidate of the American Independent Party. At the least, he wanted to become a kingmaker if the election ended without either candidate securing a majority in the Electoral College. The Democrats feared how Wallace's candidacy would affect their candidate, who appeared to be losing ground among traditional working-class constituencies throughout the country.[134]

By early 1968, the mood in Tennessee had worsened for Gore, especially among working-class whites. The members of Nashville Local 737 union held a straw vote for president, and one of Gore's supporters forwarded the results to him. It showed that George Wallace received 62.1 percent of the 870 votes cast. Johnson was far behind at 15.4 percent and Kennedy at 7.9 percent. The constituent wrote, "Albert, isn't this quite a surprise? People in all walks of life are alarmed at the present trend."[135] Clearly, the Wallace phenomenon had begun to transform politics everywhere, including Tennessee.

Despite the many problems facing the Democrats, the party faithful gathered in Chicago in August. The frontrunner for the presidential nomination was Vice President Humphrey, although Gore hoped that McGovern would sneak through at the last minute. The Gore family traveled to Chicago including Nancy, who pushed to seat Mississippi's Loyalist delegation instead of the segregated regulars. Al also joined the family, although many congressmen's children had been sent away to avoid any suggestion of cooperating with radicals planning antiwar demonstrations outside the convention center.[136] The whole atmosphere was tense, and many of the delegations split.

The divisions were especially apparent in the Tennessee delegation. The leader was Ellington, who remained close to Johnson and controlled most of the state's fifty-one votes. "The curiosity is Senator Albert Gore, the lone wolf of Tennessee politics who controls no one at all yet and who remains a fascinating, enigmatic character," one reporter wrote. He characterized Gore as "a Senator who has deeply offended, at one time or another, nearly every lobby and special interest on Capitol Hill. He has little use for consensus politics or Lyndon Johnson. He'll rock almost anybody's boat." Ellington and Gore squared off over Humphrey and McGovern, with the governor holding sway, and Gore only able to give his one vote to McGovern.[137]

While Tennessee remained firmly in Humphrey's camp, Gore made an important speech on the Vietnam War.[138] Rising on the day that Humphrey accepted the nomination, Gore made a short, albeit powerful, speech: "Mr. Chairman, fellow delegates, four years ago our party and the nominee of our party promised the people that American boys would not be sent to fight in a land war in Asia. The people made an overwhelming commitment to peace. They voted for our distinguished leader, President Lyndon B. Johnson, but they got the policies of Senator Goldwater." A load roar erupted from the antiwar delegates, forcing him to raise his arms and lower them for quiet so he could continue. The gray-haired Tennessean continued by noting that the United States had lost more than 25,000 brave troops and for what? "An erosion of the moral and spiritual base of American leadership, entanglement with the corrupt political clique in Saigon, disillusionment, despair here at home and a disastrous postponement of imperatives to improve our social ills."[139] The antiwar delegates gave him a standing ovation.

Gore left the convention disillusioned and worried. The clashes between law enforcement and protesters in the streets of Chicago alarmed him. He called them "unfortunate" and feared the disorder and its effects on his party's image. Despite his ambivalence, he promised to support Humphrey against Wallace and Nixon, telling one person that "the alternatives are to me most uninviting."[140]

Gore denounced how law enforcement had handled the unrest in Chicago, especially J. Edgar Hoover, who had promised an investigation. Yet Hoover had already criticized the protestors, leading Gore to call his judgments highly improper and unprofessional. He wrote one constituent that "I am one who believes that J. Edgar Hoover's usefulness expired a long time ago. If a few fellows like Hoover, General [Lewis] Hershey and Admiral [Hyman] Rickover would take their retirement, it would suit me fine."[141]

Such viewpoints infuriated conservative Tennesseans from both parties because they saw people such as Hoover as being the first line of defense against anarchy and the Communists. A Martin man wrote: "I am taking this means to advise you that you no longer have my support . . . It is a disheartening thing to have so much respect for a man, and then see that man go absolutely out of his head as you have done. The only thing I'm not completely sure about is whether you have turned commie or hippy or both." He also complained that "if you have any control over that son of yours you should see that he gets a hair cut." Gore thanked the man for his past support but lamented about the disagreements and hoped they would find some common ground in the future. "Now as to my son's haircut, I have always felt that one generation should be slow to impose its will in purely personal matters upon another . . . So far as I am concerned, he is free to choose to wear his hair in the style of other youngsters of his age."[142]

McGovern himself was surprised to receive Gore's support in Chicago. The South Dakota senator admitted that he did not really know Gore. "He did not reveal a lot of himself . . . he didn't open up about his personal life." They met at parties and discussed the public issues with Gore consistently making his position known as McGovern called him "always straightforward." Still, the South Dakotan characterized Gore as "something of a loner" who rarely let people see his private side, although he and Pauline had a good relationship with the Yarboroughs. Gore reminded McGovern, a professional historian, of John C. Calhoun, who could be aristocratic but always had an "enormous respect for the Senate as an institution."[143]

Others concluded that Gore endorsed McGovern because he had changed and become more identified with the Senate as an institution. A *Tennessean* editor, Wayne Whitt, emphasized that the "longer he stayed, he believed the world was his constituency, not Tennessee." David Halberstam described him as a "courtier" and admitted that the senator had "a slight tendency to overstatement, befitting a Tennessean born in his generation . . . who has never seen anything about his life or beliefs that he ought to change." He believed that it was not Gore's ego but "the U.S. Senate's ego and dignity which are on display, which is why he seems at times aloof and untouchable." The respected journalist characterized Gore as "an old-style Senator, a Roman Senator really. One can imagine him with Webster, Calhoun, and Clay. In fact, it is hard to imagine Albert as anything but a Senator."[144]

But the image of the respected senator did not always play well in Tennessee. Gilbert Merritt admitted that such a "formality and dignity did not really reach out to the UT crowd and bubba crowd."[145] The seemingly distant senator contrasted with Gore who had played the fiddle and danced during campaign stops and was much loved throughout the state for his down-home roots. His opponents began seeing this as a weakness and exploited the idea that he had lost touch.

The November election was a terrible blow to the Democrats, although Nixon won the popular vote by a very slim margin, 31,785,480 to Humphrey's 31,275,166, while Wallace took 9,906,473. However, Nixon solidly defeated Humphrey in the Electoral College by a margin of 301 to 191 with Wallace taking 46.[146]

In Tennessee, the results were especially depressing. Nixon took 37.8 percent of the vote while Wallace tallied 34 percent and Humphrey 28.1 percent. For the fourth time in the past five elections, the Republicans won Tennessee's electoral votes.[147] This was particularly distressing to the Gore family and seemed to portend the future. At Harvard, Al ran into his friend Don Gilligan whose father, John, had lost in a run for the Senate in Ohio. After expressing his sorrow over the defeat, he told him, "I'm going to be in the same position in two years. My dad's going to get beat and there's nothing we can do about it."[148]

The period of Johnson's presidency had been tumultuous for the country and Gore, especially the final two years. The Tennessean had clashed with the president over Vietnam, the Middle East, taxes, interest rates, and the presidential nomination, although they had agreed on civil rights and nuclear proliferation. The momentum for reform stalled in the period, and conservatives fought back at the local and national levels. By late 1968, the country had reached a new era of turmoil and negativity, and Gore found that swimming against the tide had significant effects, especially as he found the White House occupied by a political enemy, Richard Nixon.

# 8   TARGET NUMBER ONE

IN NOVEMBER 1970, Gore sat down and wrote his colleague, Frank Church. It was only a few days after his defeat by Republican Bill Brock in a hard, nasty campaign watched by many political observers. Despite being tired and discouraged, he remained defiant: "In this business of politics, one must live or die by the sword. Mine has been a long, honorable, and fruitful career. The people made a decision and I accept it . . ." "Even so," "I would rather to have gone down with both guns blazing for what I believed to be right as to cavil or compromise, or to whimper and run because the odds were so great. The causes for which I fought are not dead; the truth will rise again."[1]

From 1969 to 1970, Gore found himself embroiled in numerous battles that ultimately contributed to his defeat. The liberal/progressive Democratic coalition was itself in retreat, largely leaderless after the departure of LBJ and Humphrey. While Richard Nixon had won the presidency only by a small margin, he claimed a popular mandate and aggressively attacked the Democrats on many fronts—taxes, Supreme Court nominations, Vietnam, and weapons systems. Over time, Gore found himself one of the primary targets of the venom of the White House, which threw its weight behind the well-financed campaign of Rep. Bill Brock. From the start, it was a fight for his political life, and Gore knew it.

Although political prospects looked bleak for him and his party as the 1969 congressional session opened, Gore had returned to his job with his typical doggedness.[2] However, he encountered a much different Washington than the year before. Nixon, whom Gore despised, took center stage. He was not an ideologue like Barry Goldwater, but he was intensely partisan and combative and in many ways much more dangerous. He brought a legion of like-minded men into the executive branch. While there had been conflict between Gore and Johnson, it was nothing compared to what would develop between him and Nixon.

In the winter of 1969, Gore and Nixon clashed over the president's proposal to create an antiballistic missile (ABM) system. In the mid-1960s, Lyndon Johnson and Robert McNamara had proposed a limited ABM system, partly in response to a Russian plan to build one to protect Moscow. In July 1968, following the signing of the Non-Proliferation Treaty, Washington and Moscow promised future talks on the matter. Both sides feared that if either completed a system, it would disrupt the balance of power and possibly provoke a preemptive strike. Both also wanted to avoid a costly new addition to already strained military budgets. Furthermore, most scientists questioned the viability of any ABM program. The Soviet invasion of Czechoslovakia in August 1968 ended any immediate chances for substantive talks.[3]

Once in office, Nixon proposed building the Safeguard System, an arrangement of possibly twelve sites with four designed specifically to protect the Minutemen missiles. While privately unenthusiastic about the ABM system, Nixon wanted a victory on this foreign policy issue to please his party's right wing and also to use as a bargaining chip in negotiations with the Soviets. Hawkish Democrats like Richard Russell joined the team. Gore announced his opposition to the project early on, calling any deployment "a grave error." In hearings of the subcommittee on International Organization and Disarmament Affairs, Gore stated, "It is my serious conviction that the [ABM] program . . . would further endanger our security, it would make an armaments limitation agreement more difficult, if not impossible, to attain, and thus ultimately degrade our deterrent . . . [O]ur real security rests in stopping the nuclear armaments race, not promoting it."[4]

The Tennessean proved especially aggressive in the hearings that NBC and CBS taped for broadcast. During one exchange, a Defense Department witness, David Packard, produced several charts to support the administration's position. Gore jumped out of his chair and approached Packard, producing his own tables and placing them where the audience could see them. Then, he unceremoniously took the pointer from the surprised witness and proceeded to make his own presentation on how the United States already maintained a nuclear superiority over the Soviets.[5] Gore also effectively criticized the ABM system outside the committee hearings. He told the audience of *Face the Nation* that Nixon had come "down squarely . . . with the industrial-military complex." He argued that deterrence depended on power and the ability to use it but that defensive systems created the impression that the United States had retreated from its willingness to use offensive missiles, thus weakening the idea of mutual destructiveness.[6]

Despite the carping by Gore and others, the Nixon administration pressed forward. White House officials questioned their opponents' patriotism, stressing that the system would protect Americans and that the divisions at home merely strengthened the Soviet Union. They tried to bolster their position by releasing information about the Soviet development of multiple independently targetable reentry vehicles (MIRV) technology.[7] Gore, along with many of his colleagues, remained convinced of the folly of the system. He told an audience at Madison Square Garden that the president and the generals wanted to run roughshod over Congress. He angered the Nixon people when he quoted James Madison from the *Federalist Papers:* "The accumulation of all powers, legislative, executive, and judiciary, in the same hands, whether one, a few, or many, and whether hereditary, self-appointed, or elective, may justly be pronounced the very definition of tyranny." He added William Pitt's observation that "necessity is the argument of tyrants. It is the creed of slaves."[8]

He carried his arguments to the Senate floor where he allied with J. William Fulbright, Mike Mansfield, George McGovern, and Edward Kennedy (D-MA) against Robert Dole (R-KS), Henry Jackson (D-WA), and John Tower. To Gore, the Safeguard System would "lessen our security . . . by giving to the American people a false sense of security." He declared that the true measure of security for Americans was to avoid nuclear war and that the ABM system undermined the existing uneasy deterrence and threatened to escalate the arms race.[9]

In the face of mounting opposition, the Nixon administration and their hawkish allies pushed harder. The president wanted the victory badly and told one adviser, Bryce Harlow, "Make sure that all our guys are there all the time. Don't let anyone get sick. Don't let anyone go to the bathroom until it's all over." When the final vote came in August, the pro-ABM forces won a narrow victory with Vice President Spiro Agnew passing the tie-breaking vote.[10] The anti-ABM forces had anticipated defeat, but they had fought tenaciously. Until this point in the cold war, the Pentagon had faced few challenges to its weapon systems requests. Nonetheless, the narrowness of the vote signaled changes. Senator Charles Percy (R-IL) wrote Fulbright afterward that "in winning the support of half of all Senators, we established the principle that the Senate is no longer willing to accept without question the judgment of the military that a particular weapons system is vital to national survival."[11]

At the height of the ABM fight, Gore also clashed with the administration over Vietnam. During his campaign, Nixon had promised he had a "secret plan" for extricating the United States from Vietnam that would end the war on an "honorable basis." He provided few specifics other than reaching out to draft-age voters by promising to stop the draft and to create an all-volunteer army. In the meantime, he worked behind the scenes with South Vietnamese president

Nguyen Van Thieu to prevent any breakthroughs at the peace table before the November elections.[12]

Gore viewed Nixon's promises skeptically. In late March, he criticized Admiral John S. McCain, commander of the Pacific theater, who had questioned the enemy's capability to launch another offensive. Gore warned on the Senate floor that "there is a very sad lesson in this story of self-deception. A revolutionary, political war in Asia cannot be won by white westerners with acceptable risks and losses."[13]

Soon after, Gore expanded his criticism of Nixon. The *Baltimore Sun* reported that the senator wanted American people not to buy "another pig in a poke labeled 'secret negotiation.'" Yet when Nixon made his first major speech on Vietnam on May 14, Gore admitted being pleasantly surprised that he ruled out a military solution and proposed certain steps that the senator had supported for years. These included a cease-fire, international supervision of troop withdrawals, and respect for the basic concepts of the Geneva accords.[14] Despite Nixon's promises, Gore remained dubious. He told the Senate Foreign Relations Committee in mid-June that he supported any ideas that extricated the United States from Vietnam, but worried if the administration really backed such proposals: "Many times and in various ways, I tried to prevent the war from being widened and deepened, thus bloodier and harder to end. I am now doing everything I can to get us out of this horrible war as quickly, as honorably, and completely as possible."[15]

By this time, the war had become personal for Gore. In May 1969, Al had graduated from Harvard and faced a tough decision regarding military service. While sharing his parents' opposition to the war, he understood that what he did would affect his father's 1970 reelection campaign. Another important factor was that he remained registered with the draft board in Smith County, and he knew people from the area, including Walter G. Pope and Jackie Underwood, who had died in Vietnam. At the same time, his Harvard classmates had done everything possible to avoid the draft; out of the class of more than 1,200 that graduated in 1969, only two went to Vietnam.[16]

He agonized over the decision, one exacerbated by his engagement to his high school sweetheart, Mary Elizabeth "Tipper" Aitcheson. Without hesitation, his parents said that they would support whatever decision he made. As they had before, the family retreated to the solace of the farm to think and talk about it. At one point, Albert took a long walk with Al beside the Caney Fork, where they had spent so much time fishing and swimming. He remembered trying "to assist him as best I could in analyzing the situation," although he probably felt relatively powerless.[17] There were options. The Gores could have followed the example of many others and used their connections to find a slot in the Reserves or National Guard. An Alabama cousin's husband had already secured Al a place in the Alabama Guard. After some thought, Al merely responded that he appreciated the gesture, "but I believe what I'm going to do is enlist."[18]

He made the decision for several reasons. Clearly, he feared not being able to walk down Main Street in Carthage "without feeling small and guilty." He also believed that by serving, he helped his father avoid charges of disloyalty. In this way, he could help the antiwar movement by keeping in place a prominent "dove" in the Senate.[19] Without any fanfare, he traveled to a friend's home in Newark, New Jersey, and soon thereafter walked into a recruiting station. After scoring very high on the entrance exam and passing the physical, he became Private Al Gore.[20]

While Al struggled with his military service, his father faced a serious challenge on another front in the early fall. In mid-August, Nixon put forth Clement F. Haynsworth, chief judge of the Fourth Circuit Court of Appeals, to fill Fortas's vacancy on the Supreme Court. Afterward, Nixon told John Erlichman that "with this one, we'd stick it to the liberal, Ivy League clique who thought the Court was their own private playground."[21]

Almost immediately, a controversy arose. Senator Birch Bayh (D-IN) accused Haynsworth of overseeing court cases in which he had financial interests, while others complained that he belonged to segregated clubs. Meanwhile, the White House counterattacked, asking for the support of southern bar associations and the National Rifle Association. Nixon told Erlichman that "they have got to be energized. Get pro-Haynsworth speeches into the record; we've got to build a wave of support for our man." Even when some advisers told him that Haynsworth would not pass muster, Nixon responded, "If we cave on this one, they will think that if you kick Nixon you can get somewhere . . . I didn't get where I am today by running away from fights."[22]

While initially happy that Nixon had nominated a southerner, Gore soon found his enthusiasm dampened by the information regarding Haynsworth's civil rights record and business practices. The attacks on Fortas also affected Gore and others who wanted Haynsworth held to the same ethical standard. Over time, Gore joined in opposing Haynsworth, even though he understood its political costs. When the final vote occurred, Haynsworth fell 55–45, with seventeen Republicans joining thirty-eight Democrats to defeat him.[23]

The narrow victory over the ABM, Haynsworth's defeat, and the constant sniping from progressive and liberal Democrats had caused the naturally paranoid Nixon and his staff, which included Chuck Colson, Pat Buchanan, and G. Gordon Liddy, to close ranks and counterattack. They decided that Vice President Agnew would become the administration's hatchet man. Soon, he began blasting people who opposed the administration's Vietnam policies as evidence of "a spirit of national masochism encouraged by an effete corps of impudent snobs."[24]

The Agnew attacks prompted a quick response from Democrats. There had already been some questions raised regarding Agnew's financial dealings as governor of Maryland and his brash racist statements, including an occasion he spotted an Asian American reporter sleeping and asked, "What's wrong with that fat Jap?" Agnew aggravated others during a visit to Tennessee in 1968 when a reporter asked why he did not campaign in poorer areas. He quipped, "When you've seen one slum, you've seen them all." In response, Gore told some people on October 31, 1969, that Agnew was becoming "our greatest disaster next to Vietnam." The barb infuriated Agnew and other conservatives. In early November, the vice president retaliated, telling a reporter that Gore "has been inflicted on the United States far too long." He called for Gore "to be removed to some sinecure where he can simply affect those within the sound of his voice and not the whole State of Tennessee."[25] It now had become personal, and rarely did either man back away from a good fight.

Most Tennesseans who wrote Gore on the matter sided with Agnew. One constituent complained that "I am a registered Democrat, but you might be surprised to know that many Tennesseans are closer to Agnew's viewpoint than yours. We are fed-up with people getting in the streets and parading, demonstrating, and waving other flags than ours." Another condemned Gore's "citicysm [sic] and remarks about Vice-Pres. Agnew. In doing so you have attacked one of the few men in our government who has the 'guts' to stand up and be counted by 'telling it like it is' in regard to the irresponsible riff-raff who would destroy our country."[26]

Undeterred, Gore took some enjoyment in antagonizing Agnew. On the Senate floor in early December, he declared, "The Vice President has done me the honor of promising to come to Tennessee and campaign against me next year. I am grateful for this promised service and touched. There is nothing the voters of Tennessee appreciate more than having outsiders come in and instruct them on how to vote." He mocked the attacks on Agnew as "an appalling manifestation of ingratitude for public service." Then, he asked where were the vice president's fellow Republicans in rising to his defense? "Alas—except for the stentorian tones of the Vice President himself—the air is rent with silence, and, incongruous though it may seem, it now falls to a member of the Opposition to express gratitude where gratitude is due."[27]

The disagreements over policy and the attacks on Agnew ensured a strong response from the White House. The administration had already been developing a strategy built around the book *The Real Majority*, by Democratic pollsters Richard M. Scammon and Ben J. Wattenberg. In it, the authors postulated that in the 1970 congressional campaign voters would focus on issues of crime, promiscuity, and permissiveness, as well as traditional issues such as inflation. To them, the key to winning the midterm elections lay in the vote of people such as the wife of a worker in Dayton, Ohio, who would focus on issues such as riots and the rise in crime and drug use.[28]

Others had read *Emerging Republican Majority* by Kevin Philips, a political strategist who argued that the "presidential election of 1968 marked a historic occasion—the Negrophobe Deep South and modern Outer South simultaneously abandoned the Democratic Party." Philips focused on the inroads that Goldwater and George Wallace had made, especially regarding the role of race in crime, guns, and riots. One Nixon staffer wrote, "It is further pointed out that the Democrats seem to have written the South out of the Union, but the Republican Party is writing the South into the Union on an equal basis."[29]

The Nixon administration immediately made plans to attack liberal and progressive Democrats, although it embraced conservative Democrats such as Harry Byrd Jr. in Virginia for political expediency. In one meeting, Nixon told his advisers that they needed a counterploy as "the administration thrust is centrist. But now even a way-out type like McGovern is racing toward the center. We have to force them to repudiate the left, which loses them votes, or else take the left—which gives us the center."[30] The overall intent was to secure a more sympathetic Congress and to defeat his leading critics.

From the start, Nixon and his operatives zeroed in on Gore. In early December, Harry Dent sent a memo to Nixon telling him that the Senate race in Tennessee is "one of our most winnable."[31] The Republicans settled on Bill Brock as their candidate once Lamar Alexander moved out of the picture. The heir to a candy-making fortune in Chattanooga, Brock was a young member of the Tennessee conservatives who had vigorously supported Goldwater and opposed most Great Society programs and favored local control, although he had a moderate record on civil rights. He possessed a huge personal fortune, created in part by his marriage to an affluent socialite, that provided him substantial funding for the race. While he had little charisma or people skills, he had the advantage of entering a new age of politics that relied more on packaging than personal touch. Though he lacked any positive vision, he did not need it in 1970, when many people thought that the best government was the one that governed least.

The White House strategy also explored recruiting a conservative Democrat to challenge Gore. Dent wrote a colleague that "Governor Buford Ellington of Tennessee is a good friend of the President, and the Attorney General is very high on Ellington also. I am now checking to determine whether there is any possibility he may run for the Senate against Albert Gore in the primary."[32] Ellington was a viable choice. At the best, he would weaken Gore in the primary. At the worst, he would defeat Brock but give the administration a much more pliable ally in the Senate, despite his party affiliation.

To accomplish its goal of unseating Gore, the White House and the Republican National Committee (RNC) adopted several other tactics. First, Nixon dispatched Harry Treleaven, a media expert who had played a significant role in Nixon's television campaign in 1968, to Tennessee. Accompanying him was Kenneth Rietz, a young political operative with the RNC later implicated in the Watergate scandal. Rietz rented a small apartment in Nashville and organized polls and oversaw everyday operations.[33] The consultants were to coordinate the media effort with Brock. This was a modern campaign that differed significantly from any of its predecessors in Tennessee. It moved the focus from the stump, where Brock was weak, to a well-packaged multimedia campaign. Ironically, Al Gore had written his senior thesis at Harvard on "The Impact of Television on the Conduct of the Presidency, 1947–1969."[34]

The White House left nothing to chance. In early December, Jackie Gleason, an RNC operative, informed Dent that he had prepared to collect more than $500,000 from various groups, including "investments" from the Milk Producers Association and Cattlemen's Association and individuals including Helen Frick, H. Ross Perot, and Richard Mellon Scaife. He planned to circumvent existing election laws by creating a District of Columbia nonreporting committee, allowing him to avoid established limits or divulge donor names. He planned to funnel the money to the candidates in "must win" areas, including Brock and George Bush in Texas.[35]

With the opposition growing, even within his own party where Ellington had recruited his press secretary, Hudley Crockett, to challenge Gore, the senator refused to avoid controversial topics. In February 1970, Gore's subcommittee on disarmaments opened talks on the administration's plan for early deployment of Minuteman missiles. In his opening statement, he argued that the "MIRV deployment decision raises very serious questions regarding the Administration's attitude toward SALT talks and regarding its concept of our future security in the nuclear age." The committee soon submitted Senate Resolution 211, which called on Nixon to propose "an immediate suspension by the United States and the Union of Soviet Socialist Republics of flight test of multiple independently targetable reentry vehicles."[36]

The most significant controversy of the spring term related to the Supreme Court. Nixon had ordered Dent "to go out this time and find a good federal judge further south and further to the right." In January 1970, Nixon nominated another poor choice, G. Harrold Carswell. As confirmation hearings began, opponents highlighted his reversal rate of 40 percent, twice the average. Even his supporters called him "mediocre," and one witness in front of the Judiciary Committee argued that Carswell "presents more slender credentials than any nominee put forth in this century." Even people within the White House questioned the selection, as Harlow told Nixon that the senators "think Carswell's a boob, a dummy. And what counter is there to that? He is."[37]

The nomination put Gore in a terrible position. He did not want to vote against another southerner and admitted being "elated" when Nixon announced Carswell's nomination. "Now this gave me an opportunity to vote for a Southerner, freeing myself of the regional disloyalty charge," he recalled. Yet he had little time to celebrate. It came out that Carswell in 1948 had announced, "I believe that segregation of the races is proper," and that he "believed in the principles of white supremacy." His opponents also discovered that he had lied to the Judiciary Committee about his role in helping a group of whites purchase a public golf course in Tallahassee and turn it into a private "whites only" club.[38]

Gore avoided the controversy as long as possible, hoping that Nixon would withdraw the nomination or that the Judiciary Committee would reject him. Neither happened. As the Senate prepared to vote on April 8, Gore noted that "I realized full well my political life might be riding on a 'no' vote. It had become the litmus test of loyalty or disloyalty to the South, of white supremacy or civil rights for blacks with no room left for moderation or reason." As tensions mounted during the roll call, he sat at his desk and contemplated his answer. When the time came, he gave a firm "No," observing afterward that "I felt good inside." The final vote was fifty-one to forty-five against Carswell.[39]

As anticipated, his vote cost him dearly. Nixon lashed out the following day on television in a speech largely prepared by Buchanan. "I have reluctantly concluded—with the Senate as presently constituted—I cannot successfully nominate to the Supreme Court or any Federal Appellate Judge from the South who believes as I do in the strict construction of the Constitution," Nixon told the nation. Dismissing the charges of racism against the nominee, he argued that "when all the hypocrisy is stripped away, the real issue was their philosophy of strict construction of the Constitution—a philosophy that I share—and the fact that they had the misfortune of being born in the South." He emphasized that southerners deserved more representation but that he would not nominate someone from the region and "let him be subjected to the kind of malicious character assassination accorded both Judges Haynesworth [sic] and Carswell."[40]

The Haynsworth and Carswell defeats had shored up Nixon's standing in the old Confederacy. Gore and other progressives such as Ralph Yarborough had been put in a terrible position preceding an election. Many southerners characterized them as traitors and in league with the liberal northerners who easily secured the nomination of Harry Blackmun of Minnesota as Fortas's replacement. To them, the Haynsworth-Carswell debacle represented an attack on southern values, which included law and order, guns, and school prayer. Gore had made another courageous stand, but it was a fateful decision.

As Gore expected, Brock used the issue to his advantage by telling reporters that it was unfortunate that "Senator Gore has decided to place his own political future above the interests and desires of all Tennesseans." He added that votes against the two southerners "were cast despite the crisis facing America in law enforcement, drugs and crime and despite a record abuse of our lower court decisions to force school busing of our children to achieve numerical and racial balance."[41]

Gore recognized that his positions on the Supreme Court, Vietnam, arms control, and civil rights had alienated many of his constituents.[42] With the help of the *Tennessean*, he tried to improve his image. On March 22, it ran a story, "The Albert Gore Story: Tussles of a 'Combative Hillbilly.'" Author Louise Davis reported how Gore liked to go to Carthage in his old Chevrolet station wagon. "I can pick up my suit, get my hair cut, my shoes half-soled, and my car worked on all in one stop," he told her. She also shared a story Paul Harvey had told his radio listeners about how Gore had been spotted by passengers in a small plane after he had taken his clothes off to jump into the Caney Ford to rescue a prize heifer.[43]

A week later, another article, entitled "The Senator Who Risks His Neck," appeared in the *Tennessean Magazine*. Davis noted that Gore was "often obstinate, even querulous," but "a hard worker." Jack Robinson emphasized that he "can watch television, when somebody blasts him, and he gets a big kick out of it. He just laughs." She stressed Gore's fear of the influence of big business and money in politics and worried that "it might be a long time before another man from Possum Hollow could get to the Senate on his own." "He takes unpopular stands," she concluded, "but he has information the folks back home don't. Indignant letters don't worry him much. He does what he thinks best for the nation."[44]

The stories counteracted Crockett and Brock's criticisms of Gore for being out of touch. They tried to portray him as a small-town man who just happened to be a senator, a maverick representing people who respected independence. The problem was they reached only Middle Tennessee where Gore already had a strong following. His problems were in the east and west, where his support was not as strong and the media had become increasingly critical of him. To win, he needed to change the perceptions and attitudes among working- and middle-class whites in those areas.

Gore tried a tactic Estes Kefauver had employed. He assigned an assistant to read the local newspapers and report any significant events so that the senator could write a letter and note the accomplishment, including birthdays or anniversaries. The maneuver backfired as several people who received letters immediately questioned Gore's intentions. He had never acknowledged such events before and the action appeared insincere and a campaign stunt. The office soon stopped the practice.[45]

As the primary neared, Gore encountered new challenges related to the war in Vietnam. Since March, the situation in neighboring Cambodia had been unstable after General Lon Nol overthrew neutralist Prince Norodom Sihanouk. Nol received immediate recognition and secret military aid from the White House. By April 30, Nixon decided to launch an offensive into Cambodia to destroy the Central Office for South Vietnam (COSVN) and limit NVA offensive capabilities. He worried that "if when the chips are down, the world's most powerful nation acts like a pitiful helpless giant, the forces of totalitarianism and anarchy will threaten free nations and free institutions throughout the world."[46] Antiwar activists denounced the action, leading to marches and confrontations at many university campuses. Ultimately, national guardsmen in Ohio and Mississippi killed students at Kent State and Jackson State. Soon after, 100,000 protestors gathered in Washington in the first week of May to publicly criticize the invasion and the president.[47]

Doves in Congress also joined the chorus. Working in conjunction with Church, Fulbright, and others, Gore addressed the Senate and complained that the president had promised only eleven days earlier that peace was in sight. "Can it possibly be that this major military operation was not in preparation 10 days ago?" Gore asked. "If, by reason and logic, the security of the United States impels an invasion of another nation, why should we pick upon neutral, little Cambodia?" He denounced the action for merely widening the war and warned that the enemy's sanctuaries would extend from the Cambodian border to "all of Asia behind it." "Today is a sad and bloody day," he concluded.[48]

On May 6, Gore participated in a tense meeting between Nixon and the SFRC and House Foreign Affairs Committee. The Tennessean stood face to face with Nixon and complained that the invasion was "a violation of the border of a sovereign nation" by the president "without authority or even consultation with Congress." In a heated exchange, Gore asked the president whether "you base your action on the principle that the end justifies the means." Nixon responded that the invasion was an assault on sanctuaries in enemy-occupied territory, areas "controlled by an enemy that is attacking American forces."[49]

Over the next two months, doves clashed with the White House over the Cambodian invasion. John Sherman Cooper (R-KY) and Church proposed an amendment to a military sales bill, cutting the appropriations for troops in Cambodia on July 1. Another group pushed for revoking the Gulf of Tonkin Resolution. Gore supported both efforts. While the Nixon administration maneuvered to delay the Cooper-Church amendment, the Senate repealed the Tonkin resolution by a vote of 81–10. Just a few days before the effective date of implementation, the Cooper-Church amendment passed 58–37. The House, however, voted against it by a margin of two to one, and it remained bottled in committee for nearly six months.[50] Still, it was a clear signal to the White House from the Senate doves.

Nixon and the White House responded angrily to the actions of the doves. He told several congressional leaders that if "Congress undertakes to restrict me, Congress will have to assume the consequences."[51] The White House proposed the Hutson plan in July 1970, which allowed intelligence groups to use wiretaps, search mail, and burglarize offices of opponents suspected of cooperating with foreign governments. J. Edgar Hoover immediately rejected it, but the proposal highlighted Nixon's growing paranoia and desire for retribution.[52]

Nixon turned his anger on Gore as the 1970 campaign intensified. At the height of the confrontation over Cambodia, in May, the president attended a Billy Graham revival with Brock in Knoxville to show his support for the challenger. The White House planned to send others, including General Bernard Schriever, a retired four-star general and proponent of the Safeguard System, to states like Tennessee to whip up support among those who wanted a strong national defense.[53] Gore recognized the significance of such actions, noting that

"I'm astride the Southern Strategy, and he's a real bucking bronco." "I would rather not be a target, but if I must, I prefer to be No. 1."⁵⁴

Despite mounting political pressures, the family came together for a joyous occasion on May 19, 1970, when Al married Tipper at the cavernous National Cathedral. In the presence of many family members and friends, including Armand Hammer, the young couple exchanged vows with Al clad in his formal blue army uniform. They exited the chapel to the Beatles' "It's All Too Much" and traveled to Belle Haven Country Club in Virginia where the families hosted a fine reception. Afterward, they honeymooned in Hawaii before Al returned to duty at Fort Rucker, Alabama.⁵⁵

The time away from the campaign was very short. Brock continued hammering Gore rather than his primary opponent, country singer Tex Ritter. Gore's challenger in the Democratic primary also attacked him. Crockett supported the Vietnam War and stronger crime measures, and he opposed most government work programs and civil rights. He attributed "college campus disorders to a general lack of discipline." He claimed Gore had contributed to the national upheaval by opposing the war and was out of step with the mainstream voter in Tennessee. He made inroads among the Wallace Democrats, and when the balloting took place in June, he lost by a comparatively small margin of 45.2 percent to Gore's 51 percent.⁵⁶ Regardless, he had laid the groundwork for Brock's message among Democrats.

There were other ominous signs on the horizon. Gore's close friend Ralph Yarborough had lost the Texas nomination to conservative Democratic challenger Lloyd Bentsen. Yarborough and Gore had the same populist roots and held many of the same positions. That he had not been able to hold on as an incumbent in a border state with a long history of Democratic loyalty sent a clear warning sign.⁵⁷ While Crockett's attacks aided Brock, there were many people, including prominent Republicans, who worried about his chances. He lacked a real record on which to run, focusing instead on what he opposed. Nixon recognized this, observing that "Brock has voted against everything—Social Security, Appalachia, everything. While Family Assistance is not a good issue generally, it could be good for Brock. Let him be for something. On the economic issue, he has got to prove he isn't an encrusted old type."⁵⁸

Gore also recognized the political value of Brock's record. In early July, he attacked him in Brock's hometown of Chattanooga, using what he characterized as "corny" props. There were two boxes, one with his name and the other with Brock's. He loaded up his package with the interstate highway system, Social Security, and minimum wage. In the other, there was nothing. He highlighted that Brock had not represented Tennessee's interests when he consistently voted against education, veterans' benefits, and Appalachian development projects.[59] He also distributed reprints of the *Congressional Record* showing fifty issues of importance to Tennessee. It showed that Gore and Baker had voted together more than 90 percent of the time while Brock consistently voted against them. This led the Gore campaign to characterize Brock as "Mr. No No" and emphasize that the election was a choice "between a progressive Democrat and reactionary Republican."[60]

During the campaign, Gore also accentuated his roots to try and win the support of working-class laborers and farmers and to draw a significant contrast between himself and the multimillionaire. At one point, he emphasized that he had grown up with "Tennessee dirt" on his hands, "not Chattanooga chocolate." Throughout the contest, Gore continued to believe that "if you scratch a Wallace voter, you find a populist. We disagree on civil rights bills, I tell them, but I represent their economic interests."[61] Perhaps it was one of his major strengths, but the contest remained an uphill battle in which issues such as race, guns, and school prayer crossed class lines and undermined his efforts.

He also built on the Republicans' attempts to develop a theme that they were hunting a gray fox, a reference to his flowing gray mane that now had become a recognizable part of his persona. Gore began calling himself the "Gray Fox" during speeches. He liked to tell audiences, "As a boy from the hills I learned that the Gray Fox, particularly the breed from Carthage which is known as Gray Fox country—knows his way through the briar patches, can run all night and stay well ahead of the hounds."[62]

Brock countered with television and newspaper ads and even a billboard campaign. One billboard on U.S. Highway 11 inside the city limits of Sweetwater in East Tennessee announced: "Birds of a Feather Flock Together," and listed Gore's name with Kennedy, McGovern, and Fulbright. Below, it said "Elect Bill Brock." One of the most effective was one that started early and simply read in large letters "Brock." It was then changed to "Brock Believes" and then "Bill Brock Believes." Finally, it read: "Bill Brock Believes in What You Believe." All the television, radio, and print ads played on this theme.[63]

The Gore campaign denounced the tactic, although it recognized its effectiveness. Al called the billboards "subliminal smut." A campaign aide, Ted Brown, believed the billboards were "calculated to send the subliminal message that Albert Gore may not believe in God, may not believe in the white race, may not believe in America the Beautiful, but by God, Bill Brock does."[64] It was a controversial method that highlighted the challenges Gore faced in the campaign.

Gore also lacked a statewide organization with the money to match Brock's campaign. One observer noted that Gore typically traveled the state with only a press official on leave from the *Tennessean* and a UT student who was the driver. He visited towns without advance men to make appointments or gather campaign contributions. While he was still very effective as a speaker on the stump, the modern campaign was more about the media and money than the personal approach. Throughout the state, he employed fewer than ten full-time people, many less than the Brock organization. An associate emphasized, "For Albert, this is a twenty-first-century campaign. Why, he even has a schedule."[65] Still, in a state of millions spread over many small towns, farms, and cities, it was a significant challenge.

The one modern tactic that Gore utilized in his campaign was television, although with mixed results. He hired Charles Guggenheim to produce several commercials in which he hoped "people got to know him, that would be his strength."[66] One showed him astride a beautiful galloping white horse at the family farm with Al accompanying him on a bay mare. The narrator highlighted that "the closest to him value his integrity and his judgment and his determination to take the right path as he sees it . . . The people of Tennessee have learned to gauge his measure by the battles he's fought along the way . . . for TVA, tax reform, Medicare, interstate highways." Another featured him playing checkers with an older man. During the game Gore joked, "If you beat me two straight games, I'll cut you off Medicare." Another addressed the question of patriotism and showed Albert and Al sitting and talking, with the senator concluding, "Son, always love your country."[67]

The commercials sometimes backfired. Crockett had highlighted that Guggenheim was a "high-powered out-of-state image maker obviously paid by powerful out-of-state friends to try to build a new image for an out-of-touch candidate." In the case of the joke about ending Medicare, Rietz polled seniors and found some worried that Gore could and would cut their Medicare. People split on the effect of the senator riding the horse. To some, it reinforced the idea that the senator was distant and arrogant. One constituent wrote that "I saw your television ad. It confirmed my feeling that Albert is on a high horse."[68]

Gore also hurt himself when he followed the lead of others and decided to publish a book, *The Eye of the Storm: A People's Politics for the Seventies.* Part memoir, part political exposition, it was well written and outlined his ideas on a host of issues including Vietnam, energy, economics, social justice, and elections. He made his case for the populist and progressive ideals he had represented throughout his political career. While pedantic at times, it was a straightforward view of his thoughts and actions.

Problems would accompany the release of the book fairly late in the campaign. It strengthened perceptions of the distance between the senator and Nixon. Furthermore, the working-class supporters of George Wallace were very unlikely to pick up the book, and those who did found the first three chapters devoted to foreign policy, not economics. Finally, it provided his detractors with more ammunition as some reviewers seized on Gore's idea for the United States to recognize Red China and establish diplomatic relations. This reinforced the view among many that Gore was soft on communism.

In addition to these problems, Gore found himself saddled with Democratic gubernatorial candidate John Jay Hooker as the campaign heated up in the late summer. The wealthy businessman and liberal politician had run a close race against Clement in 1966. Young and handsome, he opposed the death penalty and supported civil rights, creating a strong following among Tennessee progressives and liberals. Many party regulars had flocked to his campaign because of his beliefs, as well as his ability to disperse significant patronage throughout the state.

Many people believed that Hooker and Gore needed to pool their resources. At first, the Hooker people resisted tying themselves to Gore, afraid that his positions on Vietnam, school prayer, and guns would negatively affect their candidate. Also, early on, they appeared in a good position to defeat the lackluster Republican nominee, Winfred Dunn. The Gore camp reached out to Hooker's organization, but the talks went nowhere as the senator recalled that "they felt, plainly, that I would be a load to carry, and they simply didn't want to be tied too closely to me. My assurances that I would pull my part of the load did not convince them."[69]

Suddenly the dynamics changed. In 1968, Hooker had started a chicken franchise, Minnie Pearl's. It succeeded at first but then failed miserably. Before the fall, however, Hooker had made some influential Tennesseans very rich by allowing them to buy stock low, creating, according to him, "thirty-eight [new] millionaires in the state."[70] The perceived impropriety caused his campaign to slide. The Hooker people became more open to the idea of consolidating campaigns, but it was too late. For Gore, the disclosures had made it a burden to run with Hooker on the Democratic ticket.

Gore lacked the ability to raise and spend money like Brock. By the end, Brock spent more than $1.2 million, more than twice what Gore had. Even efforts to raise contributions backfired, such as a fundraiser Edward Kennedy hosted at his home in Virginia. Brock and the Republicans jumped all over the event as an example of the ties between Gore and the liberal eastern establishment. Brock's money bought him a large, well-organized staff, including numerous special interest group committees that bought significant quantities of television, radio, and newspaper ads. One Gore supporter, Eugene Graham, complained that "Brock has all the money in the world except three or four dollars, and he knows where those are." Many of Gore's supporters agreed with his appraisal that "the major question in this campaign is can an honest, independent politician with ordinary means survive in public-relations politics of big money and deceit?"[71]

The Nixon administration played a role in the fund-raising disparity. Money from the Townhouse fund flowed into Brock's campaign as Gleason funneled contributions, typically $2,500 each, to groups such as the "Friends of Brock Committee," "Brock Boosters," "Women for Brock," and "Brock News Committee." They used the money to purchase attack ads and other campaign materials. Gleason also provided publications like "Significant Votes of Senator Gore on the Tax Reform Act of 1969," which highlighted Gore's opposition to oil depletion allowances to court wealthy donors in petroleum states. By the end of the campaign, Gleason had delivered more than $200,000 into Tennessee races, most of it to Brock. It was the most of any state, except Maryland. For his efforts, Pat Brock, brother of the candidate and campaign chairperson, would write Gleason to thank him for all his efforts.[72]

Gore's own stands in the Senate exacerbated the perception that he was out of touch with many of his constituents and led to people voting against Gore as much as supporting Brock. One of the most significant issues was race. Gore's votes on civil rights and the perception of the Democrats as the defenders of the minority community had been identified by the Republicans as the Democrats' Achilles heel. While they typically avoided overt attacks, they clearly understood how to talk about crime, school busing, and school choice to their advantage. The race card played well among various elements in Tennessee. A car dealer in Madisonville, Buster Sloan, told one reporter: "People just don't like Gore. The only people who like him are the niggers and the loafers." He bragged about going to Nashville and betting some friends about who supported Brock or Gore, telling them, "If you go up to the well dressed man, he'll be for Brock. If you go up to a bum or a nigger, he'll be for Gore."[73]

The animosity proved especially strong among industrial workers, among whom Gore's economic policies should have garnered votes. The Johnson administration's efforts to enforce equal opportunity had alienated whites, and many had turned to Wallace as their champion. In one case, workers at a Ford plant in Nashville threatened a wildcat strike when the company tried to fly the flag at half mast after the murder of Martin Luther King Jr. However, when Lurlene Wallace died, they demanded that the company lower the flag. In both cases, the company narrowly averted strikes.[74]

The racial animosities heightened as a crisis of expectations occurred among whites. Many were the first generation off the farms and had fallen into debt trying to buy homes, cars, and other consumer goods. Problems resulted when they realized that they had to pay more income taxes. One accountant expressed their frustrations, noting that "they've made about $7,000 a year in the factory and picked up another $2,000 through the soil bank. You go through their returns and they owe $1500 in taxes." He observed that when they learned that, "They get pissed off . . . [Y]ou can see them thinking. 'Where does the tax money go? Welfare. And who gets the welfare? The niggers. And who did I see on my color TV raising hell and carrying and burning some damn things? The niggers.' And so they're angry as hell."[75]

The Republicans avoided overt appeals to racism, such as playing "Dixie" until the record was worn out as Prentice Cooper had done a dozen years earlier. Instead, they employed more subtle tactics. The Republican strategists had watched the Wallace campaign closely and stolen many of its ideas. Opposing school busing, promoting school choice, regulating guns, and pushing states' rights all carried racial overtones, something every southern politician and strategist knew. They understood that many working- and middle-class whites believed that government had become a servant of African Americans. Any attack on federal power by Brock implied protection of the "southern" way of life and its traditions, which included white dominance. While Gore shared many southerners' views on issues such as school busing, the Brock campaign had his positions on civil rights, guns, and school choice, as well as perception of the Democratic Party as a tool of the minorities, on its side.[76]

Brock's followers, especially those in western Tennessee, understood the significance of the race issue, as did the Gore supporters. Over time, people in the Gore campaign (without his blessing) began withholding bumper stickers from African American voters, fearful of exacerbating the existing tensions. However, the Brock supporters, according to the *Wall Street Journal*, "have been gleefully bootlegging Gore stickers to the blacks."[77]

Compounding Gore's problems was the lukewarm response of the African American community to his candidacy, despite his efforts to reach out to them, including weekly Sunday visits during the campaign to African American churches in Memphis. Many African Americans remembered his no vote on the 1964 Civil Rights Act, and most knew that he had no African American staff members. An African American lawyer in Nashville summed up Gore's problems with the statement: "Gore does things for blacks as the poor but not for the blacks as blacks."[78]

There were other growing frustrations in the African American community. The victories in 1964 and 1965 had not ended de facto segregation, socioeconomic disparities, or the lack of business and education opportunities. The Reverend Kelly Miller Smith of Nashville told one reporter, "I'm very disenchanted. Things come up that are very basic and almost simple and you can't get it done. They put an interstate route right through the heart of the black community . . . Destroyed it . . . They couldn't go through Belle Meade (the rich white section) with an interstate but they did it to us because we're poor and black."[79] Of course, one of Gore's claims to fame was his role in the creation of the interstate highway system. While he did not influence such decisions, his identification with it hurt him.

When the Gore and Hooker people went to Memphis leaders to ask for support, they received a surprise. African American leaders had wholeheartedly supported Democrats in 1966, asking for very little money to help. However, in 1970, they demanded a huge amount of money to get out the vote. While it was common to request funds to pay for workers to man the phones, drive people to vote, and pay for advertisements, the amount was extremely high, and each faction wanted its own. David Halberstam, covering the race for *Harper's*, hypothesized that the leaders knew the mood of the African American community and asked for the exorbitant amount knowing it would be turned down, "thus preparing their own alibi in case the black vote failed."[80]

Gore's position on the Vietnam War continued to hurt him as he recognized that his opposition went "against the grain of the prevailing sentiment in Tennessee. Show Tennesseans a war and they'll fight it." Memphis mayor Henry Loeb chastised Gore, arguing that "the basic immorality is not backing our fighting men in Vietnam, and in not winning the war, and I mean it." One African American insurance adjuster told a reporter that he supported Brock because "I have a son in Vietnam, who is proud of his country and glad to fight for it. I can't see how Gore can consider pulling everybody out after everything that's already happened over there." Future GOP chairman Tom Beasley recalled that while serving in Vietnam, he reportedly found a pamphlet on a dead NVA containing statements by Americans including Gore who questioned the

U.S. role. Even though Gore had supported Beasley's appointment to West Point and been a family friend, the Democrat returned home in 1970 and became a partisan Republican.[81]

Brock also carefully blamed the lack of law and order on the Democrats' liberal attitudes that encouraged the antiwar and racial activists. "Our college campuses are infested with drug peddlers. Our courts are disrupted," he told one group, "buildings are bombed and schools threatened. Our law officers are threatened, beaten and murdered. Pornography pollutes our mailboxes . . . Rapists, robbers and burglars make our streets and home unsafe."[82] Without directly saying so, he linked Gore to all the problems, and his efforts had some effects. A telephone operator blamed "Gore's stupidity and liberal attitude" for causing "so many college riots in Tennessee. He just keeps egging it on." A Shelby County sheriff's officer admitted that "I don't like Brock." Yet he claimed, "I think he's the lesser of two evils," and told how his son at Memphis State University had hair down to his shoulders and refused to cut it, going so far as to give him a peace sign when he demanded he do so. "He keeps telling me how great Gore is, and if that's what Gore is for, then I'm not."[83]

Brock's campaign also effectively tied him to Nixon, who enjoyed a high popularity rating in Tennessee and who many conservative Democrats believed was a proponent of their ideas and values. A dockworker told a reporter that Gore had gone too far when he "voted against Nixon just for the hell of it. I didn't mind too much when he voted against Haynsworth, but he voted against Carswell too." A lawyer who admitted that Brock's record paled to that of Gore, still asserted, "The whole campaign boils down to whether or not the candidate is in favor of Nixon or against him." He added that he would vote for Brock.[84]

The White House intensified its efforts as the election approached. On September 22, Agnew visited Memphis for a Brock fund-raiser. Much to his surprise, Gore greeted him at the airport. When he saw Gore, Agnew worried aloud that he might be "headed for a citizens' arrest." During his speech in Memphis, Agnew noted that he never questioned Gore's patriotism or sincerity but believed that "he is most sincere in his mistaken belief that Tennessee is located somewhere between New York City and Hartford, Connecticut." Then, he called Gore the "Southern regional chairman of the Eastern liberal establishment" and praised Brock for being the "voice of moderate, centrist, and conservative people."[85]

Gore thoroughly enjoyed surprising Agnew. His campaign already had urged hecklers not to try to upstage the vice president, who relished confrontations. Instead, he attacked Agnew as an outsider who was "a former governor of a Union state located on the eastern seaboard. In earlier and less hospitable days, he might have been referred to as a carpetbagger by our sectional-minded folks."[86] Such portrayals influenced some Tennessee voters as pollsters saw Gore receive a bump upward after the visit.

As a follow-up, Nixon made an appearance in Tennessee on October 20, following other dignitaries, including William Westmoreland, who attended the Army-Tennessee game in early October. Nixon's staff carefully chose friendly territory at East Tennessee State University in Johnson City for the visit. He spoke to more than thirty thousand people who braved the rain to hear him praise Dunn and Brock for "putting principles first." Regarding the Senate race, "the President that Tennessee voted for should have a man in the United States Senate who voted with him on the big issues." On Vietnam, Nixon declared, "We are working for peace . . . My program, the program Bill Brock supports, says, 'End the war in a way that will win the peace.'" The Brock campaign videotaped the message to run it on all the major stations and smaller segments for commercials that ran through election day.[87]

Despite the White House efforts, Gore made up ground as the election went into its final stages. A large undecided vote remained, especially among Wallace supporters who resisted voting Republican despite their distaste for some of Gore's positions. Gore gained more support among workers and seniors as he reminded them of the two candidates' records on issues such as Social Security, the TVA, and public works. Furthermore, in debates Gore crushed Brock, who did little to persuade voters that he had a positive voting record on anything.

The final week was crucial, and Brock and the Republicans prepared a last-minute media blitz. Rietz told David Broder of the *Washington Post* that "we had 18 per cent undecided in our polls—mostly Wallacites who were anti-Gore but not pro-Brock or Republican." He reported that "now we're really going after the undecided with the four big issues we've saved for the last ten days—prayer, busing, gun control, and the judges."[88]

With the election closing, the well-funded Brock campaign flooded the media. Waiting until the end was a strategic maneuver because, at the least, many of the ads distorted the facts. With only a few days remaining and limited resources, the Gore campaign could not answer all the charges. Instead of maintaining its momentum, the Gore camp found itself on the defensive, as Halberstam observed Brock's "ads are hitting away daily at the most emotional issues."[89]

In late October, Republican strategists also had Baker submit a rider to the Equal Rights Amendment to allow for voluntary prayer in public buildings.

Again, Gore voted against it as he had twice before. Within three days, there was a full-page ad in the *Nashville Banner* proclaiming, "Albert Gore Has Taken Position against School Prayer Three Times." It mobilized some voters; Jim Sasser, one of Gore's supporters and head of the campaign in Nashville, reported that people working the phone banks for Gore received numerous queries on why the senator opposed school prayer. It was also very likely that on the Sunday preceding the election more than a few pastors commented about the senator's transgressions. According to Sasser, the "amendment put Brock over the top."[90]

A few years later, Gore complained that "in the new politics of the right, the people of a state or region are carefully surveyed not to determine their needs or aspirations, but to assess their fears, hates, and prejudices and then an expensive campaign is tailor-made to exploit the worst in them."[91] He was largely correct; conservatives, working in close alliance with the emerging Christian right, employed the model throughout the 1970s and 1980s against progressive and liberal Democrats. The frustration with the Brock campaign carried over to Gore's supporters. Eugene Graham told a reporter, "You know, I'd really like to beat these bastards. Not for Albert, not for myself, not for the Democratic Party, but just to show that the people have sense and can't be fooled by a lot of cheap lies."[92]

Until the end, Gore hoped for a miracle. His backers believed the working-class and African American votes would make the difference if the voter turnout in eastern Tennessee was low. However, the returns in early November showed East Tennessee went to Brock by a 60 percent edge while Middle Tennessee held for Gore with 62 percent. This centered the race on western Tennessee. There, Brock captured Shelby County and the surrounding areas with 55 percent, leading Gore's campaign manager, Tim Schaeffer, to observe, "Senator, it doesn't look too good." In the final numbers, the margin was 559,000 (52.1 percent) for Brock to 513,000 (47.9 percent) for Gore.[93]

On election night, the Gore family, including Al who was on leave after receiving orders to go to Vietnam, gathered at the Hermitage Hotel in Nashville. The Gores were stoic as the final results arrived, although Albert vigorously ordered the television turned off when Reagan appeared on it. Over time, Albert and Pauline tried to console the younger people. To one observer, Pauline almost looked relieved, although it was clear that the defeat shook Al a great deal. The senator resisted personally congratulating Brock, angry over the scurrilous campaign the victor had waged. When he finally made his concession speech that night, he quoted poet Edwin Markham: "Defeat may serve as well as victory to shake the soul and let the glory out." He acknowledged that the odds had been against him, but "we had to make the fight because the issues were so important and the stakes so high. I told the truth as I saw it . . . The causes for which we fought are not dead. The truth shall rise again."[94]

There is much speculation about the meaning of the last statement. Some believed Gore had passed the torch to his son, who would in the future reclaim the family position in Tennessee politics. Others thought it implied that the truth about Brock, Nixon, and Agnew would eventually emerge. However, his son stressed that it meant that the South would continue to evolve and that the mean-spirited conservatism represented by Brock and Nixon and their Bourbon attitudes would eventually fall into disfavor.[95] No one knows for sure, although the story and its predictions have evolved into legend over the years.

The whole campaign left Gore bitter and disillusioned. The very next day, Albert and Al took a canoe and paddled along the Caney Fork. His son characterized him as near despair, fatigued after months of hard campaigning. "What would you do if you had 32 years of service to the people given to the highest of your ability, always doing what you thought was right, and had been unceremoniously turned out of office?" he asked Al. Without hesitating, his son responded, "I'd take the 32 years, Dad."[96]

That same day, a constituent called the house. Pauline picked up, and the caller began to complain about the senator's position on Vietnam. With little fanfare, she replied before slamming down the phone: "I have listened to the likes of you for thirty-two years, and I don't want to hear it this morning!"[97]

Gore's defeat, along with Yarborough's, further signaled a change at the national level. Liberals and progressives retained their positions in states in the Northeast, upper Midwest, and West, but they increasingly found themselves under fire in most states outside those regions. This was particularly true in the South, where the conservatives clearly had launched an offensive in some areas, especially in the border states such as Tennessee and Texas, and won some significant victories. The Nixon White House and its political operatives built on the Wallace insurgency and harnessed its energy, and conservatives within the Democratic Party regained some power. The patterns established in the 1970 election regarding issues of race and states' rights laid the groundwork for future Republican inroads into the region, especially during the 1980s.

Yet there were some signs that Nixon's "southern strategy" had not been an overall success. Democrats gained nine seats in the House from southern states. In gubernatorial races, Jimmy Carter in Georgia, Reubin Askew in Florida, Dale Bumpers in Arkansas, and John C. West in South Carolina had all emerged victorious. They had taken progressive positions on race and won. Carter expressed his feeling that "the time for racial discrimination is over."[98] However, it would take several years and the Watergate scandal to reestablish the tradition in Tennessee with Jim Sasser and Al Gore.

Senator Gore returned to Washington for several more weeks, where he continued to receive support from his friends. "Just as I sometimes think I understand the electorate, I get a jolt such as this, and I am more puzzled than ever," Fulbright wrote Gore. Yet one Washington reporter commented that Gore was withdrawn and appeared overwhelmed by the defeat. "Albert Gore, who loved the Senate in every manifestation, sits staring straight ahead, wan and wistful. For some of the others, the last hours make the Senate easy to leave. For him, nothing helps."[99]

He would make several more speeches on issues such as school prayer and receive adulation from some of his colleagues, including Ted Kennedy, who called him one of the Senate's "giants," comparing him to Webster, Calhoun, and Clay. "If we see more clearly today on any of dozens of difficult issues, it is because we stand on the shoulders of giants like Albert Gore."[100]

Nevertheless, when January came, it was a sad time for the entire family with the forced retirement and worry over Al, who had gone to Vietnam. For years, Gore would admit that he "was promoted to private life by a marginal error on the part of the people of Tennessee."[101] At the age of sixty-three he faced a life without politics for the first time in many years. He had some choices to make, although most people did not believe that he would simply return home to become a gentleman farmer.

# 9  LIFE OUT OF THE LIMELIGHT

AL GORE RECALLED his father's 1970 loss as "a very painful experience for me, because he fought on principle and he was rejected. That coupled with the feeling that so many of my peers and I had that the country had seriously lost its way, caused me to write [to Tipper] . . . 'I'm losing my former sense of optimism about where our country is headed.'"[1] It would take him many more years to shake the experience, and the dark cloud of defeat would shape many aspects of his own public persona when he entered politics in the mid-1970s.

The election had left the Gore family disenchanted. It was a bitter defeat at the hands of a person the elder Gore saw as the archetype of everything wrong with the South. Despite his anguish and bitterness, however, Gore would rebound. Though sixty-three years old, he was not content to retire to his farm in Carthage, and neither was Pauline. They wanted new adventures and soon began a new chapter in their lives, one that extended for another twenty-seven years and encompassed a new career and support for the political aspirations of their son, who would return from Vietnam to take up the family's political banner.

Initially, Gore filled his days teaching part-time at the Vanderbilt law school, writing a book, and working with the Council for a Livable World, headed by former Senate Foreign Relations Committee adviser Carl Marcy. There, Gore led a disarmament lobby group and traveled across the country making speeches on the topic, especially to university students. As a result, several friends told him, "You are more popular in defeat than you might have been in victory."[2]

Despite appearing fairly comfortable financially, Albert and Pauline continued to worry about their future. Gore had liquidated the cattle business with Armand Hammer in 1968, showing a profit of less than a thousand dollars after expenses. Soon after the defeat, he told Jim Sasser that he was thankful for the congressional pension because it was his only source of income. Part of the problem was that Gore was not an especially good manager of money. His investments, most in the Smith County area, rarely paid significant dividends.[3]

After looking around for a year, Albert and Pauline decided the best path to secure financial independence lay in practicing law. In Nashville, they joined with George Barrett, Jack Mitchell, and Lionel Barrett to form a firm. They also signed on with Washington's Peabody, Rivlin, Cladouhos, and Lambert, headed by former Massachusetts governor Endicott Peabody. The firm special-ized in international trade and finance law, which nicely fit the Gores' interests. Pauline promised that she would have her own cases but said she would help Albert if he needed it.[4]

As he started his new jobs, Gore also made a comparatively unprecedented promise. He submitted a sworn affidavit to the Senate secretary that he would not lobby Congress "on the behalf of a private client." While acknowledging that it was a common practice, "I am not engaged in and shall not engage in lobbying to influence the passage of legislation by the U.S. Congress . . . that I have not participated nor shall I participate in the distribution of fees that have or that may be derived from lobbying by other members of or associates of said firm."[5]

Despite having a new career outside of politics, Gore found time to speak out on national issues. In summer 1971 the Nixon administration tried prevent-ing the publication of the "Pentagon Papers," which outlined deceptions by the Kennedy and Johnson administrations regarding Vietnam. Gore supported ef-forts by the *New York Times* to publish the information and responded to the White House argument that the documents were classified by declaring that "there was nothing in it that would harm the United States. It is only political protection that brought about its classification." He indicated that the papers revealed deceitfulness of previous administrations and added "the deception is still under way."[6]

He also dabbled in party politics. He initially predicted that Senator Ed-mund Muskie would win the Democratic nomination for president in 1972, al-though he supported George McGovern. He told one group that people "turn to the President for a sense that things will be all right . . . The President is supposed to be a take-charge man, a doer, a turner of the wheels . . . The Nixon administration has been a notably do-nothing administration . . . Nixon doesn't fulfill the nation's needs."[7]

At other times, Gore played a small role in state politics. As an elder states-man of the Tennessee Democrats, he was asked by some young, aspiring politi-cians for assistance. A representative case was Bob Clement, who decided to run for the Public Service Commission in 1972. The young son of the former gov-ernor visited Carthage, hoping Gore would provide him with names to contact to facilitate his candidacy. The retired senator disappointed him, concentrating on telling stories and discussing national politics. As Clement prepared to leave, however, Pauline pulled him aside and proceeded to give him information on almost every important leader in the state. As was often the case, Pauline was the keeper of the nuts and bolts information on Tennessee.[8]

The senator also focused on business. In 1972, he received a major push from Hammer after the law practices floundered as family and friends continually asked for free advice and the Gores often provided it.[9] In September 1972, Island Creek Coal Company, a subsidiary of Occidental, named Gore as its new chairman. In political terms, it made no sense for Hammer to have Gore work for him. The Tennessean had alienated many in his own party, and the Republicans in control hated him, but Gore had earned Hammer's gratitude for helping renegotiate a TVA contract that had not included proper escalation provisions. He also appreciated Gore's loyalty.

With the new job, Gore garnered a six-figure salary and many perks, providing him and Pauline with some financial stability. With his former Senate aide, Bill Allen, serving as general counsel and Stonie Barker handling the day-to-day operations from the company's headquarters in Lexington, Kentucky, Gore began a new career.[10] Some criticized Gore for joining Island Creek Coal. The *Nashville Banner* ran the headline "Populist Gore Joins Corporate Elite." Gore was unapologetic, telling one person that "since I had been turned out to pasture, I decided to go graze the tall grass."[11] He stressed that joining the company allowed him to enjoy "the irony of being a southern populist who has become a big business executive." Pauline was just as adamant. When someone complained about Gore deserting his populist roots, she firmly replied: "Albert served the people of Tennessee as best he could serve and as long as allowed. And now it is time for Albert to look out for his own interest."[12]

His tenure sparked some controversy, especially regarding the company's environmental record. Gore never shared his son's dedication to the environment, arguing, "Ecology is now a household word, but many of those who use it do not seem aware of the fact that by definition ecology is tied to economics, that man's well-being is tied to his being; that although preservation of an unsullied crystal stream, a purer atmosphere, a virgin tract of forest, or an unblemished landscape are noble goals, they are not the noblest . . . [T]he noblest is to provide man with stuff of his existence . . . Before we can recreate we must create." His general counsel, Bill Allen, observed that Gore was not a "raving environmentalist" but a practical man.[13]

Gore concentrated on what Hammer hired him to do, and that was to make a profit. Island Creek Coal was guilty of numerous environmental violations, including illegal dumping into rivers and creeks. The creation of the Environmental Protection Agency (EPA) during the Nixon administration had increased oversight and contributed to more awareness of the issues. Gore never focused on these problems, leaving the day-to-day operations to Barker. Still, his failure to deal with Island Creek's violations diminished his otherwise progressive legacy.

As he took the job at Island Creek, Gore finished *Let the Glory Out: My South and Its Politics.* The book, part memoir and part political essay, appeared in the fall of 1972. He told a reporter, "I haven't attacked anyone. I told the story. I chronicled the events as I lived them. I sought to be perfectly honest." "My fondest hope of this endeavor is that it may inspire some idealistic youths to worthy public service . . . especially in my native hills where the need for education and conscientious leadership is so great." Despite his denials, the book opened with a biting attack on Nixon and the Republicans. He complained that the party of Lincoln had allied with "conservative" southern Democrats "to exploit racial prejudices," and Nixon in particular "competed for the racist element of Wallace's constituency." He chastised Nixon for his "needless and cruel prolongation of the Vietnam War" and claimed "his incredible pretension of winning the war while withdrawing from it, is a prayer to the ghost of Robert E. Lee."[14]

The majority of the book emphasized Gore's view of the South and its future. He incorporated significant works by southern historians such as V. O. Key and Dewey Grantham and argued that the "South's story has been largely, but not entirely, a story of its betrayal by political and cultural leaders." These "New Bourbons," as Gore characterized them, had relied on racism to divide the classes and keep them from focusing on issues such as education, equal pay, workers' rights, and a myriad of social and economic problems. "Conscience and courage might have stemmed the tide toward reaction, economic depression, and political oppression, but conscience and courage were seldom found in Southern Bourbon politicians."[15]

The patterns had continued into the 1970s when politicians in places like Mississippi and South Carolina concentrated on race and states' rights rather than important topics. Gore wrote that "a plea for home rule was a plea for apathy. Let the states do it, if it should be done at all; let the local governments do it alone, if it is to be done—which really meant that very little of anything would be done."[16] To him, this was a fundamental crutch of the southern conservatives, including Strom Thurmond, Richard Russell, and Harry Byrd, as well as the mantra of new leaders of the movement such as Jesse Helms in North Carolina.

Despite his pessimistic view of southern history, Gore believed that populism, progressivism, and the New Deal had helped undermine the power of the southern Bourbons. He argued that the Nixon people had overestimated the value of the race card among the Wallace voters and postulated that "when they overcome their racism, they support governments that try to meet their needs." He took heart in the election of Reubin Askew, Jimmy Carter, and Dale Bumpers, whom he described as "a different breed from the Faubuses, Bilbos, Talmadges, and Wallaces of the past." They promoted progressive programs and civil rights and still won election by significant margins. "United in hope and in trust instead of divided in prejudice and fear, they will help the nation lift the shades of the past from the new day."[17]

The book stirred controversy. Of course, Republicans did not like the denunciations of their racism and chauvinism. According to the *Nashville Tennessean*, the Ellington camp resented being "sketched in less than flattering terms" for their role in the defeat of Gore and Hooker in 1970. The *Tennessean* concluded that the book would undoubtedly be "a hotly-discussed political topic in the next few months."[18]

Gore's optimism about the Democrats' chances in 1972 proved unwarranted. Nixon easily defeated McGovern with 60.7 percent of the vote to McGovern's 37.5 percent. The South followed the national trend: Nixon won 67.7 percent to 29.7 percent in Tennessee, while in Mississippi it was 78.2 percent to 19.6 percent. In almost every southern state, the Republican vote exceeded 65 percent.[19] It was a crushing defeat and one hailed by many as a sign of the strength of Nixon's strategy.

Although the Democrats had lost the presidential election badly, no dramatic shift in favor of the Republicans occurred in Congress. The Democrats continued controlling the Senate and House, and some ominous signs of future problems appeared. During the campaign, five men broke into the Democratic Party headquarters at the Watergate Building, several with close White House ties, including G. Gordon Liddy and James McCord. Furthermore, Agnew was under investigation for taking bribes as governor of Maryland. After the election, however, Nixon's popularity rating exceeded 70 percent, and *Time* chose him and Kissinger as its "men of the year" in February 1973.[20]

While remaining interested in politics, Gore concentrated on Island Creek Coal and helped negotiate a contract with the Nigerian government to purchase $5 billion in liquified natural gas to help offset the shortages gripping the country after the Arab nations embargoed oil and gas following the Israeli victory in the Yom Kippur War in October 1973. He also announced that the company would build a large coal-gas plant in western Kentucky just 100 miles north of

Nashville. It was hoped that such actions would help the country through the energy emergency.[21]

Before long, a constitutional crisis arose. In April 1973, Nixon noted that "we kept one step ahead of the sheriff . . . that's what we're doing." The administration had attempted to use hush money, with the president's knowledge and encouragement, to prevent the Watergate defendants from breaking their silence about the White House's responsibility in the break-in. Despite such efforts, McCord had broken ranks and helped initiate a congressional investigation by Senator Sam Ervin of North Carolina, whom Nixon described as a "senile old shit" and "slick southern asshole." Howard Baker was the ranking Republican, but Nixon worried about his independent tendencies. The Senate committee appointed a special prosecutor, Archibald Cox, and the *Washington Post* conducted an extensive investigation into the whole affair. In the meantime, prosecution for bribery and misconduct forced Agnew to resign, and Gerald Ford replaced him. Soon, Nixon fired Cox in the Saturday Night Massacre orchestrated by Robert Bork of the Justice Department, but the dismissal created a backlash, as hundreds of thousands of letters flooded the White House. In the meantime, Nixon's approval rating dropped to 17 percent.[22]

Gore watched carefully as the events unfolded. During an interview on one television show, he told the host that "the tide of events, history and the pressure of public opinion have reached such avalanche proportions that I am confident Richard M. Nixon will not be president a year from now." He added that "as a citizen of Tennessee, I believe my congressman should vote for impeachment." Also, he criticized Nixon for trying "to forge a police state . . . whose agents sought to rig a presidential election by subverting our democratic processes."[23]

Gore thought the Watergate scandal would assist the Democrats in 1974, especially on the state level. "The people of Tennessee have now tried a cold, spendthrift, high flying Republican state administration, dumb-do-nothing Republican representation in Congress and an odd assortment of pusillanimous Republican state legislators . . . I am convinced the people have had a belly full of it, and they are ready for a Democratic governor in 1974." Still, he warned that the Democrats should not rely on the scandal but concentrate on "sound, progressive, honest, middle-of-the-road issues" that served the majority of Tennesseans.[24]

His condemnations of Nixon intensified as more facts came to light in 1974. By June, he told delegates at the Tennessee Democratic convention that Nixon had mocked American virtues and that he "must go." He accused Nixon of trying to avoid prosecution by hiding behind "some undefined, inherent power that places him above the law which applies to all other men." He could not help himself and added that he had warned Tennesseans four years earlier about Nixon. "Well, history has now validated everything I said to the people of Tennessee. The Truth is rising and rising with a vengeance."[25]

While focusing on Nixon, Gore saved most of his venom for Brock. Mincing no words, he called for the removal of "that sanctimonious albatross of deceit from that high mountain in Chattanooga." He criticized the state's congressional Republicans for failing to raise their voices in protest regarding Watergate and Vietnam. "Many decent citizens, especially enlightened Republicans, must feel shamed and repulsed that our country would suffer through two of its greatest tragedies without the voice of a single Republican congressman from Tennessee being raised in reproof." Finally, he noted the absence of Republicans from many key votes, quipping that "being absent is the best service they can render to Tennessee and to the country."[26]

Gore saw his predictions start to come true in 1974. Agnew had resigned in response to criminal charges of accepting bribes. Nixon followed soon after Congress began hearings on impeachment articles. In Tennessee, Democrat Ray Blanton won the governor's mansion. The Democrats appeared on the rise everywhere, including the South, where people began to mention Georgia governor Jimmy Carter as a possible presidential candidate.[27]

While speaking out on politics, Gore continued to expend a great deal of energy on his job at Island Creek Coal. He traveled back and forth between the farm and an apartment in Lexington. In between, he made numerous trips to Occidental's headquarters in Los Angeles. It was a challenging job for anyone but especially for someone nearing retirement age. Still, he was full of energy, and his hobbies and other interests most likely would not have been enough to sustain him, so he continued.

As the 1976 elections neared, Gore found himself believing that his hope for a New South was being realized. The increased urbanization combined with a more forceful African American leadership had an effect in mobilizing a strong Democratic constituency. The backlash from Watergate and the disillusionment with the Nixon administration and Republicans in general made it appear that the Democrats might return to power in the region.

A standard-bearer for the new southern Democrat arose in the Gore family. Since his return from Vietnam, Al had been very active in everything except politics; as Pauline noted, "his father's defeat was very traumatic to him." Furthermore, his father had warned him about politics that "I would think twice about it, son. It's a long hard road."[28] For several years he worked as an investigative reporter for the *Tennessean* and found time to attend divinity school, where he tried to answer questions about his spirituality and human nature. Partly at his parents' insistence, he tried Vanderbilt Law School, although with poor results. However, in late February 1976, Al received a call from John Seigenthaler informing him that Joe Evins of the Fourth District planned to announce his retirement from the House. Over a weekend, he decided to run for the seat.[29]

One of Al's greatest dilemmas was how to deal with his father during his candidacy. Like so many sons, he wanted to escape his father's shadow. He recognized that his father's positions on Vietnam, civil rights, school prayer, and other issues could hurt him in the conservative areas of the twenty-five-county Fourth District. After he made his decision, he phoned his parents in California. His father took the call, worried that the late hour indicated an accident. After telling Albert that he intended to run for the seat, he added, "I must be my own man. I must become my own man. I must not be your candidate." While hurt that his son would not want him to campaign directly with him, Gore replied: "Well, son. I'll vote for you."[30]

Despite the request that his father avoid publicly campaigning, Pauline remembered that "my role as a political woman again changed abruptly. Though Albert was asked by Al not to campaign, I was under no such injunction."[31] Albert and Pauline returned to Carthage to hold a strategy meeting with supporters, who soon spread out across the district to deliver letters to Democratic leaders announcing Gore's candidacy, although only after Pauline had gone over several drafts and picked them apart. On March 1, Al stood at the steps of the Smith County courthouse just as his father had done years before. The twenty-seven-year-old had to excuse himself momentarily to throw up because of nerves, but he then made a brief speech indicating he wanted people to vote not on the basis of his name, but rather "I want to speak on the issues, and the people of the Fourth District are perfectly capable of judging me on this basis."[32]

Gore faced a tough campaign against eight other candidates. By far, the most imposing was the majority leader of the Tennessee state house, Stanley Rogers. He had built up a large campaign war chest and had the support of many of the party establishment including future governor Ned McWherter. Al worked hard to push his campaign of "Rekindling the American Spirit." He moved to the right to offset his father's perceived liberalism, as well as his own ties to the eastern establishment. He resisted additional gun registration, labeled homosexuality "abnormal," and opposed public funding of abortion.

This strategy paid dividends, and even the *Nashville Banner* ultimately extended its endorsement.[33]

Al proved as indefatigable a campaigner as his father. Always in a dark suit with a red tie to appear older than his years, he traveled throughout the district and stopped anywhere he could draw a crowd. He would sprint a couple of hundred yards to shake hands with a farmer or climb a pole to talk with an electric technician. In one case, he stopped at a garage to shake the hands of the mechanics but soon bolted out after realizing that it was an infamous chop shop. He and Tipper also attended their fair share of fish fries and bake sales. One reporter stressed that "he was just a bulldog, a tenacious campaigner. He just flat was everywhere at every time."[34]

The family actively supported Al's candidacy, especially Nancy, who tromped all over the southern parts of the district near the Alabama line, consistently asking local politicians, "So, what are you going to do for my little brother, Al?" The senator also played a behind-the-scenes role. In one case, Al had tried to recruit an important lawyer in Putnam County, John Maddux, as a campaign leader, but he declined. Soon, Maddux received a call from Albert, who asked to visit with him. The old politician arrived at his house with an antique that Pauline had selected. They talked for a while, as the senator reminisced about how much he had liked Maddux's father, who had been a member of the Tennessee legislature. Before leaving, he stressed: "I want you to help Al. He's hurting here in Putnam County." In short order, Maddux became a co-chair of Al's campaign.[35]

Despite Al's fears about his father's record hurting him, it had a positive effect in many ways, including his identification with important issues such as the TVA.[36] When Al told a family friend, Walter King Robinson, that "I don't want people voting for me because I'm Albert Gore's son," Robinson merely replied, "That's probably the only reason they will vote for you." Others have argued that the senator's legacy was a deciding factor; Stanley Rogers later observed, "I think there was strong sentiment within the Democratic Party that they had let Senator Gore down. A vote for the son was somewhat of a payback for what they had failed to do for the senator."[37]

Every vote mattered as the campaign went down to the wire. Rogers ran a strong campaign, tying Gore to his father and Hammer and Occidental Petroleum. On the night of the primary, however, Gore won by 3,500 votes out of 115,000 cast. He stood on the platform with his parents and family and empathized with the other candidates because "my family and I know the bitterness of defeat. I have a family that teaches you what public service is all about. That is what my family has taught me. I consider the office of congressman a sacred trust." That night, Albert finally spoke out publicly: "You elected me to Congress when I was twenty-nine years old [actually thirty], and you elected Al at the age of twenty-eight. He's starting out one year earlier than I did, so maybe that means he'll go one step further."[38]

Because Al faced no real challenger in the general election, the family focused much of its energies on supporting Jim Sasser for the Senate. Since the day Brock had defeated Gore in 1970, Sasser had promised to return the favor.[39] The son of a Soil Conservation Agency agent, he had attended rural schools and seen poverty, which "instilled in me a sense of injustice of the economic system." Gore and Kefauver had served as role models, and Sasser described Gore as "one of the best campaigners I have ever seen." His wife Mary and Nancy had become friends at Vanderbilt, and Sasser had become close to the family and helped organize Gore's campaign in Middle Tennessee in 1970.[40]

After Gore's defeat, Sasser worked as a lawyer and in 1973 became chairman of the Tennessee Democratic Executive Committee. Through hard work, which included creating a full-time staff and developing direct mailings and a newsletter, he revitalized the party. By 1976, he resigned his position and began a campaign to win the Democratic nomination and face Brock in the general election.

Traveling the state in a Winnebago, he reached out to farmers and workers, asking: "How can a millionaire know the plight of the poor, the uneducated, the jobless, the sick?" Brock's conservatism, he argued, ensured that he "ignored the needs of Tennesseans" while finding himself more "compatible with the profit motives of the oil companies." He challenged Brock to disclose his financial standing. Brock refused because of his wife's significant holdings, and when Sasser produced Brock's 1975 tax return, it showed him only paying $2,026 on more than $50,000 of income. Buttons soon appeared with the slogan "I Paid More Taxes than Brock." A *Tennessean* investigation also uncovered that Brock had hidden his involvement in an Atlanta real estate scheme that involved more than $13 million and included offices rented to federal government agencies.[41]

Throughout the campaign, Gore strongly supported Sasser, stressing that "he stands for the right things." He pointed out that with Jimmy Carter appearing to be headed to the White House, Tennessee would suffer if it continued to have two Republicans in the Senate. He also reminded people that both of the Republicans were from East Tennessee, which he called contrary to well-founded tradition in Tennessee history. Finally, he emphasized that Sasser stood in contrast to those public officials who had done little to help the economy.

"Jim is a good father, a devoted husband, a fine citizen and trustworthy man. Jim Sasser is one of whom we can be proud and I urge you to go to the polls on Nov. 2 and vote for him."[42]

On election day, the Democrats swept in Tennessee and the South. Tennessee Democrats rejoiced as Sasser defeated Brock by more than 78,000 votes, and Carter took 56 percent of the vote to Ford's 43 percent in the state. Overall, Carter took 56 percent of the southern vote and won the electoral votes of all the southern states. It appeared that Senator Gore's hopes for a New South were maturing.[43]

Following the Democratic victory, Gore found himself back in government. In May 1977, Carter picked Gore to serve with Thomas Farmer and Pennsylvania governor William Scranton on an Executive Intelligence Oversight Board. President Ford had created the organization in March 1976 in response to the 1974 Church Committee Hearings into abuses by the CIA and FBI. Its charge was to gather information and make recommendations regarding activities and possible reforms of the two agencies. Gore stressed that "it's strictly a personal liaison with the President" and that "our function is to advise the President and President alone."[44] There were several occasions on which Carter and Gore interacted. In January 1978, the board asked to discuss several issues with the president. These included developing procedures for reporting "illegal" or "improper" agency actions to Congress and new legislation in the Senate Intelligence Committee that would increase executive oversight. It praised the agencies' cooperation but sought to improve communication between the groups.[45]

Gore also used his access to the president to influence energy policy. In February 1979 he wrote Carter that "the loss of oil from Iran has seriously jeopardized the adequacy of liquid fuel supply for the United States and for our allies." To combat the energy crisis, he pushed conservation, use of the strategic oil reserves to reduce prices, maximizing of coal production, and preparations for a rationing system. For the long term, he encouraged the development of Mexican and Chinese natural resources, reduced impediments to the construction of new nuclear reactors, and increased emphasis on renewable energy. He stressed that Iran demonstrated "our national danger of depending so largely on oil imports, especially from small and perhaps vulnerable sources."[46]

Stuart Eizenstat, Carter's assistant for Domestic Affairs and Policy, replied to Gore. He agreed with many of Gore's recommendations and underscored that a rationing plan had been submitted to Congress but that the House had rejected it. He also noted that the president agreed with Gore's emphasis on developing natural resources in China. The administration wanted to accelerate the process of normalization of U.S.-Chinese relations to facilitate economic exchanges.[47] Gore continued to lobby for more coal production, even though he recognized it would negatively affect the petroleum holdings of Occidental. In August 1980, Hammer and Gore visited with Eizenstat and recommended that the government increase support for the coal export program, which especially affected Island Creek since it did a lot of business in Western Europe.[48]

Gore also spoke in favor of administration proposals, especially arms control. During the final debates on SALT II in the fall 1979, he supported the treaty in the face of hawks such as Senator Henry Jackson (D-WA), who believed the limits would allow the Soviets to launch a first strike and win a nuclear war.[49] He told one audience that SALT II did not guarantee arms reductions or strategic advantage. Instead, "it seeks to permit each country to continue to dissuade the others from attack by what Winston Churchill described as 'a balance of terror' without bankrupting each other in the process." While acknowledging that SALT II would not reduce international competition, "its defeat might well be a more serious pregnancy. A stunning victory for those who believe in rekindling the Cold War."[50]

Gore also found time to speak out on other issues. When asked in April 1980 about the Vietnam War, he responded that it remained a "troubling" question. He continued to believe that the United States should never have been involved and that "it was a horrible error—strategically, politically and morally. Our national security was not involved." He felt his stand had been validated by the events that had led to U.S. withdrawal, "and I think I've been vindicated in the minds of the people of Tennessee. Everywhere I go now I'm warmly received, I'm not the divisive character I was ten years ago."[51]

As the Carter administration ended and Ronald Reagan took office, however, Gore became increasingly less vocal on political issues. "I am in business and my son is in public life. He makes all the political statements for the Gore family." He stressed that he was much too busy to miss political life and that it now was in the hands of a younger generation.[52] His decision reflected the changing of the guard in the family, and he watched his son increase his stature in the Democratic Party through his work in the House of Representatives. Al used his committee assignments to accomplish what Rep. Leon Panetta (D-CA) characterized as the "ability to take a few issues and to convert them into press interest and headlines."[53] These included arms control, consumer protections, and environmental issues that were not the most exciting, but he established himself as a diligent worker who learned every detail and fought tenaciously for his position.[54] He followed his father's path and concentrated on comparatively narrow and oftentimes complicated issues that could aid his progress through the ranks.

Gore proudly watched his son rise to prominence. "It is enormously satisfying to both his mother and to me. Like all proud parents, we always believed our son had a great deal on the ball, so to speak . . . His success has been beyond, well, I should say equal to our dreams." He bragged that his son felt "an identity with the mass of people, the working people. I always thought I had such an identification . . . I don't see him refighting any battles that I have fought. It's a different kind of world." He acknowledged being pleased "to believe our basic moral, legal and philosophical beliefs are very similar."[55]

Not all issues found agreement in the family. In one case, Al led an investigation of a company associated with Occidental's dumping of toxic waste into the Love Canal in New York. Nevertheless, Gore encouraged his son to do what he believed was right, telling one person that "there are some people at Occidental who wish I didn't have a son. But I think my son has been right in most instances. Sure he steps on our toes every now and then, but we have a lot of toes and perhaps they need stepping on sometimes . . . I would be disappointed if he didn't pursue the public interest with diligence and conscience."[56]

Al took other positions that differed from those of his father. While he emphasized that his father had traveled the state throughout his career, he knew there was a perception that he had lost contact with his constituency.[57] In response, Al returned to his district each week and tried to hold an average of five open meetings each visit. "And I did that mainly because that felt like the right thing to do, but I think it's fair to say that the importance of keeping in touch in a way that couldn't be missed by anyone or couldn't be misrepresented by anyone was probably a lesson I learned from my father."[58]

While Al climbed the political ladder, Albert remained an active businessman. After two and a half years of negotiations and five meetings between Gore and Chinese premier Deng Xiaoping, the Chinese government signed a contract with Island Creek to build a mine in Mongolia in April 1982. Construction began in April 1983 with a three-year completion date. Once finished, it became one of the world's largest coal mines.[59]

About the same time, the family received a shock. After a visit to the Vanderbilt University Medical Center, Nancy returned home to report that she had lung cancer. While only forty-four, she had smoked heavily. Since joining Frank Hunger in Greenville to support him in his law practice and rising political career, she had become a gourmet cook, helped at the local Boys' Club, and started a day-care center. She also became friends with men such as Hodding Carter III, who became Carter's assistant secretary of state. She read the *Washington Post* every day to keep abreast of politics. She was a doting aunt, constantly worrying about her brother's four children, and she always helped his campaigns, remaining with Frank a trusted adviser and companion to Al.[60]

The family rallied to her side. Over the next two years, she flew back and forth between Greenville and Nashville for treatments. At one point, the doctors told the family that her condition was so bad that they should try to make peace with her impending death. Pauline simply responded that "that's not an option." Al learned everything he could about cancer and searched vainly for new treatments. One friend noted that Nancy "would never let you talk as if this thing was never going to be whipped. That was never part of the equation."[61]

As Nancy endured chemotherapy and other treatments, Al made a momentous decision. When Howard Baker announced his intention to retire from the Senate, Al announced that he would seek the position. Even though weak from the treatments, Nancy mustered enough energy to be with Al at the Nashville airport on May 30, 1984, when he kicked off the campaign. Wearing a wig to cover her hair loss, she proudly backed her brother. It would be her last public appearance.[62]

Days before she died on July 11, 1984, Nancy remained optimistic. Three days earlier, she called a friend to tell her about a new treatment and her plans for a long trip. The day before, she called her housekeeper in Greenville and told her that "I'm coming home tomorrow." The family was by her side, including her brother, who had flown back from campaigning in eastern Tennessee. After her death, Tipper Gore noted that Al had lost a "mediator, adviser, powerful supporter, and loving critic."[63]

The funeral took place at the family home in Carthage. Everyone was visibly shaken. Nancy's casket stood in the living room, and the senator manned the doors. The first person he allowed in was Nancy's housekeeper, Rosie White. "You all just step back. Miss Rosie will be the first one to come in," he told everyone. In the sitting area, Pauline asked: "What will we do?" A friend responded, "We will try to have the kind of courage she had." After a service performed by Nancy's long-time friend, Jane Holmes Dixon, the family laid her to rest in the Smith County Memorial Gardens.[64]

The entire event ultimately had a sobering effect on the family.[65] That Senator Gore had always taken great pride in his tobacco crops created anguish and guilt. Soon after, Al joined in a campaign to place stronger warning labels on cigarette packages, despite continuing to take money from tobacco companies through the 1990 campaign. He also still tried to find a middle ground on the issue in his home state where tobacco remained an important product, although he became a very vocal critic of the tobacco industry after 1992 when he moved into national office. His father also underwent a transformation over time. He told how he sold his allotment when Albert III visited the farm and asked what he was watering. When his grandfather replied tobacco, the young man asked: "Isn't that what killed Aunt Nancy?" That moment "drove it home" about the crop. While there are debates on how much longer it took to finally end the practice, the Gore family realized that it had to leave the business.[66]

During the summer of 1984, Al campaigned arduously for the Senate seat. Once again, Al asked his father and mother to remain behind the scenes. He wanted to continue to be his own man and, at the height of Reagan's popularity, feared alienating those with an animosity toward his father's perceived liberalism. As a result, Gore ran more to the center on issues of abortion, gun control, and arms control and fought to avoid the term "liberal."[67]

Still, his parents actively backed his campaign. In early 1983, several Memphis area supporters including Mike Cody, Charles Crawford, Walter Armstrong, and Tom Prewitt Sr. met with Al at the Memphis Country Club for an organizational meeting. As the meeting opened, Prewitt commented to Al that "we know your father and your mother, and we're here because of your mother." Yet many of these men and others from throughout the state characterized themselves as "Gore men" and went to great lengths to provide political and financial support to the younger Gore.[68]

During the campaign, Albert and Pauline worked to win support from prominent Democrats, and Al insisted that all campaign material contain the name Albert Gore Jr. At the opening of the campaign in Carthage, the grandchildren handed out old campaign buttons from the 1952 campaign against McKellar. Al also borrowed his father's 1952 campaign strategy and never bothered mentioning his opponent, Victor Ashe, but rather stated, "The central question is who can best serve Tennessee in the U.S. Senate."[69]

Albert maintained that throughout the campaign, Al made all the decisions and remained his own man.[70] However, Albert constantly provided his son with advice. The senator encouraged Al to avoid debating the former state senator Ashe because he had no national record, thus making Al a "sitting duck." Furthermore, he wanted Al to emphasize who would be the most effective, responsive candidate and one who would avoid being a "rubber stamp" for Reagan. Albert's own approach with his son was sometimes more heavy-handed. A reporter who observed a conversation between the two during the campaign noted that "whenever Gore would say something, his father would say, 'You don't know anything about that. This is how it works.' It was humiliating. Gore never disagreed with him. He just sat there and took it."[71]

As victory appeared imminent in November, a *Banner* reporter noted that Albert had maintained a low profile but that "on the rare occasions he's shown up to witness the campaign the excitement in his eyes has given him away . . . [F]ourteen years after his retirement Albert Gore Sr. can barely contain himself in an election year."[72] Once Al won his victory, the senator gave interviews. In one he emphasized that "every blacksmith takes some pleasure in the idea of his son becoming a blacksmith." The elder Gore stressed that he had gone to the Senate a relative unknown but that his son was already recognized for his positions on arms control and consumer protection. "I don't know of any other congressman who has been seen as much on national television news in the last few years," he crowed.[73]

The victory had been sweet. Al crushed Ashe, taking over 61 percent of the vote to 34 percent for his opponent, even though Reagan destroyed Walter Mondale in the presidential race. It was a joyous occasion in the Gore household. Albert had taken his Senate chair with him when he left Washington. After some rummaging around, they found it and returned it with Al. The day of the swearing in, Albert and Al entered the Senate victoriously. Both celebrated the reestablishment of the family position in the highest legislative body in the country.

As Al took his seat, he gravitated toward a new group of Democrats that had formed the Democratic Leadership Council (DLC). Its members were primarily southern and included many young southern progressive Democrats such as Richard Gephardt of Missouri, Chuck Robb of Virginia, and Bill Clinton of Arkansas. The 1984 Mondale fiasco and perceptions that the national party had moved so far to the left as to make their positions in the South untenable made the group declare their intentions to rescue the party from "liberal fundamentalism" and reinvent the party. The movement began as a caucus and over time formed the Progressive Policy Institute to promote its ideas. The members wanted to avoid the perception of the Democratic Party as soft on crime, weak on national security issues, pro-big government, and hostage to special interest groups such as labor and minorities.[74]

The DLC reflected the transformation that had been ongoing in the Democratic Party in the South since the 1960s. Progressive Democrats such as Gore and Yarborough had been labeled liberals, although their policies on race, gun control, school prayer, and foreign affairs reflected a moderate position that often clashed with the party's liberal wing. They passed the mantle to Jimmy Carter, whose policies, often grounded in the southern progressive heritage, helped him win the national election, the only one for a Democrat between 1968 and 1992. For many southern Democrats, especially those in the border states, the DLC presented an attractive alternative. While it rejected racism and intolerance and supported liberal ideas on the environment, for the most part, its program promoted traditional southern progressive and liberal positions that had existed throughout the twentieth century.

As Al's stature grew in the Senate during his first two years, the elder Gore continued to exert a great deal of influence over him. After Christmas dinner at home in Carthage in 1986, he called Al into his study. Behind closed doors, he unveiled his plan for his son's presidential candidacy in 1988. He told the thirty-eight-year-old Al that he had the youth and charisma of a Jack Kennedy, but more important, he could carry the South, especially with the advent of Super Tuesday, which included early primaries in twenty southern and border states. Al hesitated, although one Gore campaign staffer observed that Albert "had a naked, desperate desire to see his boy be president." Al mulled it over and eventually agreed. On hearing the news, Albert noted that "I yelled like a Comanche."[75]

Unlike previous campaigns, Gore turned his father and mother loose, as he no longer feared a backlash regarding his father's positions. By that time Albert was a hero to many Democrats. Furthermore, Al was only thirty-nine, and he needed to demonstrate some maturity in the national arena, something aided by his father's presence. He listened to his father on many issues, typically during talks at Albert and Pauline's apartment in the Methodist Building, although one staffer emphasized that "Gore did not gratuitously offer advice." When he did, "Al had a certain skepticism of his father like all sons."[76] Nevertheless, Albert played an important role in the campaign.

Throughout the campaign, Albert remained one of Al's loudest cheerleaders. During an early stop in April, the elder Gore emphasized that "Al has the makings of a president. He is the most exciting, charismatic candidate in the race, and he has the unusual combination of a down-to-earth personality and a keen intellect. He also has a wonderful sense of humor." He continued to hammer home his belief that it was time for change and used the transition from Eisenhower to Kennedy as his starting point: "I think the sentiment for a generational change of leadership is stronger now than it was then." The elder Gore downplayed his role in the campaign, calling politics a young man's game. "The most important contribution my wife and I can make," he told a reporter, "is to give Al and Tipper the peace of mind of knowing their children are well cared for and that is what we plan to do."[77]

As the campaign unfolded, Pauline and Albert helped their son with strategy. They pushed Al to focus on reaching mainstream America, which required taking moderate positions on issues such as defense, foreign policy, and guns, and rejecting the "politics of defeat, complacency, and doubt." In particular, Albert concentrated on international relations, where Al had more experience than his chief competitor, Massachusetts governor Michael Dukakis.[78] All policy choices did not require dismissing traditional Democrat positions, and Albert continued to project his son as the champion of the "working men and women," someone determined to create a better package for them to create "better understanding and prevent misrepresentation by Republican operatives." Gore realized that Super Tuesday would make or break his son, and that his fate depended on his taking the South. "We've got to get the Dixiecrats back in the Democratic Party, and we're playing damn hard ball. Later in the campaign, after [Al] has won the nomination, people will see the other side of his record come through," he told a reporter.[79]

Albert also played an important role in states such as Iowa, where the senator's down-home charm worked well with the farmers and Democratic Party members who dominated the caucuses. Al had to concentrate on other states, including the first primary in New Hampshire. A *Time* reporter emphasized that "Albert Sr. has been vigorously campaigning [in Iowa] as a surrogate for his son. By this week he will have hit all 99 counties in the state, giving his hillbilly speeches to elect his boy to the White House." Pauline also played a role. As Al prepared for a forum in Iowa, she passed him a note that had only three words: "Smile, Relax, Attack." She also liked to brag about her husband and son that "I trained them both, and I did a better job on my son than I did on my husband."[80]

Throughout the campaign, Albert and Pauline worked tirelessly, traveling to thirty-eight states and giving more than a thousand speeches in support of their son. At one point, the senator bragged, "I've been through 35 states, and I have 13 to go." An observer commented that as Al ran for president, "Gore, Sr., now 79, but still with fire in the belly, is working full time in the campaign." Another person stressed that "Albert Sr. sees in Al Jr. the fulfillment of his own dreams."[81]

Despite a vigorous campaign, Gore lost to Dukakis. He had done well in the Super Tuesday primaries, especially in the southern border states and the West, but Jesse Jackson had undermined his position in the Deep South, taking important states including Virginia, Georgia, and Alabama. Gore held out until destroyed by a debacle in New York, caused in large part by the support of the controversial mayor of New York City, Ed Koch. By April 21, he withdrew from the campaign, calling his effort "horrible." Yet, when asked if he would do it again, he responded: "Oh, yeah."[82]

The Gore family rallied to support Dukakis in his battle against George H. W. Bush. "Americans should rise up to be free people and elect officials on their merits and qualifications . . . lifting the level of campaigns and not focusing on the trivial," Albert told one person. He focused on campaign finances, calling for "a free election—free of special interest and PAC money." In particular he called for a ban on private monies in campaigns, which he characterized as a "threat to democracy." He denounced existing campaign finance laws as riddled with loopholes that allowed people with money to gain access to power.[83]

Al and Albert tried rallying Tennesseans to support the Democratic nominee. When the Massachusetts governor visited Nashville in June 1988, they joined him on a platform in the Hermitage Hotel to endorse Dukakis. Al commented: "I think Mike Dukakis' image here in the South and all across the country is very different from what a lot of people thought it was going to be when the campaign began. I think he moved beyond the old labels . . . I was pleased to see not only Mike Dukakis but all of us learn from each other." In the end, Dukakis paid a tribute to the elder Gore, calling him "my hero in the 50s and 60s. He gave us an example of courage, independence and integrity— the likes of which we have not often had in this country."[84]

Despite the family efforts, the 1988 campaign ended badly for the Democrats. The Bush team fought hard, utilizing hot-button issues such as race through the racially charged Willie Horton commercials to paint Dukakis as a liberal Democrat who would be weak on defense and crime and pander to the minority groups. Designed in large part by Lee Atwater, a Dixiecrat Republican from South Carolina, the strategy worked.[85] When the people went to the polls, Bush won easily. He took 53.4 percent of the vote and 426 of the electoral votes to only 45.6 percent and 111 for Dukakis. It was another devastating defeat for the Democrats that reinforced the views of the DLC and the need for change.

Albert continued to work part-time and support his son. In 1990, Al easily held his seat in the Senate, polling over 70 percent of the vote. Talk remained of another run for the presidency in 1992, but a severe accident involving his son Albert III, and Tipper's corresponding battles with depression, kept the Tennessean from actively seeking the position.

The former senator also spent a lot of time inculcating a new generation of Gores with his ideas. In particular, he had a close relationship with Karenna, Al and Tipper's eldest daughter. During the summers, she stayed at the family farm. Like her father, she worked hard and focused on raising cattle for show. Gore was tough on her, always reminding her that she was a "Tennessee girl" or a "Gore girl" and admonishing her not "to be a sissy." She later recalled that he provided her with many life lessons. One of the most memorable was when they took a car ride down to South Carthage to inspect some construction projects. At one point, he told her to introduce herself to the workers. When one withheld his hand, complaining that it was dirty, Albert instructed her to go ahead and "you tell him, that's OK—I'm a Democrat."[86]

His father's populist impulse also remained with Al. Cooperating with Tom Downey, he proposed a middle-class tax cut, the Working Family Tax Relief Act. It reduced taxes for over 30 million workers by creating an $800 child tax credit to replace the existing $2,300 personal exemption. Unlike most proposals, it paid for itself by levying an 11 percent surtax on incomes exceeding $250,000. Like his father, Al faced an uphill battle in the debates, and in the face of the Republican (and some Democratic) opposition, the proposal ultimately went nowhere.[87]

Al also managed to aggravate large vested interests, primarily the fossil fuel industry, with the publication of his book, *Earth in the Balance*. In it, he focused on environmental issues, particularly the role of carbon dioxide produced by the internal combustion engine in the greenhouse effect that had intensified global warming. It also looked at other issues that his father had supported, including population control. While controversial, the book established him as an ardent defender of the environment and an opponent of many powerful special interests.[88] It also kept him in the national spotlight and won significant support from politically powerful environmental groups.

In the summer 1992, Arkansas governor Bill Clinton garnered the Democratic nomination. The Gore family had watched from the sidelines as Clinton won even amid rumors of affairs and business misdeeds. The affable and likeable Clinton and Al had been concurrent members of the DLC but never really developed a close relationship. However, when Clinton went looking for a vice-presidential nominee, Gore made it to the short list because he would strengthen Clinton's credentials in foreign policy and the environment and balance the integrity question.

There were apprehensions in the Gore family. Pauline and Albert clearly believed that their son was a better person to head the ticket. Pauline later told a reporter that "Bill came up in a very provincial atmosphere. And even though he went to Yale, and he went to Oxford, you don't undo or move out of that provincial atmosphere that has influenced you in your early life." In particular, Pauline expressed doubts about Clinton's character. In the 1980s, during a discussion about him between Frank Hunger and Al, she told them: "Bill Clinton is not a nice person. Don't associate too closely with him." Others around the family also worried about Al aligning with Clinton. One former Gore aide who also later worked for Clinton, Roy Neel, noted that the Arkansas governor was an "instinctive politician" and that "instinctive politicians seduce the public, but they inevitably make monumental mistakes, because they tend to rely only on their instincts."[89]

Al asked for his father's advice. "Well, son, your country's in deep trouble," the elder Gore responded. "Your political party is in deep trouble. And by your own analysis, the world in which we live is under severe threat. If your party and the presidential nominee of your party ask you to give to your country, your party, and your world your talents such as they are, the question of duty comes up." After digesting the advice, Al simply replied: "Thank you, Dad."[90]

The courtship process began in June 1992. At Clinton's request, Harry McPherson, the former Johnson aide, visited Albert and Pauline's apartment in the Methodist Building and met with Al. Soon, a personal meeting between Gore and Clinton occurred, one that marked a developing friendship.[91] A deciding factor was a phone call between Martin Peretz, publisher of the *New Republic* and Al's former adviser at Harvard, and Clinton. He made the important point that "this is a man that will not knife you in the back. This is not a gossiper. This is someone whose own views about personal honor would guarantee that you would not have someone who was cooking up trouble against you."[92]

The courtship concluded late one night in June when Clinton phoned and told Gore: "I just think you could be a wonderful president." Al hesitated to call his parents, fearing that they would be asleep. They were not as they had stayed up nearly all night watching CNN. When the news broke around 4 A.M., the elder Gores celebrated heartily.[93]

The following day, Albert and Pauline watched their son join Clinton in Little Rock to make the official announcement. Al gave a speech accepting Clinton's offer and highlighting the challenges of the campaign and the choices before the nation. Clinton followed and emphasized that his decision contrasted greatly to George Bush's poor choice of Dan Quayle as vice president four years earlier. Immediately after, Al called his father in Carthage who told his son, "It was wonderful. Nothing wooden about it!" The family was ecstatic. According to one observer, "The vice presidency was also the job the father had sought, and getting on the ticket would be a family victory, a closing out of unfinished business, and would lift him one step closer to the ultimate prize."[94]

Afterward, Gore gladly provided interviews with anyone who would listen. He bragged that his son had the best of all worlds between his rural upbringing and his association with Washington political society. "Did you see him on the television today? He didn't have anything written, no notes," he bragged. He also stressed that he grew up Baptist, and that "he was reared the right way," although the senator admitted, "We aren't saints." He concluded, "When I looked at those two men this morning, handsome, stalwart young men, with careers of success and accomplishment and wives of equal intelligence, I said, 'Here is a political ticket.' "[95]

During the 1992 campaign, Albert and Pauline actively campaigned for their son and Clinton. Pauline remarked that after Clinton asked Al to share the ticket, "Albert took off and I could hardly catch him . . . All Albert wanted was for someone to say 'go.' He was in seventh heaven." She added, tongue in cheek, "You reach a certain age and you don't mind telling people how old you are. Albert doesn't mind telling people how old he is—and he doesn't mind telling people how old I am."[96]

During the 1992 Democratic National Convention, the elder Gore continued to enjoy his son's success. Consultants developed a special multimedia presentation that included Ted Kennedy, Birch Bayh, Jim Sasser, and Eugene McCarthy highlighting Albert's accomplishments and impact. Throughout the convention, Albert remained a constant source of pride and irritation for his son. As Al practiced his speech the day before his big night, the senator overheard it and told his son that it was horrible and encouraged him to be extemporaneous and put his heart into it. His son ignored the advice and stayed with the original.[97]

The next night, a near crisis occurred. Pauline and Albert visited Al backstage right before his speech. Then, they proceeded to a lift elevator to go to their seats. As it moved upward, the lift jammed. For a moment, the parents were stunned. Then, the eighty-four-year-old Albert proceeded to try to climb over the rail and down the lift. He was not about to miss his son's grand entrance. Pauline shouted to him, "Oh, Albert!" and stopped him. Fortunately, electricians arrived and fixed the problem. Soon, Albert and Pauline took their seats to watch their son in one of his greatest moments.[98]

The speech included references to his parents in which Al acknowledged their importance. He noted that 1992 was the Year of the Woman and the "46th anniversary of the year my mother, born in a time when women weren't even allowed to vote, became one of the first women to graduate from Vanderbilt Law School." He also highlighted his father's humble origins and how he rose to become a senator and near vice presidential nominee. "And growing up, I watched him stand courageously for civil rights, economic opportunity and a government that worked for ordinary people."[99]

The voice of his father came through loud and clear in the speech. He chastised Bush and Quayle for ignoring the majority of Americans, especially those "victims of AIDS, of crime, of poverty, of ignorance, of hatred, and harassment." "They have nourished and appeased tyranny and endangered America's deepest interests while betraying our cherished ideals. It is time for them to go," he told the audience to thunderous ovations.[100] As the convention wound down, the television cameras frequently panned to Albert. Each time he realized it, he would jump to his feet and flash a victory sign. Simultaneously, Pauline would yank on his coattails to make him sit down. It was obvious that he enjoyed the limelight and had the time of his life.

After the convention, Albert and Pauline went to work for the ticket. They traveled everywhere possible, jumping on board a bus from New York to Philadelphia after the convention to go with Joey Bishop, Tony Randall, and Dr. Ruth Westheimer for a tour of elder care centers. Throughout the campaign, they concentrated on older audiences and reminded them that Democrats would continue to protect Social Security and Medicare.[101] Indefatigable, they often joined their son. Sometimes, Albert would jump onto the stage with his son and clasp his hands over his head like a prizefighter who had won the championship. At other times, he would start dancing to the music. In all areas, he thoroughly enjoyed himself, although some people worried that he stole the spotlight from his son.[102]

Albert supported his son's positions, as Al lambasted Bush as a manager of the country for the elites. On the economy, he joked that if Bush made a movie he would have to title it *Honey, I Shrunk the Economy*. He attacked the president for relying on trickle-down economics while denying average Americans protections under the Family Medical Leave Act. The president's lack of educational policies and failure to develop a coherent environmental policy also distressed him, and he loved to ask crowds: "Do you believe it's time for Bush and Quayle to go?"[103]

When the campaign ended, the Clinton-Gore ticket emerged victorious. The Democrats took 43 percent of the vote with Bush taking 37.4 percent and independent H. Ross Perot, 18.9 percent. In the Electoral College, the Democrats won by a margin of 370 to 168. With the victory, Albert boasted that "we raised him for it." At the inauguration in January, the parents stood along with their son and the rest of the family on the stage in front of the Capitol, proudly watching their heir take the oath from Justice Byron White, who used Nancy's old Bible. Al's press secretary, Marla Romash, told reporters, "I just haven't seen [Albert] stop smiling all day."[104]

The 1992 campaign mirrored the one that Senator Gore had hoped to run in 1956. He was living vicariously through his son's experience, and the eighty-five-year-old acted like there was no tomorrow. It restored his faith that the South could be redeemed from the Bourbons, and the presence of two southerners on the national ticket reinforced his belief that progress had occurred and hope remained.

Albert promised his son that even though he often resided in an apartment not too far from the White House, he would never provide "unsolicited advice." Albert and Pauline also admitted that the defeat in 1970 had been terrible, but, according to Albert, "it's extremely unlikely that a father being in the Senate could make an opportunity for his son to succeed him. As it turned out, Al Jr., soon went to the house, then the Senate . . . and Al is Vice President of the United States. So things, sometimes turn out better than one might think."[105]

The family also looked on the vice presidency as a stepping stone to the presidency. On several occasions, during interviews at the Carthage home, Gore pointed out the numerous photographs on the wall in the house. He noted that one area remained open for a purpose. Most people understood that it was for remembering a Gore presidency. "I hope to live to see it filled," he told one reporter.[106]

As Al settled into the White House, the Gore family had a scare. On October 24, an ambulance took Pauline to the George Washington University hospital. Doctors diagnosed the first of a series of strokes. This one impaired the left side of her vision and left her in the hospital for a couple of days. Albert became her primary cheerleader in the recovery process. He helped her with her therapy, oftentimes walking her back and forth across the back porch at the home in Carthage as part of the routine.[107]

While focused on her health, Pauline and Albert watched their son carefully. In the midterm elections of 1994, the Democrats suffered devastating defeats, including Jim Sasser's loss to Bill Frist. Many Democrats and more importantly many Americans had become disenchanted with Clinton during his first two years in office. He had made some disastrous policy choices on gays in the military and health care reform, and charges of corruption and sexual harassment swirled around the president and his wife. The party was in disarray in the face of the conservative southern revolution led by Newt Gingrich, who used Clinton's dismal performance to sweep new Republicans into Congress.[108]

Throughout, Al remained loyal, and in return, Clinton gave him a lot more leeway than most vice presidents, especially on matters of foreign policy and government reform. In the aftermath of the 1994 debacle, advisers noted that while upset, Al "will not stab you in the back, even if you deserve it." One consultant observed that he would not set his own course, and "he would stay there and try to make this thing work. And you wouldn't think of even suggesting it to him."[109]

The loyalty factor should not have surprised anyone. Al could step on toes with his ambitions, but like his father he was loyal to friends, even those like Armand Hammer with serious flaws. The Gores recognized that the association with Clinton hurt their son. Pauline told a reporter that Al "will be damaged politically. But the important things about Al will not be damaged. His character, his ability, his honesty, his integrity."[110] The family prized loyalty, even though it would have been very easy to distance himself from the president. In 1994, he had the support of many centrists, which would have allowed him to watch from the sidelines Clinton's demise in 1996. This might have set him up for a run in 2000. However, he would not, and there would be even greater challenges facing the family as a result of Clinton's antics in the future.

By the middle of the 1990s, Senator Gore's health declined. He began experiencing problems with his memory and some loss of coordination. People in Smith County learned to recognize his car on the roads. "He always received the right of way," Chief Sonny Carter of the Smith County Rescue Squad recalled. "You gave him wide berth." On one occasion, he went into the store. When he exited, he made his way home. One of the other patrons came out and found his car missing. Like so many others in the area, he had left his keys in the car. He saw the senator's car and realized what happened. He drove it to the Gore farm and exchanged it for his own automobile without any fanfare.[111]

Despite the health problems, the family continued to support their son as the Clinton-Gore team prepared for another run in 1996. As the campaign geared up, Clinton paid a significant tribute to the elder Gore. In February 1996, the White House staged an elaborate event to commemorate the signing of the Telecommunications Act, which removed barriers to competition in telephones and cable and promoted the further expansion of the "information superhighway," a pet project of Al's since his days in Congress. At the ceremony in the Library of Congress, Clinton chose a pen that President Eisenhower had used when he signed into law the Interstate Highway Bill in 1956. The president clearly understood the continuities and paid an important tribute to the family.[112]

Despite dire predictions of impending defeat, Clinton and Gore worked hard as the next election approached. Albert's old colleague from the Senate, Bob Dole, became the Republican standard-bearer. This time, Albert and Pauline could not hit the campaign trail like they had in 1992. The senator had a harder time walking and remembering things, but as the campaign wound down, he made some public appearances, including one at Vanderbilt where he stood and waved his cane while telling the crowd to support their native son.[113] Other public appearances followed. They were in Chicago at the Democratic National Convention when Al gave his acceptance speech and noted his love for Nancy; the story of her painful death moved his parents to tears. Much to their chagrin, people accused Al of using the family tragedy to push his political fortunes as his party decided to take on big tobacco. Still, his parents rallied around Al and when provided the opportunity made every effort to help the ticket.[114]

Clinton and Gore were reelected easily in 1996. They took 49 percent of the vote to 41 percent for Dole and Kemp and 9 percent for Perot. They crushed the Republicans in the Electoral College, winning 379 to 159. Many people had been turned off by the blatant partisanship of the Republican Congress, especially its attacks on social programs and its willingness to allow the government to shut down over budget battles. Taking a page from Harry Truman's playbook, Clinton had run successfully against Congress as much as Dole.[115] While the Republicans maintained control of Congress by a small margin, the Democratic Party regained momentum which many people believed boded well for Al Gore's run for the presidency in 2000.

As the Clinton-Gore team entered its second term, the senator's health continued to decline. He made fewer public appearances. The vice president also shielded his mother and father from journalists and writers anxious to develop his story as he appeared the likely Democratic nominee in 2000. The senator's memory had begun to fade as he neared ninety, and advisers feared that any lapses in his memory would be used by the conservative press to skewer the vice president. Although they still hosted the grandchildren and others for large celebrations including Christmas, Pauline and Albert increasingly stayed close to home.[116]

There were some exceptions. In the summer of 1997, Karenna married Andrew Schiff, a doctor and son of a prominent New York family with ties to the Republican Party—although that did not stop the Gores from welcoming him. While Pauline expressed some concern that the twenty-three-year-old was too young to marry, the family joined together at the National Cathedral in Washington to celebrate the event. In typical fashion, Albert made himself a center of attention. As the service concluded, he stood up and raised his arms and let out a loud "Joy to America." He had a grand time at the reception where he danced up a storm, much to the delight of his granddaughter.[117]

In early November 1997 the Albert Gore Center at Middle Tennessee State University hosted a conference, "Albert Gore, Tennessee, and the New South." It was a one-night affair that examined the senator's record. The speakers and members of the audience were a who's who of Tennessee politics, including Ned McWherter, Adolpho Birch, Gilbert Merritt, and John Seigenthaler. Others were family friends, such as journalists Fred Graham and David Halberstam, and each spoke about Senator Gore's contribution to the New South.

Albert and Pauline joined the large gathering, sitting in the audience in the center of the second row. After I made my presentation on Senator Gore and civil rights, I remember sitting a couple of rows behind the two. I was struck by the fact that Gore still maintained a youthful exuberance. When one of the speakers highlighted the possibility of his son being president, Albert jumped from his seat and stood up and began flashing the victory sign. All the time, Pauline pulled on his coat for him to sit down. In another poignant moment, I noticed that she reached for his hand and he took it, much like longtime sweethearts. At the reception, he remained spry, charming everyone, especially the young women. He clearly enjoyed all the attention, and you could tell that he hated for the evening to end.

Within a short time, a series of illnesses weakened Gore's health. Increasingly he stayed at home, and a nurse became a regular fixture at the house in Carthage. Whenever possible, Pauline helped him clean up and then took him to the neighbors where he would regale people with stories, especially of how he visited FDR and then left his briefcase. He liked to make the point that sometime soon young congressmen would be leaving their briefcases in his son's office.[118] Al regularly made trips home to see his father and to tend to family business, all the while facing severe stress from the aftermath of Clinton's affair with Monica Lewinsky as well as investigations into his own fund-raising practices during the 1996 campaign.

Senator Gore died with the family by his side in the late afternoon of December 5, 1998. On hearing of Gore's passing, President Clinton told reporters on Air Force One that he was "the embodiment of everything public service ought to be. He was a teacher, he was a progressive, he helped to connect the South with the rest of America . . . [T]he country has lost a great patriot, a great public servant, a man who was truly a real role model for the young people like me in the South in the 1960s."[119]

A chorus of praise arose for Gore immediately after his passing. Adolpho Birch, the first African American member of the Tennessee Supreme Court, called him a "great statesman and a great Tennessean. I think his legacy stretches a long way back to the establishment of fairness and equality in all aspects of our lives." John Jay Hooker said, "I greatly admired the fact that he stood up on the civil rights question and stood up in opposition to the war. He was a very courageous leader of the antiwar movement and he paid for it with his seat in the U.S. Senate." Former governor Ned McWherter observed that Gore chose "people over politics" and "progress over partisanship." Jane Eskind, a Nashville Democratic activist, summed up the views of many, calling Gore "a voice of reason and moderation in a period not always governed by reason and moderation."[120]

On December 8, dignitaries from the state and nation gathered for a memorial service at the War Memorial Hall in Nashville; those in attendance included President Clinton, Edward Kennedy, and former Alabama senator Howell Heflin, as well as former political foes Howard Baker and Lamar Alexander. The lower hall was full, although the upper balcony opened to the public had seats. It was unlikely that most Tennesseans even remembered the senator, and those who had close ties had long since died or moved away. Still, the audience was large and the traffic congested as car after car deposited people near the hall.[121]

At the service, Pauline stood out in a regal blue dress that contrasted with the overwhelming sea of black. In this, she set the tone for the day, which was one of celebration and remembrance of a man who had lived a long and productive life. Jane Holmes Dixon, now Episcopal Bishop of Washington, led the service. There were many speakers, including Benjamin Hooks, former director of the NAACP, who stood in front of the flag-draped coffin and commented: "Thank you for standing up against bigotry." Gore's grandchildren each participated. Karenna read a letter from her grandfather from 1970: "Young people today are apt to be skeptical of authority and politicians, but the politician who equates this with radicalism is in serious error. What is wrong with impatience with injustice? . . . This is at the very core of Democratic politics." Another granddaughter, Kristin, read a poem she composed: "We've measured our seasons by you for so many years; soft winter hair and grandmother's 'Don't hug them too hard, Grandad.'" The crowd also heard an old record of Gore playing

"Soldier's Joy" on the fiddle in 1938 in front of a crowd at Constitution Hall in Washington.[122]

The most memorable address of the day came from Al, who had worked long into the night to prepare a tribute to his father. He opened with "My father was the greatest man I ever knew in my life. Most of you know him for his public service and it could be said of him, in the words of Paul, that this man walked worthy of the vocation wherewith he was called." The vice president continued, "Of all the lessons he taught me as a father, perhaps the most powerful was the way he loved my mother. He respected her as an equal, if not more. He was proud of her. But it went way beyond that. When I was growing up, it never once occurred to me that the foundation upon which my security depended would ever shake. As I grew older, I learned from them the value of a true, loving partnership that lasts for life." Related to family, he cautioned, "Don't ever doubt the impact that fathers have on their children. Children with strong fathers learn trust early on, that their needs will be met; that they're wanted; that they have value. They can afford to be secure and confident. They will get the encouragement they need to keep on going through any rough spots they encounter in life. I learned all those things from my father. He made all the difference."[123]

The vice president, giving one of the most memorable speeches of his life, told stories about his father and his rise to power, infusing the stories with tales of practical jokes and political humor.[124] He bragged that his father "was the best speaker I ever heard. When he spoke on the Senate floor the cloakrooms emptied, the galleries began to fill, the pages sat in rapt attention." Getting emotional, he told the audience as he looked at his father's casket: "So here's what I decided I would like to say today—to that young boy with the fiddle in Possum Hollow, contemplating his future: I'm proud of the choices you made. I'm proud of the road you traveled. I'm proud of your courage, your righteousness, and your truth. I feel, in the words of the poet, because my father 'lived his soul, love is the whole and more than all' . . . Dad, your whole life has been an inspiration. I'd take the 91 years—your life brought the house down."[125]

Afterward, a motorcade headed from Nashville for Carthage down old Highway 70, which had carried Gore to Nashville for law school. Along the way, people stood to pay their last respects. Many took their hats off, and store owners exited and placed their hands over their hearts as the car carrying the senator passed. As one observer noted, "Even an ambulance pulled to the side yesterday in a gesture of respect." As the procession passed a Wilson County primary school, the young students lifted a yellow banner that read: "West Elementary is thinking of the Gores."[126]

The motorcade finally stopped at the New Salem Missionary Baptist Church in Elmwood. There the family held a service for the people who best knew Gore. There were farmers, small businessmen, teachers, and people from all over Smith County. Unlike the more solemn event in Nashville, it resembled an old country-style revival, complete with audience participation, hearty "amens" and "hallelujahs," and a beautiful rendition of "Amazing Grace."[127]

The contrast between Nashville and Elmwood helped people see the different sides of Albert Gore. On one hand, he had started in the small Baptist church with the emotion and fire-and-brimstone sermons of preachers who usually had little education or formal training. People came together as a community to break the monotony of their everyday struggles against the land and the elements. The more conventional service in War Memorial Hall reflected the man that he had become and the circles he frequented. Yet he felt most comfortable when in Smith County among those he did not have to impress and people who knew and respected him. He liked the limelight, but he also loved the home where he started.

The motorcade finally made its way to the Smith County Memorial Gardens Cemetery, where Gore's body was laid next to Nancy in Grave 3, Lot 18, Section C, with only a small headstone to note his final resting spot. In his life's journey between, he had traveled the world, met with foreign dignitaries, helped shape the national and international policy of the most powerful nation on earth, and created a political dynasty. In 1907, it was unlikely anyone would have expected so much from the son of a small farmer in the Upper Cumberland of Tennessee. The young man from Possum Hollow had lived a full and eventful ninety years.

# EPILOGUE

EVEN AFTER HIS DEATH, Senator Gore continued to exert influence on American political life through his son. Rep. Bob Clement (D-TN) recalled that Gore had told him: "Bob, I want to live to see the day when my son is elected president of the United States." "He really fought hard to stay alive," Clement noted.[1]

Had he lived two more years, he would have enjoyed the scene on August 17, 2000, at the Democratic National Convention in Los Angeles. With the party faithful watching, Al Gore entered the hall. Amid popping flashbulbs, the glare of thousands of lights, and the backdrop of red, white, and blue, he made his way to the platform. There, he greeted Tipper with a passionate kiss and proceeded to the microphone.

In his acceptance address, his father's presence was obvious. Al paid tribute to his parents several times, noting Pauline's presence in the crowd. "I grew up in a wonderful family. I have a lot to be thankful for. And the greatest gift my parents gave me was love." He emphasized that his family foundation gave him security and that the example of sixty-one years of marriage was a model for everyone. "My parents taught me that the real values in life aren't material but spiritual. They include faith and family, duty and honor . . . and trying to make the world a better place."[2]

One section of his speech focused exclusively on his father. Al talked about the man from Possum Hollow who became a teacher in a one-room schoolroom when only eighteen. Noting that his father always talked with him and Nancy about seeing the ravages on families during the Great Depression, Gore stressed: "My father didn't know whether he could help those families, but he believed he had to try. And never in the years to come, in Congress and in the United States Senate, did he lose sight of the reason he entered public service: to fight for the people, not the powerful."[3]

Throughout the speech, echoes of Albert Gore resonated in his son's voice.[4] He praised public education, called for investment in health care, promoted campaign finance reform, and pushed for middle-class tax cuts. He attacked the powerful corporations, roaring, "Big tobacco, big oil, big polluters, the pharmaceutical companies, the HMOs—sometimes you have to be willing to stand up and say no, so families can have a better life." In concluding he stressed that "in this City of Angels, we can summon the better angels of our nature. Do not rest where we are or retreat, do all we can to make America all it can become."[5]

After the convention, Gore hit the campaign trail. The fall campaign was especially tough. Gore's advantages included a strong economy and some successes during Clinton's second term. Still, he faced a significant number of obstacles. President Clinton's ethical lapses had created animosity toward the Democrats, especially among the middle class. His opponent, George W. Bush, had a massive campaign war chest that dwarfed the money available to Gore. The Republicans also were extremely aggressive in their attacks, even focusing on Albert Gore and his relationship with Armand Hammer and votes against the Civil Rights Act of 1964.[6] Furthermore, Gore had his own challenges of showing his warm and giving private side and contrasting that with his cautious and stiff public persona. He ran neck-and-neck with the Texas governor right through election day.

Throughout the campaign, Pauline remained active. Emmett Edwards, a member of Gore's Tennessee campaign election staff, told how Pauline made significant efforts to mobilize African Americans in Memphis. She gathered names, addresses, and phone numbers so that staffers could invite important members of the community, especially ministers, to luncheons and other gatherings. He characterized the eighty-nine-year-old as possessing such a "positive attitude" and an ability to "wave the flag." Every time he talked to her, he walked away with a new exuberance and energy to push harder and further for the vice president.[7]

On election day, the results poured in from across the country. Gore won the popular vote by more than 500,000 votes and only needed one electoral vote to take the presidency. But voting irregularities in Florida threw the election into disarray. In the state run by Governor Jeb Bush, brother of Gore's opponent, a challenge had occurred. While exit polls showed Gore winning, the entire event came down to fewer than a thousand votes, with charges flying of voter intimidation and fraud and many other irregularities.

For nearly six weeks, the country watched the debates over Florida. It would have been some consolation for Gore had he taken his home state of Tennessee, but he had lost it by more than 78,000 votes, with Bush winning by a 51 percent to 48 percent margin. Immediately, political pundits began trying to explain the reason for his loss. Some argued that he had not been elected in Tennessee since 1990, and more than 900,000 people had moved into the state since then. They only knew him as the vice president, not the senator. Furthermore, the same groups that had mobilized against his father, including the NRA, big business, and conservative Christians, had inundated the state with attack ads. Gore took his state for granted until it was too late. His staff had few ties to the South and did not really understand the importance of Tennessee and other southern states to victory. If they had taken only one, the whole spectacle in Florida would not have mattered.

After weeks of court battles, the U.S. Supreme Court finally ended the stalemate in Florida when it denied the Gore camp the right to a recount. On December 13, Gore made a concession address. "I know that many of my supporters are disappointed. I am too. But our disappointment must be overcome by our love of country." He told how he planned to enjoy the remainder of the holidays with friends and family and added that "I know I'll spend time in Tennessee and mend some fences, literally and figuratively . . . As for the battle that ends tonight, I do believe as my father once said, that no matter how hard the loss, defeat might serve as well as victory to shape the soul and let the glory out."[8]

# NOTES

ABBREVIATIONS

CFL  Commissioner of Labor Files, Albert Gore Center, Middle Tennessee State University, Murfreesboro, TN

*CR*  *Congressional Record*

GHC  Gore House Collection, Gore Center

GSC  Gore Senate Collection, Gore Center

NPMP  Nixon Presidential Materials Project, National Archives II, College Park, MD

OHC  Oral History Collection, Lyndon B. Johnson Presidential Library, Austin, TX

QMS  Q. M. Smith Collection, Gore Center

RSFRC  Records of the Senate Foreign Relations Committee, National Archives

SHO  Senate Historical Office, National Archives

SVR  Senate Democratic Policy Committee, "Entire Senate Voting Record of Senator Albert Gore by Subject," Gore Senate Collection, Gore Center

TD  Tape Directory for the Tribute to Al Gore, Gore Center

INTRODUCTION

1. As cited in William Doyle, *An American Insurrection: The Battle of Oxford, Mississippi, 1962* (New York: Doubleday, 2001), 54.

2. Albert A. Gore, interview by Dewey Grantham and James B. Gardner, 13 November 1976, Southern Oral History Collection, Columbia Oral History Project, New York, 91 (hereafter Grantham and Gardner interview); Albert A. Gore, *Let the Glory Out: My South and Its Politics* (New York: Viking, 1972), 103–4; Robert Mann, *The Walls of Jericho: Lyndon Johnson, Hubert Humphrey, Richard Russell, and the Struggle for Civil Rights* (New York: Harcourt, Brace, 1996), 161–65.

3. As cited in Robert A. Caro, *The Years of Lyndon Johnson: Master of the Senate* (New York: Knopf, 2002), 786.

4. *Memphis Press-Scimitar*, 24 August 1968.

5. "Albert Gore Sr., Father of the Vice President, Dies," *Yahoo! News*, 5 December 1998, http://dailynews.yahoo.com/headline...html?s-v/nm/19981205/pl/gore1.html.

6. Albert Gore Jr., "Eulogy by the Vice President at the Funeral of His Father, Former Senator Albert Gore, Sr.," Office of the Press Secretary, www.whitehouse.gov/WH/EOP/OVP/html/19981209–5823.html, accessed 9 December 1998 (hereafter Gore eulogy).

7. Alonzo L. Hamby, *Liberalism and Its Challengers: FDR to Reagan* (New York: Oxford University Press, 1985).

8. Alonzo L. Hamby, "Progressivism: A Century of Change and Rebirth," in Sidney M. Milkis and Jerome M. Mileur, eds., *Progressivism and the New Democracy* (Amherst: University of Massachusetts Press, 1999), 40–80.

9. Charles L. Fontenay, *Estes Kefauver: A Biography* (Knoxville: University of Tennessee Press, 1980); Lee Seifert Greene, *Lead Me On: Frank Goad Clement and Tennessee Politics* (Knoxville: University of Tennessee Press, 1982); Warren Ashby, *Frank Porter Graham: A Southern Liberal* (Winston-Salem, NC: J. F. Blair, 1980); Julian M. Pleasants and Augustus M. Burns, *Frank Porter Graham and the 1950 Senate Race in North Carolina* (Chapel Hill: University of North Carolina Press, 1990); Claude D. Pepper and Hays Gorey, *Pepper, Eyewitness to a Century* (New York: Harcourt Brace Jovanovich, 1987); Claude D. Pepper, *Ask Claude Pepper* (Garden City, NY: Doubleday, 1984); Patrick Cox, *Ralph W. Yarborough: The People's Senator* (Austin: University of Texas Press, 2000); Brooks Hays, *Politics Is My Parish: An Autobiography* (Baton Rouge: Louisiana State University, 1981); James T. Baker, *Brooks Hays* (Macon, GA: Mercer University Press, 1989).

10. There were southerners who were economic or international liberals but failed the litmus test of civil rights, including Fulbright, Hill, and Wright Patman of Texas. Good works on these men include Virginia Vander Veer Hamilton, *Lister Hill: Statesman from the South* (Chapel Hill: University of North Carolina Press, 1987); Randall B. Woods, *Fulbright: A Biography* (New York: Cambridge University Press, 1995); and Nancy Beck Young, *Wright Patman: Populism, Liberalism, and the American Dream* (Dallas: Southern Methodist University Press, 2000).

11. David L. Chappell, *Inside Agitators: White Southerners in the Civil Rights Movement* (Baltimore: Johns Hopkins University Press, 1994).

12. *Yahoo! News*, 5 December 1998.

13. Augustus B. Cochran III, *Democracy Heading South: National Politics in the Shadow of Dixie* (Lawrence: University Press of Kansas, 2001); Richard K. Scher, *Politics in the New South: Republicanism, Race, and Leadership in the Twentieth Century*, 2nd ed. (Armonk, NY: M. E. Sharpe, 1997); Earl Black and Merle Black, *The Rise of Southern Republicans* (Cambridge: Harvard University Press, 2002); Dan T. Carter, *From George Wallace to Newt Gingrich: Race in the Conservative Counterrevolution, 1963–1994* (Baton Rouge: Louisiana State University Press, 1996) and *The Politics of Rage: George Wallace, the Origins of the New Conservatism, and the Transformation of American Politics* (New York: Simon and Schuster, 1995); Dewey W. Grantham, *The South in Modern America: A Region at Odds* (New York: HarperCollins, 1994) and *The Life and Death of the Solid South: A Political History* (Lexington: University Press of Kentucky, 1988).

14. *Nashville Tennessean*, 7 December 1998.

15. Alexander P. Lamis, *The Two-Party South* (New York: Oxford University Press, 1984).

16. As cited in David McCullough, *Truman* (New York: Simon and Schuster, 1992), 992.


1. THE BOY FROM POSSUM HOLLOW

1. Albert A. Gore, *The Eye of the Storm: A People's Politics for the Seventies* (New York: Herder and Herder, 1970), 197.

2. Russell Baker, "Gore also Runs—But for V.P.," *New York Times Magazine*, 10 April 1960, 15.

3. *Gore Family Newsletter*, July–September 1993, 233–34.

4. Ibid., 249–51.

5. TD, Tape 1.

6. Ibid.

7. Grantham and Gardner interview, 8–9.

8. TD, Tape 1.

9. Grantham and Gardner interview, 7.

10. Cited in David Maraniss and Ellen Nakashima, *The Prince of Tennessee: The Rise of Al Gore* (New York: Simon and Schuster, 2000), 27.

11. Wilma Dykeman, *Tennessee, A Bicentennial History* (New York: W. W. Norton, 1975), 133.

12. Jeanette Keith, *Country People in the New South: Tennessee's Upper Cumberland* (Chapel Hill: University of North Carolina Press, 1995), 45–57.

13. William Lynwood Montell, *Upper Cumberland Country* (Jackson: University Press of Mississippi, 1993), 75–87.

14. Gore, *The Eye of the Storm*, 192.

15. Grantham and Gardner interview, 2.

16. Ibid.; Baker, "Gore also Runs," 113.

17. Cited in James W. Davidson et al., *Nation of Nations: A Narrative History of the American Republic*, 3rd ed. (Boston: McGraw-Hill, 1998), 272; Keith, *Country People in the New South*, 58–77.

18. Robert V. Remini, *Andrew Jackson* (New York: Twayne, 1966), 14, 88.

19. Louise Davis, "The Albert Gore Story: Tussles of a 'Combative Hillbilly,'" *Nashville Tennessean Magazine*, 29 March 1970, 5.

20. Gore, *The Eye of the Storm*, 192–93.

21. Ibid., 194, 192; Maraniss and Nakashima, *The Prince of Tennessee*, 23.

22. Cited in Maraniss and Nakashima, *The Prince of Tennessee*, 22; Grantham and Gardner interview, 2.

23. Grantham and Gardner interview, 13.

24. TD, Tape 1.

25. Gore, *The Eye of the Storm*, 194–97.

26. Ibid., 195.

27. Ibid.

28. Ibid., 195–96; TD, Tape 1.

29. Gore, *The Eye of the Storm*, 196.

30. Grantham and Gardner interview, 8, 10–11.

31. Ibid., 11.

32. Gore, *The Eye of the Storm*, 197, 198.

33. "Opening Address, Albert Gore Candidate for U.S. Senate," Carthage, Tennessee, 7 June 1952, GSC, Box 12, Gore Center.

34. Later, Gore would note, "Well, I am not too sure that they would add luster to the university." Albert A. Gore, interview by Bob Bullen, 4 February 1984, Murfreesboro, TN, videotape, Gore Center (hereafter Bullen interview).

35. Grantham and Gardner interview, 12–13.

36. Ibid., 11–12; Katherine Holden, interview by Regina Forsythe, 28 September 1995, Murfreesboro, TN, QMS.1995.110.

37. Lawrence Freeman, interview by Regina Forsythe, 3 July 1995, Murfreesboro, TN, QMS 1995.18; Rollie Holden, interview by Regina Forsythe, 29 August 1995, Murfreesboro, TN, QMS 1995.78.

38. Bullen interview; Rollie Holden, interview.

39. Baxter Hobgood, interview by Regina Forsythe, 25 July 1995, Murfreesboro, TN, QMS 1995.35; Bill Turque, *Inventing Al Gore: A Biography* (Boston: Houghton-Mifflin, 2000), 6.

40. Gore, *Let the Glory Out*, 38.

41. Ibid.; Mabel Pittard, interview by Regina Forsythe, 25 September 1995, Murfreesboro, TN, QMS.1995.106. Good studies on the 1928 election include Allan J. Lichtman, *Prejudice and the Old Politics: The Presidential Election of 1928* (Chapel Hill: University of North Carolina Press, 1979), and David Burner, *The Politics of Provincialism: The Democratic Party in Transition, 1918–1932* (Cambridge: Harvard University Press, 1986).

42. Robert C. McMath, *American Populism: A Social History, 1877–1898* (New York: Hill and Wang, 1993), 166–67.

43. Gore, *Let the Glory Out*, 31. For the impact of the party in Tennessee, see Roger L. Hart, *Redeemers, Bourbons, and Populists: Tennessee, 1870–1896* (Baton Rouge: Louisiana State University Press, 1975). Gore, *The Eye of the Storm*, 107.

44. David D. Anderson, *William Jennings Bryan* (Boston: Twayne, 1981), 11, 75–80.

45. Donald K. Springen, *William Jennings Bryan: Orator of Small-Town America* (New York: Greenwood, 1991), 27.

46. Anderson, *William Jennings Bryan*, 103–4; Fontenay, *Estes Kefauver*, 21.

47. Gore, *The Eye of the Storm*, 107.

48. Dewey W. Grantham, *Southern Progressivism: The Reconciliation of Progress and Tradition* (Knoxville: University of Tennessee Press, 1983), xv–xii.

49. In addition to Grantham's work, see William A. Link, *The Paradox of Southern Progressivism, 1880–1930* (Chapel Hill: University of North Carolina Press, 1992). Other helpful works include C. Vann Woodward, *Origins of the New South, 1877–1913* (Baton Rouge: Louisiana State University Press, 1971), 369–428, and George Brown Tindall, *The Emergence of the New South, 1913–1945* (Baton Rouge: Louisiana State University Press, 1967), 1–32.

50. Grantham, *Southern Progressivism*, 34–35.

51. Keith, *Country People in the New South*, 103–42.

52. Grantham and Gardner interview, 18; August Heckscher, *Woodrow Wilson* (New York: Charles Scribner's Sons, 1991), 1–253.

53. David D. Anderson, *Woodrow Wilson* (Boston: Twayne, 1978), 95, 96, 108.

54. Ibid., 135, 136.

55. Heckscher, *Woodrow Wilson*, 581–644.

56. David M. Kennedy, *Freedom from Fear: The American People in Depression and War, 1929–1945* (New York: Oxford University Press, 1999), 10–130.

57. Grantham and Gardner interview, 10. For more on the depression in Tennessee, see Paul H. Bergeron, Stephen V. Ash, and Jeanette Keith, *Tennesseans and Their History* (Knoxville: University of Tennessee Press, 1999), 258–65.

58. Bullen interview.

59. "O.P.A. Speech," Jackson, TN, 5 October 1945, GHC, Box 8, 4.

60. Rollie Holden, interview, 9.

61. Louise Davis, "The Senator Who Risks His Neck," *Nashville Tennessean Magazine*, 29 March 1970, 10.

62. Grantham and Gardner interview, 14.

63. Bullen interview.

64. Gore, *The Eye of the Storm*, 198–99.

65. Ibid., 199.

66. Bullen interview.

67. Ibid.

68. Ibid.

69. Gore, *The Eye of the Storm*, 199; Bullen interview.

70. Grantham and Gardner interview, 16; Gore, *The Eye of the Storm*, 200.

71. Grantham and Gardner interview, 17; Gore, *Let the Glory Out*, 39.

72. Gore, *Let the Glory Out*, 42.

73. William Leuchtenburg, *Franklin D. Roosevelt and the New Deal, 1932–1940* (New York: Harper and Row, 1963); Paul Conkin, *The New Deal*, 3rd ed. (Arlington Heights, IL: Harlan Davidson, 1992); Anthony Badger, *The New Deal: The Depression Years, 1933–1940* (New York: Farrar, Straus and Giroux, 1989).

74. Gore, *Let the Glory Out*, 42.

75. Cordell Hull, *The Memoirs of Cordell Hull* (New York: Macmillan, 1948), 1:3–166.

76. Irwin F. Gellman, *Secret Affairs: Franklin Roosevelt, Cordell Hull, and Sumner Welles* (Baltimore: Johns Hopkins University Press, 1995), 24–25.

77. Ibid., 30.

78. Grantham and Gardner interview, 5.

79. George Morris, "The Pride of Possum Hollow," *Collier's*, 30 May 1942, 23.

80. Grantham and Gardner interview, 5.

81. Ibid., 28.

82. Bullen interview; Gore, *Let the Glory Out*, 43.

83. Bullen interview.

84. Gore, *Let the Glory Out*, 44.

85. Bullen interview.

86. William R. Majors, *The End of Arcadia: Gordon Browning and Tennessee Politics* (Memphis: Memphis State University Press, 1982), 62; William D. Miller, *Mr. Crump of Memphis* (Baton Rouge: Louisiana State University Press, 1964); V. O. Key Jr., *Southern Politics in State and Nation* (New York: Knopf, 1949), 64–67; Majors, *The End of Arcadia*, 62.

87. Bullen interview; Morris, "The Pride of Possum Hollow," 23.

88. Gore eulogy.

89. Bullen interview.

90. TD, Tape 1.

91. TD, Tape 2; Hank Hillin, *Al Gore Jr.: His Life and Career* (New York: Birch Lane, 1992), 15.

92. Turque, *Inventing Al Gore*, 8; Maraniss and Nakashima, *The Prince of Tennessee*, 30.

93. *Jackson Sun*, 17 January 1993.

94. Florrie Wilkie Sanders, "Life of Women in Political Families—Pauline LaFon Gore '36," *Vanderbilt Lawyer* 24 (Spring 1994): 24; TD, Tape 2.

95. TD, Tape 2.

96. *Jackson Sun*, 17 January 1993.

97. Turque, *Inventing Al Gore*, 8.

98. Ibid.

99. Grantham and Gardner interview, 27–28; TD, Tape 2; Maraniss and Nakashima, *The Prince of Tennessee*, 30.

100. Maraniss and Nakashima, *The Prince of Tennessee*, 32–33; David Halberstam, interview, 22 November 2002, Tempe, AZ [interviews are by author unless otherwise specified].

101. Pamela Hess, "Perils of Pauline Gore," *George*, September 1998, 95; Gore eulogy.

102. TD, Tape 2; Grantham and Gardner interview, 26–27.

103. Hess, "Perils of Pauline Gore," 95, 94.

104. TD, Tape 1.

105. Majors, *The End of Arcadia*, 81.

106. TD, Tape 1.

107. Charles Gore to Albert Gore, 15 January 1937, CFL, Box 1.

108. C. W. Heard to Gore, 20 June 1937, CFL, Box 1.

109. TD, Tape 1; Gore, *The Eye of the Storm*, 201.

110. Jarrell to Albert Gore, 22 January 1938, CFL, Box 1; Gore to Jarrell, 29 January 1938, CFL, Box 1; Morris, "The Pride of Possum Hollow," 23.

111. Gore, *Let the Glory Out*, 57–58.

112. Hess, "Perils of Pauline Gore," 94.

113. TD, Tape 2.

114. Gore, *Let the Glory Out*, 54.

115. Alan Brinkley, *The End of Reform: New Deal Liberalism in Recession and War* (New York: Knopf, 1995), 19–21; Gore, *Let the Glory Out*, 45, 60, 43.

116. Gore, *Let the Glory Out*, 47; James T. Patterson, *Congressional Conservatism and the New Deal: The Growth of the Conservative Coalition in Congress, 1933–1939* (Lexington: University Press of Kentucky, 1967).

117. Cited in Gore, *Let the Glory Out*, 45.

118. Ibid., 33–34.

119. Ibid., 58.

120. TD, Tape 1.

121. TD, Tape 2.

122. Morris, "The Pride of Possum Hollow," 44.

123. O'Donnell to Nation and Business, "Interview with Congressman Gore," 30 October 1941, *Newsweek* Archives, Washington, DC [hereafter O'Donnell interview].

124. Gore, *The Eye of the Storm*, 202.

125. TD, Tape 1.

126. O'Donnell interview; Maraniss and Nakashima, *The Prince of Tennessee*, 25–26.

127. Morris, "The Pride of Possum Hollow," 44.

128. Gore, *The Eye of the Storm*, 203.

129. *Yahoo!News*, 8 December 1998.


## 2 · MR. GORE GOES TO WASHINGTON

1. Gore, *Let the Glory Out*, 61–62.

2. As cited in Doris Kearns, *Lyndon Johnson and the American Dream* (New York: St. Martin's, 1976), 89.

3. Hillin, *Al Gore Jr.*, 12.

4. Ibid.

5. *Carthage Courier*, 29 April 1996. The relationship between Gore and Hull was mainly limited to Gore's admiration for and emulation of the elder statesman. There is some, albeit not a large quantity of, correspondence in Hull's papers in the Library of Congress demonstrating that the two did not enjoy a particularly close relationship of everyday interaction or anything resembling it. Still, Hull clearly influenced the young congressman and his views. Papers of Cordell Hull, Library of Congress, Washington, D.C. Fontenay, *Estes Kefauver*, 101.

6. Gore, *The Eye of the Storm*, 203.

7. Patterson, *Congressional Conservatism and the New Deal*, 288–337; Leuchtenberg, *Franklin D. Roosevelt and the New Deal*, 271–74; Gore, *The Eye of the Storm*, 203–4.

8. *New York Times*, 20 April 1939; Gore, *The Eye of the Storm*, 204.

9. Morris, "The Pride of Possum Hollow," 44; Gore, *Let the Glory Out*, 60.

10. O'Donnell interview, 4; *CR*, 3 August 1939, H10955–56.

11. *Current Biography*, 1952, 213–14.

12. Quoted in Thomas G. Paterson, J. Garry Clifford, and Kenneth J. Hagan, *American Foreign Policy: A History Since 1900*, 3rd ed. (Lexington, MA: D.C. Heath, 1991), 377. Robert A. Divine, *The Reluctant Belligerent: American Entry into World War II*, 2nd ed. (New York: Knopf, 1979), 69–78; Justus D. Doenecke and John E. Wilz, *From Isolation to War, 1931–1941*, 2nd ed. (Arlington Heights, IL: Harlan Davidson, 1991), 53–60; Wayne S. Cole, *Roosevelt and the Isolationists, 1932–1945* (Lincoln: University of Nebraska Press, 1983), 187–296.

13. Paterson, Clifford, and Hagan, *American Foreign Policy*, 378; Robert Divine, *The Illusion of Neutrality* (Chicago: University of Chicago Press, 1962), 318.

14. Gore, *Let the Glory Out*, 63; *CR*, 1 November 1939, H1203.

15. William L. O'Neill, *A Democracy at War: America's Fight at Home and Abroad in World War II* (Cambridge: Harvard University Press, 1993), 18.

16. Michael A. Butler, *Cautious Visionary: Cordell Hull and Trade Reform, 1933–1937* (Kent, OH: Kent State University Press, 1998), 1–14; Edward S. Kaplan, *American Trade Policy, 1923–1995* (Westport, CT: Greenwood, 1996), 43–44.

17. Lloyd C. Gardner, *Economic Aspects of New Deal Diplomacy* (Madison: University of Wisconsin Press, 1964), 42.

18. *CR*, 31 January 1940, H816; Kaplan, *American Trade Policy*, 50.

19. *CR*, 28 February 1940, H2112.

20. *CR*, 22 October 1940, H2290–91.

21. Ibid.

22. Divine, *The Reluctant Belligerent*, 93–96; Wayne S. Cole, *America First: The Battle Against Intervention, 1940–1941* (Madison: University of Wisconsin Press, 1953), 46.

23. Gore, *The Eye of the Storm*, 210; Gore, *Let the Glory Out*, 52.

24. Al Gore, interview by Douglas Brinkley, 10 July 1999, New Orleans, LA.

25. Grantham, *The South in Modern America*, 153–56.

26. Fontenay, *Estes Kefauver*, 106–7.

27. *CR*, 30 July 1940, H9719.

28. Ibid.

29. Warren F. Kimball, *Forged in War: Roosevelt, Churchill, and the Second World War* (New York: William Morrow, 1997), 73–76; Doenecke and Wilz, *From Isolation to War*, 102–3.

30. Paterson, Clifford, and Hagan, *American Foreign Policy*, 380; Divine, *The Reluctant Belligerent*, 110; David Porter, *The Seventy-Sixth Congress and World War II, 1939–1940* (Columbia: University of Missouri Press, 1979), 171–72. Wheeler quote from Cole, *America First*, 46. Taft quote from Doenecke and Wilz, *From Isolation to War*, 103; Justus D. Doenecke, *Storm on the Horizon: The Challenge to American Intervention, 1939–1941* (New York: Rowman and Littlefield, 2000), 167.

31. Grantham and Gardner interview, 38; WSM Transcripts, 2 February 1941, GHC, Box 1.

32. Waldo Heinrichs, *Threshold of War: Franklin D. Roosevelt and American Entry into World War II* (New York: Oxford University Press, 1988), 11; WSM Transcripts, 16 March 1941, GHC, Box 1.

33. Luther Patrick to Eleanor Roosevelt, 27 March 1941, Papers of Eleanor Roosevelt, File: Social Events at the White House, Box 984, Franklin D. Roosevelt Library, Hyde Park, NY.

34. John W. Jeffries, *Wartime America: The World War II Home Front* (Chicago: Ivan R. Dees, 1996), 27.

35. Albert A. Gore, "Inflation and Price Control," speech on *National Farm and Home Hour*, 11 October 1941, p. 6, GHC, Speeches, Box 7.

36. Notes of House Banking and Currency Committee, 6 October 1941, Committee Reports, RG 233, File 77A-F3.1-HR77A-F4.1, National Archives; Gore, "Inflation and Price Control," 4, GHC.

37. O'Donnell interview, 1.

38. *CR*, 26 November 1941, H9082, H9180, H9981.

39. *CR*, 24 November 1941, H9182.

40. *CR*, 26 November 1941, H9065; John Kenneth Galbraith, *A Life in Our Times: Memoirs* (Boston: Houghton-Mifflin, 1981), 144.

41. Jonathan G. Utley, *Going to War with Japan, 1937–1941* (Knoxville: University of Tennessee Press, 1985), 102–82; WSM Transcripts, 19 October 1941, GHC, Box 1.

42. WSM Transcripts, 7 December 1941, GHC, Box 1.

43. Cole, *Roosevelt and the Isolationists*, 506.

44. O'Neill, *A Democracy at War*, 105–19.

45. *New York Times*, 26 March 1942, 25 March 1942; WSM Transcripts, 24 March 1942, GHC, Box 1.

46. "Can We Head Off Serious Inflation?" on *Wake-Up America*, 3 May 1942, GHC, Speeches, Box 7.

47. *New York Times*, 25 March 1942.

48. Sanders, "Life of Women in Political Families—Pauline LaFon Gore," 24.

49. John W. Dower, *War without Mercy: Race and Power in the Pacific War* (New York: Pantheon, 1986), 36.

50. Greg Robinson, *By Order of the President: FDR and the Internment of Japanese Americans* (Cambridge: Harvard University Press, 2001), 73–124.

51. WSM Transcripts, 22 February 1942, GHC, Box 1.

52. WSM Transcripts, 9 May 1942, GHC, Box 1.

53. Cited in David D. Lee, *Sergeant York: An American Hero* (Lexington: University Press of Kentucky, 1985), 120.

54. Gore to Roosevelt, 27 May 1942; FDR to M. H. McIntyre, 28 May 1942; M. H. McIntyre, 28 May 1942; all in OF 300, Democratic National Committee Files, Folder: Tennessee, 1933–1945, FDR Library.

55. Milton to Graves, 15 May 1942, Henry Morgenthau Papers, Microfilm 152, Diary, Book 528, pp. 409–11, FDR Library.

56. Richard Rhodes, *The Making of the Atomic Bomb* (New York: Simon and Schuster, 1986), 303–14, 486–87; Bullen interview.

57. David E. Lilienthal, *The Journals of David E. Lilienthal*, vol. 2: *The Atomic Energy Years, 1945–1950* (New York: Harper and Row, 1966), 396; Bullen interview.

58. Albert Gore, "Canada Did It," *Saturday Evening Post*, 6 June 1942, 18, 44; *Washington Daily News*, 30 April 1942.

59. WSM Transcripts, 27 September 1942, GHC, Box 2.

60. *CR*, 18 January 1943, H219.

61. Grantham and Gardner interview, 37.

62. *CR*, 11 March 1943, H1867.

63. Ibid., H1891.

64. Jeffries, *Wartime America*, 33; John M. Blum, *V Was for Victory: American Politics and Culture during World War II* (New York: Harcourt Brace Jovanovich, 1976), 242–43.

65. *CR*, 25 March 1943, H2504.

66. Albert Gore, "Two-Way Trade and Peace," *Collier's*, 24 April 1943, 20.

67. Ibid., 60.

68. James B. Atleson, *Labor and Wartime State: Labor Relations and Law during World War II* (Urbana: University of Illinois Press, 1998), 188–90.

69. WSM Transcripts, 2 May 1943, GHC, Box 2.

70. Atleson, *Labor and Wartime State*, 194–97; *CR*, 2 June 1943, H5229.

71. Roland Young, *Congressional Politics in the Second World War* (New York: Columbia University Press, 1956), 63–67; WSM Transcripts, 27 June 1943, GHC, Box 2; Jeffries, *Wartime America*, 25.

72. Albert Gore, "Gallatin War Bond Rally," 15 May 1943, GHC, Speeches, Box 7; *Chattanooga Times*, 18 June 1943.

73. Cited in Woods, *Fulbright*, 80; WSM Transcripts, 21 May 1943, GHC, Box 2.

74. Young, *Congressional Politics in the Second World War*, 193; Thomas A. Bailey, *A Diplomatic History of the American People*, 8th ed. (New York: Appleton-Century-Crofts, 1969), 767.

75. *CR*, 20 September 1943, H7670–71; Albert A. Gore, "Should the Treaty Authority of the U.S. Senate Be Curtailed?" *Congressional Digest* 22 (October 1943): 243.

76. Young, *Congressional Politics in the Second World War*, 193; Gaddis Smith, *American Diplomacy during the Second World War, 1941–1945*, 2nd ed. (New York: Knopf, 1985), 140.

77. WSM Transcripts, 3 October 1943, GHC, Box 2.

78. Albert Gore, "Our Situation as One Member of Congress Sees It," Nashville, 6 December 1943, GHC, Speeches, Box 8; Caroline Pruden, "Tennessee and the Formative Years of the United Nations: A Case Study of Southern Opinion," *Tennessee Historical Quarterly* 52 (Spring 1993): 6.

79. *New York Times*, 14 January 1944; WSM Transcripts, 23 January 1944, GHC, Box 2.

80. Young, *Congressional Politics during the Second World War*, 213–17; Jeffries, *Wartime America*, 158–59.

81. *CR*, 17 May 1944, H4623; Young, *Congressional Politics during the Second World War*, 217.

82. Cited in Young, *Congressional Politics in the Second World War*, 173. Fish ultimately published two books on the topic of what FDR accomplished: *FDR: The Other Side of the Coin: How We Were Tricked into World War II* (New York: Vantage, 1976) and *Tragic Deception: FDR and America's Involvement in World War II* (Old Greenwich, CT: Devin-Adair, 1983). In *Memoir of an American Patriot* (Lanham, MD: Regnery Gateway, 1991), he repeated the charges.

83. *CR*, 19 May 1944, H4747; Young, *Congressional Politics in the Second World War*, 173–74.

84. Jeffries, *Wartime America*, 165–66.

85. *CR*, 5 June 1944, H2800.

86. Ibid., H2801.

87. Donoho to Roosevelt, 12 June 1944, OF 300, Democratic National Committee Files, Folder: Tennessee, 1933–1945, FDR Library.

88. Albert Gore, "Campaign Speech, 1944," n.d., GHC, Speeches, Box 8.

89. Albert Gore, "For Lasting Peace—Roosevelt or Dewey," Columbus, OH, 8 October 1944, GHC, Speeches, Box 8.

90. Jeffries, *Wartime America*, 166–67; Young, *Congressional Politics in the Second World War*, 24–25.

91. *CR*, 4 December 1944, H8751; WSM Transcripts, 3 December 1944, GHC, Box 2.

92. Bryce Harlow, interview by Michael L. Gillette, 23 February 1979, OHC. Harlow recalled in 1979 that the whole process was "a political charade, but that's the way politics is done oftentimes, and used to be done a lot more than it is done today."

93. *Current Biography*, 1952, 213.

94. *CR*, 19 March 1945, H2451.

95. Ibid., H2452.

96. Ibid., H2454.

97. Ibid., H2455.

98. Ibid.

99. *New York Times*, 5 March 1945.

100. *CR*, 19 March 1945, H2455.

101. Ibid., H2453.

102. Ibid.

103. Ibid., H2456.

104. Cited in Woods, *Fulbright*, 103.

105. WSM Transcripts, 15 April 1945, GHC, Box 3; Gore, *Let the Glory Out*, 65.

3. IN THE NEW WORLD OF ATOMS, THE COLD WAR,
   AND THE FAIR DEAL

1. Grantham and Gardner interview, 41.

2. WSM Transcripts, 15 April 1945, GHC, Box 3.

3. Ibid.; Grantham and Gardner interview, 40.

4. Gary B. Oshower, *The United Nations and the United States* (New York: Twayne, 1998), 26–29.

5. Albert Gore, "Crossville Commencement Address," 20 April 1945, Crossville, TN, GHC, Speeches, Box 8; Pruden, "Tennessee and the Formative Years of the United Nations," 3–12.

6. WSM Transcripts, 1 May 1945, GHC, Box 3.

7. Young, *Congressional Politics in the Second World War*, 194–96.

8. Edwin P. Hoyt, *Japan's War: The Great Pacific Conflict, 1853–1952* (New York: McGraw-Hill, 1986), 397–412; Bullen interview.

9. Bullen interview.

10. Herbert Feis, *The Atomic Bomb and the End of World War II* (Princeton: Princeton University Press, 1966), 121–46.

11. The argument became controversial in 1965 after the publication of the first edition of Gar Alperovitz's *Atomic Diplomacy: Hiroshima and Potsdam: The Use of the Atomic Bomb and the American Confrontation with Soviet Power*, 2nd ed. (Boulder: Pluto Press, 1994).

12. Bullen interview.

13. Donald R. McCoy, *The Presidency of Harry S. Truman* (Lawrence: University Press of Kansas, 1984), 41–66; Lawrence S. Wittner, *One World or None* (Stanford: Stanford University Press, 1993), 58; Albert A. Gore, "O.P.A. Speech," 5 October 1945, Jackson, TN, GHC, Speeches, Box 8.

14. Baruch to Gore, 24 January 1945, GHC, Personal, Box 5; *CR*, 14 November 1945, H A4872–73.

15. Robert J. Donovan, *Conflict and Crisis: The Presidency of Harry S. Truman, 1945–1948* (New York: W. W. Norton, 1977), 229–38.

16. *CR*, 10 December 1945, H11778–81; *New York Times*, 11 December 1945.

17. *New York Times*, 24 February 1946, 2 February 1946; *CR*, 21 February 1946, H A895.

18. *New York Times*, 24 February 1946.

19. Albert A. Gore, "Speech to Sutton Country, Ohio Democratic Women's Federation," 14 February 1946, Akron, OH, GHC, Speeches, Box 8.

20. A. Wigfall Green, *The Man Bilbo* (Westport, CT: Greenwood, 1976), 101; John Egerton, *Speak Now against the Day: The Generation before the Civil Rights Movement* (New York: Knopf, 1994), 401; Green, *The Man Bilbo*, 98.

21. WSM Transcripts, 1 May 1945, GHC, Box 3.

22. WSM Transcripts, 22 December 1946, GHC, Box 3.

23. Fontenay, *Estes Kefauver*, 9.

24. Beverly Witten, secretary to Albert Gore, to Matthew J. Connelly, secretary to Harry Truman, 9 August 1946, Official Files, Box 322; Albert Gore to Harry S. Truman, 29 June 1946, General File, Box 2594; Notes of Meeting between Gore and Truman, 21 September 1945, President's Personal File, Box 6, Harry S. Truman Library, Independence, MO.

25. Susan M. Hartmann, *Truman and the 80th Congress* (Columbia: University of Missouri Press, 1971), 4–11.

26. Cited ibid., 11.

27. Baruch to Gore, 12 February 1947, GHC, Personal, Box 5; WSM Transcripts, 13 July 1947, GHC, Box 3; *CR*, 5 February 1947, H810–11; 27 March 1947, H2751–52.

28. WSM Transcripts, 2 February 1947, GHC, Box 3.

29. "TVA Gordon Clapp Confirmation," 6 February 1947, GHC, Speeches, Box 9; WSM Transcripts, 2 February 1947, GHC, Box 3; McCullough, *Truman*, 538–39; Alonzo L. Hamby, *Beyond the New Deal: Harry S. Truman and American Liberalism* (New York: Columbia University Press, 1973), 183.

30. Cited in John L. Gaddis, *Strategies of Containment: A Critical Appraisal of Postwar American National Security Policy* (New York: Oxford University Press, 1982), 20–21.

31. Cited in Thomas G. Paterson and Dennis Merrill, *Major Problems in American Foreign Relations* (Lexington, MA: D. C. Heath, 1995), 2:258. Walter LaFeber, *America, Russia, and the Cold War, 1945–1992*, 7th ed. (New York: McGraw-Hill, 1993), 49–58; John L. Gaddis, *The United States and the Origins of the Cold War, 1941–1947* (New York: Columbia University Press, 1972), 346–52; Theodore A. Couloumbis, *The United States, Greece, and Turkey* (New York: Praeger, 1983), 7–22.

32. WSM Transcripts, 16 March 1947, GHC, Box 3.

33. R. Alton Lee, *Truman and Taft-Hartley: A Question of Mandate* (Lexington: University Press of Kentucky, 1966), 49–79, 99; Hamby, *Beyond the New Deal*, 184.

34. LaFeber, *America, Russia, and the Cold War*, 70–72.

35. Michael J. Hogan, *The Marshall Plan: America, Britain, and the Reconstruction of Western Europe, 1947–1952* (New York: Cambridge University Press, 1987), 26–87; Hogan, *A Cross of*

*Iron: Harry S. Truman and the Origins of the National Security State, 1945–1954* (New York: Cambridge University Press, 1998), 90; Hartman, *Truman and the 80th Congress*, 159.

36. WSM Transcripts, 7 December 1947, 14 December 1947, GHC, Box 3.

37. Imanuel Wexler, *The Marshall Plan Revisited: The European Recovery Program in Economic Perspective* (Westport, CT: Greenwood, 1983), 249–55.

38. WSM Transcripts, 4 January 1948, GHC, Box 4.

39. WSM Transcripts, 29 February 1948, GHC, Box 4.

40. Grantham and Gardner interview, 34.

41. Turque, *Inventing Al Gore*, 4.

42. Ibid., 4–5.

43. Fontenay, *Estes Kefauver*, 137–38.

44. Ibid., 147.

45. Ibid., 153.

46. Grantham and Gardner interview, 39; Ted Brown, interview, 7 November 1997, Murfreesboro, TN.

47. Grantham and Gardner interview, 39.

48. WSM Transcripts, 27 June 1948, GHC, Box 4.

49. John C. Culver and John Hyde, *American Dreamer: The Life and Times of Henry A. Wallace* (New York: W. W. Norton, 2000), 456–509; Kari Frederickson, *The Dixiecrat Revolt and the End of the Solid South, 1932–1968* (Chapel Hill: University of North Carolina Press, 2001), 118–86; Donald R. McCoy and Richard Ruetten, *Quest and Response: Minority Rights and the Truman Administration* (Lawrence: University Press of Kansas, 1973), 134–37.

50. As cited in Zachary Karabell, *The Last Campaign: How Harry Truman Won the 1948 Election* (New York: Knopf, 2000), 210–11.

51. WSM Transcripts, 3 October 1948, GHC, Box 4.

52. Karabell, *The Last Campaign*, 254.

53. WSM Transcripts, 7 November 1948, GHC, Box 4.

54. Gore, *Let the Glory Out*, 66–69.

55. WSM Transcripts, 16 January 1949, GHC, Box 4, Gore Center.

56. Thomas G. Paterson, *On Every Front: The Making and Unmaking of the Cold War*, revised edition (New York: W. W. Norton, 1992), 84–85; WSM Transcripts, 11 July 1948, GHC, Box 4; LaFeber, *America, Russia, and the Cold War*, 82; Stephen E. Ambrose and Douglas G. Brinkley, *Rise to Globalism: American Foreign Policy Since 1938*, 8th ed. (New York: Penguin, 1997), 102–4.

57. WSM Transcripts, 3 April 1949, GHC, Box 4.

58. Melvyn P. Leffler, *A Preponderance of Power: National Security, the Truman Administration, and the Cold War* (Stanford: Stanford University Press, 1992), 408–18.

59. WSM Transcripts, 31 July 1949, GHC, Box 4.

60. Reo M. Christenson, *The Brannan Plan: Farm Politics and Policy* (Ann Arbor: University of Michigan Press, 1959), 15–16.

61. Ibid., 3–4; Hamby, *Beyond the New Deal*, 305.

62. *CR*, 20 July 1949, H9857; WSM Transcripts, 17 July 1949, GHC, Box 4.

63. *CR*, 20 July 1949, H9857–58.

64. Allen J. Matusow, *Farm Policies and Politics in the Truman Years* (Cambridge: Harvard University Press, 1967), 209–10; *New York Times*, 22 July 1949; "People of the Week," *Life*, 1 August 1949, 27.

65. WSM Transcripts, 24 July 1949, GHC, Box 4.

66. McCoy and Rutten, *Quest and Response*, 179.

67. WSM Transcripts, 26 February 1950, GHC, Box 4.

68. Gore, *The Eye of the Storm*, 207–208.

69. Gore to Harry Woodbury, 20 February 1950, GHC, Personal, unfiled.

70. Alan D. Harper, *The Politics of Loyalty: The White House and the Communist Issue, 1946–1952* (Westport, CT: Greenwood, 1969); Richard M. Freeland, *The Truman Doctrine and the Origins of McCarthyism: Foreign Policy, Domestic Politics, and Internal Security, 1946–1948* (New York: New York University Press, 1985); Allen Weinstein, *Perjury: The Hiss-Chambers Case*, 2nd ed. (New York: Random House, 1997).

71. Robert Griffith, *The Politics of Fear: Joseph R. McCarthy and the Senate*, 2nd ed. (Amherst: University of Massachusetts Press, 1987), 48–49, 52–67. Other good books on McCarthy include David M. Oshinsky, *A Conspiracy So Immense: The World of Joe McCarthy* (New York: Free Press, 1983); Thomas C. Reeves, *The Life and Times of Joe McCarthy: A Biography* (New York: Stein and Day, 1982); Roberta Strauss Fuerelicht, *Joe McCarthy and McCarthyism: The Hate that Haunts America* (New York: McGraw-Hill, 1972); and Donald F. Crosby, *God, Church, and Flag: Senator Joseph R. McCarthy and the Catholic Church, 1950–1957* (Chapel Hill: University of North Carolina Press, 1978).

72. Griffith, *The Politics of Fear*, 67–68; WSM Transcripts, 19 March 1950, GHC, Box 4.

73. WSM transcripts, 1 April 1950, GHC, Box 4.

74. Bruce Cumings, *The Origins of the Korean War: Liberation and Emergence of Separate Regimes, 1945–1947* (Princeton: Princeton University Press, 1981), and *The Origins of the Korean War: The Roaring of the Cataract, 1947–1950* (Princeton: Princeton University Press, 1990); Leffler, *A Preponderance of Power*, 366.

75. Rosemary Foot, *The Wrong War: American Policy and the Dimensions of the Korean Conflict, 1950–1953* (Ithaca: Cornell University Press, 1985); Burton Kaufman, *The Korean War: Challenges in Crisis, Credibility, and Command* (Philadelphia: Temple University Press, 1986); Sergei Goncharov, John W. Lewis, and Xue Litai, *Uncertain Partners: Stalin, Mao, and the Korean War* (Stanford: Stanford University Press, 1993); William Stueck, *The Road to Confrontation: United States Policy toward China and Korea, 1947–1950* (Chapel Hill: University of North Carolina Press, 1981).

76. WSM Transcripts, 2 July 1950, GHC, Box 4.

77. Gore to Wilson, 15 September 1950, GHC, Personal, Box 5.

78. Gore to Wilson, 27 September 1950, GHC, Personal, Box 5.

79. Cassell to Gore, 10 November 1950, GHC, Personal, Box 5.

80. Pauline Gore, Speech to the Crossville Women's Club, 19 November 1950, GHC, Speeches, Box 11; Woodall to Gore, 31 January 1951, GHC, Personal, Box 5.

81. Wilson to Gore, 21 February 1951, GHC, Personal, Box 5.

82. William Stueck, *The Korean War: An International History* (Princeton: Princeton University Press, 1995), 127–203.

83. Mrs. John Bauhofer to Gore, 16 January 1951, GHC, Correspondence, Box 14.

84. Albert Gore, Speech to Southern Agriculture Workers' Convention, 5 February 1951, GHC, Speeches, Box 11.

85. Stueck, *The Korean War*, 182–87.

86. Russell Brothers to Gore, 13 April 1951; T. G. Burchett to Gore, 12 April 1951, GHC, Correspondence, Box 14.

87. WSM Transcripts, 1951 [no specific date given], GHC, Box 4; Gore to Otto Britt, 19 April 1951, GHC, Correspondence, Box 14.

88. Gore to Truman, 14 April 1951, Official File, Box 1528, Folder 692-A, Truman Library.

89. Howard Jones, *Crucible of Power: A History of American Foreign Relations from 1897* (Wilmington, DE: Scholarly Resources, 2001), 304.

90. Gore to Meeman, 16 November 1951, GHC, Personal, Box 6.

91. Gore to Ahlgren, 29 November 1951, GHC, Personal, Box 6.

92. Albert Gore to the Kefauver Rally, 12 December 1951, GHC, Speeches, Box 11.

93. Albert Gore to Tennessee Newspapers, 3 February 1952, GHC, Newspapers, Box 12; *New York Times*, 3 February 1952; Gore to Baruch, 27 February 1952, GHC, Personal, Box 6.

94. Bullen interview; Gore to Tennessee Newspapers, GHC.

95. *CR*, 25 March 1952, H2868–71; *New York Times*, 25 June 1952; Gore to O. R. Galliher, 5 June 1952, GHC, General Files, Box 23.

96. Albert Gore, "Opening Address, Albert Gore Candidate for U.S. Senate," 7 June 1952, GHC, Speeches, Box 12.

97. Ibid.

98. Gore, *Let the Glory Out*, 52, 77.

99. Ibid., 77.

100. Grantham and Gardner interview, 58.

101. "44 v. 83," *Time*, 11 August 1952, 20.

102. *Nashville Banner*, 31 October 1984.

103. *New York Times*, 7 August 1952.

104. Cited in Miller, *Mr. Crump of Memphis*, 345.

105. "44 v. 83," 20; "Upsets in the Senate: Old-Timers Lose Out . . . Younger Men Win in Three States, Threaten in Others," *U.S. News and World Report*, 22 August 1952, 54.

106. Greene, *Lead Me On*.

107. Gore spent a total of $50,000 on the campaign, a rather large sum for those days. Bullen interview.

108. John Patrick Diggins, *The Proud Decades: America in War and Peace, 1941–1960* (New York: W. W. Norton, 1988), 122.

109. Gore to Edgar Webster, 29 September 1952, GHC, General Files, Box 24.

110. Anthony Summers, *The Arrogance of Power: The Secret World of Richard Nixon* (New York: Viking, 2000), 118–19.

111. Gore also highlighted that only $190 of the $18,000 had gone to Nixon's anticommunist activities. Gore to Helen Boyd, 29 September 1952, GHC, General Files, Box 24.

112. Jonathan Aitken, *Nixon: A Life* (London: Weidenfeld and Nicolson, 1993), 210–20.

113. Gore to Nat Williams, 13 October 1952; Gore to Littrell Rust, 11 October 1952, GHC, General Files, Box 24.

114. Stephen E. Ambrose, *Eisenhower: Soldier, General of the Army, President-Elect, 1890–1952* (New York: Simon and Schuster, 1983), 1:571.

115. Gore to Baruch, 10 November 1952, GHC, Personal, Box 6.


4. JOINING THE MILLIONAIRES' CLUB

1. Davis, "The Senator Who Risks His Neck," 7.

2. True to his country roots, when he took the oath of office, Gore hosted a buffet in the caucus room in the Senate office building. The main course was a ham from a pig raised at his farm. *Nashville Tennessean*, 2 January 1953.

3. Gore to Johnson, 12 January 1953, LBJ Congressional File, Box 44, Lyndon B. Johnson Library, Austin, TX.

4. Johnson to Gore, 12 January 1953, LBJ Congressional File, Box 44.

5. Gore to Ahlgren, 3 February 1953, GSC, Personal: Frank Ahlgren.

6. Richard H. Immerman, *John Foster Dulles: Piety, Pragmatism, and Power in U.S. Foreign Policy* (Wilmington, DE: Scholarly Resources, 1999), 41–44.

7. Gore to Talonis, 28 February 1953, GSC, Special: Henry Lodge.

8. Nathaniel R. Howard, ed., *The Basic Papers of George M. Humphrey as Secretary of the Treasury, 1953–1957* (Cleveland: Case Western Reserve Historical Society, 1965), xxv–xxviii; Chester Pach Jr. and Elmo Richardson, *The Presidency of Dwight D. Eisenhower*, rev. ed. (Lawrence: University Press of Kansas, 1991), 34.

9. Gore, *Let the Glory Out*, 109–10.

10. Robert Dallek, *Lone Star Rising: Lyndon Johnson and His Times, 1908–1960* (New York: Oxford University Press, 1998), 431.

11. Gore to Hull, 23 April 1953, GSC, Personal: Cordell Hull.

12. *Chattanooga Times*, 28 April 1953.

13. Gore to Charles Gore, 3 June 1953, GSC, Personal: Mr. Gore.

14. Robert Robinson to Gore, 12 June 1953, GSC, Personal: Mr. Gore; Pauline Gore to Neil Howard, 18 August 1953, GSC, Personal: Mrs. Gore.

15. Gore, *Let the Glory Out*, 191.

16. William Allen, interview, 26 July 1996, Lexington, KY; David Halberstam, "The End of a Populist," *Harper's*, January 1971, 42; Jack Robinson Sr., interview, 3 November 1998, Nashville; Halberstam, "The End of a Populist," 167.

17. *CR*, 6 May 1953, S4625–28.

18. Speech to Democratic Rally, Knoxville, 29 August 1953, GSC, Research, Commerce: Tight Money.

19. Steve Weinberg, *Armand Hammer: The Untold Story* (Boston: Little, Brown, 1989); Carl Blumay with Henry Edwards, *The Dark Side of Power: The Real Armand Hammer* (New York: Simon and Schuster, 1992); Edward Jay Epstein, *Dossier: The Secret History of Armand Hammer* (New York: Random House, 1996).

20. Maraniss and Nakashima, *The Prince of Tennessee*, 37.

21. Hammer to Gore, 14 October 1953, GSC, Personal: Mr. Gore.

22. Hammer to Gore, 26 October 1953, GSC, Personal: Mr. Gore; Jack Robinson Sr., interview, 16 November 1998, Nashville

23. Bob Zelnick, *Gore: A Political Life* (Washington, DC: Regency Press, 1999), 21–25.

24. John Seigenthaler, interview, 24 September 2001, Nashville.

25. Gore to Clement, 18 January 1954, GSC, Personal: Mr. Gore.

26. Gore to Johnson, 27 February 1954, LBJ Congressional File, Box 44.

27. Ibid.

28. Gore to Meeman, 11 February 1954, GSC, Personal: Edward Meeman.

29. Blanche Wiesen Cook, *The Declassified Eisenhower: A Divided Legacy* (Garden City, NY: Doubleday, 1981); Fred Greenstein, *The Hidden-Hand Presidency: Eisenhower as Leader* (New York: Basic Books, 1982).

30. Hendon to Tolson, 20 January 1947; Hoover to Gore, 26 February 1951; Albert Gore Sr. FBI files, FBI Archives, Washington, DC.

31. L. B. Nichols to Tolson, memo, 18 March 1954, Albert Gore Sr. FBI files.

32. Ibid.

33. George C. Herring, *America's Longest War: The United States and Vietnam, 1950–1975*, 3rd ed. (New York: McGraw-Hill, 1996), 3–29; Lloyd Gardner, *Approaching Vietnam: From World War II through Dienbienphu* (New York: W. W. Norton, 1988), 21–280.

34. Stanley Karnow, *Vietnam: A History* (New York: Penguin, 1986), 190–98.

35. George Donelson Moss, *Vietnam: An American Ordeal*, 4th ed. (Upper Saddle River, NJ: Prentice-Hall, 2002), 62–65.

36. Gore to Howard Parsons, 14 April 1954, GSC, Special: Indochina, Policy.

37. *Spartanburg (SC) Herald*, 19 April 1954.

38. Gore to C. C. Smith, 6 May 1954, GSC, Special: Indochina, Policy.

39. Mann, *The Walls of Jericho*, 154. Jack Greenberg, *Crusaders in the Courts: How a Dedicated Band of Lawyers Fought for the Civil Rights Revolution* (New York: Basic Books, 1994), 197–99; James T. Patterson, *Brown v. Board of Education: A Civil Rights Milestone and Its Troubled Legacy* (New York: Oxford University Press, 2001), 46–69.

40. Aldon D. Morris, *The Origins of the Civil Rights Movement: Black Communities Organizing for Change* (New York: Free Press, 1984), 27; Mann, *The Walls of Jericho*, 155.

41. Gore to Johnson, 28 May 1954, GSC, Legislative: Judiciary, Civil Rights.

42. Ibid.

43. Gore to James R. Falls, 11 September 1954, GSC, Legislative: Judiciary, Civil Rights.

44. Gore, *Let the Glory Out*, 84–85.

45. *Life*, 21 June 1954, 20.

46. "Gore's Challenge," *New Republic*, 21 June 1954, 5; *Life*, 21 June 1954, 20.

47. "Gore's Chances," *New Republic*, 28 June 1954, 4.

48. Gore, *Let the Glory Out*, 80.

49. Aaron Wildavsky, *Dixon-Yates: A Study in Power Politics* (New Haven: Yale University Press, 1962), 81–93.

50. Ibid., 103.

51. Ibid., 104–105; *Oklahoma City Times*, 27 July 1954.

52. Gore to Thomas H. Allen, 21 June 1954, GSC, Department: AEC, TVA; *CR*, 16 July 1954, S10714, S10845; *New York Times*, 20 July 1954.

53. *New York Times*, 22 July 1954; Wildavsky, *Dixon-Yates*, 112–15.

54. *New York Times*, 27 July 1954.

55. Clinton P. Anderson, *Outsider in the Senate: Senator Clinton Anderson's Memoirs* (New York: World Publishing Company, 1970), 191; Eugene Zuckert and Arnold Kramish, *Atomic Energy for Your Business* (New York: D. McKay, 1956), 137; Wildavsky, *Dixon-Yates*, 117.

56. Wildavsky, *Dixon-Yates*, 119.

57. Harry Asquith to Gore, 16 August 1954, GSC, Politics: Campaign Help, 1958 Campaign.

58. Cited in James B. Gardner, "Political Leadership in a Period of Transition: Frank G. Clement, Albert Gore, Estes Kefauver, and Tennessee Politics, 1948–1956" (Ph.D. diss., Vanderbilt University, 1978), 466; *Memphis Commercial Appeal*, 7 August 1954.

59. *Knoxville News-Sentinel*, 6 June 1954.

60. Gore transcript, 1 September 1954, GSC, Politics: DNC, Correspondence.

61. *Daily Oklahoman*, 8 October 1954.

62. Dallek, *Lone Star Rising*, 462.

63. Gore, *Let the Glory Out*, 168, 124.

64. Baker, "Gore also Runs," 114; George A. Smathers, interview by Donald A. Ritchie, 1 August–24 October 1989, 60, SHO; Halberstam, "The End of a Populist," 37.

65. Arthur Herman, *Joseph McCarthy: Reexamining the Life and Legacy of America's Most Hated Senator* (New York: Free Press, 2000), 238–57.

66. Gore to Lucille Collins, 25 June 1954, GSC, Special: Joseph McCarthy, General; Gore to McClellan, 26 June 1954, GSC, Personal: Mr. Gore.

67. Rev. R. T. Johnson to Gore, December 1954; Williams to Allen, 24 November 1954, GSC, Special: Joseph McCarthy, Censure Motion.

68. Gore to James Corn, 11 December 1954, GSC, Special: Joseph McCarthy, Censure Motion; Thomas C. Reeves, *The Life and Times of Joseph McCarthy: A Biography*, 2nd ed. (New York: Madison Books, 1997), 654–63.

69. *New York Times*, 28 January 1955, 12 February 1955.

70. *New York Times*, 19 February 1955.

71. Wildavsky, *Dixon-Yates*, 255; Legislative Meeting supplementary notes, 28 June 1955, DDE Papers, Legislative Meeting Series, Ann Whitman File, Box 2, Eisenhower Library.

72. Gore to William Sturdevant, 6 July 1955, GSC, Department: AEC, TVA; Jason Leonard Finkle, *The President Makes a Decision: A Study of Dixon-Yates* (Ann Arbor: Institute of Public Administration, 1960), 191–98.

73. Cited in Wildavsky, *Dixon-Yates*, 265.

74. Eisenhower to Leonard Finder, 15 July 1955, DDE Papers, DDE Diary Series, Whitman File, Box 11.

75. Gardner, "Political Leadership in a Period of Transition," 466.

76. *Orlando Sentinel*, 11 September 1955.

77. Grantham and Gardner interview, 70.

78. Numan V. Bartley, *The Rise of Massive Resistance: Race and Politics in the South During the 1950s*, 2nd ed. (Baton Rouge: Louisiana State University Press, 1997), 82–107.

79. Ibid., 109; Francis M. Wilhoit, *The Politics of Massive Resistance* (New York: George Braziller, 1973), 76–78.

80. Woods, *Fulbright*, 207–8; Gore, *Let the Glory Out*, 102–3.

81. Robert A. Caro, *The Years of Lyndon Johnson: Master of the Senate* (New York: Knopf, 2002), 786–87; Tony Badger, "Southerners Who Refused to Sign the Southern Manifesto," *Historical Journal*, 42 (1999): 517–19; John A. Goldsmith, *Colleagues: Richard B. Russell and His Apprentice, Lyndon B. Johnson* (Washington, DC: Seven Locks Press, 1993), 51–52.

82. Gore, *Let the Glory Out*, 103–4; Grantham and Gardner interview, 92.

83. Vander Veer Hamilton, *Lister Hill*, 213.

84. Grantham and Gardner interview, 91; Gore, *Let the Glory Out*, 103–4; Mann, *The Walls of Jericho*, 161–65.

85. Constituent to Gore, 21 March 1956; Constituent to Gore, 14 March 1956; Constituent to Gore, n.d., GSC, Issue Mail: Southern Manifesto.

86. Cited in Gilbert C. Fite, *Richard Russell Jr.: Senator from Georgia* (Chapel Hill: University of North Carolina Press, 1991), 333–34.

87. Baker, *Brooks Hays*, i.

88. President's Advisory Committee on a National Highway Program, "A 10-Year National Highway Program: A Report to the President," January 1955, Reports to the Senate Committee on Public Works, Senate 84-A-F14, RG 233, File 1, National Archives.

89. Dwight D. Eisenhower to Congress, 22 February 1955, Reports to the Senate Committee on Public Works, Senate 84-A-F14, RG 233, File 2.

90. *U.S. News and World Report*, 4 March 1955, 14.

91. *New York Times*, 22 February 1955.

92. Statement to Governor's Forum, 4 May 1955, GSC, Legislation: Public Works, Highways.

93. Lyndon B. Johnson, "Statement by Senator Johnson on the Highway Bill by Senators Harry F. Byrd and Albert Gore," 22 May 1955, Pre-Presidential Papers, Box 306, LBJ Library; *CR*, 20 May 1955, S6714–21; 23 May 1955, S6775–86, S6788–91, S6795–6808, S6967–81; 25 May 1955, S6983–92, S7000, S7011–13, S7016–22.

94. Tom Lewis, *Divided Highways: Building the Interstate Highways, Transforming American Life* (New York: Viking, 1997), 120.

95. Ibid., 122.

96. Ibid., 216.

97. Gore to Johnson, 2 May 1956, GSC, Politics: Correspondence, Senators.

98. Albert Gore, speech before the State Democratic Convention, Hartford, CT, 6 July 1956, Post-Presidential Name File, Box 76, Truman Library.

99. Porter McKeever, *Adlai Stevenson: His Life and Legacy* (New York: William Morrow, 1989), 375–78; Wilma Dykeman, "Too Much Talent in Tennessee?" *Harper's*, March 1955, 49; *New York Times*, 15 August 1956.

100. George E. Reedy, interview by Michael L. Gillette, 17 August 1983, p. 7, OHC.

101. Earle C. Clements, interview by Michael L. Gillette, 24 October 1974, p. 22, OHC; Theodore C. Sorenson, *Kennedy* (New York: Harper and Row, 1965), 89; James H. Rowe Jr., interview by Michael L. Gillette, 9 December 1983, p. 14, OHC.

102. Gore, *Let the Glory Out*, 95.

103. Cited in Fontenay, *Estes Kefauver*, 275; Wayne Whitt, interview, 25 September 2001, Nashville.

104. Gore, *Let the Glory Out*, 95; Theodore Sorenson, interview, 18 October 1998, Phoenix; Sorenson, *Kennedy*, 91.

105. Gore to Fulbright, 18 September 1956, Papers of J. William Fulbright, BCN 77, J. William Fulbright Collection, University of Arkansas Library, Fayetteville; Gore to Spark-man, 22 August 1956, GSC, Politics: Democratic Convention, Alabama; Johnson to Gore, 30 August 1956, GSC, Politics: Democratic Convention, Texas.

106. Gore eulogy.

107. Robert A. Divine, *Blowing on the Wind: The Nuclear Test Ban Debate, 1954–1960* (New York: Oxford University Press, 1978), 72.

108. Gore, *Let the Glory Out*, 98–99.

109. Ibid., 99.

110. *Evening Star* (Washington), 1 October 1956.

111. Turque, *Inventing Al Gore*, 25.

112. Ibid.

113. *U.S. News and World Report*, 24 February 1956, 16; "A Senate Probe for Lobbies," *Business Week*, 25 February 1956, 30–31; *CR*, 22 February 1956, S3113.

114. *New York Times*, 1 March 1956, 11 March 1956.

115. Gore to Johnson, 22 August 1956, GSC, Politics: Democratic Convention, Texas; Johnson to Gore, 30 August 1956, LBJ U.S. Senate File, Box 70, LBJ Library.

116. *U.S. News and World Report*, 19 October 1956, 22.

117. Gore, *Let the Glory Out*, 97.

118. Pearson to Moore, 24 November 1956; Pearson to Jim Blevins, n.d., Papers of Drew Pearson, Box 3, LBJ Library.

119. Pach and Richardson, *The Presidency of Dwight D. Eisenhower*, 126.

120. *Chattanooga Times*, October 1957 supplement; Dewey W. Grantham, *Recent America: The United States Since 1945*, 2nd ed. (Wheeling, IL: Harlan Davidson, 1998), 93; Geoffrey Perret, *Eisenhower* (New York: Random House, 1999), 541.


### 5. A TIME OF PERIL ON MANY FRONTS

1. Gore, *Let the Glory Out*, 115.

2. Constituent to Gore, 12 February 1957; Sims Crownover to Gore, 21 February 1957, GSC, Academy Files: Air Force, Negro Applicant.

3. Gore to O. P. Dugan, 12 February 1957, GSC, Academy Files: Air Force, Negro Applicant.

4. Al Gore, interview by author, 24 September 2001, Nashville.

5. *New York Times*, 3 February 1957.

6. Ibid.; *CR*, 7 February 1957, S1729–33.

7. *Chattanooga Times*, 3 March 1957; *Baltimore Sun*, 5 March 1957.

8. Dykeman, "Too Much Talent for Tennessee?" 53.

9. Gore to Jim K. Gore, 9 May 1957, GSC, Politics: Campaign Help, 1958 Campaign; *Cannon County (TN) Courier*, 15 November 1957.

10. Louise Davis, "Pancakes and Protocol: Vivacious Mrs. Albert Gore Thrives on the Washington Whirl," *Nashville Tennessean Magazine*, 12 May 1957, 12–15.

11. Johnson to Allen, 29 April 1957, LBJ Congressional File, Box 44.

12. Anne Hodges Morgan, *Robert S. Kerr: The Senate Years* (Norman: University of Oklahoma Press, 1977), vii, 40.

13. Gore, *Let the Glory Out*, 124; Jesse R. Nichols, interview by Donald A. Ritchie, 26 March–12 April 1994, p. 70, SHO.

14. Albert Gore, "The Secretary of the Treasury: A Study of the Use of Public Office for Private Advancement," 12 March 1957, GSC, Research: Conflict of Interest, George Humphrey.

15. Howard, *The Basic Papers of George M. Humphrey*, xxv–xxviii; Pach and Richardson, *The Presidency of Dwight D. Eisenhower*, 34.

16. "Statement of Senator Albert Gore at Public Hearing of the Committee on Finance," 11 July 1957, GSC, Legislative: Finance, Tight Money Policy.

17. Constituent to Gore, 19 July 1957, GSC, Legislative: Judiciary, Civil Rights; Gore to Roy C. Wallow, 26 July 1957, GSC, Issue Mail: Civil Rights.

18. Gore to Roy C. Wallow; Gore to Ahlgren, 25 July 1956, GSC, Media: Newspaper, Newspaper Editor.

19. Gore to D. L. Lansden, 17 July 1957, GSC, Legislative: Judiciary, Civil Rights; *CR*, 22 July 1957–23 July 1957, S12325, S12441; 31 July 1957–1 August 1957, S13146, S13293, S13300, S13314–16; Chappell, *Inside Agitators*, 160.

20. Gore, *The Eye of the Storm*, 131–32.

21. Gore, *Let the Glory Out*, 118, 130; Gore, *The Eye of the Storm*, 130, 132.

22. Maraniss and Nakashima, *The Prince of Tennessee*, 34.

23. Al Gore, interview; Maraniss and Nakashima, *The Prince of Tennessee*, 41.

24. *Detroit Free Press*, 9 February 1958.

25. Gore to John Knight, 15 February 1958, GSC, Media: Newspaper, Editors' Correspondence.

26. Gore to John Spence, 31 March 1958, GSC, Media: Newspaper, Editors' Correspondence.

27. *Akron Beacon Journal*, 20 April 1958; Gore to Clyde Mann, 29 April 1958, GSC, Media: Newspaper, Editors' Correspondence.

28. *St. Petersburg Times*, 7 May 1958; clipping, 8 May 1958, GSC, Media: Newspaper.

29. *Washington Star*, 6 June 1958.

30. *Nashville Tennessean*, 5 June 1958.

31. Cited in Greene, *Lead Me On*, 46–47.

32. Don Oberdorfer, telephone interview by author, 18 January 2002; Baker, "Gore Also Runs," 15; Gore, *Let the Glory Out*, 112.

33. Pete Daniel, *Lost Revolutions: The South in the 1950s* (Chapel Hill: University of North Carolina Press, 2000), 261.

34. Numan V. Bartley, *The New South, 1945–1980: The Story of the South's Modernization* (Baton Rouge: Louisiana State University Press, 1995), 225–35.

35. Baker, "Gore Also Runs," 15; *Knoxville Journal*, 7 July 1958.

36. *Knoxville News-Sentinel*, 27 July 1958; Seigenthaler, interview.

37. *St. Louis Post-Dispatch*, 4 July 1958.

38. *Washington Post*, 9 August 1958.

39. Davis, "The Senator Who Risks His Neck," 10; *Washington Post*, 9 August 1958.

40. Gore, *Let the Glory Out*, 113; Baker, "Gore Also Runs," 15; Gore to John W. Carmody, 16 August 1958, Papers of John W. Carmody, Correspondence, Box 187, FDR Library.

41. *Washington Post*, 9 August 1958; *U.S. News and World Report*, 22 August 1958, 49.

42. No title, n.d., GSC, Research: AEC, Fall Out #1.

43. Eisenhower to Baruch, 3 July 1957, DDE Papers, White House Central Files, Box 526.

44. *New York Herald Tribune*, 16 November 1958; *Memphis Commercial Appeal*, 20 October 1958.

45. Bryce Harlow, memo, 18 November 1958, DDE Papers, DDE Diary Series, Whitman File, Box 37.

46. *Time*, 3 November 1958, 17.

47. Perret, *Eisenhower*, 556; Pach and Richardson, *The Presidency of Dwight D. Eisenhower*, 183–85.

48. Greene, *Lead Me On*, 182; Gore, *Let the Glory Out*, 114.

49. Gore to Marquis Childs, 18 February 1959, GSC, Research: Commerce, Interest Rates; Gore to Johnson, 13 May 1959, LBJ Papers, Papers of the Democratic Leader, Box 366; Gore, *Let the Glory Out*, 132; B. E. Hobgood, Superintendent of Murfreesboro Schools, to Gore, 9 May 1959, GSC, Department: HEW, Education.

50. Bergeron, Ash, and Keith, *Tennesseans and Their History*, 294–95.

51. Copy of the article, Papers of Drew Pearson, Box 3.

52. Gore to Creed C. Black, 14 March 1959, GSC, Media: Newspaper, Editors' Correspondence.

53. Gore to Foley, 12 June 1959, GSC, Politics: DNC.

54. Speech, 5 June 1959, GSC, Research: Commerce, Tight Money.

55. Johnson to Gore, 15 September 1959; Johnson to Gore, 16 June 1959, LBJ U.S. Senate File, Box 71.

56. Karenna Gore Schiff, telephone interview, 1 April 2002; Memorandum of Travel, 16 September 1959, November–December 1960, RSFRC, RG 46, Box 162.

57. Joint Statement of Senator Albert Gore and Senator Gale W. McGee, November 1959, DDE Papers, White House Central Files, Box 579.

58. "Articles by Albert M. Colegrove, Scripps-Howard Staff Writer, Regarding the Foreign Aid Program in Vietnam," RSFRC, RG 46, Box 169.

59. Gore, *Let the Glory Out*, 121–22.

60. *Washington Daily News*, 11 December 1959.

61. Gore to Editor of the *Washington Post*, 10 January 1960, RSFRC, RG 46, Box 169.

62. Ibid.

63. Speech for delivery on Senate Floor, 7 March 1960, GSC, Research: Foreign Policy, Dictators.

64. *Baltimore Sun*, 18 December 1959.

65. Robert D. Johnson, "The Origins of Dissent: Senate Liberals and Vietnam, 1959–1964," *Pacific Historical Review* (1996): 249–75.

66. *Chicago Sun-Times*, 17 December 1959; statement to Princeton Luncheon, 20 March 1960, GSC, Special: Birth Control, General.

67. *Chicago Sun-Times*, 17 December 1959.

68. James T. Lappan to Gore, 17 December 1959, GSC, Special: Birth Control, General.

69. Francis R. Valeo, interview by Donald Ritchie, 1985–86, p. 205, SHO.

70. E. C. Rogers to Gore, 10 February 1960, GSC, Politics: DNC, Candidates.

71. Gore to Kenneth Dixon, 20 February 1960, GSC, Politics: DNC, Candidates.

72. Chappell, *Inside Agitators*, 171.

73. Constituent to Gore, 29 February 1960; Gore to Robert L. Everett Jr., 25 March 1960, GSC, Legislative: Judiciary, Civil Rights.

74. *CR*, 14 March 1960, S5428; 1 April 1960, S7138; Senate Democratic Policy Committee, "Entire Senate Voting Record of Senator Albert Gore by Subject" (hereafter SVR), 3 January 1953–13 October 1962, 93, GSC.

75. Chappell, *Inside Agitators*, 172.

76. Baker, "Gore Also Runs," 15.

77. Address of Senator Albert Gore to the National Democratic Club, New York, 4 May 1960, RSFRC, RG 46, Box 169.

78. Speech to the United Jewish Appeal, Chicago, 7 June 1960, GSC, Foreign Policy: Middle East.

79. Paul Conkin, *Big Daddy from the Pedernales: Lyndon Baines Johnson* (Boston: Twayne, 1986), 152–55.

80. Gore, *Let the Glory Out*, 140.

81. Gore to John Wheelock, 19 July 1960, GSC, Politics: DNC, Candidates.

82. Constituent to Gore, 15 July 1960, GSC, Politics: DNC, Candidates.

83. Gore to Margaret Cole, 20 July 1960; Gore to J. Harold Stephens, 23 July 1960, GSC, Politics: DNC, Candidates; *New York Herald Tribune*, 8 August 1960.

84. Gore, *Let the Glory Out*, 141.

85. Cited in David Halberstam, *The Powers That Be* (New York: Knopf, 1979), 5–6.

86. Gore to Gene Graham, 18 August 1960, GSC, Media: Newspaper, Editors' Correspondence.

87. Gore to Kennedy, 17 October 1960, Pre-Presidential Files, Box 987, John F. Kennedy Library, Boston.

88. Gore to Kennedy, 9 November 1960, Pre-Presidential Files, Box 1062, JFK Library.

## 6. LIVING IN CAMELOT

1. Gore, *Let the Glory Out,* 142.

2. Ibid., 143.

3. Sorenson, *Kennedy,* 271–72.

4. Gore, *Let the Glory Out,* 143.

5. Francis R. Valeo, *Mike Mansfield, Majority Leader: A Different Type of Senate, 1961–1973* (Armonk, NY: M. E. Sharpe, 1999), 13; Robert Dallek, *Flawed Giant: Lyndon Johnson and His Times, 1961–1973* (New York: Oxford University Press, 1998), 8.

6. Dallek, *Flawed Giant,* 8; Gore, *Let the Glory Out,* 148.

7. *CR,* 27 April 1961, S6849; 14 April 1961, S5913.

8. *CR,* 4 May 1961, S7437; 6 September 1961, S18435.

9. Douglas Frantz and David McKean, *Friends in High Places: The Rise and Fall of Clark Clifford* (Boston: Little, Brown, 1995), 170–73.

10. *Memphis Commercial Appeal,* 20 September 1961; *CR,* 25 September 1961, S21159–60.

11. Ralph Wooten to Gore, 22 September 1961; Emerson Roberts Jr. to Gore, 21 September 1961, GSC, Issue Mail: Dupont Stock; *CR,* 26 September 1961, S21348.

12. Gore to Kennedy, 3 February 1962; Gore to Joe Sir, 10 March 1962, GSC, Legislative: Finance, DuPont; Frantz and McKean, *Friends in High Places,* 202–3.

13. Elizabeth Cobbs Hoffman, *"All You Need Is Love": The Peace Corps and the Spirit of the 1960s* (Cambridge: Harvard University Press, 1998), 41.

14. Ibid., 46–48.

15. Coates Redmon, *Come As You Are: The Peace Corps Story* (New York: Harcourt Brace Jovanovich, 1986), 36–37, 216.

16. Ibid., 147.

17. Gore to Joyce Brannon, 24 April 1961, GSC, Department: ICA, Peace Corps; *CR,* 6 June 1961, S9510.

18. Stephen Rabe, *Eisenhower and Latin America: The Foreign Policy of Anticommunism and Latin America* (Chapel Hill: University of North Carolina Press, 1988), 128. Good works on the topic include Richard E. Welch Jr., *Response to Revolution: The United States and the Cuban Revolution* (Chapel Hill: University of North Carolina Press, 1985), and Thomas G. Paterson, *Contesting Castro: The United States and the Triumph of the Cuban Revolution* (New York: Oxford University Press, 1994).

19. Trumball Higgins, *The Perfect Failure: Kennedy, Eisenhower, and the CIA at the Bay of Pigs* (New York: W. W. Norton, 1987); Piero Gleijeses, "Ships in the Night: The CIA, the White House, and the Bay of Pigs," *Journal of Latin American Studies* 27 (February 1995): 1–42.

20. Gore, *Let the Glory Out,* 148–49; Peter Wyden, *Bay of Pigs: The Untold Story* (New York: Simon and Schuster, 1979), 310.

21. U.S. Congress, Senate, *Executive Session of the Senate Foreign Relations Committee,* "Briefing on the Cuban Situation," 2 May 1961, 423.

22. Gore, *Let the Glory Out,* 149.

23. *Memphis Press-Scimitar,* 19 May 1961.

24. Ibid.; *Santa Clara Register,* 20 May 1961.

25. Robert McNamara to Gore, 2 June 1961, GSC, Department: Defense, Joint Chiefs.

26. Gore to Elizabeth Jones, 8 June 1961, GSC, Department: Defense, Joint Chiefs.

27. Gore to Williams, 28 June 1961, GSC, Department: State, Kennedy-Khrushchev; Maxwell D. Taylor, *Swords and Plowshares* (New York: W. W. Norton, 1972), 189, 197.

28. Kennedy to Gore, 25 July 1961, GSC, Department: White House, President; McGeorge Bundy to Gore, 4 May 1961, Executive Files, Box 13, JFK Library; George McGovern, Special Assistant to the President and Director of Food for Peace, 20 April 1961, Executive Files, Box 12, JFK Library; Walter LaFeber, *Inevitable Revolutions: The United States in Central America*, 2nd ed. (New York: W. W. Norton, 1993), 155–56.

29. LaFeber, *America, Russia, and the Cold War*, 218.

30. Gore to Boyer, 8 August 1961; Gore to E. H. Schendel, 11 November 1961, GSC, Department: State, Berlin.

31. Statement from the Office of Albert Gore, 14 January 1962, RSFRC, RG 46, Box 163; Johnson, "The Origins of Dissent," 257.

32. *Nashville Tennessean*, 17 December 1961.

33. Kennedy to Gore, 15 December 1961, GSC, Department: State, Volta Dam; *Lagos Daily Express*, 9 February 1962.

34. *CR*, 7 September 1961, S18561–62; 29 August 1961, S A6770.

35. Geoffrey Perrett, *Jack: A Life Like No Other* (New York: Random House, 2001), 360–61; Clark M. Clifford, *Counsel to the President: A Memoir* (New York: Random House, 1991), 375–78.

36. Arthur M. Schlesinger Jr., *A Thousand Days: John F. Kennedy in the White House* (Boston: Houghton Mifflin, 1965), 635.

37. Sorenson, *Kennedy*, 451.

38. Gore, *Let the Glory Out*, 153.

39. Ibid., 153–55.

40. *CR*, 16 April 1962, S6569–70; Albert Gore, "The Coming Steel Crisis and How to Deal with It," *Harper's*, April 1962, 13–16.

41. Cited in Sorenson, *Kennedy*, 452.

42. Schlesinger, *A Thousand Days*, 941; Doyle, *An American Insurrection*; Nadine Cohodas, *The Band Played Dixie: Race and the Liberal Conscience at Ole Miss* (New York: Free Press, 1997).

43. Mann, *The Walls of Jericho*, 328–29.

44. Ibid., 329.

45. Ibid., 332–33.

46. Harvey Greene to Gore, 1 October 1962; Mrs. I. V. Walker to Gore, n.d., GSC, Issue Mail: Ole Miss Incident.

47. Gore to J. W. McGregor, 5 October 1962, GSC, Issue Mail: Ole Miss Incident.

48. Gore, *Let the Glory Out*, 69.

49. Mark J. White, *Missiles in Cuba: Kennedy, Khrushchev, Castro and the 1962 Crisis* (Chicago: Ivan R. Dee, 1997), 56, 79.

50. Gore to constituents, October 1962, GSC, Issue Mail: Cuba.

51. Cited in White, *Missiles in Cuba*, 145.

52. Fite, *Richard B. Russell Jr.*, 446; Gore to Doris Dennison, 17 November 1962, GSC, Department: State, Cuba.

53. *Charleston Gazette*, 14 June 1962.

54. Gore to Mansfield, 6 June 1962, GSC, Research: Tax, No Tax Cut.

55. Gore, *Let the Glory Out*, 170–71.

56. Ibid.

57. Cited in Robert Dallek, *An Unfinished Life: John F. Kennedy, 1917–1963* (Boston: Little, Brown, 2003), 588.

58. *Knoxville Journal*, 25 January 1963.

59. Lawrence O'Brien to Gore, 28 May 1963, Executive Files, Box 38, JFK Library.

60. Carl M. Brauer, *John F. Kennedy and the Second Reconstruction* (New York: Columbia University Press, 1977), 265–70; Hugh D. Graham, *The Civil Rights Era: Origins and Development of National Policy, 1960–1972* (New York: Oxford University Press, 1990), 79–83.

61. List, n.d., Papers of Richard B. Russell Jr., Box 18, File 12, Russell Research Center, University of Georgia.

62. Constituent to Gore, 12 June 1963, GSC, Issue Mail: Civil Rights.

63. Gore to James T. Dacus, 28 June 1963, GSC, Issue Mail: Civil Rights.

64. Robert S. Alley, *School Prayer: The Court, the Congress, and the First Amendment* (Buffalo: Prometheus Books, 1994), 107–26.

65. Constituent to Gore, 26 June 1963, GSC, Issue Mail: School Prayer.

66. Byron C. Hulsey, *Everett Dirksen and His Presidents: How a Senate Giant Shaped American Politics* (Lawrence: University Press of Kansas, 2000), 219, 225–28; Gore to Avondale Baptist Church (Chattanooga), 20 July 1963, GSC, Issue Mail: School Prayer.

67. *Nashville Banner*, 10 July 1962; Albert Gore to John Kennedy, 29 July 1963, Executive Files, Box 36, JFK Library. Allen Gore had passed away in 1956.

68. Mary Sasser, telephone interview, 13 June 2001; Jane Holmes Dixon, interview, 14 June 2001, Washington, DC.

69. Jim Sasser, interview, 12 June 2001, Washington, DC; Maraniss and Nakashima, *The Prince of Tennessee*, 196, 195.

70. For a good study of the times and women's roles, see Elaine Tyler May, *Homeward Bound: American Families in the Cold War Era* (New York: Basic Books, 1988), 114–34.

71. Holmes Dixon, interview.

72. Gilbert Merritt, interview, 26 September 2001, Nashville.

73. Turque, *Inventing Al Gore*, 30; Maraniss and Nakashima, *The Prince of Tennessee*, 199.

74. Maraniss and Nakashima, *The Prince of Tennessee*, 199; Turque, *Inventing Al Gore*, 30.

75. Cited in Kenneth T. Walsh, "Fathers and Sons," *U.S. News and World Report*, 9 August 1999, 20.

76. Dan Murphy, "The Special Bond between a Father and a Son," *Tennessee Monthly*, June 1996, 14; Hillin, *Al Gore Jr.*, 31.

77. Peter Boyer, "Gore's Dilemma," *New Yorker*, 28 November 1994, 103.

78. Gore to Kenneth Morgan, 4 September 1962, GSC, Personal: Tennessee; Turque, *Inventing Al Gore*, 32–33.

79. Turque, *Inventing Al Gore*, 32–35.

80. Ibid., 32–33.

81. Ibid., 29.

82. Cited in Maraniss and Nakashima, *The Prince of Tennessee*, 46.

83. Ibid.

84. Boyer, "Gore's Dilemma," 103; Maraniss and Nakashima, *The Prince of Tennessee*, 50.

85. Maraniss and Nakashima, *The Prince of Tennessee*, 50; Walsh, "Fathers and Sons," 20; Katherine Boo, "The Liberation of Albert Gore," *Washington Post Monthly Magazine*, 28 November 1993, 11.

86. Adrian S. Fisher, interview by Paige E. Mulhollan, 31 October 1968, OHC.

87. Gore to constituents, August 1963, GSC, Issue Mail: Test Ban Treaty; Albert Gore to William L. Clayton, 30 August 1963, Papers of William L. Clayton, Box 167, LBJ Library.

88. Michael R. Beschloss, *The Crisis Years: Kennedy and Khrushchev, 1960–1963* (New York: HarperPerennial, 1991), 636.

89. Fontenay, *Estes Kefauver*, 400–403.

90. Robinson, interview, 18 November 1998; Turque, *Inventing Al Gore*, 43–44.

91. Moss, *Vietnam: An American Ordeal*, 118–37.

92. Fredrik Logevall, *Choosing War: The Lost Chance for Peace and Escalation of War in Vietnam* (Berkeley: University of California Press, 1999), 1–74.

93. Gore, *The Eye of the Storm*, 7.

94. Herring, *America's Longest War*, 113–19.

95. Gore, *The Eye of the Storm*, 7; Johnson, "The Origins of Dissent," 270.

96. Gore to A. S. Landiss, 6 December 1963, GSC, Department: White House, Kennedy's Assassination.

97. Gore to Leon Pierce, 19 December 1963, GSC, Department: White House, Kennedy's Assassination.


7. IN THE MIDST OF THE GREAT SOCIETY AND BEYOND

1. Gore to Johnson, 23 November 1963; Johnson to Gore, 29 November 1963, GSC, Department: White House, Letters to the President.

2. Barr to Mike Manatos, 17 December 1963, White House Central Files, Box 146, LBJ Library.

3. Johnson and Dillon, telephone conversation, 8 January 1964, Telephone Conversations of Lyndon B. Johnson (hereafter Tapes), WH 6401.08, LBJ Library.

4. Dallek, *Flawed Giant*, 73; Johnson and McCarthy, telephone conversation, 6 January 1964, Tapes, WH 6401.06; Dallek, *Flawed Giant*, 74.

5. Conkin, *Big Daddy from the Pedernales*, 220–21; Dallek, *Flawed Giant*, 74–84.

6. Gore, *Let the Glory Out*, 175; Gore to constituents, 19 February 1964, GSC, Issue Mail: Medical Care.

7. Gore, *Let the Glory Out*, 174–75.

8. Cited in Woods, *Fulbright*, 328–29.

9. Constituent to Gore, 14 June 1963; Constituent to Gore, n.d., GSC, Issue Mail: Civil Rights. This was a common tactic among segregationists to attack civil rights proponents. See Jeff Woods, *Black Struggle, Red Scare: Segregation and Anti-Communism in the South, 1948–1968* (Baton Rouge: Louisiana State University Press, 2004).

10. Gore, *The Eye of the Storm*, 133–34.

11. *CR*, 11 June 1964, S13491.

12. SVR, 9 January 1963–3 October 1964, 73–112.

13. Richard Harris, "Annals of Politics: How the People Feel," *New Yorker*, 10 July 1971, 37; *CR*, 19 June 1964, S14434.

14. Gore, *Let the Glory Out*, 119; Gore, *The Eye of the Storm*, 134–35.

15. Al Gore, interview by author.

16. Gore to Joe Jared, 9 July 1964, GSC: Politics, General; Sasser, interview.

17. Dallek, *Flawed Giant*, 160; Smathers and Johnson, telephone conversation, 1 August 1964, Tapes, WH 6408.01.

18. Herring, *America's Longest War*, 134; Edwin E. Moïse, *Tonkin Gulf and the Escalation of the Vietnam War* (Chapel Hill: University of North Carolina Press, 1996), 73–142.

19. Moss, *Vietnam: An American Ordeal*, 173; Robert D. Johnson, *Ernest Gruening and the American Dissenting Tradition* (Cambridge: Harvard University Press, 1998), 254; H. R. McMaster, *Dereliction of Duty: Lyndon Johnson, Robert McNamara, the Joint Chiefs of Staff, and the Lies That Led to Vietnam* (New York: HarperCollins, 1997), 134; Ezra Y. Siff, *Why the Senate Slept: The Gulf of Tonkin Resolution and the Beginning of America's Vietnam War* (Westport, CT: Praeger, 1999), 61–62.

20. Johnson, "The Origins of Dissent," 273; *CR*, 6 August 1964, S18075.

21. George McGovern, telephone interview, 25 August 2001; Woods, *Fulbright*, 355.

22. Robert S. McNamara, James G. Blight, and Robert K. Brigham, *Argument without End: In Search of Answers to the Vietnam Tragedy* (New York: PublicAffairs, 1999), 202–4.

23. Gore, *The Eye of the Storm*, 8–9.

24. Gore, *Let the Glory Out*, 177.

25. Cited in Dallek, *Flawed Giant*, 209.

26. Gore, *Let the Glory Out*, 178–79.

27. Johnson and Gore, telephone conversation, 2 September 1964, Tapes, WH 6409.01; Manatos to O'Brien, 22 September 1964, LBJ White House Central Files, Box 55.

28. Gary A. Donaldson, *Liberalism's Last Hurrah: The Presidential Campaign of 1964* (Armonk, NY: M.E. Sharpe, 2003).

29. Gore to Johnson, n.d.; Johnson to Gore, 4 September 1964, GSC, Department: White House, Letters to the President.

30. Neal Gregory (assistant to Gore) to Paul Danaceau (DNC), 16 December 1964, GSC, Special: John Birch, General.

31. Cited in Maurice Isserman and Michael Kazin, *America Divided: The Civil War of the 1960s* (New York: Oxford University Press, 2000), 139.

32. Johnson and Gore, telephone conversation, 2 October 1964, Tapes, WH 6410.01.

33. Lyndon Johnson, "Remarks of the President at the War Memorial Building," 9 October

1964, President's Appointment File, Box 10, LBJ Library; Johnson and Ahlgren, telephone conversation, 9 October 1964, Tapes, WH 6410.04.

34. Carol Bradley, "The Gore on the Sidelines: Albert Sr. Would Love to Be Helping His Son," *Nashville Tennessean Magazine*, 31 October 1984, A15.

35. Allen, interview.

36. *Nashville Tennessean*, 1 January 1965; Gore, *Let the Glory Out*, 184.

37. Robert C. Hodges, "The Cooing of a Dove: Senator Albert Gore Sr.'s Opposition to the War in Vietnam," *Peace and Change* 22 (April 1997): 137–39.

38. *Nashville Banner*, 14 January 1965; Constituent to Gore, 5 February 1965, GSC, Issue Mail: Vietnam.

39. Gore to Mary Toomey, 18 February 1965, GSC, Department: State, Vietnam.

40. Gore and Johnson, telephone conversation, 18 March 1965, Tapes, WH 6503.09.

41. David J. Garrow, *Protest at Selma: Martin Luther King Jr. and the Voting Rights Act of 1965* (New Haven: Yale University Press, 1978).

42. SVR, 4 January 1965–23 October 1965, 74–76.

43. Gore to constituents, 25 March 1965, GSC, Issue Mail: Voting Rights.

44. SVR, 4 January 1965–23 October 1965, 13, 22–30, 74–76.

45. Albert Gore, "How to Be Rich without Paying Taxes," *New York Times Magazine*, 11 April 1965, 28–29, 86.

46. Ibid.

47. McGovern, interview; Manuel Leonardo to Johnson, 16 April 1965, LBJ White House Central Files, Box 207.

48. Russell to constituents, 8 December 1964, Russell Papers, Box 28, File 36; Dallek, *Flawed Giant*, 206.

49. Valeo, *Mike Mansfield, Majority Leader*, 248.

50. Dallek, *Flawed Giant*, 207.

51. *CR*, 7 July 1965, S15834.

52. Irwin Unger and Debi Unger, *LBJ: A Life* (New York: J. Wiley and Sons, 1999), 366.

53. Irving Bernstein, *Guns or Butter: The Presidency of Lyndon Johnson* (New York: Oxford University Press, 1996), 156.

54. Isserman and Kazin, *America Divided*, 139–45.

55. William C. Berman, *William Fulbright and the Vietnam War: The Dissent of a Political Realist* (Kent, OH: Kent State University Press, 1988), 52–53.

56. Ibid.

57. *The Vietnam Hearings* (New York: Vintage Books, 1966), 15, 43–46.

58. *Nashville Tennessean*, 17 February 1966; *The Vietnam Hearings*, 127.

59. Cited in Johnson, *Ernest Gruening and the American Dissenting Tradition*, 274.

60. Athan G. Theoharis, ed., *From the Secret Files of J. Edgar Hoover* (Chicago: Ivan R. Dee, 1991), 237.

61. Melvin Small, *Johnson, Nixon and the Doves* (New Brunswick: Rutgers University Press, 1988), 79; Pat M. Holt, interview, 203, OHC.

62. Al Gore, interview by Brinkley.

63. *CR*, 7 March 1966, S5175.

64. *Nashville Tennessean*, 2 April 1966; *CR*, 7 March 1966, S5171.

65. Glenn T. Seaborg and Benjamin S. Loeb, *Stemming the Tide: Arms Control in the Johnson Years* (Lexington, MA: Lexington Books, 1987), 111–18.

66. Gore to A. T. Harris, 5 May 1965, GSC, Department: UN, Admission of Red China; Press Conference of Senator Albert Gore, 21 January 1966, RSFRC, RG 46, Box 1.

67. Stanley D. Bachrack, *The Committee of One Million: "China Lobby" Politics, 1953–1971* (New York: Columbia University Press, 1976), 218–57.

68. *Washington Post*, 3 June 1966.

69. Gore Press Conference, 21 January 1966, RSFRC.

70. *Nashville Tennessean*, 7 December 1998.

71. *Nashville Tennessean*, 13 August 1966; *CR*, 26 August 1966, S20809.

72. *Nashville Tennessean*, 4 August 1966.

73. *CR*, 17 August 1966, S19721.

74. Heller to Johnson, 6 September 1966, LBJ White House Central Files, Box 146.

75. Cited in William H. Frist and J. Lee Annis Jr., *Tennessee Senators, 1911–2001: Portraits of Leadership in a Century of Change* (Lanham, MD: Madison Books, 1999), 127.

76. Ibid., 130–32.

77. *Nashville Tennessean*, 6 August 1966; 2 April 1966.

78. Greene, *Lead Me On*, 361.

79. Gore, *Let the Glory Out*, 197.

80. Bergeron, Ash, and Keith, *Tennesseans and Their History*, 324.

81. Gore would maintain a good friendship with Baker throughout his career and even cancel a trip to South America to personally escort him down the Senate aisle to take the oath. Gore to Fulbright, 2 December 1966, RSFRC, RG 46, Box 1.

82. Frederickson, *The Dixiecrat Revolt and the End of the Solid South*, 235–37.

83. Cited in Hulsey, *Everett Dirksen and His Presidents*, 226.

84. Gore to Constituents, 19 January 1967, GSC, Issue Mail: Prayer.

85. *New York Times*, 27 March 1967; *Washington Post*, 28 March 1967.

86. Robert Mann, *Legacy to Power: Senator Russell Long of Louisiana* (New York: Paragon House, 1992), 247–54; *CR*, 3 April 1967, S8061; 2 May 1967, S11485; 4 April 1967, S8303.

87. *Washington Post*, 18 May 1967.

88. *Human Events*, 10 June 1967; *CR*, 23 May 1967, S13463; Gore to George Chamberlin, 25 May 1967, GSC, Legislation: Finance, Election Campaigns.

89. *Nashville Tennessean*, 23 May 1967; Bill Holland to Gore, 25 June 1967, GSC, Legislation: Finance, Election Campaigns.

90. Jones, *Crucible of Power*, 371–72.

91. Thomas W. Zeiler, *Dean Rusk: Defending the American Mission Abroad* (Wilmington, DE: Scholarly Resources, 2000), 96–97; George W. Ball and Douglas B. Ball, *The Passionate Attachment: America's Involvement with Israel, 1947 to the Present* (New York: W. W. Norton, 1992), 56–61; David Schoenbaum, *The United States and Israel* (New York: Oxford University Press, 1993), 149–53, 186–87.

92. *Jerusalem Post*, 10 July 1967.

93. Johnson to Gore, 12 July 1967, National Security Files, Box 11, LBJ Library.

94. *CR*, 12 July 1967, S18499.

95. Gore to Mrs. Truman Kahn, 15 August 1967, GSC, Department: State, Middle East.

96. *CR*, 15 August 1967, S22655.

97. *Chicago Tribune*, 28 August 1967.

98. *CR*, 24 October 1967, S29801; 2 November 1967, S31078.

99. *CR*, 24 October 1967, S29802.

100. *CR*, 30 November 1967, S34355.

101. Humphrey to Gore, 16 November 1967, RSFRC, RG 46, Box 2; Gore to Humphrey, 1 December 1967, GSC, Department: Correspondence, Vice President.

102. *Memphis Commercial Appeal*, 27 October 1967; Allen to J. C. Walker, 19 December 1967, GSC, Department: State, Vietnam.

103. Constituent to Gore, 23 October 1967; Gore to Charles Warren Montgomery III, 27 October 1967, GSC, Department: State, Vietnam.

104. Bernard Schwartz, *Swann's Way: The School Busing Case and the Supreme Court* (New York: Oxford University Press, 1986), 46–66.

105. Ibid.

106. *CR*, 5 December 1967, S35081.

107. Gore to Constituents, June 1969, GSC, Legislative: Judiciary, General.

108. McGovern, interview.

109. Gore, *The Eye of the Storm*, 135–37.

110. Gore to Constituents, 26 January 1968, GSC, Issue Mail: Pueblo; Mitchell B. Lerner, *The Pueblo Incident: A Spy Ship and the Failure of American Foreign Policy* (Lawrence: University Press of Kansas, 2002).

111. William J. Duiker, *Sacred War: Nationalism and Revolution in a Divided Vietnam* (New York: McGraw-Hill, 1995), 208–18.

112. Albert Gore, "Vietnam," speech to the Borah Foundation, University of Idaho, 17 February 1968, RSFRC, RG 46, Box 2; Gore to W. C. Wofford, 15 February 1968, GSC, Department: State, Vietnam.

113. "Selected Questions and Comments of Members of the SFRC during Secretary Rusk's Appearance in Open Session, March 11–12," Papers of Clark Clifford, Box 11–12, LBJ Library.

114. Albert Gore, "Excerpts of Closing Statement during Foreign Relations Committee Hearing," 12 March 1968, GSC, Department: State, Vietnam.

115. Herring, *America's Longest War*, 215.

116. Cited in Unger and Unger, *LBJ*, 460.

117. *CR*, 1 April 1968, S8410–11.

118. Dallek, *Flawed Giant*, 517; Adam Fairclough, *To Redeem the Soul of America: The Southern Christian Leadership Conference and Martin Luther King* (Athens: University of Georgia Press, 1987), 382; Gore, *The Eye of the Storm*, 135.

119. Ramsey Clark to Gore, 4 March 1968; Arnold Aronson to Gore, 19 March 1968, GSC, Politics: Tennessee, 1968 Campaign.

120. Gore to Jesse Moores, 9 May 1968, GSC, Special: King's Death.

121. Al Gore, interview by author.

122. *CR*, 21 May 1968, S14169–80; 23 May 1968, S14744–45, S14795–96; Gore to Constituents, 12 June 1968, GSC, Issue Mail: Firearms; Constituent to Gore, June 1968, GSC, Legislative: Judiciary, Guns.

123. Unger and Unger, *LBJ*, 467; *Nashville Banner*, 10 June 1968.

124. Gore to Louie E. Spivey, 13 March 1968, GSC, Issue Mail: Poor People's March; *CR*, 24 May 1968, S14918.

125. Merle Miller, *Lyndon: An Oral Biography* (New York: G. P. Putnam's Sons, 1980), 482–83; Dallek, *Flawed Giant*, 558–60.

126. Cited in Dallek, *Flawed Giant*, 558.

127. Constituents to Gore, July 1968, GSC, Issue Mail: Supreme Court Nomination; Albert Gore, "Capitol Commentary," 1 July 1968, GSC, Legislative: Judiciary, Supreme Court Nomination.

128. *CR*, 16 September 1968, S26885.

129. Bruce Allen Murphy, *Fortas: The Rise and Ruin of a Supreme Court Justice* (New York: William Morrow, 1988), 498–511; *CR*, 30 September 1968, S28781.

130. Robert Shogan, *A Question of Judgment: The Fortas Case and the Struggle for the Supreme Court* (New York: Bobbs-Merrill, 1972), 260–61; Dallek, *Flawed Giant*, 564.

131. Carter, *The Politics of Rage*, 108–9, 195–225.

132. Ibid., 313.

133. Michael Schaller and George Rising, *The Republican Ascendancy: American Politics, 1968–2001* (Wheeling, IL: Harlan Davidson, 2002), 16–26.

134. Stephan Lesher, *George Wallace: American Populist* (New York: Addison-Wesley, 1994), 387–431.

135. Constituent to Gore, 23 March 1968, GSC, Politics: Presidential.

136. Maraniss and Nakashima, *The Prince of Tennessee*, 85–86.

137. *Memphis Press-Scimitar*, 24 August 1968.

138. Ralph Yarborough to Gore, 31 August 1968, GSC, Politics: DNC, Chicago.

139. Maraniss and Nakashima, *The Prince of Tennessee*, 87–88; Gore to Philip Livingston, 21 August 1968, GSC, Politics: DNC, Chicago.

140. Gore to Timothy Foley, 5 September 1968; Gore to Kitchey Hume, 31 August 1968, GSC, Politics: DNC, Chicago.

141. Gore to Florence Brown, 27 September 1968, GSC, Special: Law and Order; Gore to Harry Richmond, 24 September 1968, GSC, Department: Justice, FBI.

142. Constituent to Gore, 29 August 1968; Gore to Larry Yates, 5 September 1968, GSC, Politics: Tennessee.

143. McGovern, interview. Like Gore, Yarborough worked long hours, and they did not share many common interests. Cox, *Ralph W. Yarborough*, 204.

144. Whitt, interview; Halberstam, "The End of a Populist," 36–37.

145. Merritt, interview.

146. Lewis L. Gould, *1968: The Election That Changed America* (Chicago: Ivan R. Dee, 1993).

147. Numan V. Bartley and Hugh D. Graham, *Southern Elections: County and Precinct Data, 1950–1972* (Baton Rouge: Louisiana State University Press, 1978), 219.

148. Cited in Maraniss and Nakashima, *The Prince of Tennessee*, 89.

## 8. TARGET NUMBER ONE

1. Gore to Church, 12 November 1970, Papers of Frank Church, Box 2, File 13, Frank Church Collection, Boise State University Library.

2. Despite their many differences, Johnson and Gore had a rapprochement as the president left office. Johnson wrote Gore in mid-January, "As I leave the presidency, I recall the many good days we have shared, working together on the Nation's business. The Senate will always remain one of the cornerstones of my life. I hope that in the days ahead I will be able to meet with you again and talk about the State of the Nation. Thank you for your devotion to an institution we both cherish and for helping sustain me over these years." Johnson to Gore, 17 January 1969, LBJ White House Central Files, Box 207.

3. George Bunn, *Arms Control by Committee: Managing Negotiations with the Russians* (Stanford: Stanford University Press, 1992), 108.

4. Melvin Small, *The Presidency of Richard Nixon* (Lawrence: University Press of Kansas, 1999), 101–2; Gore to Arthur Hooks, 12 March 1969, GSC, Legislation: Foreign Relations, Disarmament; Albert Gore, "Opening Statement, Gore to Subcommittee on International Organization and Disarmament Affairs," 21 March 1969, RSFRC, RG 46, Box 1.

5. Woods, *Fulbright*, 520.

6. *Baltimore Sun*, 24 March 1969.

7. Stephen E. Ambrose, *Nixon: The Triumph of a Politician, 1962–1972* (New York: Simon and Schuster, 1989), 276–77.

8. Albert Gore, "Remarks of Senator Albert Gore at Madison Square Garden," 25 June 1969, RSFRC, RG 46, Box 1.

9. *CR*, 17 July 1969, S19855; 22 July 1969, S20220.

10. Aitken, *Nixon*, 434–35.

11. Cited in Woods, *Fulbright*, 525.

12. Ambrose, *Nixon*, 190, 207–9.

13. *CR*, 20 March 1969, S6966.

14. *Baltimore Sun*, 9 May 1969; Gore, *The Eye of the Storm*, 11–12.

15. Albert Gore, "The Vietnam War," 17 June 1969, RSFRC, RG 46, Box 1.

16. Maraniss and Nakashima, *The Prince of Tennessee*, 108.

17. Al Gore, interview by author; Turque, *Inventing Al Gore*, 66. A close family friend and Al's undergraduate thesis adviser, Martin Peretz, emphasized that there was "no way Al Gore would not have gone to the military." Martin Peretz, telephone interview, 23 April 2002.

18. Maraniss and Nakashima, *The Prince of Tennessee*, 109.

19. Douglas Brinkley, "Al Gore's Defining Moment," *Talk*, November 1999, 152; Bill Turque, "The Three Faces of Al Gore," *Newsweek*, 20 July 1992, 30.

20. Maraniss and Nakashima, *The Prince of Tennessee*, 114.

21. Ambrose, *Nixon*, 296.

22. Ibid., 315; Small, *The Presidency of Richard Nixon*, 168.

23. Gore, *Let the Glory Out*, 238; Aitken, *Nixon*, 391.

24. *Charleston News and Courier*, 21 October 1969.

25. Ambrose, *Nixon*, 191; Rowland Evans Jr. and Robert D. Novack, *Nixon in the White House* (New York: Random House, 1971), 315; *Washington Post*, 9 November 1969.

26. Constituent to Gore, 3 November 1969; Constituent to Gore, 1 November 1969, GSC, Issue Mail: Vice President Agnew.

27. Albert Gore, "Gratitude to the 'Veep,'" 10 December 1969, RSFRC, RG 46, Box 1.

28. Glen Moore, "Richard M. Nixon and the 1970 Midterm Elections in the South," *Southern Historian* 12 (1991): 61.

29. Kevin P. Phillips, *Emerging Republican Majority* (New Rochelle, NY: Arlington House, 1969), 36; Dent to Nixon, 8 December 1969, Nixon Presidential Materials Project (NPMP), White House Special Files: Harry S. Dent, Box 8, National Archives II, College Park, MD.

30. William Safire, *Before the Fall: An Inside View of the Pre-Watergate White House* (New York: Grosset and Dunlap, 1978), 318–19.

31. Dent to Nixon, 3 December 1969, NPMP, White House Special Files: Harry S. Dent, Box 9.

32. Dent to Peter Flanigan, 15 December 1969, NPMP, White House Special Files: Harry S. Dent, Box 3.

33. Maraniss and Nakashima, *The Prince of Tennessee*, 121.

34. Turque, *Inventing Al Gore*, 56.

35. Jackie Gleason to Dent, 3 December 1969, NPMP, White House Special Files: Harry S. Dent, Box 9.

36. Albert A. Gore, "Opening Statement by Senator Gore," 16 March 1970, RSFRC, RG 46, Box 1.

37. Small, *The Presidency of Richard Nixon*, 168, 169; John Ehrlichman, *Witness to Power: The Nixon Years* (New York: Simon and Schuster, 1982), 126.

38. Gore, *Let the Glory Out*, 239; Jonathan Schell, *The Time of Illusion* (New York: Vintage Books, 1976), 81; Evans and Novack, *Nixon in the White House*, 165.

39. Gore, *Let the Glory Out*, 239–40; Aitken, *Nixon*, 393.

40. Cited in Ehrlichman, *Witness to Power*, 128–29.

41. *New York Times*, 19 April 1970.

42. Throughout the war, the South including Tennessee had supported the military solution much more than other regions of the country did. For an excellent overview, see Joseph A. Fry, *Dixie Looks Abroad: The South and U.S. Foreign Relations, 1789–1973* (Baton Rouge: Louisiana State University Press, 2002), 269–73.

43. Davis, "The Albert Gore Story," 5, 10.

44. Davis, "The Senator Who Risks His Neck," 7, 10.

45. Brown, interview.

46. Cited in Herring, *America's Longest War*, 261.

47. Kenneth J. Heineman, *Put Your Bodies upon the Wheels: Student Revolt in the 1960s* (Chicago: Ivan R. Dee, 2001), 175–76.

48. *CR*, 1 May 1970, S13833, S13835; Leroy Ashby and Rod Gramer, *Fighting the Odds: The Life of Senator Frank Church* (Pullman: Washington State University Press, 1994), 309; Robert Mann, *A Grand Delusion: America's Descent into Vietnam* (New York: Basic Books, 2001), 659.

49. Gore, *The Eye of the Storm*, 25; Safire, *Before the Fall*, 193.

50. Woods, *Fulbright*, 568–75.

51. Henry Brandon, *The Retreat of American Power* (New York: Doubleday, 1974), 146–47.

52. Athan Theoharis, *Spying on Americans: Political Surveillance from Hoover to the Hutson Plan* (Philadelphia: Temple University Press, 1978), 13–39.

53. Moore, "Richard M. Nixon and the 1970 Midterm Elections in the South," 62; Peter Flanigan to Brock, 12 May 1970, NPMP, White House Special Files: Harry S. Dent, Box 3.

54. *New York Times*, 3 July 1970; Nancy Benac, "Gore Sr. Called Passionate Advocate," *Yahoo! News*, 6 December 1998, http://dailynews.yahoo.com/headline.../19981206/goreremembered1.html.

55. Maraniss and Nakashima, *The Prince of Tennessee*, 119.

56. Moore, "Richard M. Nixon and the 1970 Midterm Elections in the South," 63; Bartley and Graham, *Southern Elections*, 218.

57. Cox, *Ralph Yarborough*, 254–63.

58. Cited in Safire, *Before the Fall*, 320.

59. *New York Post*, 13 June 1970; *New York Times*, 3 July 1970.

60. Kelly Leiter, "Tennessee: Gore vs. the White House," *The Nation*, 26 October 1970, 397.

61. Frist and Annis, *Tennessee Senators, 1911–2001*, 167; Turque, *Inventing Al Gore*, 78.

62. Cited in Halberstam, "The End of a Populist," 42.

63. Leiter, "Tennessee," 396; Seigenthaler, interview. The Brock television commercials are available from the Julian P. Kanter Political Commercial Archive, University of Oklahoma, Norman.

64. Halberstam, "The End of a Populist," 38–39; Maraniss and Nakashima, *The Prince of Tennessee*, 121.

65. Harris, "Annals of Politics," 38.

66. Cited in Maraniss and Nakashima, *The Prince of Tennessee*, 122.

67. Cited in Turque, *Inventing Al Gore*, 75.

68. Cited in Michael S. Martin and Tony Badger, "The Anti-Gore Campaign of 1970," presented at the Tennessee Conference of Historians, Nashville, 27 September 2003, p. 3; Merritt, interview; Jim Sasser, interview.

69. *Nashville Tennessean*, 24 September 1972.

70. Halberstam, "The End of a Populist," 42–43.

71. Harris, "Annals of Politics," 37, 38.

72. Townhouse File, #807, NPMP, Records of the Watergate Special Prosecution Force, Campaign Contributions Task Force, Box 6.

73. Harris, "Annals of Politics," 36.

74. Halberstam, "The End of a Populist," 40–41.

75. Ibid., 40. Good works on the topic of the transformation of the South and the working class include Bruce Schulman, *From Cotton Belt to Sunbelt: Federal Policy, Economic Development,*

*and the Transformation of the South, 1938–1980* (New York: Oxford University Press, 1991), and Robert Emil Botsch, *We Shall Not Overcome: Populism and Southern Blue-Collar Workers* (Chapel Hill: University of North Carolina Press, 1980).

76. Carter, *From George Wallace to Newt Gingrich*, 28–46.

77. *Wall Street Journal*, 20 October 1970.

78. Halberstam, "The End of a Populist," 42.

79. Ibid., 45.

80. Merritt, interview; Halberstam, "The End of a Populist," 41.

81. *Nashville Tennessean*, 6 December 1998; Henry Loeb to William O'Hara, copy to Gore, 5 June 1970, GSC, Issue Mail: Vietnam; Leiter, "Tennessee," 398; Frist and Annis, *Tennessee Senators, 1911–2001*, 111.

82. *Wall Street Journal*, 20 October 1970.

83. Leiter, "Tennessee," 397–98.

84. Ibid.

85. *Memphis Commercial Appeal*, 23 September 1970; Moore, "Richard M. Nixon and the 1970 Midterm Elections in the South," 64–65.

86. *Nashville Tennessean*, 23 September 1970.

87. *New York Times*, 21 October 1970; *Nashville Banner*, 20 October 1970; "Tennessee—1970 Election," 20 October 1970, NPMP, White House Special Files: H.R. Haldeman, Box 123.

88. Cited in Eugene Graham, "Gore's Lost Cause," *New South*, Spring 1971, 29.

89. Halberstam, "The End of a Populist," 39.

90. J. Lee Annis Jr., *Howard Baker: Conciliator in an Age of Crisis* (New York: Madison Books, 1995), 56.

91. Gore, *Let the Glory Out*, 6.

92. Harris, "Annals of Politics," 38.

93. Maraniss and Nakashima, *The Prince of Tennessee*, 125; Numan V. Bartley and Hugh D. Graham, *Southern Politics and the Second Reconstruction* (Baltimore: Johns Hopkins University Press, 1975), 159.

94. Turque, *Inventing Al Gore*, 80; Maraniss and Nakashima, *The Prince of Tennessee*, 125; Halberstam, "The End of a Populist," 45.

95. Al Gore, interview by author.

96. Ibid.; Gore eulogy.

97. Turque, *Inventing Al Gore*, 81.

98. Grantham, *The South in Modern America*, 284; Randy Sanders, *Mighty Peculiar Elections: The New South Gubernatorial Campaigns of 1970 and the Changing Politics of Race* (Gainesville: University Press of Florida, 2002); Francis Butler Simkins and Charles Pierce Rowland, *A History of the South*, 4th ed. (New York: Knopf, 1972), 649.

99. Fulbright to Gore, 16 November 1970, Fulbright Papers, Box 3, F3; *Washington Star*, 20 December 1970.

100. *Nashville Banner*, 1 January 1971.

101. Bullen interview. He later said, "I fought for what I believe in. I would do it again." *Nashville Tennessean*, 6 December 1998.

1. Al Gore, interview by Brinkley. A great challenge of the final chapter of this book was securing the materials that existed so readily for the period before 1971. The family and Occidental have maintained the bulk of the materials, as is often the case of former Senate members, who do not transfer personal materials to the archives until after the deaths of those directly involved.

2. Carl Marcy, Oral History Interviews, p. 273, SHO; Gore, *Let the Glory Out*, 281–82.

3. Turque, *Inventing Al Gore*, 17; Jim Sasser, interview; Brown, interview.

4. *Nashville Tennessean*, 17 June 1971.

5. *Nashville Tennessean*, 14 December 1971.

6. *Nashville Tennessean*, 17 June 1971.

7. *Nashville Banner*, 8 November 1971; *Nashville Tennessean*, 16 July 1972, 2 October 1971.

8. Bob Clement, interview, 14 June 2001, Washington, DC.

9. Robinson, interview, 18 November 1998.

10. William Allen, telephone interview, 1 June 1999.

11. *Nashville Banner*, 28 September 1972; Al Gore, interview by author; *Washington Post*, 18 January 1980.

12. *Nashville Tennessean*, 6 September 1972; Jim Sasser, interview.

13. Zelnick, *Gore*, 20–21; Allen, interview.

14. *Nashville Tennessean*, 13 October 1972; Gore, *Let the Glory Out*, viii, 6–7.

15. Gore, *Let the Glory Out*, 13, 27.

16. Ibid., 33.

17. Ibid., 291, 288, 307.

18. Seigenthaler, interview; *Nashville Tennessean*, 24 September 1972.

19. Bartley and Graham, *Southern Elections*.

20. Grantham, *Recent America*, 333–34.

21. *Nashville Tennessean*, 8 November 1973.

22. Summers, *The Arrogance of Power*, 443, 446; Small, *The Presidency of Richard Nixon*, 289–90.

23. *Nashville Tennessean*, 2 November 1973; *Nashville Banner*, 1 October 1973.

24. *Nashville Banner*, 1 October 1973.

25. *Nashville Tennessean*, 9 June 1974.

26. Ibid.

27. Scher, *Politics in the New South*, 106–8.

28. Richard Stennis, "Profiles in Caution: The Several Faces of Al Gore Are All Carefully Thought Out," *Time*, 21 March 1988, 28; Walsh, "Fathers and Sons," 20.

29. Turque, *Inventing Al Gore*, 112.

30. Ibid., 113.

31. Sanders, "Life of Women in Political Families—Pauline LaFon Gore," 25.

32. Turque, *Inventing Al Gore*, 114–15.

33. Ibid., 119–20.

34. Maraniss and Nakashima, *The Prince of Tennessee*, 171–74; Turque, *Inventing Al Gore*, 124.

35. Maraniss and Nakashima, *The Prince of Tennessee*, 170.

36. Lamis, *The Two-Party South*, 171.

37. Turque, *Inventing Al Gore*, 115, 128.

38. Maraniss and Nakashima, *The Prince of Tennessee*, 175; Turque, *Inventing Al Gore*, 129.

39. Seigenthaler, interview.

40. Jim Sasser, interview.

41. Frist and Annis, *Tennessee Senators, 1911–2001*, 181–82; Larry Daughtery, telephone interview, 14 February 2002.

42. *Nashville Tennessean*, 1 November 1976.

43. Scher, *Politics in the New South*, 102.

44. *Nashville Tennessean*, 4 May 1977, 21 April 1980.

45. Thomas L. Farmer to Carter, 20 January 1978, White House Central Files, Name Files: Gore, Jimmy Carter Library, Atlanta.

46. Gore to Carter, 9 February 1979, Carter White House Central Files, Box UT-5.

47. Eizenstat to Gore, 28 March 1979, Carter White House Central Files, Box UT-5.

48. Eizenstat to Gore, 9 August 1980, Carter White House Central Files, Name Files: Gore.

49. Robert G. Kaufman, *Henry M. Jackson: A Life in Politics* (Seattle: University of Washington Press, 2000), 365–67.

50. *Nashville Tennessean*, 25 October 1979.

51. *Nashville Tennessean*, 12 April 1980.

52. *Nashville Tennessean*, 15 April 1982.

53. Maraniss and Nakashima, *The Prince of Tennessee*, 182.

54. Turque, *Inventing Al Gore*, 130–50.

55. *Nashville Banner*, 28 December 1978.

56. *Nashville Tennessean*, 21 April 1980.

57. Walsh, "Fathers and Sons," 21.

58. Al Gore, interview by Brinkley.

59. *Nashville Tennessean*, 15 April 1982.

60. Holmes Dixon, interview; Maraniss and Nakashima, *The Prince of Tennessee*, 200–202.

61. Maraniss and Nakashima, *The Prince of Tennessee*, 203.

62. Turque, *Inventing Al Gore*, 160.

63. Maraniss and Nakashima, *The Prince of Tennessee*, 203; Turque, *Inventing Al Gore*, 160.

64. Maraniss and Nakashima, *The Prince of Tennessee*, 204.

65. Turque, *Inventing Al Gore*, 301.

66. Ibid., 160–62.

67. Steve Owens, telephone interview, 20 December 2001. Owens was on Al Gore's staff while he was in the Senate in the 1980s.

68. Steve Owens, interview, 26 March 2000, Phoenix, AZ; interview, 20 December 2001.

69. Turque, *Inventing Al Gore*, 163.

70. *Nashville Tennessean*, 7 November 1984.

71. Turque, *Inventing Al Gore*, 164.

72. *Nashville Banner*, 31 October 1984.

73. *Nashville Tennessean*, 7 November 1984.

74. August B. Cochran III, *Democracy Heading South: National Politics in the Shadow of Dixie* (Lawrence: University Press of Kansas, 2001), 110.

75. Turque, *Inventing Al Gore*, 183; Dan Murphy, "The Special Bond between a Father and a Son," *Tennessee Monthly*, June 1996, 14.

76. Owens, interview, 20 December 2001.

77. *Nashville Tennessean*, 13 April 1987.

78. Strobe Talbott, "Trying to Set Himself Apart," *Time*, 19 October 1987, 18; Stennis, "Profiles in Caution," 28.

79. Stennis, "Profiles in Caution," 28; *Nashville Banner*, 20 October 1987.

80. Talbott, "Trying to Set Himself Apart," 18; Turque, *Inventing Al Gore*, 20.

81. *Nashville Tennessean*, 10 October 1988; Hugh Sidney, "Sons of the Fathers," *Time*, 7 March 1988, 22; *Nashville Banner*, 20 October 1987; Talbott, "Trying to Set Himself Apart," 17.

82. Turque, *Inventing Al Gore*, 207–12.

83. *Nashville Tennessean*, 10 October 1988.

84. *Nashville Tennessean*, 19 June 1988.

85. John Brady, *Bad Boy: The Life and Politics of Lee Atwater* (New York: Addison Wesley, 1997), 170–94.

86. Gore Schiff, interview.

87. Michael Kinsley, "Goretax," *New Republic*, 10 June 1991, 4.

88. Turque, *Inventing Al Gore*, 229–37.

89. Boyer, "Gore's Dilemma," 105; Turque, *Inventing Al Gore*, 20–21, 256.

90. Carl P. Leubsdorf, "Politics Lost a Lot of Color When Elder Gore Died," *Dallas Morning News*, 24 December 1998.

91. Maraniss and Nakashima, *The Prince of Tennessee*, 268–75.

92. Turque, *Inventing Al Gore*, 247.

93. *Nashville Tennessean*, 10 July 1992.

94. Turque, *Inventing Al Gore*, 248–49.

95. *Washington Post*, 10 July 1992.

96. *Nashville Banner*, 13 May 1993.

97. Maraniss and Nakashima, *The Prince of Tennessee*, 274.

98. Ibid., 275.

99. Al Gore, "Facing the Crisis of Spirit," *Vital Speeches of the Day* 58 (15 August 1992): 647.

100. Ibid.

101. Pam Eakes, telephone interview, 23 September 2002.

102. Murphy, "The Special Bond between a Father and a Son," 14.

103. Turque, *Inventing Al Gore*, 259–60.

104. Margaret Carlson, "We Raised Him for It: Gore's Father Wanted His Son to Finish What the Family Had Started," *Time*, 28 February 2000, 46; Turque, *Inventing Al Gore*, 265; *New York Times*, 21 January 1993.

105. Murphy, "The Special Bond between a Father and a Son," 14; Steve Barnes, "The Gores," *Active Years*, September 1993, 10.

106. Boyer, "Gore's Dilemma," 100.

107. *Nashville Tennessean*, 25 October 1993; Maraniss and Nakashima, *The Prince of Tennessee*, 292.

108. Carter, *From George Wallace to Newt Gingrich*, 102–3.

109. Boyer, "Gore's Dilemma," 104.

110. Ibid., 105, 110.

111. *Nashville Tennessean*, 7 December 1998; Gore eulogy.

112. Turque, *Inventing Al Gore*, 302.

113. Walsh, "Fathers and Sons," 21.

114. Turque, *Inventing Al Gore*, 309–11.

115. For more on the 1996 election, see James W. Ceaser and Andrew E. Busch, *Losing to Win: The 1996 Elections and American Politics* (New York: Rowman and Littlefield, 1997); Elizabeth Drew, *Showdown: The Struggle between the Gingrich Congress and the Clinton White House* (New York: Simon and Schuster, 1996); and Charles O. Jones, *Clinton and Congress, 1993–1996* (Norman: University of Oklahoma Press, 1999).

116. Peretz, interview.

117. Gore Schiff, interview.

118. Maraniss and Nakashima, *The Prince of Tennessee*, 292.

119. *Yahoo! News*, 5 December 1998.

120. *Nashville Tennessean*, 7 December 1998, 9 December 1998.

121. Turque, *Inventing Al Gore*, 352–54.

122. Steve Holland, "Sen. Albert Gore Sr. Remembered as Liberal," *Yahoo! News*, 8 December 1998, http://dailynews.yahoo.com/headline...html?2-v/nm/19981208/pl/gore/6.html; *Nashville Tennessean*, 9 December 1998.

123. Gore eulogy.

124. Martin Peretz, "Father and Son," *New Republic*, 28 December 1998, 50.

125. Gore eulogy.

126. *Nashville Tennessean*, 9 December 1998.

127. Maraniss and Nakashima, *The Prince of Tennessee*, 40–41.


EPILOGUE

1. *Nashville Tennessean*, 8 December 1998. At the same time, the loss of his father had a significant impact on Al. One of his friends, Steve Armistead, told another, Goat Thompson, "Al's having a tough time, I can tell, and if you're around him you can tell, too, since his dad died." Maraniss and Nakashima, *The Prince of Tennessee*, 292.

2. Al Gore, "Making America All It Can Be," *Vital Speeches of the Day* 66 (1 September 2000): 675.

3. Ibid., 678.

4. Throughout the campaign, Gore made references to his father and his influence, telling one interviewer: "Well, I'm part of a tradition that ties together Cordell Hull and Franklin Roosevelt and my father, and Harry Truman and John Kennedy—a populist Democrat that

believes in the dignity of representative democracy and tries hard to make it work." Al Gore, interview by Brinkley.

5. Gore, "Making America All It Can Be," 677, 675, 679.

6. The attacks opened with the publication of Zelnick's *Gore: A Political Life.* The poorly researched and mistake-filled book on Gore was published by Regnery Press, an organization that specialized—in the words of the publisher—in "authors who confront the status quo of political correctness." Other attacks included John J. Miller, "What a Père: Gore Sr. in Jr's Mind," *National Review,* 26 July 1999, 26–28, and Richard Lowry, "Spawn: Every Bit His Father's Son," *National Review,* 14 August 2000, 22–25.

7. Emmett Edwards, telephone interview, 17 December 2001.

8. Al Gore, "The Common Good of All Americans," *Vital Speeches of the Day* 67 (1 January 2000): 163.

# Defending HST on the Bench,

helped Frank Wilson "us f Ball fan"

McKellar race: a friend told him he
lost Tipton cy for shaking hands w/ blacks

10 or 12 speeches a day ) Thinking Gellee/McK
                                Never some more Care

Conflict in Senate w/ LBJ. } → no good committee
                                                    chairs

The convention vice presidential race- Estes Beat JFK & G
'56 agin Prentice Cooper — Se/144 - race
previews

For JFK & LBJ in 60 / Anti Dillon / Anti LBJ
                                        ni Cover

Treated son as an adult }

Vietnam — Regretted Tonkin Gulf resolution
              joins mansfield, F'Brite
1966    opposes war — Mansfield, F'Brite
                                            morse

He asked Al "What would you do - 32 yrs &
turned out?" "I'd take the 32 years Dad

Dreams for Al — Terrific thrill in
                    Clinton Gore victory
quote Al on election
                    will - p 213
              "Let The story out."

# BIBLIOGRAPHY

ARCHIVES AND SPECIAL COLLEC

Carl Albert Center, University of Oklahoma
  Papers of Helen Gahagan Douglas
  Papers of Robert Kerr
Jimmy Carter Library, Atlanta
  White House Central Files
Frank Church Collection, Boise State Uni~~...~~
  Papers of Frank Church
Dwight D. Eisenhower Library, Abilene, KS
  Dwight D. Eisenhower Papers
Federal Bureau of Investigation Archives, Washington, DC
  Files on Albert Gore Sr.
J. William Fulbright Collection, University of Arkansas, Fayetteville
  Papers of J. William Fulbright
Albert Gore Center, Middle Tennessee State University, Murfreesboro
  Commissioner of Labor Files
  Gore House Collection
  Gore Senate Collection
  WSM Transcripts
Harvard University Library, Cambridge, MA
  Papers of Joseph Buttinger
Lyndon B. Johnson Library, Austin, TX
  Papers of William Clayton
  Papers of Clark Clifford
  Papers of the Democratic Leader
  Lyndon B. Johnson Congressional File
  Lyndon B. Johnson United States Senate File
  National Security Files
  Oral History Collection
  Papers of Drew Pearson
  Pre-Presidential Papers
  President's Appointment File
  Telephone Conversations of Lyndon B. Johnson
  White House Central Files
Julian P. Kanter Political Commercial Archive, University of Oklahoma, Norman

Kefauver Collection, Universi~~...~~
Papers of Estes Kefauver
John F. Kennedy Librar~~...~~
Executive Files
Pre-Presidentia~~...~~
Library of Con~~...~~
Papers of~~...~~
Nationa~~...~~
Re~~...~~

...y of Tennessee, Knoxville

..., Boston

...Files
...gress, Washington, DC
...Cordell Hull
...Archives, Washington, DC
...ords of the Joint Committee on Atomic Energy
Records of the Senate Foreign Relations Committee
Reports to the Senate Committee on Public Works
*Newsweek* Archives, Washington, DC
Nixon Presidential Material Project, National Archives II, College Park, MD
Annotated News Summaries
White House Special Files
Records of Watergate Special Prosecution Force
Franklin D. Roosevelt Library, Hyde Park, NY
Papers of John W. Carmody
Democratic National Committee Papers
Papers of Henry Morgenthau
Richard B. Russell Jr. Center, University of Georgia, Athens
Papers of Richard B. Russell Jr.
Harry S. Truman Library, Independence, MO
Official Files
Post-Presidential Name File


INTERVIEWS BY AUTHOR

Allen, William. 26 July 1996, Lexington, KY.
———. 1 June 1999, telephone.
Brown, Ted. 7 November 1997, Murfreesboro, TN.
Clement, Bob. 14 June 2001, Washington, DC.
Daughtery, Larry. 14 February 2002, telephone.
Dixon, Jane Holmes. 14 June 2001, telephone.
Eakes, Pam. 23 September 2002, telephone.
Edwards, Emmett. 17 December 2001, telephone.
Gore, Albert, Jr. 24 September 2001, Nashville.
Halberstam, David. 22 November 2002, Tempe, AZ.
McGovern, George. 24 August 2001, telephone.
Merritt, Gilbert. 26 September 2001, Nashville.
Oberdorfer, Don. 18 January 2002, telephone.
Owens, Steve. 20 December 2001, telephone.

————. 26 March 2000, Phoenix.

Peretz, Martin. 23 April 2002, telephone.

Robinson, Jack, Sr. 3 November 1998, Nashville.

————. 16 November 2000, Nashville.

Sasser, Jim. 12 June 2001, Washington, DC.

Sasser, Mary. 13 June 2001, telephone.

Schiff, Karenna Gore. 11 April 2002, telephone.

Seigenthaler, John. 24–25 September 2001, Nashville.

Sorenson, Theodore. 18 October 1998, Phoenix.

Whitt, Wayne. 25 September 2001, Nashville.


ADDITIONAL INTERVIEWS

Clements, Earle C. Interview by Michael L. Gillette, 24 October 1974. Oral History Collection, Lyndon B. Johnson Presidential Library, Austin, TX.

Fisher, Adrian S. Interview by Paige E. Mulhollan, 31 October 1968. Oral History Collection, LBJ Library.

Freeman, Lawrence. Interview by Regina Forsythe, 3 July 1995, Murfreesboro, TN. Q. M. Smith Collection, QMS 1995.18, Albert Gore Center, Middle Tennessee State University, Murfreesboro.

Gore, Albert A., Sr. Interview, Carthage, Tennessee. Tape Directory for Tribute to Albert Gore, Gore Center.

————. Interview by Bob Bullen, 4 February 1984, Murfreesboro, TN. Videotape, Gore Center.

————. Interview by Dewey Grantham and James B. Gardner, 13 November 1976. Southern Oral History Collection, Columbia Oral History Project, New York.

————. Interview by Kenneth O'Donnell, 30 October 1941. O'Donnell to Nation and Business, "Interview with Congressman Gore," *Newsweek* Archives, Washington, DC.

Gore, Albert A., Jr. Interview by Douglas Brinkley, 4 September 1999, New Orleans.

Harlow, Bryce. Interview by Michael L. Gillette, 23 February 1979. Oral History Collection, LBJ Library.

Hobgood, Baxter. Interview by Regina Forsythe, 25 July 1995, Murfreesboro, TN. Q. M. Smith Collection, QMS 1995.35, Gore Center.

Holden, Katherine. Interview by Regina Forsythe, 28 September 1998, Murfreesboro, TN. Q. M. Smith Collection, QMS.1995.110, Gore Center.

Holden, Rollie. Interview by Regina Forsythe, 29 August 1995, Murfreesboro, TN. Q. M. Smith Collection, QMS 1995.78, Gore Center.

Holt, Pat M. Oral History Interviews, Senate Historical Office, Washington, DC.

Marcy, Carl. Interview by Donald A. Ritchie, 14 September–16 November, 1983. Oral History Interviews, Senate Historical Office, Washington, DC.

Nichols, Jesse R. Interview by Donald A. Ritchie, 26 March–12 April 1994. Oral History Interviews, Senate Historical Office, Washington, DC.

Pittard, Mabel. Interview by Regina Forsythe, 25 September 1995, Murfreesboro, TN. Q. M. Smith Collection, QMS.1995.106, Gore Center.

Reedy, George E. Interview by Michael L. Gillette, 17 August 1983. Oral History Collection, LBJ Library.

Rowe, James H., Jr. Interview by Michael L. Gillette, 9 December 1983. Oral History Collection, LBJ Library.

Smathers, George A. Interview by Donald A. Ritchie, 1 August–24 October 1989. Oral History Interviews, Senate Historical Office, Washington, DC.

Valeo, Francis R. Oral History Interviews by Donald J. Ritchie, 1985–86. Senate Historical Office, Washington, DC.


GOVERNMENT PUBLICATIONS

*Congressional Record*
*Executive Sessions of the Senate Foreign Relations Committee*
*Hearings, International Development and Security* (Senate Foreign Relations Committee)


MEMOIRS, PERSONAL ACCOUNTS, AND PRIVATE PAPERS (PUBLISHED)

Anderson, Clinton P. *Outsider in the Senate: Senator Clinton Anderson's Memoirs.* New York: World Publishing Company, 1970.

Clifford, Clark. *Counsel to the President: A Memoir.* New York: Random House, 1991.

Fish, Hamilton. *Memoir of an American Patriot.* Lanham, MD: Regnery Gateway, 1991.

Galbraith, John Kenneth. *A Life in Our Times: Memoirs.* Boston: Houghton-Mifflin, 1981.

Gore, Albert A. *The Eye of the Storm: A People's Politics for the Seventies.* New York: Herder and Herder, 1970.

———. *Let the Glory Out: My South and Its Politics.* New York: Viking, 1972.

Howard, Nathaniel R., ed. *The Basic Papers of George M. Humphrey as Secretary of Treasury, 1953–1957.* Cleveland: Case Western Reserve Historical Society, 1965.

Hull, Cordell. *The Memoirs of Cordell Hull.* Vol. 1. New York: Macmillan, 1948.

Johnson, Walter, ed. *The Papers of Adlai E. Stevenson: Continuing Education and the Unfinished Business of American Society, 1957–1961,* vol. 7. Boston: Little, Brown, 1977.

Lilienthal, David E. *The Journals of David E. Lilienthal.* 7 vols. New York: Harper and Row, 1964–1983.


BOOKS

Aitken, Jonathan. *Nixon: A Life.* London: Weidenfeld and Nicolson, 1993.

Alley, Robert S. *School Prayer: The Court, the Congress, and the First Amendment.* Buffalo: Prometheus Books, 1994.

Alperovitz, Gar. *Atomic Diplomacy: Hiroshima and Potsdam: The Uses of the Atomic Bomb and the American Confrontation with Soviet Power.* 2nd ed. Boulder: Pluto Press, 1994.

Ambrose, Stephen E. *Eisenhower: Soldier, General of the Army, President-Elect, 1890–1952*. New York: Simon and Schuster, 1983.

———. *Nixon: The Triumph of a Politician, 1962–1972*. New York: Simon and Schuster, 1989.

Ambrose, Stephen E., and Douglas G. Brinkley. *Rise to Globalism: American Foreign Policy Since 1938*. 8th ed. New York: Penguin, 1997.

Anderson, David D. *William Jennings Bryan*. Boston: Twayne, 1981.

———. *Woodrow Wilson*. Boston: Twayne, 1978.

Annis, J. Lee, Jr. *Howard Baker: Conciliator in an Age of Crisis*. New York: Madison Books, 1995.

Ashby, Leroy, and Rod Gramer. *Fighting the Odds: The Life of Senator Frank Church*. Pullman: Washington State University Press, 1994.

Ashby, Warren. *Frank Porter Graham: A Southern Liberal*. Winston-Salem, NC: J. F. Blair, 1980.

Atleson, James B. *Labor and Wartime State: Labor Relations and Law during World War II*. Urbana: University of Illinois Press, 1998.

Bachrack, Stanley D. *The Committee of One Million: China Lobby Politics, 1958–1971*. New York: Columbia University Press, 1976.

Badger, Anthony. *The New Deal: The Depression Years, 1933–1940*. New York: Farrar, Straus and Giroux, 1989.

Bailey, Thomas A. *A Diplomatic History of the American People*. 8th ed. New York: Appleton-Century-Crofts, 1969.

Baker, James Thomas. *Brooks Hays*. Macon, GA: Mercer University Press, 1989.

Ball, George W., and Douglas B. Ball. *The Passionate Attachment: America's Involvement with Israel, 1947 to the Present*. New York: W. W. Norton, 1992.

Balz, Dan, and Ronald Brownstein. *Storming the Gates: Protest Politics and the Republican Revival*. Boston: Little, Brown, 1996.

Bartley, Numan V. *The New South, 1945–1980: The Story of the South's Modernization*. Baton Rouge: Louisiana State University Press, 1995.

———. *The Rise of Massive Resistance: Race and Politics in the South during the 1950s*. 2nd ed. Baton Rouge: Louisiana State University Press, 1997.

Bartley, Numan V., and Hugh D. Graham. *Southern Elections: County and Precinct Data, 1950–1972*. Baton Rouge: Louisiana State University Press, 1978.

———. *Southern Politics and the Second Reconstruction*. Baltimore: Johns Hopkins University Press, 1975.

Bergeron, Paul H., Stephen V. Ash, and Jeanette Keith. *Tennesseans and Their History*. Knoxville: University of Tennessee Press, 1999.

Berman, William C. *William Fulbright and the Vietnam War: The Dissent of a Political Realist*. Kent, OH: Kent State University Press, 1988.

Bernstein, Irving. *Guns or Butter: The Presidency of Lyndon Johnson*. New York: Oxford University Press, 1996.

Beschloss, Michael R. *The Crisis Years: Kennedy and Khrushchev, 1960–63*. New York: Harper-Perennial, 1991.

Black, Earl, and Merle Black. *The Rise of Southern Republicans*. Cambridge: Harvard University Press, 2002.

Blum, John M. *V Was for Victory: American Politics and Culture during World War II*. New York: Harcourt Brace Jovanovich, 1976.

Blumay, Carl, with Henry Edwards. *The Dark Side of Power: The Real Armand Hammer*. New York: Simon and Schuster, 1992.

Botsch, Robert Emil. *We Shall Not Overcome: Populism and Southern Blue-Collar Workers*. Chapel Hill: University of North Carolina Press, 1980.

Brady, John. *Bad Boy: The Life and Politics of Lee Atwater*. New York: Addison Wesley, 1997.

Brandon, Henry. *The Retreat of American Power*. New York: Doubleday, 1974.

Brauer, Carl M. *John F. Kennedy and the Second Reconstruction*. New York: Columbia University Press, 1977.

Brinkley, Alan. *The End of Reform: New Deal Liberalism in Recession and War*. New York: Knopf, 1995.

Bunn, George. *Arms Control by Committee: Managing Negotiations with the Russians*. Stanford: Stanford University Press, 1992.

Burner, David. *The Politics of Provincialism: The Democratic Party in Transition, 1918–1932*. Cambridge: Harvard University Press, 1986.

Butler, Michael A. *Cautious Visionary: Cordell Hull and Trade Reform, 1933–1937*. Kent, OH: Kent State University Press, 1998.

Caro, Robert A. *The Years of Lyndon Johnson: Master of the Senate*. New York: Knopf, 2002.

Carter, Dan T. *From George Wallace to Newt Gingrich: Race in the Conservative Counterrevolution, 1963–1994*. Baton Rouge: Louisiana State University Press, 1996.

———. *The Politics of Rage: George Wallace, the Origins of the New Conservatism, and the Transformation of American Politics*. New York: Simon and Schuster, 1995.

Ceaser, James W., and Andrew E. Busch. *Losing to Win: The 1996 Elections and American Politics*. New York: Rowman and Littlefield, 1997.

Chappell, David L. *Inside Agitators: White Southerners in the Civil Rights Movement*. Baltimore: Johns Hopkins University Press, 1994.

Christenson, Reo M. *The Brannan Plan: Farm Politics and Policy*. Ann Arbor: University of Michigan Press, 1959.

Cobbs Hoffman, Elizabeth. *"All You Need Is Love": The Peace Corps and the Spirit of the 1960s*. Cambridge: Harvard University Press, 1998.

Cochran, Augustus B., III. *Democracy Heading South: National Politics in the Shadow of Dixie*. Lawrence: University Press of Kansas, 2001.

Cohen, Warren I. *A History of Sino-American Relations*. 4th ed. New York: Columbia University Press, 2000.

Cohodas, Nadine. *The Band Played Dixie: Race and the Liberal Conscience at Ole Miss*. New York: Free Press, 1997.

Cole, Wayne S. *America First: The Battle against Intervention, 1940–1941*. Madison: University of Wisconsin Press, 1953.

———. *Roosevelt and the Isolationists, 1932–1945*. Lincoln: University of Nebraska Press, 1983.

Conkin, Paul. *Big Daddy from the Pedernales: Lyndon Baines Johnson*. Boston: Twayne, 1986.

———. *The New Deal*. 3rd ed. Arlington Heights, IL: Harlan Davidson, 1992.

Cook, Blanche Wiesen. *The Declassified Eisenhower: A Divided Legacy*. Garden City, NY: Doubleday, 1981.

Couloumbis, Theodore A. *The United States, Greece, and Turkey*. New York: Praeger, 1983.

Cox, Patrick. *Ralph W. Yarborough: The People's Senator*. Austin: University of Texas Press, 2001.

Crosby, Donald F. *God, Church, and Flag: Senator Joseph R. McCarthy and the Catholic Church, 1950–1957*. Chapel Hill: University of North Carolina Press, 1978.

Culver, John C., and John Hyde. *American Dreamer: The Life and Times of Henry A. Wallace*. New York: W. W. Norton, 2000.

Cumings, Bruce. *The Origins of the Korean War: Liberation and Emergence of Separate Regimes, 1945–1947*. Princeton: Princeton University Press, 1981.

———. *The Origins of the Korean War: The Roaring of the Cataract, 1947–1950*. Princeton: Princeton University Press, 1990.

Dallek, Robert. *Lone Star Rising: Lyndon Johnson and His Times, 1908–1960*. New York: Oxford University Press, 1991.

———. *Flawed Giant: Lyndon Johnson and His Times, 1961–1973*. New York: Oxford University Press, 1998.

———. *An Unfinished Life: John F. Kennedy, 1917–1963*. Boston: Little, Brown, 2003.

Daniel, Pete. *Lost Revolutions: The South in the 1950s*. Chapel Hill: University of North Carolina Press, 2000.

Davidson, James W., et al. *Nation of Nations: A Narrative History of the American Republic*. 3rd ed. Boston: McGraw-Hill, 1998.

Dennis, Michael. *Lessons in Progress: State Universities and Progressivism in the New South, 1880–1920*. Urbana: University of Illinois Press, 2001.

Diggins, John Patrick. *The Proud Decades: America in War and Peace, 1941–1960*. New York: W. W. Norton, 1988.

Divine, Robert A. *Blowing on the Wind: The Nuclear Test Ban Debate, 1954–1960*. New York: Oxford University Press, 1978.

———. *The Reluctant Belligerent: American Entry into World War II*. 2nd ed. New York: Knopf, 1979.

Doenecke, Justus D. *Storm on the Horizon: The Challenge to American Intervention, 1939–1941*. New York: Rowman and Littlefield, 2000.

Doenecke, Justus D., and John E. Wilz. *From Isolation to War, 1931–1941*. 2nd ed. Arlington Heights, IL: Harlan Davidson, 1991.

Donaldson, Gary A. *Liberalism's Last Hurrah: The Presidential Campaign of 1964*. Armonk, NY: M. E. Sharpe, 2003.

Donovan, Robert J. *Conflict and Crisis: The Presidency of Harry S. Truman, 1945–1948*. New York: W. W. Norton, 1977.

Dower, John W. *War without Mercy: Race and Power in the Pacific War*. New York: Pantheon, 1986.

Doyle, William. *An American Insurrection: The Battle of Oxford, Mississippi, 1962*. New York: Doubleday, 2001.

Drew, Elizabeth. *Showdown: The Struggle between the Gingrich Congress and the Clinton White House*. New York: Simon and Schuster, 1996.

Duiker, William J. *Sacred War: Nationalism and Revolution in a Divided Vietnam*. New York: McGraw-Hill, 1995.

Dykeman, Wilma. *Tennessee: A Bicentennial History*. New York: W. W. Norton, 1975.

Egerton, John. *Speak Now against the Day: The Generation before the Civil Rights Movement in the South*. New York: Knopf, 1994.

Ehrlichman, John. *Witness to Power: The Nixon Years*. New York: Simon and Schuster, 1982.

Epstein, Edward Jay. *Dossier: The Secret History of Armand Hammer*. New York: Random House, 1996.

Evans, Rowland, Jr., and Robert D. Novack. *Nixon in the White House*. New York: Random House, 1971.

Fairclough, Adam. *To Redeem the Soul of America: The Southern Christian Leadership Conference and Martin Luther King*. Athens: University of Georgia Press, 1987.

Feis, Herbert. *The Atomic Bomb and the End of World War II*. Princeton: Princeton University Press, 1966.

Ferrell, Robert H. *Harry S. Truman: A Life*. Columbia: University of Missouri Press, 1994.

Finch, Philip. *God, Guts, and Guns*. New York: Seaview/Putnam, 1983.

Finkle, Jason Leonard. *The President Makes a Decision: A Study of Dixon-Yates*. Ann Arbor: Institute of Public Administration, 1960.

Fish, Hamilton. *FDR: The Other Side of the Coin: How We Were Tricked into World War II*. New York: Vantage, 1976.

————. *Tragic Deception: FDR and America's Involvement in World War II*. Old Greenwich, CT: Devin-Adair, 1983.

Fite, Gilbert C. *Richard Russell Jr.: Senator from Georgia*. Chapel Hill: University of North Carolina Press, 1991.

Fontenay, Charles L. *Estes Kefauver: A Biography*. Knoxville: University of Tennessee Press, 1980.

Foot, Rosemary. *The Wrong War: American Policy and the Dimensions of the Korean Conflict, 1950–1953*. Ithaca: Cornell University Press, 1985.

Frantz, Douglas, and David McKean. *Friends in High Places: The Rise and Fall of Clark Clifford*. Boston: Little, Brown, 1995.

Frederickson, Kari. *The Dixiecrat Revolt and the End of the Solid South, 1932–1968*. Chapel Hill: University of North Carolina Press, 2001.

Freeland, Richard M. *The Truman Doctrine and the Origins of McCarthyism: Foreign Policy, Domestic Politics, and Internal Security, 1946–1948*. New York: New York University Press, 1985.

Frist, William H., and J. Lee Annis Jr. *Tennessee Senators, 1911–2001: Portraits of Leadership in a Century of Change*. Lanham, MD: Madison Books, 1999.

Fry, Joseph A. *Dixie Looks Abroad: The South and U.S. Foreign Policy, 1789–1993*. Baton Rouge: Louisiana State University Press, 2002.

Fulbright, J. William. *The Arrogance of Power*. New York: Random House, 1966.

Gaddis, John L. *Strategies of Containment: A Critical Appraisal of Postwar American National Security Policy*. New York: Oxford University Press, 1982.

———. *The United States and the Origins of the Cold War, 1941–1947.* New York: Columbia University Press, 1972.

Gardner, James B. "Political Leadership in a Period of Transition: Frank G. Clement, Albert Gore, Estes Kefauver, and Tennessee Politics, 1948–1956." Ph.D. diss., Vanderbilt University, 1978.

Gardner, Lloyd. *Approaching Vietnam: From World War II through Dienbienphu.* New York: W. W. Norton, 1988.

———. *Economic Aspects of New Deal Diplomacy.* Madison: University of Wisconsin Press, 1964.

Garrow, David J. *Protest at Selma: Martin Luther King Jr. and the Voting Rights Act of 1965.* New Haven: Yale University Press, 1978.

Gellman, Irwin F. *Secret Affairs: Franklin Roosevelt, Cordell Hull, and Sumner Welles.* Baltimore: Johns Hopkins University Press, 1995.

Goldsmith, John A. *Colleagues: Richard B. Russell and His Apprentice, Lyndon B. Johnson.* Washington, DC: Seven Locks Press, 1993.

Goncharov, Sergei, John W. Lewis, and Xue Litai, *Uncertain Partners: Stalin, Mao, and the Korean War.* Stanford: Stanford University Press, 1993.

Gould, Lewis L. *1968: The Election that Changed America.* Chicago: Ivan R. Dee, 1993.

Graham, Hugh D. *The Civil Rights Era: Origins and Development of National Policy, 1960–1972.* New York: Oxford University Press, 1990.

Grantham, Dewey W. *The Life and Death of the Solid South: A Political History.* Lexington: University Press of Kentucky, 1988.

———. *Recent America: The United States Since 1945.* 2nd ed. Wheeling, IL: Harlan Davidson, 1998.

———. *The South in Modern America: A Region at Odds.* New York: HarperCollins, 1994.

———. *Southern Progressivism: The Reconciliation of Progress and Tradition.* Knoxville: University of Tennessee Press, 1983.

Green, A. Wigfall. *The Man Bilbo.* Westport, CT: Greenwood, 1976.

Greenberg, Jack. *Crusaders in the Courts: How a Dedicated Band of Lawyers Fought for the Civil Rights Revolution.* New York: Basic Books, 1994.

Greene, Lee Seifert. *Lead Me On: Frank Goad Clement and Tennessee Politics.* Knoxville: University of Tennessee Press, 1982.

Greenstein, Fred. *The Hidden-Hand Presidency: Eisenhower as Leader.* New York: Basic Books, 1982.

Griffith, Robert. *The Politics of Fear: Joseph R. McCarthy and the Senate.* 2nd ed. Amherst: University of Massachusetts Press, 1987.

Halberstam, David. *The Powers That Be.* New York: Knopf, 1979.

Hamby, Alonzo L. *Beyond the New Deal: Harry S. Truman and American Liberalism.* New York: Columbia University Press, 1973.

———. *Liberalism and Its Challengers: FDR to Reagan.* New York: Oxford University Press, 1985.

Harper, Alan D. *The Politics of Loyalty: The White House and the Communist Issue, 1946–1952.* Westport, CT: Greenwood, 1969.

Hart, Roger L. *Redeemers, Bourbons, and Populists: Tennessee, 1870–1896.* Baton Rouge: Louisiana State University Press, 1975.

Hartmann, Susan M. *Truman and the 80th Congress.* Columbia: University of Missouri Press, 1971.

Hays, Brooks. *Politics Is My Parish: An Autobiography.* Baton Rouge: Louisiana State University Press, 1981.

Heckscher, August. *Woodrow Wilson.* New York: Charles Scribner's Sons, 1991.

Heineman, Kenneth J. *Put Your Bodies upon the Wheels: Student Revolt in the 1960s.* Chicago: Ivan R. Dee, 2001.

Heinrichs, Waldo. *Threshold of War: Franklin D. Roosevelt and American Entry into World War II.* New York: Oxford University Press, 1988.

Herman, Arthur. *Joseph McCarthy: Reexamining the Life and Legacy of America's Most Hated Senator.* New York: Free Press, 2000.

Herring, George C. *America's Longest War: The United States and Vietnam, 1950–1975.* 3rd ed. New York: McGraw-Hill, 1996.

Higgins, Trumball. *The Perfect Failure: Kennedy, Eisenhower, and the CIA at the Bay of Pigs.* New York: W. W. Norton, 1987.

Hillin, Hank. *Al Gore Jr.: His Life and Career.* New York: Birch Lane, 1992.

Hogan, Michael. *A Cross of Iron: Harry S. Truman and the Origins of the National Security State, 1945–1954.* New York: Cambridge University Press, 1998.

Hoyt, Edwin P. *Japan's War: The Great Pacific Conflict, 1853–1952.* New York: McGraw-Hill, 1986.

Hulsey, Byron C. *Everett Dirksen and His Presidents: How a Senate Giant Shaped American Politics.* Lawrence: University Press of Kansas, 2000.

Immerman, Richard H. *John Foster Dulles: Piety, Pragmatism, and Power in U.S. Foreign Policy.* Wilmington, DE: Scholarly Resources, 1999.

Isserman, Maurice, and Michael Kazin. *America Divided: The Civil War of the 1960s.* New York: Oxford University Press, 2000.

Jeffries, John W. *Wartime America: The World War II Homefront.* Chicago: Ivan R. Dee, 1996.

Johnson, Robert D. *Ernest Gruening and the American Dissenting Tradition.* Cambridge: Harvard University Press, 1998.

Jones, Charles O. *Clinton and Congress, 1993–1996.* Norman: University of Oklahoma Press, 1999.

Jones, Howard. *Crucible of Power: A History of U.S. Foreign Relations Since 1897.* Wilmington, DE: Scholarly Resources, 2001.

Kaplan, Edward S. *American Trade Policy, 1923–1995.* Westport, CT: Greenwood, 1996.

Karabell, Zachary. *The Last Campaign: How Harry Truman Won the 1948 Election.* New York: Knopf, 2000.

Karnow, Stanley. *Vietnam: A History.* New York: Penguin, 1986.

Kaufman, Burton. *The Korean War: Challenges in Crisis, Credibility, and Command.* Philadelphia: Temple University Press, 1986.

Kaufman, Robert G. *Henry M. Jackson: A Life in Politics.* Seattle: University of Washington Press, 2000.

Kearns Goodwin, Doris. *Lyndon Johnson and the American Dream*. New York: St. Martin's, 1976.

Keith, Jeanette. *Country People in the New South: Tennessee's Upper Cumberland*. Chapel Hill: University of North Carolina Press, 1995.

Kennedy, David M. *Freedom from Fear: The American People in Depression and War, 1929–1945*. New York: Oxford University Press, 1999.

Key, V. O, Jr. *Southern Politics in State and Nation*. New York: Knopf, 1949.

Kimball, Warren F. *Forged in War: Roosevelt, Churchill, and the Second World War*. New York: William Morrow, 1997.

LaFeber, Walter. *America, Russia, and the Cold War, 1945–1992*. 7th ed. New York: McGraw-Hill, 1993.

———. *Inevitable Revolutions: The United States and Central America*. 2nd ed. New York: W. W. Norton, 1993.

Lamis, Alexander P. *The Two-Party South*. New York: Oxford University Press, 1984.

Lee, Alton. *Truman and Taft-Hartley: A Question of Mandate*. Lexington: University Press of Kentucky, 1966.

Lee, David D. *Sergeant York: An American Hero*. Lexington: University Press of Kentucky, 1985.

Leffler, Melvyn P. *A Preponderance of Power: National Security, the Truman Administration, and the Cold War*. Stanford: Stanford University Press, 1992.

Lerner, Mitchell B. *The Pueblo Incident: A Spy Ship and the Failure of American Foreign Policy*. Lawrence: University Press of Kansas, 2002.

Lesher, Stephan. *George Wallace: American Populist*. New York: Addison-Wesley, 1994.

Leuchtenberg, William. *Franklin D. Roosevelt and the New Deal, 1932–1940*. New York: Harper and Row, 1963.

Lewis, Tom. *Divided Highways: Building the Interstate Highways, Transforming American Life*. New York: Viking, 1997.

Lichtman, Allan J. *Prejudice and the Old Politics: The Presidential Election of 1928*. Chapel Hill: University of North Carolina Press, 1979.

Link, William A. *The Paradox of Southern Progressivism, 1880–1930*. Chapel Hill: University of North Carolina Press, 1992.

Logevall, Fredrik. *Choosing War: The Lost Chance for Peace and Escalation of War in Vietnam*. Berkeley: University of California Press, 1999.

McCoy, Donald R. *The Presidency of Harry S. Truman*. Lawrence: University Press of Kansas, 1984.

McCoy, Donald R., and Richard Ruetten. *Quest and Response: Minority Rights and the Truman Administration*. Lawrence: University Press of Kansas, 1973.

McCullough, David G. *Truman*. New York: Simon and Schuster, 1992.

McKeever, Porter. *Adlai Stevenson: His Life and Legacy*. New York: William Morrow, 1989.

McMaster, H. R. *Dereliction of Duty: Lyndon Johnson, Robert McNamara, the Joint Chiefs of Staff, and the Lies That Led to Vietnam*. New York: HarperCollins, 1997.

McMath, Robert C. *American Populism: A Social History, 1877–1898*. New York: Hill and Wang, 1993.

McNamara, Robert S., James G. Blight, and Robert K. Brigham. *Argument without End: In Search of Answers to the Vietnam Tragedy*. New York: PublicAffairs, 1999.

Majors, William R. *The End of Arcadia: Gordon Browning and Tennessee Politics*. Memphis: Memphis State University Press, 1982.

Mann, Robert. *A Grand Delusion: America's Descent into Vietnam*. New York: Basic Books, 2001.

———. *Legacy to Power: Senator Russell Long of Louisiana*. New York: Paragon House, 1992.

———. *The Walls of Jericho: Lyndon Johnson, Hubert Humphrey, Richard Russell, and the Struggle for Civil Rights*. New York: Harcourt, Brace, 1996.

Maraniss, David, and Ellen Nakashima. *The Prince of Tennessee: The Rise of Al Gore*. New York: Simon and Schuster, 2000.

Matusow, Allen J. *Farm Policies and Politics in the Truman Years*. Cambridge: Harvard University Press, 1967.

———. *Nixon's Economy: Booms, Bust, Dollars, and Votes*. Lawrence: University Press of Kansas, 1998.

May, Elaine Tyler. *Homeward Bound: American Families in the Cold War Era*. New York: Basic Books, 1988.

Miller, Merle. *Lyndon: An Oral Biography*. New York: G. P. Putnam's Sons, 1980.

Miller, William D. *Mr. Crump of Memphis*. Baton Rouge: Louisiana State University Press, 1964.

Moïse, Edwin E. *Tonkin Gulf and the Escalation of the Vietnam War*. Chapel Hill: University of North Carolina Press, 1996.

Montell, William Lynwood. *Upper Cumberland Country*. Jackson: University Press of Mississippi, 1993.

Morgan, Anne Hodges. *Robert S. Kerr: The Senate Years*. Norman: University of Oklahoma Press, 1977.

Morris, Aldon D. *The Origins of the Civil Rights Movement: Black Communities Organizing for Change*. New York: Free Press, 1984.

Moss, George Donelson. *Vietnam: An American Ordeal*. 4th ed. Upper Saddle River, NJ: Prentice-Hall, 2002.

Murphy, Bruce Allen. *Fortas: The Rise and Ruin of a Supreme Court Justice*. New York: William Morrow, 1988.

O'Neill, William L. *A Democracy at War: America's Fight at Home and Abroad in World War II*. Cambridge: Harvard University Press, 1993.

Oshinsky, David M. *A Conspiracy So Immense: The World of Joe McCarthy*. New York: Free Press, 1983.

Oshower, Gary B. *The United Nations and the United States*. New York: Twayne, 1998.

Pach, Chester, Jr., and Elmo Richardson. *The Presidency of Dwight D. Eisenhower*. Revised ed. Lawrence: University Press of Kansas, 1991.

Paterson, Thomas G. *Contesting Castro: The United States and the Triumph of the Cuban Revolution*. New York: Oxford University Press, 1994.

———. *On Every Front: The Making and Unmaking of the Cold War*. Revised ed. New York: W. W. Norton, 1992.

Paterson, Thomas G., J. Garry Clifford, and Kenneth J. Hagan. *American Foreign Policy: A History Since 1900*. 3rd ed. Lexington, MA: D. C. Heath, 1991.

Paterson, Thomas G., and Dennis Merrill. *Major Problems in American Foreign Relations*. Lexington, MA: D. C. Heath, 1995.

Patterson, James T. *Brown v. Board of Education: A Civil Rights Milestone and Its Troubled Legacy*. New York: Oxford University Press, 2001.

———. *Congressional Conservatism and the New Deal: The Growth of the Conservative Coalition in Congress, 1933–1939*. Lexington: University Press of Kentucky, 1967.

Pepper, Claude. *Ask Claude Pepper*. Garden City, NY: Doubleday, 1984.

Pepper, Claude D., and Hays Gorey. *Pepper, Eyewitness to a Century*. New York: Harcourt Brace Jovanovich, 1987.

Perret, Geoffrey. *Eisenhower*. New York: Random House, 1999.

———. *Jack: A Life Like No Other*. New York: Random House, 2001.

Phillips, Kevin P. *The Emerging Republican Majority*. New Rochelle, NY: Arlington House, 1969.

Pleasants, Julian M., and Augustus M. Burns. *Frank Porter Graham and the 1950 Senate Race in North Carolina*. Chapel Hill: University of North Carolina Press, 1990.

Porter, David. *The Seventy-Sixth Congress and World War II, 1939–1940*. Columbia: University of Missouri Press, 1979.

Rabe, Stephen. *Eisenhower and Latin America: The Foreign Policy of Anticommunism and Latin America*. Chapel Hill: University of North Carolina Press, 1988.

Redmon, Coates. *Come As You Are: The Peace Corps Story*. New York: Harcourt Brace Jovanovich, 1986.

Reeves, Thomas C. *The Life and Times of Joseph McCarthy: A Biography*. 2nd ed. New York: Madison Books, 1997.

Remini, Robert V. *Andrew Jackson*. New York: Twayne, 1966.

Rhodes, Richard. *The Making of the Atomic Bomb*. New York: Simon and Schuster, 1986.

Robinson, Greg. *By Order of the President: FDR and the Internment of Japanese Americans*. Cambridge: Harvard University Press, 2001.

Safire, William. *Before the Fall: An Inside View of the Pre-Watergate White House*. New York: Grosset and Dunlap, 1978.

Sanders, Randy. *Mighty Peculiar Elections: The New South Gubernatorial Campaigns of 1970 and the Changing Politics of Race*. Gainesville: University Press of Florida, 2002.

Schaller, Michael. *The United States and China in the Twentieth Century*. 2nd ed. New York: Oxford University Press, 1990.

Schaller, Michael, and George Rising, *The Republican Ascendancy: American Politics, 1968–2001*. Wheeling, IL: Harlan Davidson, 2002.

Schell, Jonathan. *The Time of Illusion*. New York: Vintage Books, 1976.

Scher, Richard K. *Politics in the New South: Republicanism, Race, and Leadership in the Twentieth Century*. 2nd ed. Armonk, NY: M. E. Sharpe, 1997.

Schlesinger, Arthur M., Jr. *A Thousand Days: John F. Kennedy in the White House*. Boston: Houghton-Mifflin, 1965.

Schoenbaum, David. *The United States and Israel*. New York: Oxford University Press, 1993.

Schulman, Bruce. *From Cotton Belt to Sunbelt: Federal Policy, Economic Development, and the Transformation of the South, 1938–1980*. New York: Oxford University Press, 1991.

Schwartz, Bernard. *Swann's Way: The School Busing Case and the Supreme Court*. New York: Oxford University Press, 1986.

Seaborg, Glenn T., and Benjamin S. Loeb. *Stemming the Tide: Arms Control in the Johnson Years*. Lexington, MA: Lexington Books, 1987.

Shogan, Robert. *A Question of Judgment: The Fortas Case and the Struggle for the Supreme Court*. New York: Bobbs-Merrill, 1972.

Siff, Ezra Y. *Why the Senate Slept: The Gulf of Tonkin Resolution and the Beginning of America's Vietnam War*. Westport, CT: Praeger, 1999.

Simkins, Francis Butler, and Charles Pierce Rowland. *A History of the South*. 4th ed. New York: Knopf, 1972.

Small, Melvin. *Johnson, Nixon, and the Doves*. New Brunswick: Rutgers University Press, 1988.

———. *The Presidency of Richard Nixon*. Lawrence: University Press of Kansas, 1999.

Smith, Gaddis. *American Diplomacy during the Second World War, 1941–1945*. 2nd ed. New York: Knopf, 1985.

Sorenson, Theodore C. *Kennedy*. New York: Harper and Row, 1965.

Springen, Donald K. *William Jennings Bryan: Orator of Small-Town America*. New York: Greenwood, 1991.

Strauss Fuerelicht, Roberta. *Joe McCarthy and McCarthyism: The Hate That Haunts America*. New York: McGraw-Hill, 1972.

Stueck, William. *The Korean War: An International History*. Princeton: Princeton University Press, 1995.

———. *The Road to Confrontation: United States Policy toward China and Korea, 1947–1950*. Chapel Hill: University of North Carolina Press, 1981.

Summers, Anthony, with Robbyn Swan. *The Arrogance of Power: The Secret World of Richard Nixon*. New York: Viking, 2000.

Taylor, Maxwell D. *Swords and Plowshares*. New York: W. W. Norton, 1972.

Theoharis, Athan G. *Spying on Americans: Political Surveillance from Hoover to the Hutson Plan*. Philadelphia: Temple University Press, 1978.

———, ed. *From the Secret Files of J. Edgar Hoover*. Chicago: Ivan R. Dee, 1991.

Tindall, George Brown. *The Emergence of the New South, 1913–1945*. Baton Rouge: Louisiana State University Press, 1967.

Turque, Bill. *Inventing Al Gore: A Biography*. Boston: Houghton-Mifflin, 2000.

Unger, Irwin, and Debi Unger. *LBJ: A Life*. New York: J. Wiley and Sons, 1999.

Utley, Jonathan G. *Going to War with Japan, 1937–1941*. Knoxville: University of Tennessee Press, 1985.

Valeo, Francis R. *Mike Mansfield, Majority Leader: A Different Type of Senate, 1961–1973*. Armonk, NY: M. E. Sharpe, 1999.

Vander Veer Hamilton, Virginia. *Lister Hill: Statesman from the South*. Chapel Hill: University of North Carolina Press, 1987.

*The Vietnam Hearings.* New York: Vintage Books, 1966.

Walker, J. Samuel. *Henry Wallace and American Foreign Policy.* Westport, CT: Greenwood, 1976.

Weinberg, Steve. *Armand Hammer: The Untold Story.* Boston: Little, Brown, 1989.

Weinstein, Allen. *Perjury: The Hiss-Chambers Case.* 2nd ed. New York: Random House, 1997.

Welch, Richard E., Jr. *Response to Revolution: The United States and the Cuban Revolution, 1959–1961.* Chapel Hill: University of North Carolina Press, 1985.

Wexler, Imanuel. *The Marshall Plan Revisited: The European Recovery Program in Economic Perspective.* Westport, CT: Greenwood, 1983.

White, Graham, and John Maze. *Henry A. Wallace: His Search for a New World Order.* Chapel Hill: University of North Carolina Press, 1995.

White, Mark J. *Missiles in Cuba: Kennedy, Khrushchev, Castro, and the 1962 Crisis.* Chicago: Ivan R. Dee, 1997.

Wildavsky, Aaron. *Dixon-Yates: A Study in Power Politics.* New Haven: Yale University Press, 1962.

Wilhoit, Francis M. *The Politics of Massive Resistance.* New York: George Braziller, 1973.

Wittner, Lawrence S. *One World or None.* Stanford: Stanford University Press, 1993.

Woods, Jeff. *Black Struggle, Red Scare: Segregation and Anti-Communism in the South, 1948–1968.* Baton Rouge: Louisiana State University Press, 2004.

Woods, Randall. *Fulbright: A Biography.* New York: Cambridge University Press, 1995.

Woodward, C. Vann. *Origins of the New South, 1877–1913.* Baton Rouge: Louisiana State University Press, 1971.

Wyden, Peter. *Bay of Pigs: The Untold Story.* New York: Simon and Schuster, 1979.

Young, Nancy Beck. *Wright Patman: Populism, Liberalism, and the American Dream.* Dallas: Southern Methodist University Press, 2000.

Young, Roland. *Congressional Politics in the Second World War.* New York: Columbia University Press, 1956.

Zeiler, Thomas W. *Dean Rusk: Defending the American Mission Abroad.* Wilmington, DE: Scholarly Resources, 2000.

Zelnick, Bob. *Gore: A Political Life.* Washington, DC: Regnery Press, 1999.

Zuckert, Eugene, and Arnold Kramish. *Atomic Energy for Your Business.* New York: D. McKay, 1956.

ARTICLES

Badger, Anthony. "Southerners Who Refused to Sign the Southern Manifesto." *Historical Journal* 42 (1999): 517–19.

Baker, Russell. "Gore Also Runs—But for V.P." *New York Times Magazine,* 10 April 1960, 15.

Barnes, Steve. "The Gores," *Active Years,* September 1993, 10.

Boo, Katherine. "The Liberation of Albert Gore.." *Washington Post Monthly Magazine,* 28 November 1993, 11.

Boyer, Peter. "Gore's Dilemma." *New Yorker,* 28 November 1994, 103.

Bradley, Carol. "The Gore on the Sidelines: Albert Sr. Would Love to Be Helping His Son." *Nashville Tennessean Magazine*, 31 October 1984, A15.

Brinkley, Douglas. "Al Gore's Defining Moment." *Talk*, November 1999, 152.

Carlson, Margaret. "A Certain Nervous Look." *Time*, 4 April 1955, 16.

———. "We Raised Him for It: Gore's Father Wanted His Son to Finish What the Family Had Started." *Time*, 28 February 2000, 46.

Davis, Louise. "The Albert Gore Story: Tussles of a 'Combative Hillbilly,'" *Nashville Tennessean Magazine*, 22 March 1970, 5.

———. "Pancakes and Protocol: Vivacious Mrs. Albert Gore Thrives on the Washington Whirl." *Nashville Tennessean Magazine*, 12 May 1957, 12–15.

———. "The Senator Who Risks His Neck." *Nashville Tennessee Magazine*, 29 March 1970, 10.

Dykeman, Wilma. "Too Much Talent in Tennessee?" *Harper's*, March 1955, 49.

"44 v. 83." *Time*, 11 August 1952, 20.

Gleijeses, Piero. "Ships in the Night: The CIA, the White House, and the Bay of Pigs." *Journal of Latin American Studies* 27 (February 1995): 1–42.

Gore, Albert. "The Atom Goes to Sea." *Atomizer* 4 (May 1955): 3–5.

———. "Canada Did It." *Saturday Evening Post*, 6 June 1942, 18, 44.

———. "The Coming Steel Crisis and How to Deal with It." *Harper's*, April 1962, 13–16.

———. "How to Be Rich without Paying Taxes." *New York Times Magazine*, 11 April 1965, 28–29, 86.

———. "Is the Present Federal Civilian Atomic Energy Field Sound?" *Congressional Digest* 36 (January 1957): 13.

———. "Should the Treaty Authority of the U.S. Senate Be Curtailed?" *Congressional Digest* 22 (October 1943): 243.

———. "Two-Way Trade and Peace." *Collier's*, 24 April 1943, 20.

Gore, Albert A, Jr. "The Common Good of All Americans." *Vital Speeches of the Day* 67 (1 January 2000): 163.

———. "Eulogy by the Vice President at the Funeral of His Father, Former Senator Albert Gore, Sr." Office of the Press Secretary, www.whitehouse.gov/WH/EOP/OVP/html/19981209–5823.html.

———. "Facing the Crisis of Spirit." *Vital Speeches of the Day* 58 (15 August 1992): 647.

———. "Making America All It Can Be." *Vital Speeches of the Day* 66 (1 September 2000): 675.

"Gore's Challenge." *New Republic*, 21 June 1954, 5.

"Gore's Chances." *New Republic*, 28 June 1954, 4.

Graham, Eugene. "Gore's Lost Cause." *New South*, Spring 1971, 29.

Halberstam, David. "The End of a Populist." *Harper's*, January 1971, 42.

Hamby, Alonzo L. "Progressivism: A Century of Change and Rebirth." In Sidney M. Milkis and Jerome M. Mileur, eds., *Progressivism and the New Democracy*. Amherst: University of Massachusetts Press, 1999.

Harris, Richard. "Annals of Politics: How the People Feel." *New Yorker*, 10 July 1971, 37.

Hess, Pamela. "Perils of Pauline Gore." *George*, September 1998, 95.

Hodges, Robert C. "The Cooing of a Dove: Senator Albert Gore Sr.'s Opposition to the War in Vietnam." *Peace and Change* 22 (April 1997): 137–39.

Johnson, Robert D. "The Origins of Dissent: Senate Liberals and Vietnam, 1959–1964." *Pacific Historical Review* 65 (1996): 249–75.

Kinsley, Michael. "Goretax." *New Republic*, 10 June 1991, 4.

Leiter, Kelly. "Tennessee: Gore vs. the White House." *The Nation*, 26 October 1970, 397.

Leubsdorf, Carl P. "Politics Lost a Lot of Color When Elder Gore Died." *Dallas Morning News*, 24 December 1998.

Lowry, Richard. "Spawn: Every Bit His Father's Son." *National Review*, 14 August 2000, 22–25.

Martin, Michael S., and Tony Badger. "The Anti-Gore Campaign of 1970." Presented at the Tennessee Conference of Historians, Nashville, 27 September 2003.

Miller, John J. "What a Père: Gore Sr. in Jr.'s Mind." *National Review*, 26 July 1999, 26–28.

Moore, Glen. "Richard M. Nixon and the 1970 Midterm Elections in the South." *Southern Historian* 12 (1991): 61.

Morris, George. "The Pride of Possum Hollow." *Collier's*, 30 May 1942, 23.

Murphy, Dan. "The Special Bond between a Father and a Son." *Tennessee Monthly*, June 1996, 14.

"A New Farm Bill Tops Congressional List." *Life*, 23 January 1956, 46–47.

People of the Week. *Life*, 1 August 1949, 27.

Peretz, Martin. "Father and Son." *New Republic*, 28 December 1998, 50.

Pruden, Caroline. "Tennessee and the Formative Years of the United Nations: A Case Study of Southern Opinion." *Tennessee Historical Quarterly* 52 (Spring 1993): 6.

Sanders, Florrie Wilkie. "Life of Women in Political Families—Pauline LaFon Gore '36." *Vanderbilt Lawyer* 24 (Spring 1994): 24.

"A Senate Probe for Lobbies." *Business Week*, 25 February 1956, 30–31.

Sidney, Hugh. "Sons of the Fathers." *Time*, 7 March 1988, 22.

Stennis, Richard. "Profiles in Caution: The Several Faces of Al Gore Are All Carefully Thought Out." *Time*, 21 March 1988, 28.

Talbott, Strobe. "Trying to Set Himself Apart." *Time*, 19 October 1987, 18.

Turque, Bill. "The Three Faces of Al Gore." *Newsweek*, 20 July 1992, 30.

"Upsets in the Senate: Old-Timers Lose Out . . . Younger Men Win in Three States, Threaten in Others." *U.S. News and World Report*, 22 August 1952, 54.

Walsh, Kenneth T. "Fathers and Sons." *U.S. News and World Report*, 9 August 1999, 20.

NEWSPAPERS, NEWS MAGAZINES, AND NEWSLETTERS

In addition to the large metropolitan newspapers of the time in New York, Chicago, Detroit, Dallas, and Washington, D.C., as well as widely circulated weeklies and magazines such as *Time* and *Newsweek*, I consulted the following publications:

*Akron Beacon Journal*
*Baltimore Sun*
*Cannon County (TN) Courier*
*Carthage (TN) Courier*

*Charleston (SC) Gazette*
*Charleston (SC) News and Courier*
*Chattanooga News Free Press*
*Chattanooga Times*
*Daily Oklahoman* (Oklahoma City)
*Gore Family Newsletter*
*Human Events*
*Jackson (MS) Sun*
*Jerusalem Post*
*Knoxville Journal*
*Knoxville News-Sentinel*
*Lagos (Nigeria) Daily Express*
*Memphis Commercial Appeal*
*Memphis Press-Scimitar*
*Nashville Banner*
*Nashville Tennessean*
*Oklahoma City Times*
*Orlando Sentinel*
*Santa Clara Register*
*Spartanburg (SC) Herald*
*St. Louis Post-Dispatch*
*St. Petersburg Times*
*Yahoo! News*

# INDEX

Abernathy, Ralph, 210
Abernathy, Thomas (D-MS), 115
Acheson, Dean, 92, 149
African Americans, 5, 74, 75, 87, 96, 112,
    113, 134, 135, 139, 144, 148, 153, 167, 184,
    185, 187, 190, 193, 200, 210, 268, 272. *See
    also* civil rights
Agee, Berry, 12
Agency for International Development
    (AID), 166
Agnew, Spiro, 219, 222, 239, 247
Agricultural Adjustment Act (AAA), 26, 36,
    85
Ahlgren, Frank, 94, 102, 139, 191
Aid to Families with Dependent Children
    (AFDC), 183
Aiken, George (R-VT), 85
Air Force (U.S.), 135, 167, 174
Alexander, Holmes, 192
Alexander, Lamar (R-TN), 223, 268
Alexandria, Tenn., 22
Algeria, 208
Allen, Bill, 106, 167, 243
Alliance for Progress, 165
America First Committee, 48, 78
American Independent Party, 213
American Medical Association (AMA), 189
American Socialist Party, 107
American University, 212
Americans for Constitutional Action, 213
Anderson, Clinton (D-NM), 116, 120, 131
antiballistic missile (ABM) system, 217–19
Anti-Defamation League, 87,
Appalachian Mountains, 41
Appalachian Regional Development Act, 183

Arab-Israeli wars, 154
Arkansas National Guard, 144
Arlington, Va., 41, 55
Armey, Dick (R-TX), 6
Armistead, Donna, 177
Armstrong, Walter, 255
Army of the Republic of Vietnam (ARVN),
    180, 207, 208
Ashe, Victor, 255, 256
Askew, Reubin, 5, 239, 245
Asquith, Harry, 117
Atkins, Hobart, 98, 100
Atlantic City, 189
atomic bomb, 69
Atomic Energy Act of 1954, 121
Atomic Energy Commission (AEC), 55, 115,
    116, 121
atomic testing, 129, 130, 144, 147, 165
Atwater, Lee, 259
Autobahn, 65, 125

Bachman, Nathan (D-TN), 29
Baker, Howard, Jr. (R-TN), 179, 200, 230,
    237, 246, 254, 268
Baker, Howard, Sr. (R-TN), 90
Baker, Russell, 119, 154
Baltimore, 210
Bangkok, 132
Baptists (Southern), 10, 11, 30, 175, 262
Barker, Stonie, 243, 244
Barkley, Alben (D-KY), 82, 93, 127
Barnett, Ross, 7, 113, 168
Barr, Bob (R-GA), 6
Barrett, George, 241
Barrett, Lionel, 241

Bartlett, Charles, 10

Baruch, Bernard, 50, 72, 75, 100, 107, 147

Bass, Ross (D-TN), 179, 199, 200

Batista, Fulgencio, 151, 162

Battle of Britain, 48

Bay of Pigs, 163, 164

Bayh, Birch (D-IN), 221, 262

Beasley, Tom, 234, 236

Bedford County, 143

Bell Hunt, Ocie, 41, 87

Belle Haven Country Club, 229

Bennett, Charles E. (D-FL), 87

Bentsen, Lloyd (D-TX), 229

Berlin, 84, 165

Berlin Crisis (1961), 165

Bethlehem Steel, 57, 167

Biddle, Francis, 61

Bilbo, Theodore (D-MS), 74, 75, 88, 245

Birch, Adolpho, 267, 268

Birmingham, Ala., 168

Bishop, Joey, 263

Bissel, Richard, 163

Black, Creed, 149

Blackmun, Harry, 226

Blanton, Ray, 247

Bloom, Sol (D-NY), 42, 43

Blough, Roger, 166, 167

Bolling, Dick, 155

Borah Foundation, 208

Bork, Robert, 246

*Bradley v. Richmond School Board*, 206

Brannan, Charles F., 85, 86

Brannan plan, 86, 87, 95

Brazil, 138

Brezhnev, Leonid, 198

Bricker, John (R-OH), 62

Bridge, Styles (R-NH), 89, 131

Brock, Pat, 233

Brock, William (Bill), III (R-TN), xiii, 211, 217, 223–34, 236–39, 247, 250, 251

Broder, David, 237

Brown, Theodore, Jr., xiv, 230

*Brown v. the Board of Education*, 112, 113, 123, 124

Browning, Gordon, 6, 28–30, 33–34, 37, 81, 94, 98

Brownsville, Tenn., 124

Brussels World Fair, 142, 145

Bryan, William Jennings, 18–19, 21, 138

Buchanan, Pat, 222, 225

Buddhists, 179, 180

Bumpers, Dale (D-AR), 5, 239, 245

Burdick, Eugene, 161

Burger, Warren, 211

Bush, George H. W., 224, 259, 261, 263

Bush, George W., xiii

Bush, Jeb, 272

Bush, Prescott (R-CT), 107, 125

busing, 206, 207

Butler, Paul, 153

Button, Fred, 144

Byrd, Harry (D-VA), 1, 123, 183, 223, 244

Byrdstown, Tenn., 14

Byrnes, James, 76, 112


Calhoun, John C., 215, 216

Cambodia, 227, 228

Camp Shelby, 61

campaign finance reform, 131–33, 135, 136

Canada, 55, 138

Caney Fork River, 122, 176, 220, 226, 239

Caperhart, Homer (R-IN), 137, 164

Carswell, G. Harrold, 225, 226, 236

Carter, Hodding, III, 254

Carter, Jimmy, 239, 240, 245, 247, 250, 251, 257

Carter, Sonny, 265

Carthage, Tenn., 9, 23–26, 29, 37, 41–43, 56, 59, 97, 141, 174, 176, 177, 198, 221, 226, 241, 242, 248, 254, 264, 267, 269, 270

Cash, June Carter, 47

Castle Heights Military Academy, 176

Castro, Fidel, 151, 162, 163

Cattlemen's Association, 224
Celotex Corporation, 52
Central High School (Little Rock), 144
Central Intelligence Agency (CIA), 163, 164, 251
Central Office for South Vietnam (COSVN), 227
Cessna Aircraft Company, 52
Chattanooga, Tenn., 124, 174, 223, 229
Chautauqua speaking circuit, 19
Cheney, Dick, xiii
Christian Right, 238, 273
Church, Frank (D-ID), 164, 188, 204, 217, 227, 228
Church Committee, 251
Church of Christ, 30
Churchill, Winston, 48, 252
civil rights, 6, 7, 74, 75, 85, 87, 88, 96, 100, 112, 122, 144, 167, 193. *See also* African Americans
Civil Rights Acts: of 1957, 139, 140; of 1960, 153, 154; of 1964, 171, 172, 184–86, 190, 199, 235, 272; of 1968, 209
Civilian Conservation Corps (CCC), 26
Clapp, Gordon, 76
Clark, Joseph (D-PA), 151, 159
Clark, Ramsey, 209, 211
Clay, General Lucius, 125
Clay, Henry, 216, 240
Clayton Anti-Trust Bill, 21
Cleary, Father Edward J., 190
Clement, Bob, 7, 242, 271
Clement, Frank, 4, 6, 98, 108, 117, 121, 127, 136, 142–44, 199, 200, 201, 232
Clements, Earle (D-KY), 128
Cleveland, Tenn., 145
Clifford, Clark, 155, 208
Clinton, Bill, 5, 129, 256, 260, 261, 265–68, 272
Clinton, Tenn., 144, 149
Cody, Mike, 255
Coggins, Christine, 149

Colegrove, Albert M., 150
Colson, Chuck, 222
Communist China, 92, 110, 112, 180, 185, 195–98, 205, 208, 232, 251
Communists, 88, 130, 163, 185, 215
Compton College, 194
COMSTAT, 179
Connally, Tom (D-TX), 60, 71
Connecticut Democratic Convention, 127
conservatism, southern, 6
Constitution (U.S.), 88, 193, 211, 226
Constitution Hall, 39, 169
Continental Army, 8,
Coolidge, Calvin, 22
Cooper, John C. (R-KY), 228
Cooper, Prentice, 64, 143–46, 157
Cooper-Church amendment, 228
Coral Sea, battle of, 54,
Corrupt Practices Act, 135
Council for a Livable World, 241
court-packing scheme, 36
Cox, Archibald, 246
Cox, Eugene (D-GA), 35
Crawford, Charles, 255
Crockett, Davy, 11
Crockett, Hudley, 224, 227, 229, 231
Crossville High School, 70, 91, 98
Crownover, Sims, 134
Crump, Edward, 6, 28–29, 37, 80, 81, 94, 96, 98
Cuba, 19, 151, 162, 163, 168, 169, 170
Cuban missile crisis, 169
Culkin, Francis (R-NY), 45
Cumberland Law School, 26
Cumberland River, 8, 23, 27, 29
Curtis, Carl T. (R-NE), 135
Czechoslovakia, 84, 218

Dahlbert, Bror, 52
Dallas, Tex., 181
Daniel, Price (D-TX), 103, 104
Daniel plan, 104

Daugherty, Larry, xv, 6
Davis, John, 178
Davis, Louise, 136, 226
"Day of Infamy" speech, 52
DeLoach, Carl, 110
Democratic Caucus, 187
Democratic Congressional Wives Forum, 137
Democratic Leadership Council (DLC), 256, 257, 259, 260
Democratic National Committee, 73, 117, 118
Democratic National Conventions: 1952, 99; 1956, 127–29, 133; 1960, 149, 155; 1964, 189, 190; 1968, 214, 215; 1992, 262; 1996, 266; 2000, 271
Democratic Party, 4, 22, 26, 36, 73, 83, 101, 110, 130, 143, 148, 150, 153, 161, 181, 189, 223, 239, 252, 256, 258
Dent, Harry, 223–25
Department of Defense, 166, 218
Department of Health, Education, and Welfare (HEW), 149, 194, 211
destroyer-base deal, 47
Detroit, Mich., 8, 23, 24
Dewey, Thomas E., 62–64, 82, 83
DeWitt, John L., 53
Diem, Ngo Dinh, 112, 151, 179, 180
Dienbienphu, 111
Dies, Martin (D-TX), 35
Dillon, Douglas, 158, 159, 161, 182, 192, 193
Dirksen, Everett (R-IL), 173, 187, 200, 201
Disney, Wesley E. (D-OK), 57
District of Columbia, 224
District of Columbia Committee, 102
Dixiecrat Party, 82, 83, 123
Dixon, Edgar, 115
Dixon-Yates contract, 115, 120–22, 133, 136
Dodd, Christopher (D-CT), 199
Dodge, Joseph, 115
Dole, Robert (R-KS), 219, 266
Donnelly, Ignatius, 18

Donoho, James, 63
Douglas, Paul (D-IL), 3, 5, 110, 153, 159
Downey, Tom (D-NY), 260
Dukakis, Michael, 258, 259
Dulles, John Foster, 102, 110
Dunn, Winfred, 232, 237
DuPont, Corporation, 160, 161
Dykeman, Wilma, 136

80th Congress, 75, 82
East Tennessee State University, 237
Eastland, James (D-MS), 6, 112, 211
Eaton, Clement, 20
Edelsberg, Herman, 87
Edwards, Emmett, xv, 272
Edwards, John, 5
Egypt, 93, 150, 202
Einstein, Albert, 55
Eisenhower, Dwight D.: civil rights, 139, 140, 144; Dixon-Yates, 115, 116, 121, 122; election of 1952, 99, 100; election of 1956, 132, 133; interstate highway system, 125, 126; military industrial complex, 134; Vietnam War, 110, 111; mentioned, 65, 66, 103, 106, 114, 147, 148, 152, 157, 162, 163, 257, 265
Eisenhower, John, 132
Eizenstat, Stuart, 252
Elementary and Secondary Education Act, 183
Ellington, Buford, 146, 148, 184, 200, 214, 224
"Emergency Steel Act of 1962," 167
Environmental Protection Agency (EPA), 243
Equal Rights Amendment, 237
Erlichman, John, 221
Ervin, Sam (D-NC), 123, 124, 185, 246
Eskind, Jane, 268
Ethiopia, 165
Evans, Sillman, Jr., 128
Evers, Medgar, 167
Evins, Joe (D-TN), 248

Fair Deal, 5, 79, 83, 101
Fair Employment Practices Committee (FEPC), 74, 81, 87, 96, 100
Fair Labor Standards Bill, 35
Family Medical Leave Act, 263
Farmer, Thomas, 251
Faubus, Orval, 7, 144, 146, 245
Faulkner, William, 1
Federal Bureau of Investigation (FBI), 107, 108, 110, 196, 251
Federal Communications Commission (FCC), 202
Federal Deposit Insurance Corporation (FDIC), 26
Federal Housing Administration (FHA), 199
Federal National Mortgage Association, 199
Federal Reserve, 103, 199
Federal Reserve Act, 21
*Federalist Papers*, 219
Fentress County, 55
Fifteenth Amendment, 130, 193
filibuster, 74, 116, 212
First Amendment, 172
First Boston Corporation, 115, 121
Fish, Hamilton (R-NY), 49, 62, 74
Fogarty, John (D-RI), 64
"Food for Peace Program," 165
Food Stamp Act, 183
Ford, Gerald, 246
Ford, Harold, Jr., 7
Ford, Henry, II, 170, 171, 197
Ford Motors, 170
Fort Meade, 64
Fort Ogelthorpe, 61
Fort Rucker, 229
Fortas, Abe, 211, 212, 221
Fourteen Points, 21
Fourth Congressional District (TN), 25, 27, 37–39, 54, 55, 74, 85, 248
Fourth Neutrality Act, 44
Fowler, Henry, 192, 193
Fowler, Jon, 199

France, 44, 46, 78, 84, 110–12, 192, 208
Franco-American Alliance, 84
Freeman, Lawrence, 16
Frick, Helen, 224
Frist, Bill (R-TN), 264
Fulbright, J. William (D-AR): civil rights, 124; Vietnam, 187, 196, 227; mentioned, 1, 21, 59, 60, 105, 115, 148, 155, 178, 219, 230, 240
Fulbright resolution, 60

Galbraith, John Kenneth, 51, 158
Gardenhire, Joseph M., 23
Garner, John Nance, 39
General Motors, 160
Geneva, 147
Geneva Accords (1954), 112
George, Walter (D-GA), 36
Georgia Federation of Labor and CIO, 34
Gephardt, Richard (D-MO), 256
Germany, 44, 46, 52, 55, 65–67, 69
Ghana, 165, 166
GI Bill of Rights (also GI Bill), 61
Giap, Vo Nguyen, 111
Gilligan, Don, 216
Gingrich, Newt (R-GA), 6, 265
Glass, Carter (D-VA), 36
Gleason, Jackie, 224, 233
Goldwater, Barry (R-AZ), 131, 135, 184, 217, 223
Gordon, Bart (D-TN), 7
Gore, Al: xi, xii, 2, 5, 7, 8, 32, 79, 80, 108, 128, 129, 167, 175, 176, 197, 214, 216, 224, 229, 231
—elections: 1958, 145; 1970, 221, 238–41; 1976, 249, 250; 1984, 255, 256; 1988 presidential primary, 257–59; 1992, 262–64; 1996, 266, 267; 2000, xiii, 271–73
—military service: 220, 221, 240, 247
—relationships: with father, 117, 141, 176–78, 215, 239, 248, 253, 269–71; with mother, 131, 136, 247–49, 262, 263; with Nancy, 175, 249, 254

Gore, Al (*continued*)

—views: abortion, xiii, 249, 255; arms control, 252, 255; civil rights, 186; consumer protection, 252; environment, 252; gun control, xiii, 248, 255; homosexuality, 249; national defense, xiii; school prayer, xiii; taxes, 260;Vietnam, 197

Gore, Albert: ancestors, 8, 9; athleticism, 12; atomic weapons, 55, 129, 130, 147; battles against Crump machine, 6, 28, 29; campaigns for Al, 249, 255–59, 261–63; campaign finance reform, 131–33, 135, 136, 201, 202; career as a teacher, 14, 15; cattle business, 107, 108, 122; childhood, 8–13; college education, 11, 15–17; commissioner of labor, 33–36; death, 267–70; Dixon-Yates contract, 115, 116, 120–22, 133, 136, 144; energy policy, 251, 252; environmental record, 243, 244; *The Eye of the Storm: A People's Politics for the Seventies,* 231–32; family finances, 104; family planning, 148; farm price support, 85, 86; fiddle playing, 12, 13, 38, 39, 49, 98, 105; Great Depression, 22, 24, 28; gun control, xiii; inflation, 193; intelligence oversight, 251; interest rates, 106, 138, 139, 149, 157, 182, 193, 198, 199; internment of the Japanese, 53, 54; interstate highway system, 125–27, 133, 144, 198; labor, 33, 34, 58, 59, 77, 78, 131; *Let the Glory Out: My South and Its Politics,* 244, 245; lobbying efforts, 242; maverick nature, 43, 50, 51, 59, 77, 86, 87, 158, 161, 166, 226, 227; Medicare, 189, 190, 194, 195, 231; minimum wage, 141; practice of law, 33; price and wage controls, 50, 51, 55, 56, 72; public education, 46, 84, 85, 191; public works, 7, 142, 183, 191, 237; race for the vice presidency in 1956, 127–29; race for the vice presidency in 1960, 142, 143; radio shows, 47, 52, 64, 67, 69, 78; reciprocal trade, 42, 45, 57; school prayer, xiii, 172, 173, 184, 201, 238; sense

of humor, 29, 137, 138; Social Security, 4, 34, 36, 77, 189, 191, 237; steel crisis of 1962, 166, 167; superintendent of schools, 25, 28, 31; Supreme Court nominations, 211, 212, 221, 225, 226; taxes, 3, 4, 56, 57, 75, 84, 101, 103, 118, 142, 144, 157, 159, 160, 170, 171, 182, 190, 194, 197, 231; Tennessee Valley Authority, 47, 48, 76, 77, 96, 114, 115, 237; tobacco farming, 254; vouchers, xiii; war profiteers, 52, 53; World War II, 53–55, 58, 60, 61, 63–66

—civil rights: Air Force Academy appointments, 134, 148; *Brown* decision, 112, 113, 123; busing, 206, 207; 1957 Civil Rights Bill, 139, 140; 1960 Civil Rights Bill, 153; 1964 Civil Rights Bill, 171, 172, 184–86, 190; 1968 Civil Rights Bill, 209; Clinton, Tenn., 144, 149; FEPC, 74, 81, 87, 96, 100; Ole Miss incident, 167, 168; poll tax, 75, 139; Southern Manifesto, 1, 2, 123, 124, 134, 143, 146; Voting Rights Act of 1965, 193; mentioned, 6, 7, 75, 87, 88, 122, 123, 133, 182, 233, 234

—clashes: with Eisenhower administration, 103, 106, 109, 114–16, 118, 121, 122, 124, 125, 138, 142, 147; with FBI, 110, 215; with Kennedy, 158, 161, 166, 170; with LBJ, 182, 192–94, 196, 198, 199, 205–207, 214; with Nixon, 100, 110, 217, 218, 219, 232; with Strom Thurmond, 1, 2, 82, 83

—elections: superintendent of schools, 22, 23, 25; 1938, 37–40; 1942, 54; 1944, 63, 64; 1952, 88, 90, 91, 94–98; 1958, 143–47; 1964, 184, 187, 189–91; 1970, xiii, 217, 223, 224, 227–39, 241

—foreign policy views: ABM, 217–19; China, 4, 197; Cuba, 162–65, 169, 170; family planning and population control, 148, 152, 153; Korean War, 90, 92, 93, 112; Marshall Plan, 78; Middle East, 93, 94, 150, 155, 203, 204; NATO, 4; nuclear disarmament, 224, 225, 241; nuclear proliferation, 197,

198; Nuclear Test Ban Treaty (1963), 178, 198; Peace Corps, 161, 162; road to World War II, 44, 47–49, 51; Soviet Union, 77, 90; Truman Doctrine, 77; trade, 45, 57; United Nations, 4, 59, 60, 70, 90; Vietnam War, 110–12, 148, 150–52, 179, 180, 182, 187–90, 192, 196, 197, 199, 201, 205–208, 214, 219–21, 227, 228, 235–37, 252

—influences upon: Andrew Jackson, 11, 12, 46; Thomas Jefferson, 11, 12, 46; New Deal, 25, 26, 29, 34–36; parents, 9, 12, 13; populism, 18, 19; progressivism, 19–21; religion, 10, 11, 30, 46; Franklin Roosevelt, 41, 47, 67, 68, 119; Woodrow Wilson, 20, 21

—relationships: with Spiro Agnew, 222, 223, 236, 237; with Frank Clement, 117; with Al Gore, 80, 117, 176, 186, 220, 248, 253, 264, 271, 272; with Karenna Gore, 259, 266, 267; with Nancy Gore, 174, 175, 176, 186; with Pauline Gore, 30, 31, 32, 35, 37, 42, 81, 91, 97, 105, 106, 136, 137, 175, 176, 267; with Armand Hammer, 107, 108; with Cordell Hull, 26–28, 47, 49, 96; with Lyndon Johnson, 102, 107, 118, 119, 127, 130, 150, 159, 178, 182–84, 187, 191–94, 196, 198–99, 205–207, 209; with Estes Kefauver, 80–82, 88, 94, 95, 136, 179, 180; with John Kennedy, 155–58, 166–68, 170, 171, 181; with Robert Kerr, 137, 138; with Joseph McCarthy, 89, 90; with Richard Nixon, 99, 100, 182, 217, 232, 236, 244, 246, 247; with Harry Truman, 69, 78, 79, 141, 150

Gore, Albert, III, 255, 259
Gore, Allen, 9, 22, 27
Gore, Arkley, 15, 34
Gore, Charlie, 15, 34, 104
Gore, Grace, 9
Gore, John, 8
Gore, Karenna, xv, 259, 266, 268
Gore, Laura Bettie, 9

Gore, Margie (Denny), 9, 173
Gore, Mary Elizabeth "Tipper" (Aitcheson), 220, 229, 241, 249, 254, 258, 259
Gore, Mounce, 9
Gore, Nancy: battle with cancer, 253–55, 266; education, 173, 174; leads 1964 reelection campaign, 184; Peace Corps, 162; relationship with Al, 175, 176, 249, 254; mentioned, 35, 55, 79, 142, 145, 149, 214, 250, 264, 270
Gore, Pauline LaFon: education, 30–32; and Eleanor Roosevelt, 53; family background, 30; family finances, 104; influence on husband, 32, 35, 91, 105, 176, 177, 267; newspaper views of, 136; personality, 30–32; political adviser, 91, 130, 145, 150, 165, 187, 191, 202, 238, 242, 243, 249, 255, 258, 263, 272; practice of law, 33, 35, 242; race issues, 87, 88; relationship with Al, 32, 131, 136; relationship with Nancy, 130, 131, 141; speaker on issues, 130; views of Clinton, 260, 261; mentioned, 41, 53, 61, 79, 80, 106, 214, 239, 241, 265, 266, 268, 269, 271
Gore, Reggie, 9, 10, 12
Gore Center, 267
Grace, Eugene, 57
Graham, Billy, 228
Graham, Bob (D-FL), 5
Graham, Eugene, 233, 238
Graham, Frank Porter, 4
Graham, Fred, 174, 267
Graham, Gene, 156
Graham, Katherine, 182
Grantham, Dewey, 244
Graves, Harold N., 54
Great Britain, 44, 47, 48, 78, 84, 208
Great Depression, 21–22, 29, 41, 42, 51, 85, 106
"Great Society," 5, 183, 189, 190, 193–95, 213, 223
Green v. County School Board, 206

Greuning, Ernest (D-AK), 151, 188

Griffin, Robert (R-MI), 4, 211, 212

Guggenheim, Charles, 231

Guirion, David Ben, 155

Gulf of Tonkin Resolution, 187, 189, 192, 196, 228


Hackett, Donald Lee, 13, 39

Halberstam, David, 32, 119, 216, 235, 267

Halsey, William "Bull," 53

Hamilton, Alexander, 11

Hammer, Armand, 107, 108, 229, 241, 243, 249, 252, 265, 272

Hanna, Mark, 138

Harding, Warren G., 22, 64

Hargis, Billy James, 213

Harlow, Bryce, 64, 219

Harness, Forest (R-IN), 62

Harvey, Paul, 226

Haynsworth, Clement F., 221, 236

Hays, Brooks (D-AR), 4, 73, 79, 124

Health, Education, and Welfare (HEW), Department of. *See* Department of Health, Education, and Welfare (HEW)

Heard, Alexander, 132

Heard, C. W., 34

Heflin, Howell (D-AL), 5, 268

Heinshohn, A. G., 144

Heller, Walter, 199

Helms, Jesse (R-NC), 6

Henderson, Leon, 49, 55

Henderson Bill, 50

Hermitage Hotel, 238, 259

Hershey, Lewis, 215

Highway Trust Fund, 126

Hill, Lister (D-AL), 1, 124, 172, 190

Hillan, Hank, 176

Hiroshima, 71

Hitler, Adolf, 54, 58, 65, 90

Ho Chi Minh, 110, 170, 206

Hoffman, Clare (R-MI), 60, 87

Holden, Katherine, 16

Holden, Rollie, 17, 23

Holifield, Chet (D-CA), 121

Holmes Dixon, Jane, 174, 254, 268

Holt, Pat, 196

Holton Arms, 173

Hooker, John Jay, 232, 235

Hooks, Benjamin, 200

Hoover, Herbert, 17, 22, 63, 83, 228

Hoover, J. Edgar, 110, 215

Hope, Clifford (R-KS), 85

Horton, Willie, 259

House Banking and Currency Committee, 42, 49

House Foreign Affairs Committee, 228

House of Representatives, 26, 59

House Un-American Activities Committee (HUAC), 88

House Ways and Means Committee, 75, 114

Howell, Sally, 47

Huffines, Lee, 23–25

Hughes, Rowland, 121

Hull, Cordell, 3, 15, 21, 26–28, 42, 45, 51, 70, 79

Humphrey, George, 103, 106, 110, 127

Humphrey, Hubert (D-MN), 101, 127, 128, 138, 139, 162, 178, 182, 189, 205, 214–16

Hunger, Frank, 174, 253, 254, 261

Hutson plan, 228


India, 152, 208

Indochina, 110, 111

Internal Revenue Service (IRS), 52

International Business Machines (IBM), 159, 160

Interparliamentary Union, 132

interstate highway system, 125–27, 198, 265

Island Creek Coal Company, 243–45, 247, 252

Israel, 93, 94, 150, 155, 203, 204, 245

Italy, 73, 78

Iwo Jima, 71

Jack and Heintz, 53

Jackson, Andrew, 11, 12, 18, 149

Jackson, Henry (D-WA), 102, 219, 252

Jackson, Jesse, 258

Jackson, Tenn., 30, 31, 72, 95

Jackson County, 9

Jackson State University, 227

Jamestown, Tenn., 38

Janeway, Eliot, 204

Japan, 51–53, 56, 69, 71, 72, 90, 150, 205

Jefferson, Thomas, 11, 12, 46, 73

Jenner, William (R-IN), 115

Jewish-Americans, 79

Jewish Community Relations Council, 204

Job Corps, 183

John Birch Society, 190, 213

Johnson, Andrew, 69

Johnson, Hiram (R-CA), 64

Johnson, Hugh, 112

Johnson, Lady Bird, 130

Johnson, Lyndon: ambivalent relationship with Gore, 102, 118, 119, 127, 178, 182, 187, 190–93, 196; becomes president, 181, 182; cattle ties to Gore, 107, 150; civil rights, 184–86, 190, 193, 209; as a deal maker, 44, 116; on death of FDR, 67; Great Society programs, 183, 189, 190, 193–95; influence of populism, 18; Middle East, 203–204; presidential aspirations, 122; presidential election of 1964, 188–90, 212; presidential election of 1968, 208–209; Supreme Courts, 211–12; taxes, 171, 182, 183, 194; as vice president, 155, 157; Vietnam, 187–89, 192, 195–97, 205–207; mentioned, 1, 2, 41, 64, 79, 101, 104, 108, 115, 126, 128–31, 149, 200, 213, 214, 217

Johnson, Sam, 41

Joint Chiefs of Staff, 163, 164

Joint Committee on Atomic Energy, 102

Jordan, 93, 150, 203

Jordan, Barbara (D-TX), 5

Judiciary Committee Subcommittee on Anti-trust and Monopoly Legislation (JSAM), 115

Jupiter missiles, 169

Kai-shek, Chiang, 197

Kaiser and Reynolds, 166

Kefauver, Diane, 179

Kefauver, Estes (D-TN): on civil rights, 74, 75, 113, 123, 134, 144, 149, 153; competition with Gore, 79, 80, 88, 136; death, 179; Dixon-Yates, 115, 121; 1948 senate race, 80, 81; run for presidency in 1952, 94, 95, 99; run for vice presidency in 1956, 127–29, 155; mentioned, 1, 4, 6, 19, 42, 54, 64, 101, 122, 130, 143, 184, 199, 227

Kemp, Jack (R-NY), 266

Kennan, George, 76, 149, 196, 205

Kennedy, Edward (D-MA), 219, 230, 233, 240, 262, 268

Kennedy, John F.: assassination, 158, 181, 182; clash at Ole Miss, 167, 168; 1960 election, 155–57; foreign policy, 161, 162, 165, 166, 169, 170, 178; run for vice presidency in 1956, 127–29; steel crisis of 1962, 166, 167; Vietnam, 179, 180; work in the Senate with Gore, 131; mentioned, 2, 5, 81, 102, 105, 159, 190, 257

Kennedy, Joseph, 158

Kennedy, Robert (D-NY), 168, 169, 189, 208, 213

Kent, Frank, 54

Kent State University, 227

Kenya, 165

Kenyon, Dorothy, 89

Kerr, Robert (D-OK), 107, 137, 138

Key, V. O., 244

Keynesian economics, 3

Khrushchev, Nikita, 165, 166

King, Martin Luther, Jr., 209, 234

Kissinger, Henry, 245

Knight, John, 141

Knowland, William (R-CA), 116

Knoxville, Tenn., 107, 127, 144, 145, 183, 228

Knutson, Walter (R-MN), 57, 75, 76, 78

Knutson plan, 76

Korean War, 90, 92, 93, 99, 103, 111

Ku Klux Klan, xiii, 1, 74, 123

Kuykendall, Dan, 187, 190

Ky, Nguyen Cao, 196, 208


Laos, 165, 179

labor, 33, 34, 58, 59, 77, 78

LaFon, Everett, 97

LaFon, Maude, 30

LaFon, Thelma, 30

LaFon, Whit, 30, 31, 91

Lambertson, William P. (R-KS), 56

Langer, William (R-ND), 115

Leadership Conference on Civil Rights, 209

League of Nations, 19, 21, 70, 90

Lebanon, Tenn., 198

Ledbetter, Orpha, 14, 15

Lederer, William, 161

Lee, Harper, 141

Lehman, Herbert (D-NY), 101

LeMay, Curtis, 164

Lemnitzer, Lyman, 163, 164

lend-lease bill (HR 1776), 48, 49

Lenin, Vladimir, 107

Lewinsky, Monica, 267

Lewis, John L., 58, 59

Lexington, Ky., 183, 243, 247

liberalism, 3, 4, 73, 182, 248; southern, 3, 5, 154

Liberia, 74, 165

Libya, 165

Liddy, G. Gordon, 222, 245

Lilienthal, David, 55

Lincoln, Abraham, 11, 69, 244

Litchford, Mary, 11

Little Creek, Tenn., 16

Little Rock, Ark., 144, 145

Lodge, Henry Cabot, Jr., 103, 180

Loeb, Henry, 235

Long, Russell (D-LA), 185, 201, 202

Los Angeles, 71, 213, 247

Lott, Trent (R-MS), 6

Love Canal, 253

Lowenstein, Jim, 208

Loyalist delegation (MS), 214

*Lum v. Rice*, 123


McCain, Admiral John S., 220

McCarthy, Eugene (D-MI), 2, 183

McCarthy, Joseph (R-WI), 88–90, 93, 102, 119, 120, 208

McClellan, John (D-AR), 6, 115, 120, 131, 172, 211

McClellan Crime Bill, 210

McCord, James Nance, 148

McCord, James, 245, 246

McGee, Gale (D-WY), 150, 151

McGill, Ralph, 124

McGovern, George (D-SD), 2, 3, 188, 194, 207, 214, 215, 219, 223, 230

McKellar, Kenneth (D-TN), 6, 34, 37, 48, 69, 76, 80, 95–98, 102

McNamara, Robert, 161, 164, 180

MacArthur, Douglas, 71, 92, 93

Maddux, John, 249

Madison County, 30

Madison, James, 219

Madisonville, Tenn., 19, 233

Manatos, Mike, 196

Manchuria, 90, 92

Manhattan Project, 55, 71

Manila, 71

Mann, Clyde, 142

Mansfield, Mike (D-MT), 3, 102, 131, 135, 152, 159, 170, 195

Mao Zedong, 110

Marcy, Carl, 241

Markham, Edwin, 238

Marshall, George C., 78

Marshall, Thurgood, 154

Marshall Plan, 78
Martin, Joe (R-MA), 43
Martin, Tenn., 215
Martin, William M., Jr., 103
massive resistance, 1, 123
Medicare, 3, 182, 189, 190, 194, 195, 231
Meeman, Edward, 109
Mellon, Andrew, 22, 127
Mellon Scaife, Richard, 224
Memphis, Tenn., 172, 206, 209, 211, 235,
    272
Memphis State University, 236
Meredith, James, 167, 168
Merriman, Walter, 29
Merritt, Gilbert, xv, 174, 175, 216, 267
Methodist Building, 257, 261
Miami, 192
Michner, Earl (R-MI), 51
Middle East, 93, 202–205
Middle South Utilities Company, 115
Middle Tennessee State Teachers' College
    (MTSTC). See Middle Tennessee State
    University (MTSU)
Middle Tennessee State University (MTSU),
    xiii, 8, 14, 16, 47, 267
Milk Producers' Association, 224
Miller Smith, Kelly, 235
Mills, Wilbur (D-FL), 189, 194
Milton, George Fort, 54
Mine Inspection Law, 34
Minh, Duong Van, 180
Minuteman missiles, 224
Mitchell, J. Ridley, 25, 29, 37
Mitchell, Jack, 241
Mitchell, John, 212
Mitchell, John A., 81
Mondale, Walter (D-MN), 256
Monroney, Mike (D-OK), 2, 50, 73, 79, 105,
    107
Moore, John, 132
Morgenthau, Henry, Jr., 48, 67
Morse, Wayne (I-OR), 2, 107, 114, 137, 151,
    188, 196

Moscow, 76, 152, 169
Moyers, Bill, 161, 190
multiple independently targetable reentry ve-
    hicles (MIRV), 219, 224
Murfreesboro, Tenn., xiii, 14, 39, 46
Murray, Tom (D-TN), 91
Muskie, Edmund (D-ME), 242
Mussolini, Benito, 54, 90

Nagasaki, 71
Nance, Steve, 34
Nashville, 8, 22, 30, 35, 47, 127, 130, 175,
    191, 213, 238, 241, 246, 254, 259, 269
Nasser, Gamal Abdel, 203
National Association for the Advancement of
    Colored People (NAACP), 139, 140, 167,
    268
National Democratic Club, 154
National Governors' Forum, 125
National Guard, 144
National Rifle Association, 210, 221, 273
National Security Council, 169
National Unemployment Act, 34
Nationalist China, 92, 197, 198
Naval Affairs Committee, 52
Neal, Jim, xiii, xiv
Neel, Roy, 261
Nehru, Jawaharlal, 152
"New Bourbons," 169, 244, 245
New Deal, 5, 25–27, 29, 36, 38, 41, 69, 72,
    73, 75, 76, 78, 83, 88, 99, 101, 123, 245
New Delhi, 152
New Market, Va., 8
New Mexico, 55
New York World's Fair (1938), 42, 43
Newark, N.J., 221
Nigeria, 245
Nineteenth Amendment, 21
Nixon, Richard: ABM, 217–19; "Checkers"
    speech, 100; election of 1952, 99, 100; elec-
    tion of 1960, 155–56; election of 1968, 215,
    216; environmental record, 243; Southern

Nixon, Richard (*continued*)
Strategy, 229, 239; Supreme Court nominations, 221, 225, 226; Vietnam War, 111, 219, 227, 237, 241, 244; Watergate, 245, 246; mentioned, 99, 118, 211, 212, 223
Nkrumah, Kwame, 165, 166
Nol, Lon, 227
Non-Proliferation Treaty, 218
North Atlantic Treaty Organization (NATO), 4, 84, 198
North Vietnamese Army (NVA), 207, 227
North Korea, 90, 92
North Vietnam, 187, 195
Nuckolls, Nell Lowe, 30

O'Daniel, "Pappy," 38
Oak Ridge, 55, 96
Oberdorfer, Don, 143
Occidental Petroleum Company, 108, 126, 243, 247, 249, 252, 253
Office of Price Control, 49
Ohio Women Democrats, 73
Okinawa, 71
Old Hickory, Tenn., 24
Oswald, Lee Harvey, 181
Oxford incident, 168, 169

Packard, David, 218
Pahlavi Mohammad, Shah Reza, 151
Palestine, 79
Palestine Liberation Organization (PLO), 203
Palestinian refugees, 94, 150, 203
Panetta, Leon (D-CA), 252
Paris, Tenn., 164
Patrick, Luther (D-AL), 49
Payne, Mattie Lucy, 176, 178
Peabody, Endicott, 242
Peabody, Rivlin, Cladouhos, and Lambert, 241
Peace Corps, 161, 162, 175
Pearson, Drew, 132, 149, 170

Pearl Harbor, 51, 53, 62
Pentagon, 164, 219
Pentagon Papers, 242
Pepper, Claude (D-FL), 4
Percy, Charles (R-IL), 219
Peress, Irving, 119
Peretz, Martin, 261
Perot, H. Ross, 224
Peru, 143
Peters, Charles, 175
Philippines, 19
Philips, Kevin, 223
Pitt, William, 219
Pittard, Mabel, 17
Pleasant Shade, Tenn., 16, 27
*Plessy v. Ferguson*, 112, 123
Poland, 44
Polk, James, 11, 12
poll tax, 75
Poor People's March, 210
Pope, Walter G., 220
populism, 3, 18, 19, 26, 41, 46, 118, 119, 139, 245
Possum Hollow, Tenn., 8–10, 13, 14, 198, 227, 269–71
Price Control Act, 56
price controls, 50, 51, 55, 56, 70
Priest, Percy (D-TN), 96
Prince Edward County, Va., 206
Progressive Party, 82
Progressive Policy Institute, 256
progressivism, 3, 19, 20, 26, 27, 46, 73, 239, 245
public education, 46, 84, 85
*Pueblo* incident, 207
Putnam County, 249

Quayle, Dan, 261, 263

Randall, Tony, 263
Rayburn, Sam (D-TX), 43, 55, 56, 64, 73, 118, 129, 156

Reagan, Ronald, 189, 213, 238, 252, 255, 256

reciprocal trade, 42, 45, 57, 114

Reciprocal Trade Agreement (1933), 45, 114

Red Cross, 203

Red Scare, 120

Reece, B. Carroll (R-TN), 81

Reed, Daniel (R-NY), 60

Reed, Wash, 61

Reedy, George, 128

Republican Party, 6, 73, 82, 83, 100, 107,
108, 150, 154, 159, 191, 200

Rhee, Syngman, 151

Rhodesia, 165, 208

Ribicoff, Abraham (D-CT), 194

Richardson, Admiral J. O., 62

Rickover, Admiral Hyman, 215

Ridgway, Matthew, 92

Rietz, Kenneth, 224, 231

Ritter, "Tex," 229

Robinson, Jack, Sr., xiv, 106, 226

Robinson, Walter King, 249

Robb, Chuck (D-VA), 5, 256

Rockefeller, Nelson, 160

Rogers, Stanley, 248

Romash, Marla, 264

Rome, Tennessee, 22

Roosevelt, Eleanor, 40, 53, 74

Roosevelt, Franklin D.: atomic bomb, 55;
death of, 67, 68; first meeting, 41; foreign
affairs, 44, 48, 52; Gore's military service in
WWII, 61, 63, 64; mentioned, 6, 21, 25,
26, 35, 36, 46, 50–54, 56, 69, 107, 267. *See
also* New Deal

Roosevelt, James, 56

Rowe, Jim, 128

Ruml, Beardsley, 57

Ruml Plan, 57

Rusk, Dean, 180, 196, 208

Russell, Richard (D-GA), 1, 7, 113, 168, 170,
185, 187, 194, 195, 218

safeguard system, 218, 219, 228

Saigon, 214

St. Alban's, 130, 175, 176, 178

Saltonstall, Leverett (R-MA), 103

Sasser, Jim, xiv, 173, 174, 238, 240, 241, 250,
262, 264

Sasser, Mary, xiv, 5, 7, 173, 174, 250

Saturday Night Massacre, 246

Scammon, Richard M., 223

Schaeffer, Tim, 238

Schiff, Andrew, 266

Schiffler, Andrew (R-WV), 48

Schlesinger, Arthur, Jr., 166

school prayer, xiii, 172, 173

Schriever, General Bernard, 228

Scott County, 90

Scranton, William, 251

Securities and Exchange Commission (SEC),
26

Seigenthaler, John, xv, 248, 267

Selective Service Board, 134

Senate Appropriations Committee, 97

Senate Armed Services Committee, 195

Senate Finance Committee, 114, 127, 138,
157, 170, 183

Senate Foreign Relations Committee: executive sessions, 179; staff views of Gore, 152;
subcommittee on Africa, 165; Senate Judiciary Committee, 212, 225; mentioned, 64,
89, 102, 127, 148, 157, 162, 180, 196, 208,
220, 228

Senate Post Office, 149

Senate Public Works Committee, 76, 102,
125

Seventeenth Amendment, 21

17th parallel, 112

Shelby County, 98, 135, 172, 200, 237

Shelbyville, 143

Shriver, Sargent, 161

Sihanouk, Norodom, 227

Sixteenth Amendment, 21

Sloan, Buster, 233

Smathers, George (D-FL), 119, 187

Smith, Adam, 160

Smith, Al, 16

Smith, General W. B., 66

Smith-Connally Act, 59

Smith County, 8, 9, 16, 23, 25, 31, 108, 109, 241, 265, 270

Social Security, 4, 34, 36, 77, 189

Soil Conservation Agency, 250

Sorenson, Theodore, 129, 158, 163

South Korea, 90

South Vietnam, 151, 152, 179, 180, 181, 187, 196, 205, 208, 241, 245

Southern Citizens' Council, 1, 123

Southern Manifesto, 1, 2, 123, 124, 143, 146, 199

Southern States Industrial Council, 35

Southern Strategy, 229, 239

Soviet Union, 66, 69, 71, 73, 76–78, 84, 90, 93, 107, 147, 161, 162, 165, 177, 178, 197, 203, 205, 208, 225

Sparkman, John (D-AL), 99, 129

Spence, John, 142

Stalin, Josef, 78, 103

Starnes, Joe (D-AL), 48

State Department, 27, 89

Steagall, Henry (D-AL), 50

Steagall plan, 50, 86

Stennis, John (D-MS), 195

Stettinius, Edward, Jr., 70

Stevenson, Adlai, Jr., 19

Stevenson, Jr., Adlai, 7, 99, 127–29, 132, 169

Stewart, Tom (D-TN), 76, 80, 81

Stilwell, Joseph, 71

Strategic Arms Limitations Agreement I (SALT I), 225

Strategic Arms Limitations Agreement II (SALT II), 252

Straus, Nathan, 43

Sudan, 165

Super Tuesday, 258

Supreme Court, 1, 172, 211, 212, 273

Swann, Theodore, 36

Syria, 93

Taft, Robert (R-OH), 49, 75, 78, 79, 104

Taft-Hartley Act, 77, 78, 99

Talmadge, Herman (D-MS), 6, 245

tariffs, 27, 45, 46

Tax Executives' Institute, 160

Taylor, Maxwell, 163, 164

Telecommunications Act, 265

Tennessee Association of Broadcasters, 202

Tennessee Democratic Executive Committee, 250

Tennessee General Assembly, 9

Tennessee Independents, 144

Tennessee Valley Authority (TVA), 4, 26, 29, 36, 38, 39, 47, 48, 76, 77, 114, 115, 171, 191, 237

Tet offensive, 207, 208

Thieu, Nguyen Van, 208, 220

38th parallel, 90, 92

Thompson, Gordon, 176

Thornberry, Homer, 211

Thurmond, Strom (R-SC), 1, 2, 6, 82, 83, 88, 123, 144, 185, 191, 211, 244

Tipton County, 97

Tobey, Frank, 121

Tokyo, 71

Tompkinsville, Ky., 35

Topeka, Kans., 109

Tower, John (R-TX), 172, 185, 219

Treleaven, Harry, 224

Trousdale County, 63

Truman, Harry: election of 1948, 79, 82, 83; first meeting with Gore, 70; foreign policy with the Soviets, 76, 77, 84; Korean War, 90–92; Medicare, 195; Vietnam, 110; mentioned, 7, 69, 73, 75, 86, 101, 116, 141, 266

Truman Doctrine, 77

Tuley, Bill, 24

Turkey, 169

Twentieth Century Reformation, 213

Tydings, Millard (D-MD), 36

Underwood, Jackie, 220

Union College, 31

United Jewish Appeal, 154
United Mine Workers (UMW), 58, 59
United Nations, 3, 4, 59, 60, 70, 73, 90, 92, 103, 197, 203
United Nations Commission on Women, 89
University of Alabama, 212
University of Idaho, 208
University of Mississippi, 167, 168
University of North Carolina (Chapel Hill), 20, 132
University of Tennessee, 15, 90, 216
Upper Cumberland, 7, 8, 10, 12, 26, 27, 45, 74, 106, 125
U.S. Housing Authority, 43
U.S. Steel, 166
U.S. Treasury, 86, 125
*U.S.S. Maddox*, 187
*U.S.S. Turner Joy*, 187

Valeo, Frank, 152, 159
Vandenberg, Arthur (R-MI), 44, 71
Vanderbilt Law School, 31, 32, 171, 173, 241, 248, 263
Vanderbilt University, 35, 250, 266
Vaughn, Henry, 97
Venezuela, 162
Veterans' Administration (VA), 199
Viet Cong, 179, 205, 207
Viet Minh, 110–12
Vietnam War, 4, 110, 111, 112, 148, 150–52, 179, 180, 182, 187–90, 192, 193, 195–97, 199, 200, 205, 206–208, 214, 219–21, 227, 228, 235, 236, 242, 247
Vishinsky, Andrei Y., 103
Volta River, 165
vouchers, xiii

Wagner Act, 26
Wake Island directive, 93
Wall Street, 148, 158, 159
Wallace, George, 6, 172, 213, 223, 232, 234, 244, 245

Wallace, Henry, 82, 83
Wallace, Lurlene, 213, 234
War Department, 64
War Memorial Hall, 269, 270
Warren, Earl, 112
Warren Court, 112, 168, 206
Warsaw Pact, 198
Washington, George, 11
Watergate, 224, 245–47
Watertown, 22
Watson, Thomas J., 159
Wattenberg, Ben J., 223
Watts riots, 195
Weakley County, 30
Webb, Robley D., 75
Webster, Daniel, 216, 240
Welch, Joseph, 119
Wenzell, A. H., 115, 121
West, John C., 5, 239
West Germany, 78, 150
Westheimer, Dr. Ruth, 263
Westmoreland, William, 205, 237
Whalen, Grover, 43
Wheeler, Bill, 60
Wheeler, Burton (D-MT), 48
Wheeling, W.Va., 88
Wherry, Kenneth (R-NE), 89
White, Justice Byron, 254
White, Rosie, 254
White, William S., 142, 143, 145
Whitt, Wayne, xv, 215
Wilkins, Roy, 140, 209
Williams, Franklin, 161
Willkie, Wendell, 46
Wilson, Frank, 90, 91
Wilson, Woodrow, 3, 20, 21, 122
Woodall, Jack, 91
Woodbury, Harry, 88
Woods, George, 115
Working Family Tax Relief Act, 260
World War I, 61, 66, 70, 177
World War II, xi, 3, 93, 177, 197

WSM radio, 47, 52, 64, 67, 69, 89

Xiaoping, Deng, 253

Yalu River, 92
Yarborough, Ralph (D-TX), 4, 18, 226, 229,
239, 256
Yates, Eugene, 115
Yom Kippur War, 245

York, Alvin, 14, 54, 60
Young, Andrew (D-GA), 5
Young Democrats (TN), 28
Young Men's Christian Association (YMCA),
8, 30
Young Women's Christian Association
(YWCA), 30, 31

Zuckert, Eugene, 115

Pauline LaFon — East & West

*[handwritten annotations]* In the foreword SL acknowledges that his father could be stubborn — esp. on principal.

"God, Guts, Guns = Repub platform" — Bumper sticker
An old Klan saying "6 - 6 - 6"

Preface → Hull was a major early influence.
You quote Larry D "LAST 2 New Deal FDR Demos."
paved way for other young, liberal Southerners

one room school house | fiddle... farm

tobacco his plant | poor - UT - MTSU
flunked practice teaching
you'd beat me next time
The loss to Hufflines.

Canar..tir "... death bed endorsement.
Bursy's son...? later | VP Garner's advice Not my

Congress at age 32 | Spoke against FDR's housing Bill. speeches ......

Hull's influence!

Backs Truman in '48
Hates McCarthy